More Damning than Slaughter

T0327088

More Damning
than Slaughter

Desertion *in the*
Confederate Army

Mark A. Weitz

UNIVERSITY OF NEBRASKA PRESS • LINCOLN AND LONDON

© 2005 by the University of
Nebraska Press
All rights reserved
Manufactured in the United
States of America

⊗

Set in Minion
and Copperplate
by Kim Essman.
Designed by Ray Boeche.

Library of Congress
Cataloging-in-Publication
Data
Weitz, Mark A., 1957–
More damning than slaughter :
desertion in the Confederate
Army / Mark A. Weitz.
p. cm.
Includes bibliographical
references and index.
ISBN-13: 978-0-8032-4797-0 (cl.: alk. paper)
ISBN-10: 0-8032-4797-4 (cl.: alk. paper)
ISBN-13: 978-0-8032-2080-5 (pa.: alk. paper)
1. United States—History—Civil War,
1861–1865—Desertions.   2. Confederate
States of America. Army—History.   3. Soldiers
—Confederate States of America—History.
4. Military deserters—Confederate States
of America—History.   5. Desertion, Military
—Confederate States of America—History.
I. Title.
E545.W458 2005
973.7'8–dc22
2005004044

CONTENTS

In May 1865, Gen. Edmund Kirby Smith looked to Texas as the last hope of the Confederacy. Once the master of "Kirby Smithdom," a vast area of the Confederate trans-Mississippi free of Union control, Smith found himself pushed into the Lone Star state with one last shot to stop the Union invader. With what remained of the trans-Mississippi army in Texas, Smith believed he could carry on the fight. From Shreveport, Louisiana, he tried to rally his small army, and in a circular addressed simply to his soldiers he laid out the situation. The revolution was in crisis. Robert E. Lee and his army were prisoners of war, and any hope the Confederacy had of survival depended on the efforts of this western army. He believed they possessed the means to continue resistance and that if the four-year-long struggle were to have any meaning, this army had to step up, protect their homes and their honor, and keep fighting. He begged the men to "stand by your colors—maintain your discipline . . . the numbers—the discipline and the efficiency of this army will secure to our country terms, that a proud people can with honor accept."[1]

The objective of the war had changed: peace with honor had replaced absolute victory. But regardless of the goal, the war continued, and Smith looked to his soldiers to do their duty. Within thirty days Smith had surrendered. The instrument of his defeat was not the Union army but rather his own troops. Before his eyes, what remained of the army deserted en masse and dissolved into the Texas countryside. Smith found his soldiers' conduct appalling and said so in a May 30 proclamation that came four days after his official surrender. In words that could not mask his disappointment, Smith lashed out at the faceless men who were to have been the instrument of resistance but instead had disbanded and headed home, taking their weapons and equipment with them. "I am left a commander without an army, a general without troops, you have made your choice. It was unwise and unpatriotic but it is final. I pray you not live to regret it." Smith was certain there would be a price, predicting that "the enemy will now possess your country and dictate his own laws. You have voluntarily destroyed your organizations and thrown away all means of resistance. Your present duty is pain, return to your families. Resume the occupations of peace."[2]

Despite the surrender of Lee at Appomattox and of Joseph Johnston twelve days later, Smith believed that the war was not over as long as an army remained in the field. The last official battle would come in June 1865, at Palmetto Ranch in southern Texas. Thus the dissolution of Smith's army marked perhaps the best example of mass desertion during the Civil War. An entire army had deserted, and with it had disappeared any hope of further resistance. It would be difficult to argue that desertion had not destroyed what remained of the Confederate army.

In hindsight, the Texas desertion is easily dismissed as insignificant. The war was effectively over. Smith deplored his men for abandoning the fight, but had they stayed he would soon have found himself with an army but without a cause. While the Texans may have been the last and perhaps most dramatic instance of desertion, the problem had plagued the Confederate military for most of the war. And hence to treat it as an isolated incident is to misunderstand it.

Admittedly, Confederate desertion has proved difficult to define. When did men desert? Was there any pattern based on what army they were in, where they were fighting, or what state they were from? How many actually deserted and—one of the most pondered questions—why? Perhaps the most important question has never been answered: Did desertion hurt the Confederate cause? If so, how badly? That is the question this book seeks to answer, and in the process of doing so it seeks to make some sense of desertion from the Confederate army.

As far back as the Romans, desertion has been recognized as potentially more damaging than any other form of troop attrition. Some of the most illustrious military leaders of the Western world have called desertion a disease, a cancer, a malignancy. Desertion not only depletes an army of soldiers but spreads to those who remain, undermining their morale and eroding unit cohesion. Napoleon, Frederick the Great, and others offered advice on how to prevent desertion and how to deal with it once it surfaced. The most common preventative was constant activity, either drill or fatigue duty.[3] Yet despite the attention given to the subject, there is little evidence that desertion destroyed any of these armies. Defeat, if and when it came, was most often at the hands of a superior military force in the field, confronting an army outnumbered not from desertion but from slaughter. In some cases, like that of Frederick the Great, defeat came only with the commander's own death. Desertion therefore posed but one of a number of military discipline problems, including drinking, fighting, pillaging civilians, and malingering. Discipline itself was but one concern among many for a commander grappling with problems of supply, intelligence, and recruitment. Thus historically desertion was troublesome but not damning.

Many scholars and popular historians believe that desertion in the Confederate army was a minor problem, one that never seriously affected the Confederacy's ability to wage war, and one that has been drastically overstated. They condemn the notion that desertion served as a vivid example of weakened or destroyed Confederate nationalism. They point to Lee's Army of Northern Virginia, perhaps the single greatest unifying factor in the Confederacy, as evidence of unwavering devotion among soldiers whose morale, although tested, never broke. Faced with evidence of declining will, both at home and on the battlefield, proponents of Confederate strength emphasize those who stayed rather than what they see as a minority who lost hope. They demand to be shown that desertion actually hurt.[4]

Part of the difficulty in defining Confederate desertion and its effect on the war comes from the official sources and the scholarship based on those sources since the end of the war. This problem is most acutely felt in trying to determine the actual number of deserters and the patterns that flow directly from the numbers. The official number of deserters from the Confederate army is 103,400. That figure comes from the records, compiled at the end of the war, that now make up the vast collection of Confederate soldiers' service records on deposit with the National Archives.[5] Compiled by state and regiment, the records consist of one, sometimes two, service record cards for each soldier, indicating his last status, whether killed, wounded, captured, or mustered out. Included within that information is whether he was absent without leave (AWOL) or had deserted. In some cases the information reflects where and when a man deserted, but in many cases it says only "deserted." In most instances, no indication is given whether he returned or where he went when he deserted—home, North, to the Union army, perhaps to another unit within the Confederate army. There is no way to determine if desertion or AWOL served as a designation of last resort for a soldier who could not otherwise be accounted for. More importantly, the official number of deserters seems inconsistent with evidence from letters, diaries, reports, and newspapers that indicates desertion was much more frequent.

The official numbers in the Confederate service records were assembled from information in a variety of sources compiled both during and after the war, and they did not benefit from contemporary sources that at one time existed and might have shed light on the desertion question. One of the best examples is the report of Col. William H. Fowler of Alabama. Originally a captain in the Fifth Alabama Artillery stationed in Mobile, Fowler was promoted to colonel and transferred to Montgomery, where he became a statistician. On December 8, 1863, he received a commission from the Alabama legislature to compile a record of all Alabama troops. The desire to preserve the deeds of Alabama's soldiers had shown itself as early as 1862 but found renewed interest as 1863 came to a close. Fowler systematically contacted officers in the Army of Tennessee from the company level and above in January 1864, informing them of his efforts and providing forms with specific instructions, including the designation of deserters with an "x." After working diligently for most of 1864, Fowler assembled complete records for Alabama soldiers in the Army of Tennessee. Next he turned to the Army of Northern Virginia, in which far fewer Alabama troops served. When the war ended in April 1865, Fowler was still working on the Army of Northern Virginia, and he completed his work within the year. However, as the Confederate government fled Montgomery in the last days of the war, Fowler's records for the Army of Tennessee were lost. All that remains today are his records for Alabama soldiers in the Army of Northern Virginia. Any hope that Fowler would re-create his data, or at least provide his own recollections of his work, died when he was assassinated in Texas in 1867.[6]

Fowler's report indicated that several other Confederate states had begun to compile similar records. Virginia, North Carolina, and South Carolina had followed Alabama's example with zeal, apparently devoting even more money to the project than Alabama had.[7] However, if they began such endeavors, either the projects were never completed or their fruits were lost, just as most of Fowler's work fell victim to the disarray during the last days of the Confederacy.

A greater problem is that, based on contemporary observations, Confederate records seem suspect, even when intact. The responsibility for accumulating accurate numbers on Confederate troop strength fell to the company surgeons and their morning reports. In April 1863, the Confederate surgeon general, Samuel P. Moore, issued a directive to all medical officers regarding the proper way to complete reports of sick and wounded. The reports reaching Richmond were "incomplete and ineffective," he complained, "and wholly unsuited to establish accurate and reliable statistics concerning the prevalence of disease throughout the army." However, the information was more than just a tool for tracking disease; the instructions made it clear that the medical officers were to prepare quarterly reports indicating "returned to duty, furloughed, discharged, deserted and died." Medical officers at the company level became responsible for recording all casualty figures, including desertion, and the accuracy of Confederate desertion numbers therefore depended on how well these men did their job. We do not know if the quality of the reporting process improved after Moore's order, but the primary data collector continued to be a lower-level medical officer.[8]

The troop strength numbers accumulated in the field found their way to the center of Confederate military record keeping, the Adjutant and Inspector General's Office. Little is known of Gen. Samuel Cooper, the man who occupied this office throughout the war, but from the observations of those around him it is possible to draw conclusions regarding the efficiency of this record-keeping branch of the Confederacy. Robert Garlick Hill Kean served as head of the Confederate Bureau of War for most of the conflict. He began the war as a private and fought at First Manassas. Several months later he was promoted to captain and took his position in one of the nine bureaus of the War Department, where he served until the end the war. From this vantage point, Kean observed almost every prominent Confederate government figure, including Samuel Cooper.[9]

Kean did not hide his contempt for Cooper, and perhaps that feeling may have colored his opinion. But by the summer of 1863, Kean believed Cooper should be relieved and that he survived only because Jefferson Davis allowed him to stay. Kean was critical of Davis for retaining Cooper, calling it a case of "West Pointism"—a reference to the president's preference for West Point officers. Kean also criticized Davis's need to have accommodating men around him, even if they were of lesser talent. Whether or not it was colored by a personal dislike for Cooper or Davis, Kean's evaluation of Cooper's record keeping was harsh: "As Inspector General one would suppose that the office highest in rank, the official keeper of the rolls whose specific duty it is to know the state of the army and compel proper returns, would in two and a half years have got some complete returns." According to Kean, it was common knowledge that Cooper had no clear picture of the strength of Lee's army, the force nearest to him and most stationary. Worse, he had no accurate count of the strength of the armies in the trans-Mississippi. Kean claimed there had never been a time when Cooper could provide even a "tolerably close guess" of the whole force on the rolls of the army. Why not? According to Kean, Cooper was never there, and not one document a week showed any indication that Cooper had personally attended to the matter.[10]

Troop strength was determined by taking the number of total troops and subtracting the number of those discharged, dead, furloughed, sick, wounded, captured, and deserted. Moore's directive to Confederate medical officers and

Kean's criticism of Cooper occur within a three-month period in the late spring and summer of 1863. We have no reason to believe that record keeping improved dramatically, so it is difficult to trust desertion numbers compiled by the Confederate army for all of its troops. The record-keeping deficiency not only affects numbers but also skews state and county patterns, making it difficult to determine points of high and low frequency.

While broad Confederate numbers on desertion are problematic, more narrow figures do exist. The problem is determining the extent to which these figures are part of the official number or are in addition to it. From July 1863 until the end of the war, the Union army kept records of Confederate soldiers who deserted into its lines and swore the oath of allegiance. This register identifies more than thirty thousand Confederate deserters and makes it possible to track desertion by state, county, unit, army, and time period. Some of these men are part of the larger desertion number, while many are in addition to the traditional figure for Confederate desertion. In some instances, men listed in Confederate service records or muster rolls as "AWOL since . . ." appear as deserters to the enemy in the Union register.[11] On its face the register accounts for less than a third of the total number of Confederate deserters, depending on whether they are a subset of the larger numbers, partially contained within the larger number, or a completely different set of men altogether.

Union records reflect two other groups of Confederate soldiers that, although not designated as deserters in Union records, clearly fall under this category. Confederate POWs held in Union camps had the opportunity to apply to take the oath of allegiance and secure their release. Once released they fell into two groups: those who enlisted to fight with the Union in theaters unrelated to the war and those who returned to civilian life, remaining in the North or making their way home. Those who entered the Union army were sent west and fought Indians for the remainder of the war. These men, referred to as "Galvanized Yankees," had been re-coated and switched sides.[12] Those choosing the civilian route sometimes went home and sometimes returned to the Confederate army, having sworn the oath only "from the teeth out" to escape the rigors of prison life. Regardless of how the Confederate government would have viewed these men, in the eyes of their comrades they were deserters. The clearest proof of this comes from Union correspondence and Confederate diaries and letters. Men swearing the oath had to apply by signing a roster posted within the prison camps, thereby allowing everyone to know who was willing to forsake the cause and swear allegiance to the Union. Both Union and Confederate records reveal that loyal Confederate prisoners threatened and sometimes took the lives of oath takers. The situation grew so severe that Union camp commanders tried to move these men out of the camps, though they had to settle for separate billeting.[13]

Prisoners of war who took the oath, while deserters, are a relatively small group. Prisoners—even those willing to renounce their loyalty to the Confederacy—posed more of a risk for Union officials. Unlike deserters, they were in Union custody involuntarily, and many had expected to be paroled and released until the exchange program broke down in late 1863. Determining the strength of their commitment to the Union was difficult. As the war progressed the office of the commissary general of prisoners became more reluctant to release POWs and made the process more difficult before abating the program completely. However, despite the smaller numbers, these men make up a portion of the total picture. Not only do they demonstrate a different form of desertion, but they exemplify the variety of ways men could desert from the Confederate army.[14]

Hospitals provided yet another route to freedom. Morning reports of company medical officers were not the only source of desertion data compiled by doctors and surgeons. As the war progressed the fighting intensified, bringing heavy casualties and the need for a hospital system to accommodate the sick and wounded. The hospitals in both the Army of Northern Virginia and the Army of Tennessee proved to be easy avenues of escape for men healthy enough to desert. Samuel H. Stout, the assistant surgeon general in charge of the Army of Tennessee, faced the need to constantly move the sick and wounded as the Union army pushed deeper into the South. Not only did his mobile hospital network give men the opportunity to desert while in transit, but his receiving hospitals funneled men further south to sites safe from Union occupation—and too close to home for some soldiers to resist the temptation to desert. Figures exist for desertion from Army of Northern Virginia hospitals. While the numbers for the Army of Tennessee have not been totaled, Stout's hospital registers make the task possible.[15]

Desertion numbers also appear sporadically among certain units or in particular places. For example, a Mississippi record lists seventy-five deserters held by the local sheriffs of Chickasaw County from July 1863 to July 1864. Louisiana records provide a list of 149 deserters from the Confederate army dated December 9, 1862. The Louisiana ledger provides name, rank, physical description, civilian occupation, unit designation, and a space for comments. The information appears to have been prepared in contemplation of some form of newspaper publication, because a notation at the bottom sets out a reward of thirty dollars for each deserter returned to the army. Records from the Union prison in occupied Natchez, Mississippi, provide a descriptive list of twenty-seven Confederate deserters who took the oath of allegiance to the United States, with notations that several were sent North after taking the oath. The same document lists fourteen Confederate POWs who swore the oath of allegiance to the Union and were released. While all three sources are helpful in a limited sense, particularly in trying to understand the local ramifications of Confederate desertion, they provide only small pieces of a much larger picture.[16]

Published primary-source documents likewise offer a mixed blessing. An extensive compilation of North Carolina troops lists each man, identifying deserters by name. First published in seven volumes between 1966 and 1977, the data on North Carolina artillery, cavalry, and infantry are drawn mainly from the compiled military service records in Record Group 109 at the National Archives. The compilers made sure to point out that those service records were a compilation of muster rolls, prison records, payrolls, hospital records, inspection reports, parole rolls, and other "records containing service information." The volumes were updated and expanded beginning in 1988, and while the information is much easier to access, it is not substantially different from that contained in Record Group 109. The record is nevertheless extremely useful and forms the basis of perhaps the best study to date on North Carolina desertion.[17]

The sooner after the war that records were compiled, the more problematic the information within them becomes. Louisiana's Confederate soldier records were assembled by Andrew B. Booth, the commissioner of the state's military records, and published in 1920. In the first sentence of his introduction, Booth states that "it is reasonably certain there is not extant a complete and perfect record of the individual members of any Louisiana Confederate States Army Command." The best records were apparently those kept on Louisiana soldiers in the Army of Northern Virginia, where (Robert Garlick Hill Kean's comments notwithstanding) the muster rolls and returns were more accurate. Booth then revealed two key characteristics of the Confederate military: the widespread problem of desertion and the deplorable condition of Confederate service records. He lamented that "a very large number" of soldiers were AWOL at the final surrender of their respective commands and consequently not listed as present on the final roll. Booth admitted that those soldiers absent are solely to blame. But he argued that some men indeed served honorably, and that now "the burden is upon them to prove their devotion to duty, and the state of Confederate records makes that task difficult if not insurmountable." For soldiers in the Trans-Mississippi Department the burden was greater because Confederate muster rolls for that army were burned in Shreveport when Smith surrendered in May 1865, a fate similar to that suffered by Fowler's Army of Tennessee records for Alabama troops. Booth believed that the desertion of some served only to enhance the dedication to duty of those who remained, or as he put it, "nerved them to stand the final test of Soldierly Honor." Booth further contended that the majority of desertion occurred at the end of the war, after Lee's surrender, as men deserted in droves to return to their homes. His introduction chronicles, through official letters and circulars, the month-long process whereby Smith's army self-destructed from desertion, from group desertions of ten to twenty in April to four hundred trying to desert Galveston by mid-May.[18]

Booth's position is not in and of itself a problem, nor is it hard to understand his sentiment toward the soldiers of his state. His project became possible when the captured Confederate records, held by the United States War Department, were finally released for public access. What he described is Record Group 109, and as with troop compilations from other states, it formed the basis of the Louisiana record. However, what is troubling is his analysis of how to view men who appear to have deserted in 1865 in light of the lack of otherwise good records. He argues that "where all the record the Government has of a soldier is good and no faltering or neglect of duty is found recorded against him, and his service is shown to the end of 1864; great charity should be exercised toward him." The intent is noble, but given the predisposition against marring a soldier's good name, the data are somewhat suspect.[19]

While the Louisiana records admit to a bias against dishonoring a soldier, more troublesome is the collection devoted to South Carolina troops compiled early in the twentieth century. A review of its three volumes reveals that no South Carolina troops deserted. There were many listed as AWOL for more than a year, but they never deserted. However, other records, including some of those already discussed, indicate that such was not the case. Part of the problem with studying desertion in the South is that the notion that men deserted continues to carry a stigma in a region where the memory of the war is important but often skewed, particularly where scholarship and published primary sources emerged while Confederate veterans or their immediate families remained alive. Confederate pension applications carried an averment that the soldier had never deserted, and records identifying deserters, although they did exist, particularly at the regimental level, threatened monetary stipends as well as personal reputations.[20]

What makes the quantitative data confusing is that the numbers simply cannot be reconciled with the letters, diaries, official reports, and other material of
the time that not only point to desertion as much larger and more widespread
but indicate that it genuinely hurt the Confederate cause, both at the front
and at home. Smith's letters and proclamation give few if any numbers, but
his words reveal that desertion destroyed his army. In virtually every part of
the Confederate army from 1862 to the close of the war, the desertion situation
appears critical at some stage of the conflict. This suggests that the story goes
beyond the numbers that can be derived from the available records. Perhaps
the quest for an exact number is not only pointless but overlooks the more
obvious fact, namely, that desertion was widespread and its effects hurt. Can
we count every deserter? No. Did desertion and its many ramifications undermine the Confederate war effort? Yes. The difficulty is in making the argument
without hard statistical data, a difficulty borne out by the secondary literature
on desertion.

The source problem is reflected in the work on desertion since the war.
Studies devoted exclusively to desertion are both scarce and narrow. This is
not to suggest that the work is not of good quality; it simply means that
source limitations have dictated a particular approach to studying desertion,
an approach that this study will adopt in part and reject in part. Only three
book-length studies exist, two of which are more than eighty years old. Only
Ella Lonn's 1928 work looks at desertion broadly. However, Lonn's focus is so
broad, encompassing both Union and Confederate desertion, that the book is
most useful as a place from which to begin studying desertion. In many cases
Lonn identifies excellent sources, but she analyzes them only peripherally. The
other two books are state studies of Alabama and Georgia. The focus of each is
who deserted, from where, when, and the reasons for desertion. Implicit in all
three books is the notion that desertion hurt the Confederacy, but Lonn's book
may actually argue that in raw numbers the effect was not so great, and the two
state studies make it difficult to draw conclusions regarding the impact on the
Confederacy as a whole. Both state studies clearly argue that military service—
service that became compulsory and open-ended—severely undermined local
communities, but neither can address the degree to which the subsequent desertion undermined the overall Confederate war effort.[21]

With so few book-length studies, most literature on desertion is found either
in parts of larger works dealing with the war or a certain aspect of it, or in smaller
journal articles devoted to specific units or geographic regions. There are a few

articles dealing with desertion on a state level. The periodical literature reflects the same early disfavor for the subject. The first appears in 1950, a short, obscure piece in an obscure journal. Until the 1980s there is little academic attention on the subject. The periodical literature reflects the need to get at desertion locally. This body of work covers both the Union and Confederate armies and sees desertion as the product of different factors, ranging from home-front concerns and community influences to poor food and clothing, morale problems within units, and loss of unit integrity due to change of officers or unit designation. North Carolina figures prominently in this literature. As the state contributing the most combat troops to the war, suffering the highest casualty numbers, and counting units among the most courageous of the war, it lives with the stigma of having the highest number of deserters. While the periodical literature suggests that desertion harmed the war effort, it does not address the question head-on. Causation, not harm, tends to be the main focus.[22]

This study is possible because the South did lose the war. The reality of defeat begs the question of why. Part of the answer to whether desertion hurt or crippled the Confederate war effort lies in accepting that precise numbers are impossible. In some ways we judge the sophistication of a civilization, or a nation, by its record keeping, and the Confederacy's, while probably the best it could have been under the circumstances, was lacking. Some of what was assembled and compiled did not survive the war, or if it did survive, it fell victim to inadequate storage in the years following the war. The remainder of the answer lies in believing that the extent and nature of the harm to the Confederacy can be measured and determined without precise numbers.

A starting point is also to accept that no single factor caused the demise of the Confederacy, not even desertion. Rather, it was a series of factors, working in concert, that ultimately undermined the Southern war effort. The question becomes where, if at all, desertion fit into the mix. To paraphrase Vegetius, a Roman military historian of the fourth century c.e., was desertion more harmful to the Confederate army than slaughter? Death, not desertion, claimed such men as Stonewall Jackson, William Dorsey Pender, and Patrick Cleburne. Thousands of crack combat troops died the same way, or from diseases contracted in camps. Did desertion merely take the weak, the slackers, ridding the army of numbers without really diminishing its quality?

Studies to date suggest that deserters were not cowards, or at least most of them were not. When it struck, desertion took quality soldiers and undermined good units. The limited evidence available suggests that when desertion swept through Georgians in 1863–64 it took seasoned soldiers, veterans of almost two years of fighting in the West's most bitter struggles. North Carolina units racked by desertion performed admirably, even heroically, in the field. But the issue of whether desertion hurt the Confederate army is in many ways different from a larger issue of whether desertion hurt the "Confederacy." The evidence suggests not only that desertion undermined the army's fighting effectiveness but that the worst part of desertion was that its effects spread from the army into other parts of the struggle. Perhaps the analogy to a disease is more appropriate than one might imagine. The problem is that traditionally the army has been seen as the "body." The reality, at least in the Confederacy, is that the army, or armies, were but organs within the larger body. The disease that began in the army did not stay there. In one way or another, it spread. In some ways it is ironic that desertion, a military crime, may have been more damaging to the civilian world than it was to the military.

Throughout this study, desertion takes on the qualities of a disease, one that starts in the only place it technically can, the military. However, once the army becomes infected the disease spreads to other organs of the body and infests vital parts of the Confederacy, not the least of which would be the Confederate civilian home front. It would be impossible to determine if desertion alone could have destroyed the Confederacy, since it never had the opportunity to operate alone. Instead, it began to weaken the Confederacy as other political, economic, and social problems developed. Desertion certainly did not destroy all Confederate armies in the same way that it did Smith's, at least not for the brunt of the war. However, acting with other conditions, desertion would weaken some parts of the Confederacy and destroy others, including certain parts of its military machine.

In many ways the Confederacy was predisposed to the problem. At some level devotion to military duty is always tested, particularly in war. What becomes evident is that the Confederacy, and therefore its military, lacked certain characteristics or conditions that would otherwise have strengthened or ensured loyalty to the service. Apologists' arguments notwithstanding, the Confederacy simply did not engender within its soldiers the same sense of nationalism that the Union did. Much is made of the distinction between North and South in terms of industry versus agriculture. However, what is forgotten is the effect of this divergent development on society. The South, much more so than the North, was a region dominated by localism. Loyalty in some cases existed as high as the state level, but by and large it was local communities that dominated people's minds and hearts. Combine this proclivity for the local with the fact that the "Confederacy" as a nation did not exist until two months prior to the war, and that when it did come into being it was formed out of seven Deep South states, in three of which secession was bitterly contested. Thus not only were the people less inclined to attach to something national, but the nation hardly reflected the people being asked to embrace it.

The signs were there early. Some zealously enlisted, but not everyone embraced the cause. Conscription left men and communities with no real choice, and they chose to fight together rather than be drafted and separated. But men who went to war together could likewise leave together, particularly given the conflict that war would present in its third year. In some ways the problem ran much deeper than just a weak attachment to the Confederacy. The South's army would be made up of soldiers very much like those who served in previous American armies. Agriculture created a nation of farmers that became an army of farmers. While much of the South belonged to regional and national markets, some of it did not, and the South's agrarian army would find itself confronted with many of the same problems its Revolutionary and colonial predecessors had faced. In a very real sense, Confederate desertion was a peculiarly American practice, one that had been around for a hundred years and flowed directly from agrarian armies fighting in and around home.

This, then, is a story of the Confederacy from its inception to its ultimate collapse. It is told from the vantage point of its soldiers who confronted conflicting loyalties, physical hardship, death, and the Union military. However, while desertion may have begun as a national military problem, it would not be restricted to the nation or the military. It became the problem of state and local governments that not only struggled to maintain the army's fighting effectiveness but found that desertion undermined the welfare and safety of the civilian communities. The voice of desertion therefore resonates from people other than soldiers. Men and women far removed from the battlefield add their own perspective to the problem. They not only add insight into the size and nature of Confederate desertion but also demonstrate the degree to which its effects spread beyond the army itself. Finally, the story begins with those who had long since passed to dust, men who helped fight some of the Republic's earliest conflicts and knew firsthand the challenges faced by a government and military seeking to assemble and maintain an army drawn from the heart of an agrarian population.

More Damning than Slaughter

1. THE AMERICAN PRACTICE

Desertion, it seems, has been with America from the time it formed armies. But while military leaders have struggled to control the problem, virtually no efforts were made to analyze desertion as an aspect of military science. Beginning in 1802, the U.S. government trained its professional officer corps at West Point, where cadets mastered mathematics, terrain, and, to a lesser degree, current military tactics and strategy. Such an education left little time for learning how to actually lead men in battle. Those lessons came in the field, and prior to the Civil War that meant commanding small bodies of troops in posts scattered across the growing western frontier.

With little real war and only Indian conflicts as an ongoing problem, desertion between 1812 and 1846 was a problem of the peacetime army. Causes of desertion varied: low pay, mediocre food, and poor clothing attracted few U.S. citizens to the army, leaving the ranks to be filled by immigrants who had been unable to find work. With service conditions harsh, desertion ran high in the 1820s and 1830s. The frontier nature of service also left field officers isolated from Washington DC, with a wide latitude to punish insubordination in the ranks. The routine use of harsh and "illegal" punishment for offenses other than desertion may have driven peacetime soldiers to desert. A notice published in the *Army and Navy Chronicle* in May 1839 indicated that the American public saw limits to proper punishment, even for deserters. An article that first appeared in the *Detroit Morning Post* told of two soldiers who were drummed out of the service after being whipped and branded and having their heads shaved. There was no objection to the drumming out of deserters, but the paper condemned whipping and branding as "utterly disgraceful to the service and the country." Death and imprisonment were acceptable, but whipping and branding were deemed cruel and unusual under the Eighth Amendment.[1]

War came, most notably in 1812 and 1846, and with it came desertion. During the War of 1812, 205 men were executed for desertion—clear evidence that the problem existed. America's most famous deserters—to the extent that desertion can bring acclaim—the San Patricos, deserted during the Mexican War. However, the commonly told story of this battalion conceals much of the truth. The Mexican War remains the foreign conflict with the highest desertion rate for American soldiers. The emphasis on the Irish unit conceals the fact that 8.3 percent of all U.S. soldiers deserted during the war. Although desertion from the San Patricos did occur, not all were Irish-born, and the desertion itself was not the mass exodus of legend. The desertion ran from November 1845 to August 1847. Of the seventy-one men tried for deserting and joining the enemy, fewer than half were Irish, and contrary to the famous stone plaque left in their honor, these men were not martyrs who died for Mexico. Fifty were hung, several were shot, and nineteen escaped death when their sentences were commuted. Reasons for their desertion ranged from poor food, incidence of disease, harsh military punishment, the inability to receive Catholic sacraments, the offer of land from the Mexican government, and the pull from Mexican women with whom several soldiers had fallen in love.[2]

The U.S. Army left Mexico knowing that men had deserted, but it never seriously tried to analyze why. The Irish not only served as a way to rationalize the problem but also fed a growing sense of nativism in American society. To the degree that the war could have provided lessons for subsequent conflicts, including the civil war that loomed on the horizon, those lessons were lost on a military community that returned to the business of peacetime service and policing the frontier. During the Civil War the two sides brought more than 3 million men into the ranks of volunteer armies. Desertion, an inconvenience for the U.S. regular army in the nineteenth century, became much more of a problem, particularly for the South. To the extent that Civil War civilian and military leaders learned anything about desertion from the Mexican War, the importance of those lessons was no doubt muted by the fact that America quickly won a convincing victory, with a small army showing skill and tactics lauded by the acknowledged military master of the day, Frenchman Henri Jomini.

After April 1865 there was no real effort to learn from the experiences of the Civil War. To the extent that anyone addressed the problem it came in trying to justify what had happened, like Zebulon Vance's postwar speeches trying to place the conduct of North Carolina's troops into some kind of understandable context. As the reality of the death and destruction began to sink in, the war found a comfortable place in the South's literature of the lost cause. Both sides struggled to explain what could only be characterized as a national tragedy. An in-depth examination of men who abandoned the fight simply did not fit into the agenda of either side.

Following the Civil War the size of the U.S. Army shrank, and once again it found its niche in policing the American frontier. Added to the traditional U.S. soldier was a new fighting man, the African American buffalo soldier. In military circles the topic of desertion saw an increase in interest, judging by the amount of periodical literature that emerged during the period. While desertion continued to be troublesome, statistical data compiled between the end of the Civil War and the end of the nineteenth century provided no consistent picture of the problem. Some studies indicated that between 1865 and 1891 desertion was as low as 14 percent, while others placed it as high as 33 percent. The graduating essay of Lt. William D. McAnaney from the U.S. Infantry and Cavalry School, published in 1889, claimed that from 1884 to 1889, 42 percent of U.S. soldiers deserted. What is most revealing about the literature, including McAnaney's essay, is that it shows that the military genuinely tried to understand desertion in the early 1880s and that these efforts simply failed. In 1882 the adjutant general's office issued General Order no. 130, directing department commanders to file annual reports on desertion and try to address the question, why do men desert? The reports for 1883 and 1884 assigned cause in roughly 33 percent of the cases, but among the causes frequently listed was "dissatisfaction." McAnaney noted in his essay that to say a man deserts from dissatisfaction is like saying that "a man is blind because he cannot see." Thus in more than 80 percent of the cases, the reports filed over a two-year period pursuant to the adjutant general office's order failed to identify a cause. The 1889 report concluded that men deserted from monotony, from unnecessary restraints of the military, and from the low social position held by enlisted men. While McAnaney's essay does not offer a great deal of insight into desertion, the fact that it was published at all is significant. A notation at the bottom of the first page speaks volumes about the importance of desertion and how long it took for the U.S. military to realize that it was a reality for any army. After explaining that the essay was one of five recommended for publication, the board of reviewing instructors stated, "The topics of graduating essays are generally restricted to subjects relating to strategy, tactics, and military history, but any important theme relating to military administration or our National military policy is allowed, subject to the approval of the commanding officer of the school."[3] As a topic, desertion had finally arrived, but it was too late to do the Confederacy any good.

Seventy-five years after the end of the Civil War, the U.S. Army finally tried to understand desertion in the army. In 1920, Col. E. N. Woodbury published a study of desertion in the army from 1831 through World War I. Buried almost since its completion, the report to the Morale Division of the War Department was limited to desertion from the regular army. Unfortunately, that precludes any usefulness for the Civil War period, since the regular army made up such a small percentage of the Union army and none of the Confederate army. More importantly, Woodbury identified "war" as the condition most likely to cause desertion, confirming his study's primary focus on peacetime desertion. After claiming that forty-five out of every one hundred soldiers deserted during the Civil War, Woodbury never discussed Civil War desertion again. However, even had he been so inclined, his study would most likely have failed to resolve the question of Confederate Civil War desertion, at least insofar as causation was concerned.[4]

Woodbury's study, like those in the 1880s, focused on preventing desertion and thus had a contemporary rather than purely historical focus. It also came at the point where for the first time in American history more people lived in urban areas than in rural areas, an evolution that began before the Civil War. Unlike the men in Woodbury's study, Southern soldiers were neither career soldiers nor urban dwellers. By occupation many were farmers, most were rural, and many were from newly or sparsely settled areas of the South. Woodbury attempted to unravel desertion's mysteries by looking at the small professional army that dominated America's military for more than eighty years from 1831. To find the answers to Confederate Civil War desertion he needed to go back much further, to the provincial and continental armies of eighteenth-century colonial America.

The American Civil War enjoys an aura of exceptionalism. There have been many civil wars throughout history—some as bloody and many that lasted as long or longer—but none are as revered in popular culture or as closely scrutinized by academics both at home and abroad. Part of the fascination seems to lie in a perception of "firsts" or "best." Military historians marvel at the killing power of the new rifled musket and the change in tactics it brought to the battlefield. Jackson and Lee revolutionized warfare. Sherman and Grant brought total war to North America. Heavy casualties revolutionized battlefield medicine. River warfare brought ironclads, rams, and submarines. In short, a host of innovations came from the war. Political historians point to the vast new powers exercised at the federal level that enabled the North to prevail. The freeing of 4.5 million slaves makes the war one of emancipation and elevates the conflict beyond a mere political or economic struggle between divergent interests. While some of this praise is well deserved, desertion during the American Civil War, particularly among Confederate troops, found many of its roots in an American military and civilian culture that began a hundred years earlier, when America first began to organize militarily beyond the local militia level. What would prove unique, however, would be the effect of desertion on the Southern war effort and the fissures in the Confederate government and Southern society that desertion brought into focus.

With but a few notable and brief examples, the story of the American soldier until the twentieth century is one of men fighting at home. In many cases, battlefield and home front were the same place. In most cases, even if the battlefield was not in one's own backyard, it was never far from home. The close physical proximity to home brought equally close emotional attachments among soldiers, their families, and their communities. This attachment, when combined with the hardships of war and soldiering, strongly undermined the cohesiveness of American armies in the eighteenth and nineteenth centuries.

This is not to suggest that the civilian quality of American soldiers prevented them from performing as professionals on the battlefield. It is an American trait to be able to draw from its civilian population, rapidly build a large and effective fighting force, train it, and have it perform brilliantly in battle. When the war ends, the army dissolves back into the civilian community. This was certainly the case in the American Civil War.[5] What this suggests, however, is that as the rigors of war begin to take their toll, soldiers predisposed to desert will experience a pull from home that may not only draw them in a direction to which they are already inclined but may also make it easier for them to desert and survive.

In January 1777, George Washington's army settled in at Morristown, New Jersey, for what promised to be a miserable winter. All the ingredients of despair existed, including poor housing, lack of food, and the all too recent memories of war, memories that, despite victories at Trenton and Princeton, remained haunted by defeat and retreat. The results, if not predictable, were certainly not unexpected. In growing numbers the soldiers opted for what had become the "American practice," followed the example of many who had preceded them, and deserted.[6]

Despite his best efforts, Washington could use only his personal leadership qualities and the limited tools his civilian government left at his disposal. Then he could only watch and wait. He had seen it all before, not just in this war, but in another. Twenty years before, as a colonel commanding Virginia colonial troops in the Seven Years' War, Washington first encountered the problem of maintaining an army composed of farmers fighting on their home soil within close proximity to their homes and communities. What he knew in 1777 was that the "American practice" had existed since the earliest days of organized colonial armies. What not even Washington could have known or suspected was that almost a century after he first encountered desertion as an American problem his Southern military descendants would face the same problem, with many of the same causes, as the Confederacy struggled to keep its own "revolutionary" army in the field.

The Seven Years' War provided the first opportunity to examine the conduct of American soldiers in a formal military setting over a sustained period. Almost from its inception the "American practice" made itself known. By the fall and winter of 1755, Washington and his contemporaries in the army and government discovered that raising an army and keeping it in the field presented two different problems. Desertion had already become a problem, and military men advocated that it be "quashed as much as lies in our power." As it increased toward the end of 1755, Washington placed a portion of the blame at the feet of officers, specifically their mismanagement and inactivity at dealing with the problem. However, he was not naive, and he had known for some time that the military was only partly at fault. In August 1755, shortly after Braddock's defeat, Washington received a letter from Virginia attorney John Martin. Martin pleaded with Washington to pardon three members of the prestigious Virginia Blues who had deserted, claiming, "Smith has a sweetheart & 2 children here & Barker a wife which I presume were the loadstones [*sic*] that attracted them." Martin's entreaties offered an early recognition that home held a heavy draw. While Virginia governor Robert Dinwiddie offered to pardon all deserters who returned by September 20, 1755, few accepted and Washington wasted no time in making his feelings known. Punish those civilians who aid and abet desertion with heavy fines and corporal punishment. Yes, civilians seduce soldiers, but they also harbor them and assist them with every necessary means of escape. Although they could not punish the solicitation, they had to crush the facilitation. Washington's military subordinates agreed: punish those who harbor the deserters.[7]

Deserters themselves also had to be severely punished. By 1756 standing orders declared any man taken beyond one mile from town without leave was to be deemed a deserter. Yet punishment seemed unclear and at times nonexistent. Some questioned the wisdom of hanging a man who deserted and returned of his own accord, while Washington insisted that "things are not being rightly settled for punishing deserters" and suggested going "on with the old way and whipping stoutly." The militia posed even greater problems, not only deserting in large numbers, sometimes fifty at a time, but avoiding punishment by reenlisting in the Virginia Regulars.[8]

Thus, while desertion posed a problem, a related problem became the unwillingness to severely punish the conduct. Washington insisted on putting deserters to death, claiming that without severe punishment he could not stop the practice. Governor Dinwiddie intervened when possible to ameliorate such sentences. Even after giving Washington the maximum authority that existed under the more harsh British establishment, Dinwiddie asked that army regulations be applied "with tenderness as the exigency of affairs may require." Washington steadfastly maintained what Robert E. Lee, Braxton Bragg, and others would later argue to Jefferson Davis: leniency breeds contempt, and without the death sentence there is little hope of deterring men from deserting.[9]

Washington and the American colonial authorities were never able to stop desertion in the provincial armies. According to orderly books kept at the time, punishment ranged from death to five hundred lashes, penalties consistent with British military law. Not only did colonial authorities have to contend with the draw from home and the assistance that came with it, but as the war progressed, some units fell into neglect and even their officers insisted that unless troops were properly fed, clothed, and equipped, desertion would be unavoidable.[10] America survived the Seven Years' War in great part because of the presence of the British army and its strict military discipline. Twenty years later that same army would be Washington's foe, and the problem of desertion would still be there.

In many ways, the Continental army's response to desertion reflected both an acknowledgment and an ignorance of the lessons of the Seven Years' War. The problem began almost immediately. Inadequate provisions, including food, plagued the army in 1776. Much as occurred during the American Civil War, speculation also caused unrest as civilians actually worked against the cause for the desire of money. Gen. Horatio Gates pointed out the disease and its causes: "Everything about this army is infected with pestilence: the cloaths, the blanketts, the Air & the Ground they walk upon." Smallpox seemed to be the major threat. As men deserted, most headed straight for home, and even Washington doubted their willingness to return voluntarily despite governmental offers of pardon.[11]

Desertion during the American Revolution foreshadowed many of the problems the Confederate army would face. Recapturing deserters forced colonial authorities to venture into local communities assisted by local militias. Just as during the Civil War, it became apparent to the military that without local assistance deserters would be lost to the army, and if the local community resisted efforts to recapture these men the task became even more arduous. Leniency plagued the Continental army just as it would the South's forces eighty-five years later. Despite the early severity of the problem and the fact that it occurred throughout the army, the penalty remained limited to corporal punishment, ranging from fifteen to thirty-nine lashes, a penalty that often was never meted out. In many cases officers found "some favorable circumstances appearing in the person's behalf" that justified mitigation.[12] Leniency would come to haunt the Confederate army as well.

Like the Confederate army, the Continental army consisted of soldiers recruited from states and communities under circumstances where those local and regional loyalties continued to override the need for national cohesion. Going beyond mere jealousy, the situation involved money and perhaps privilege. Just as the exemption and substitute rules of the Civil War undermined morale, state governments allowed "vast bounty [to be] given for substitutes in the militia." The New Hampshire government offered local militiamen as much as fifty dollars to enlist, an inducement that infuriated regular soldiers who volunteered out of patriotism.[13]

The first revolution brought with it other conduct that the Confederacy would struggle with in the second. Desertion to the enemy, a major problem for the Confederacy as the war dragged on, had been a problem for Washington's army as well. Closely connected to this problem became the practice of inducing the enemy to desert. One of the few death sentences meted out early in the Revolutionary War fell upon Peter Buise, convicted of desertion and of being found near the "enemy's sentinels."[14] In a letter to John Hancock, Washington insisted that the government simply did not understand colonial soldiers:

> When men are irritated & the passions inflamed, they fly hastily, and cheerfully to arms, but after the first emotions are over, to expect, among such people as compose the bulk of an army, that they are influenced by any

THE AMERICAN PRACTICE

other principles than those of interest, is to look for what never did & I fear
never will happen. . . . [Even an officer] makes you the same reply . . . that
his pay will not support him and he cannot ruin himself and his family
to serve his country, when every member of the community is equally
interested and benefitted by his labours—The few therefore, who act upon
Principles of disinterestedness, are, comparatively speaking—no more than
a drop in the Ocean. . . . To place any dependence on militia, is, assuredly,
resting upon a broken staff . . . the sudden change in their manner of living
(particularly in their lodging) brings on sickness in many, impatience in all;
& such an unconquerable desire of returning to their respective homes that
it not only produces shameful & scandalous desertions among themselves,
but infuses the like spirit in others. [15]

What made sense in 1776 applied equally in 1861. While the Confederate army would be a far cry from either the colonial militia or the Continental army, even with its superior combat skills and training the bulk of its soldiers would continue to be farmers not so far removed from home with an unconquerable desire to return, a desire that would be fueled by the growing realization that, like their revolutionary forefathers, they could not both fight for their country and provide for their families. [16]

Washington's army survived its struggle in the North, but desertion remained a problem. The inability to keep the army properly supplied, particularly in the winter months, made desertion a tempting option for New Yorkers, Pennsylvanians, and New Englanders camped so close to home when wives and families were drawing upon their sense of duty. As the theater of war shifted south, Gens. Nathanael Greene and Daniel Morgan faced the same dilemma. Greene offered a simple solution: "[Allow me to] hang one of these fellows in the face of the troops without the form of a tryal. . . . I will have one hung up this afternoon where the army are to march by." Many of Greene's fellow officers agreed that executing deserters was the only remedy. [17] When the fighting in the Revolutionary War moved south, the conflict came to more closely resemble the Civil War eighty years later. The British campaign into South Carolina eventually took it through North Carolina and Virginia, creating many of the conditions and fears that surfaced as the Union moved into the South in 1862. It was more than simply lack of clothing and supplies that drove colonial desertion. The presence of the enemy and the actual and potential damage it brought on the region compelled many men to abandon the fight. Desertion patterns during the Revolution mirrored those of the Civil War as soldiers from western

North Carolina's Salsbury district deserted in huge numbers. Of even greater significance were men otherwise willing to join the service who refused to do so because the enemy was active in the country and plundering their property.[18]

The day after Christmas in 1780, John Honeycut, a North Carolinia soldier, wrote General Greene to beg for a pardon. Honeycut, who enlisted in August 1779 and deserted that October, had a wife and seven small children. He discovered what Confederate deserters learned years later: that deserting was but part of the problem, that once one escaped, it had to be safe to return or desertion was all for naught. The man conceded he deserted without knowing the danger and went home to his family but found it was not safe there. Even after returning home prior to his recapture, he lived in fear for his life from colonial authorities.[19]

Southern families of the Civil War era, particularly those of yeomen, resembled colonial American family units like Honeycut's. Young men came from large families, many with younger children, and worked in subsistence or semi-subsistence households where the male work component was essential. While western North Carolina was far from totally isolated during the Civil War, during colonial times it was only beginning to develop the local and regional trade networks that would be more advanced by the 1860s. Many parts of the mountain South were not as developed as western North Carolina by 1860, and in many ways they resembled the region a hundred years earlier. Honeycut's desertion would be typical of many soldiers who, fighting near home or close enough to home to feel they could safely reach it, opted to desert. However, like Honeycut, many found, either by observing others or through personal experience, that safety remained a key factor. Similarly, during the Civil War, so long as the Confederacy controlled the roads, towns, and countryside, desertion remained risky, even after one returned home. North Carolina families described men "laying out" (hiding) near home to escape the sweep of Confederate home guards. Fear of recapture in turn drove another aspect of Confederate desertion that mirrored Honeycut's experience: desertion to the enemy. However, deserting to the Union required renouncing the Confederate cause and brought with it issues of dishonor and shame that might follow a soldier into civilian life upon his return.[20]

Added to this situation was the fear, unique to Southerners, that large segments of the slave population would be released to prey upon homes and communities, a fear that caused Southern slaveholders to watch their slaves more carefully. Slavery was but one element that the Revolutionary South shared with the Civil War South. Greene found that the region itself was far weaker and lacking in basic resources to fight the war than had been initially represented. Calling the South's war-making capacity "greatly magnified and over rated," he claimed that "a false principle of pride of having the Country thought powerful have led people to believe it was so." Such would also be the case during the Civil War. Southern perceptions of the region's economic and military power proved inflated, and while the army certainly fought as effectively as any other American army before or since, the South's leadership vastly overestimated its economic condition. The young nation's inability to provide for both soldier and civilian proved its undoing and the source of much of its desertion problem. Men were left with no choice but to desert, particularly around harvest time. Five years to the day after the signing of the Declaration of Independence, General Lafayette wrote Greene to tell him that his militia was deserting because of the harvest. Eighty-three years later, regimental records for the Seventeenth Alabama would show men leaving the ranks at harvest time, only some of them to return when the harvest was over.[21]

Desertion during the Revolution continued up to and even beyond the end of the war; then, like the army itself, it disappeared with the return of peace. However, the lessons of America's two great wars of the eighteenth century remained as guides for government and military leaders in the nineteenth century. America of the eighteenth century was agrarian and, in the South particularly, sparsely populated. Regardless of the nation's need, its soldiers remained seasonal soldiers, men capable of providing military service who recognized that their labor was irreplaceable at home. In addition, service was contractual, not indefinite. Men followed into war community leaders who led by deference, not with an iron hand. A change in leadership, a failure to provide certain necessities, or the threat of campaigning beyond the locality or region they had agreed to serve in resulted in desertion.[22]

To say that the North and the South developed differently in the years between the Revolution and the Civil War is to state a truism. Many of those differences formed the source of much of the rhetoric that surrounded the schism between the sections as the war drew progressively closer. Lost in the discussion of the population shift, or rather the North's greater industrial growth, is what this meant in terms of each region's ability to wage war and the types of soldiers each would bring to the conflict. From a military standpoint, the North's development meant that by 1861 it would have a "disposable" male population.

Immigration, industrialization, and mechanized agriculture created a pool of soldiers that could be taken away without severely undermining Northern society's ability to continue. While loved ones would miss those who went to war, life would go on without an appreciable drop in the standard of living. While some households remained "economic units," a growing trend in the North was a move away from this model of the family and toward a less economic and more nurturing concept. Even among Northern farm families, the size of the population meant that the nation could relieve a family of some sons without taking every one of them. At the onset of the war, Northern society would resemble America's military future much more than its past.

In many ways, the South of 1860 continued to resemble the America of the late eighteenth and early nineteenth centuries. First, its white population combined with its preferred form of agriculture to create a potential pool of men who could hardly be called disposable. The South's cotton production, which made that commodity king in the 1850s, was not the result of the efforts of the vast majority of white Southerners. While Southern farmers well below the planter status took part in cotton manufacturing, the degree and purpose of this participation differed significantly from that of their wealthier neighbors. The wealthy made up barely 3 percent of the population, and while this class would figure significantly in the South's progression into war, it would not contribute to the same degree to the army that would ultimately do the fighting.[23] To find the Southern soldier one must go down the food chain into that vast sea of men referred to as yeomen and poor whites. These men and their sons would form the backbone of the Southern army, an army of farmers, men whose lives were as governed by the seasons as the lives of their fathers and grandfathers before them. These men could not be spared in the same way as their Northern counterparts without affecting the quality of their families' lives—and often those families' very survival.

While few contest the agrarian, semi-subsistence character of most of the Confederate army, studies on the social makeup of the Southern soldier are less numerous than one might imagine. The largest study encompasses nine thousand soldiers from seven states in twenty-eight regiments. By far the leading occupation was farmer, with fifty-six hundred men (62 percent) claiming that occupation. The data listed only eleven planters, suggesting that planters might be included in the farmer category. A smaller study encompassed only 390 soldiers. Of that group, 56 percent of the enlisted men claimed farming as their occupation. The smaller study delineated between planters and farmers, lowering the percentage of men likely to be simple farmers. However, its data group was drawn from men who left written records of their experience, which may have excluded men within the farming category because they were not literate and left no record of their experiences.[24]

The key category is enlisted men. A study of Georgia deserters indicated that more than 93 percent of the deserters were from the enlisted ranks, with almost all of those men being privates. The studies of Confederate soldiers may have actually understated the percentage of farmers. Neither indicates when the men enlisted. Although Southerners enthusiastically answered the call in 1861, not all joined. The 1862 Conscription Act left men with the choice of enlisting or being drafted. Many, particularly in regions with mountains or swamps where most worked as farmers and where almost no planters lived, enlisted in 1862.[25] In either case, the Confederate army was made up mostly of yeomen who left farms and families that were dependent on them for essential labor. While social studies of the Confederate army may be limited, the makeup of the Confederate army can be ascertained by looking at the region before the war. Without question, it was almost exclusively agricultural, mostly smaller farms.

What this suggests is that the same factors that existed in colonial society in the South continued to exist in the Civil War South. The "loadstones" of home, family, and community that drew colonial soldiers home would exert a similar pull on Confederate soldiers. This does not mean that Confederate soldiers were automatically going to desert. What it means is that once the hardships that are an inherent part of soldiering and war began to take their toll, the opportunity that home afforded to escape combined with the perception that home not only afforded certain comforts but also stood on the verge of ruin. For many men, the nation they were fighting for proved unwilling or unable to provide what their families needed when they went to war. Studies of immigration to America suggest that pulling up stakes and leaving home for a new land and new opportunity required both a push and a pull. The push came from conditions where they were, and the pull was exerted by the chance for something better.[26] Desertion in the Confederate army would follow a similar dynamic. The push would come from wartime conditions and experiences foreign to most soldiers; the pull would come from home, a place very much like the place their ancestors left when they went to war against the French and later the British. If desertion can be likened to a disease, it had not infected Confederate soldiers the moment they joined the army; rather, they were at a high risk of contracting the disease.

So long as the war went well, home remained secure and distant, families fed and duty clear, men remained healthy. But when the fortunes of war slid or became unclear, when camp life brought disease and death or its monotony drew men's thoughts to home, a home not secure, a family not well fed, these things wore down soldiers' immunity and produced a disease that spread beyond the ranks of the army into the Confederacy as a whole.[27]

Woodbury missed the point. War alone does not drive desertion. After the Civil War, U.S. Army desertion in time of war would be remarkably low. The Spanish-American War, World Wars I and II, the Korean War, and even the Vietnam War would witness desertion rates below 6 percent, some lower than 2 percent.[28] The statistics for the U.S. Army in the post–Civil War era showed that desertion in peacetime was much more prevalent than during any American war after 1865. However, even if his conclusions are flawed and his unwillingness to tackle the Civil War diminishes the usefulness of his study, Woodbury still provides insight into understanding Confederate desertion. First, if he is correct in his assertion that desertion rates during the war were 45 percent, that alone is revolutionary. Second, and just as important, his study and those since suggest that even if the Confederate number of 103,400 deserters is correct, given the size of the Confederate army, the desertion rate was higher than for any previous American war. Thus the potential that desertion hurt the Confederacy exists in the high number alone.[29]

Aside from numbers, Woodbury suggests several aspects of desertion that have significance for the Civil War. Even in 1920 he recognized the importance of the public perception of desertion as a crime and conceded that "the attitude of the public toward deserters and desertion has a great effect on the amount of desertion." Unfortunately, he also had to admit that the attitude taken by civilians toward deserters in 1920 was not a matter of record. During the Civil War that would not be the case, and although what people thought about deserters and desertion was not the subject of a pure statistical analysis, it was clearly articulated. Perhaps Woodbury's greatest contribution was his suggestion that desertion is a progressive process, that one can see it coming by lesser military infractions that begin with simple indifference to duty and escalate to absence without leave, which then becomes permanent.[30]

To follow the analogy of desertion as a disease further, the fact that Confederate soldiers may have been susceptible to desertion does not mean desertion was a foregone conclusion. Certain factors could overcome or at least ameliorate the potential to desert. One factor is patriotism, or a broader sense of nationalism. Before following the progress of desertion, one must look at the extent to which the Confederacy itself, by infusing in its soldiers a sense of nation or country, could override the compulsion to leave when it appeared that the two duties— one to nation and the other to home and family—came into conflict.

In May 1861, E. N. Edwards, president of the North Carolina State Secession Convention, wrote Jefferson Davis to announce the Tarheel state's arrival into the newly formed Confederate States of America. Edwards's short note expressed his desire that the new nation be "strengthened by all the kindred ties of climate, pursuits and institutions, may perpetually 'promote the general welfare and secure the blessings of liberty' to our people and their posterity." By the end of the month the young nation would be complete. Its eleven states, driven from the Union by the sectionalism that dominated America for the preceding fifteen years, now faced the task of turning their collective resistance into a unit that would bind a widespread and diverse population to a common cause.[1]

Edwards's reference to "kindred ties of climate, pursuits and institutions" actually identified some of the attributes of nationalism. But from the beginning, Southerners perceived these attributes in terms of region or section, not nation. William Moore moved from Leon County, Florida, to Shreveport, Louisiana, where he became a member of the Shreveport Greys. Immediately following South Carolina's secession he began keeping a diary. The first entry defined the challenge that faced the Confederacy. Moore believed that within twelve months everyone would know the horrors of war; he was reconciled "to approaching events and whatever the South accepts, I accept her fate as mine." Four months later Henrietta Embree of Belton, Texas, lamented that one family, Americans, would now have to meet in battle, but her heart was truly "with the south . . . she is brave and will not submit nor would I have her now." But the South was not a nation; at best it was a place, a diverse place. The question remained: Were the attributes Edwards spoke of sufficient to create a sense of "nation" among people who in many ways did not share climate, pursuits, or institutions? More importantly, could the South, a region, become the Confederacy, a nation, with sufficient strength and devotion from its citizens and soldiers to meet the challenge of war?[2]

Since 1980 a wave of scholarly literature has been devoted to the existence, strength, success, and failure of Confederate nationalism. The efforts to get a grasp on the Confederacy as a "nation" have clearly helped to define the parameters of the debate, but the existence and shape of Confederate nationalism remain an open question. In the estimation of one historian, a large part of the problem is that "the yardsticks used to measure nationalism's presence or absence have been too abundant, too variegated, and often too vague to give historians sufficient grounds for conclusive agreement." In addition, scholars disagree on how to define nationalism.[3] Thus we must define Confederate nationalism before we can determine if it existed. That question begs a more basic one: What is nationalism?

On one level nationalism is structural. Does a geopolitical entity exercise some form of centralized control and authority over its citizenry? In 1861 some people in both the North and the South conceded the structural nationalism of the Confederacy. It raised armies and navies and conducted war. Its congress passed laws that affected people living in every Confederate state, and its courts administered justice throughout the Confederacy.[4] Likewise, historians have pointed to some of these same attributes of the Confederacy's structural existence as a type of nationalism.[5] However, nationalism is more than structure; it also involves some sense of shared belief or ideology. For the Confederacy, nationalism in a nonstructural sense would prove crucial, because many of the actions taken by the Confederate government as the war progressed would serve to undermine people's sense of loyalty to the nation and its cause.[6]

What, then, is ideological nationalism? Dictionary definitions vary. One describes it as a "devotion to the interest or culture of a nation"; another calls it "loyalty and devotion to a nation, a sense of national consciousness exalting one nation above all others and placing primary emphasis on promotion of its culture and interests as opposed to those of other nations or supranational groups."[7] The definitions are even more disparate when historians try to define the term. One discussion of nationalism begins, "For purposes of this study, nationalism is defined as . . ." One definition calls nationalism a "voluntary, collective identification with a nation and a commitment to that nation." Benedict Anderson describes it as an "imagined political community . . . a deep horizontal comradeship . . . that makes it possible over the last two centuries, for so many millions of people . . . [to be] willing to die for such limited imaginings." Hans Kohn, seeking to draw a comparison between Prussian/German nationalism in the 1860s and Confederate nationalism, draws on an older concept and calls it "a state of mind, in which the supreme loyalty of the individual is to the nation-state. It is characterized by a deep attachment to one's native soil, to local tradition, and to established territorial authority and is marked by certain common objective factors such as common descent, language, territory, political identity, customs, and traditions"—in effect, Edwards's "kindred ties." Kohn's definition emphasizes the existence of a thriving corporate will, a state of mind inspiring or motivating the large majority of people and professing to inspire all of its members. David Potter argues against overemphasizing common culture, instead suggesting that nationalism in general and Confederate nationalism in particular are best understood as a "community of interest."[8]

The South in 1861 seemed to possess many of the attributes necessary to build Confederate nationalism. In theory it should have been able to sustain a national identity as well as the North did, whether common culture or common interest was the key component of wartime unity. Even with the differences of culture within the South, as this and other studies point out, the existence of a common enemy and a common fate (if defeated) should have provided the basis of a collective will. However, what seems clear is that whatever bound the South together as a region or a section before the war did not readily translate into the glue necessary to bind the Confederacy into a cohesive unit once it went to war. Historians of the antebellum South point to the notion of Herrenvolk democracy to explain how the South united its economically disparate white classes into a unified front in support of slavery, an institution from which most did not directly benefit economically. Race, or rather democracy within the master white race, unified antebellum Southerners. While the theory has merit, some historians point to the constant underlying tension and conflict among whites that made Herrenvolk democracy far from a panacea of Southern antebellum harmony.[9] Regardless of which side is correct, race as an antebellum bond among whites would lose its adhesive powers when the Confederacy went to war.

Given the difficulty of finding one definition of nationalism, where have historians found a shared ideology, a collective identification with a nation, or a shared sense of will or commitment? Some have found it in the expressions of "nation" by Southerners in their letters and diaries of the time. For many of these people the Army of Northern Virginia became a symbol of the new nation, and their will crumbled only after that army surrendered. Both as a symbol of the new nation and as a culture around which Southerners cultivate an allegiance, the Confederate flag has been offered as the basis of Confederate nationalism. Another study finds that religion and a belief that the Confederacy was "God's chosen people" provided common ideological ground upon which Southerners could conceptualize themselves as a nation. Slavery remained a key component of this ideology as Southerners strove to make slavery consistent with Scripture. In the end, however, this and other nationalistic beliefs proved inadequate to the task of sustaining people's beliefs in the Confederacy and its cause under the stress of war.[10]

Notwithstanding all of these indications of nationalism, real Southern nationalism would come later, in the wake of defeat, and Confederate nationalism during the war would be an inchoate project that occupied the efforts of its leaders throughout the conflict. In many ways the Confederacy functioned as a nation, at least on the surface, but drafting, taxing, mobilizing, and building a war machine could not engender common will where it did not already exist.[11] The irony of the Confederacy lies in the fact that in trying to build a national identity, it strained what collective will may have existed. As the war dragged on, any strength soldiers could have drawn from a shared sense of national identity to sustain the effort simply would not keep them in the field.

Nationalism is tied to desertion. In a war, particularly one for independence, an army is not only an extension of the fledgling nation but in many ways its most important tool and symbol of national identity. That was certainly the case in the American Revolution, and this was a common historical experience that both North and South drew heavily upon. The Continental army became a symbol of the new nation, something with which all citizens could identify.[12] Likewise, the Confederate military drew men to its ranks from across the South, and some of the individual armies became symbols of a cause and nation badly in need of unifying forces.[13] The ability of these men to continue fighting or their willingness to give up the cause would not only affect the army but would in turn affect the civilian population, particularly civilian morale in the states and regions where these men came from. Collectively, soldiers might be a symbol of nationalism, but without a sense of nationalism themselves, or some other unifying motivation, they could easily become a symbol of disunity. The Confederacy's quest to build a nation, along with the factors that served to unite its people in the absence of such a force, reveal that a true nation is greater than the sum of its parts and that kindred ties of climate, pursuits, and institutions may define a section or a region but, at least in this case, did not make a nation. The soldiers who made up its army felt an allegiance, but it was not to the

Confederacy, and their inability to see themselves as Confederate would make it easier for them to desert when the time came.

In the South, transforming sectionalism into nationalism ran into trouble from the beginning. Fifteen states made up the antebellum South, and when the dust cleared and the sides were drawn at the close of the summer of 1861, four states—Missouri, Kentucky, Maryland, and Delaware, all slave states— had already rejected membership in the new nation. Four others would not secede until after the war began. Thus to the extent that kindred ties existed among the fifteen slave states prior to 1860, those ties did not bind, or at least not sufficiently. The four border states showed a lack of common will among Southern states, but because so few men from the border states enlisted in the Confederate service, they are not a part of the desertion story. The four states of the upper South—Arkansas, Tennessee, North Carolina, and Virginia— however, contributed significantly to the Confederate army, and the inability of a national identity to sustain men from these states and those of the lower South is important to the story.

The notion that the South was divided prior to the war is hardly a new one. The changes in the border states during the antebellum period altered those places to the degree that by the outset of the war they no longer shared a common bond with their more southern neighbors. However, the real divisions existed within the Confederacy, divisions defined in many ways by the very factors that Edwards identified as kindred ties: climate, pursuits, and institutions.[14]

In reality, Southern nationalism was no more cohesive that its wartime muta-tion, Confederate nationalism. The South was not one cohesive unit, nor were its predominant political subdivisions, the states, cohesive units. There were many "Souths." Alabama, Arkansas, Georgia, North Carolina, Tennessee, and Virginia all had at least two and as many as five distinct geographical regions prior to the war. These regions were defined by geography and climate, differences that in turn dictated pursuits and institutions. Mountains, swamps, and piney woods carved the South into unique places and set them apart from the black belt regions where slavery and plantation farming thrived. To say that the entire South was agricultural and therefore bound by a common pursuit is to ignore the differences in agriculture that existed and thereby to fail to understand that different kinds of people emerged from these regions.[15]

The Ozarks of Arkansas, the Smokeys of eastern Tennessee, and the Ap-palachians, running from Alabama and Georgia in the south through western North Carolina and north into Virginia, created subcultures and communities that, although Southern, did not share the same means of subsistence and worldview as their lower Piedmont and black belt kin. This is not to suggest that all these mountain regions were isolated, backward areas completely detached from the world around them. In fact, some were integral parts of thriving regional markets themselves tied to national and international commerce. Western North Carolina had been developing since colonial times, and by the eve of the Civil War it enjoyed a thriving economic relationship with the lower portion of the state, parts of South Carolina, and eastern Tennessee. However, its geography would preclude an active participation in the most sacred of Southern institutions, slave-driven plantation farming. Appalachian North Carolina would embrace slavery, not as a central part of its economy but as a speculative investment during the war, as slaveholders in the eastern part of the state began to sell and move their slaves into the mountains for protection.[16] Eastern Tennessee was anything but backward. When the realities of difference emerged and resistance to Confederate will came from this region, it was not from ignorant mountain dwellers but rather a pastoral revolt from people in the mountain valleys and towns.[17]

Mountains are not necessarily the determiner of sophistication, although they can be. In nineteenth-century America they also dictated streams of commerce that in turn developed kindred and economic ties. For the South, that did not necessarily mean ties with other Southerners. Gettysburg, Pennsylvania, destined to become in the minds of many the crossroads of the Civil War, was a crossroads of a different kind prior to 1860. As the center of a thriving tannery business and wagon manufacturing, it looked for its economic well-being not north but south, into Maryland and West Virginia, regions that depended upon Northern commerce and manufacturing for essentials. Just as the Shenandoah Valley provided an avenue of invasion for both armies during the war, it served as a conduit of commerce prior to the war.[18]

Mountains also isolate and allow people to develop apart from the mainstream of society. Northwest Georgia, the region known at one time as Cherokee County, did not begin serious development until after 1832. Many of its first settlers, gold rushers, hurried off to California when the gold played out. By 1861 it demonstrated social and political attributes far different than those found in the lower Piedmont and black belt regions of the state. Northeast Alabama likewise existed as a subregion of Alabama, connected by few roads and no railroads to the remainder of the state. Arkansas is best described as a frontier when the war began. Even its flat regions and river bottom land were vastly rural, sparsely populated areas even by nineteenth-century standards, with no decent roads, poor railroads, and a vastly underdeveloped infrastructure. Its mountains in the northwest part of the state represented the edge of a frontier and were home to a crude, illiterate, volatile, and hard-fisted yeomanry living in a subsistence-level economy that shared little with those in the regions below them.[19]

Mountains not only isolated; whether or not a region was part of a larger network, mountains meant different climate, and climate meant different agriculture. Simply put, cotton would not grow in the South's higher elevations; temperature and rainfall dictated a different growing season, and that in turn pushed these regions into different agriculture. Food crops, not cotton, dominated the mountain areas. Smaller acreage and more difficult land to clear and farm necessitated larger families and created a world of non-cash, semi-subsistence-based farmers in regions throughout the South. In short, while most people claimed agriculture as their pursuit, it was not always the same pursuit. The key to Southern sectionalism, and many argue to secession, lay in making slavery more than an economic institution. Slavery became the foundation of a political mind-set that bound diverse groups together. While Herrenvolk democracy, the allegiance to "every white man's best government," may have eased the tensions of class and region during peacetime, the further removed one was from the actual economic benefits of the institution, the less bonded one felt to slavery. Thus, to the degree that Confederate nationalism depended upon slavery as an institution to act as a tie among its citizens, it based itself on a foundation that most of its people did not directly benefit from economically. The peacetime benefit flowed from a sense of belonging to the superior race, but even in areas where slavery was strong the tensions between slaveholders and non-slaveholders festered beneath the surface. When war came, it would take more than slavery to bind the poor to the cause.[20]

One did not have to go to the mountains to find difference within the South. Not only did the swampland of Florida, southeast Georgia, southeast Alabama, and Mississippi prove inhospitable for both cotton and other cash-crop agriculture, but slavery, both as an economic system and a basis for Confederate nationalism, likewise disappeared deep into the soft, marshy ground and scraggly pine forests of these regions in the heart of the lower South. Not only did these areas not support slave-based agriculture, but they offered a hard living to those hearty enough to endure the elements, which made the people within them some of the poorest in the South. From 1810, the settlers who flocked to

Alabama were predominantly yeoman farmers; they owned no slaves and had little hope of increasing their lot in life. For most of these people, wealth and fame neither existed nor were sought. Thus, from the inception of statehood in 1819, the mixture of planter and small farmer in Alabama made class conflict a possibility.[21] In some instances, these regions passively resisted the Confederacy; in others, like Jones County, Mississippi—"the Free State of Jones"—witnessed a rebellion of its own during the war, waged in part by Confederate deserters. Jones County reflected the lack of cohesion that existed within states, a problem that found its roots in the way the area developed decades before.[22]

Conflict existed not only within states but between them, and like many of the internal disputes within states, these conflicts had begun long before the war. Alabama and Mississippi had originally been one territory that split prior to statehood. Disputes arose between the Mississippi River settlements that controlled the government and those near the Tombigbee that struggled for more power. One citizen admitted that "nature never . . . designed the two counties to be under the same government." The large territory was split in part because the South saw a benefit in having two states. But the reality was that the people were simply different.[23]

As the South prepared for war, the prospect of fulfilling Edwards's hope that climate, pursuits, and institutions would bind the Confederacy together and ensure both liberty and prosperity already looked bleak. Louisiana, for example, was no more unified than Alabama or Mississippi. It existed as a land of confused loyalties and long-held enmity among its own people that would not only make allegiance to the Confederacy difficult but would later lead to violence within the state. Francophone Arcadians distrusted incoming Anglo-Celtic settlers, while other groups like the Germans of Lac Des Allemands and the scattered pockets of free blacks stood isolated and distrustful. Cotton growers, those most likely to embrace the new nation, took over the northern parts of Louisiana, driving out the former inhabitants, while foreign and newcomer capitalists controlled the wealthy sugar plantations in the south.[24]

To make matters more difficult, pockets within the South, some characterized by geographic differences but others that did not exhibit geographic, climatic, or institutional differences, refused to relinquish their allegiance to the Union. For these people nationalism did exist, a sense of duty to the only nation they had ever known. Lost in the debate over Confederate nationalism is the fact that for some, engendering a sense of nation based upon allegiance to the Confederacy first required severing that same connection to the Union. One Alabama man spoke for many when he said, "I was born and raised in the Union and I expect to die with a Union principal [*sic*] in me[.] I will die before I will take an oath to support the Southern Confederacy." Arkansas provided a good example of this conflict in loyalty. Even in areas south of the Ozarks, a large portion of the population felt a persistent attachment to the Union. What ultimately prevailed was an even deeper unwillingness to go to war with the rest of the South— sufficient to drive secession, but hardly the stuff of nationalism. In every state but South Carolina there was significant opposition to secession, and although this resistance was eventually overcome, departure from the Union did not guarantee a subsequent bonding of the disparate parts.[25]

Men of at least eight of the eleven Confederate States enlisted and fought in the Union army against the Confederacy. This does not take into account those who would later take advantage of a Union program that allowed them to leave prison and enlist in the army to fight elsewhere. By some estimates a total of 47,118 men from the South enlisted in the Union army, with more than half of those coming from Tennessee. Other studies show the number to be as high as 100,000, with men from ten Southern states joining the Union army. The Union raised six regiments of white troops in certain pro-Union areas of Alabama. Arkansas contributed fourteen white regiments, more than 8,000 troops. In contrast, Confederate recruiting efforts in the North yielded very poor results.[26] Military service is the greatest sacrifice a sovereign or nation can demand of a citizen. Between 50,000 and 100,000 Southern men not only refused to embrace the Confederacy but clung to the Union and its institutions despite finding themselves isolated within the rebellion.

Distance, geography, climate, and politics proved formidable obstacles to national unity. Confederate nationalism did not exist when the war began, at least not the unified corporate will that we associate with modern nationalism. True, some "national" feelings did exist, and men frequently wrote of laying themselves "upon the altar of their country" or acting in defense of the nation.[27] But feelings of allegiance expressed by some soldiers still do not rise to the level of nationalism embraced by all citizens and soldiers. Given the limited sources available to historians, a precise breakdown of those who actually identified themselves as Confederates may not be possible. Even the strongest evidence pointing to the existence of a vibrant Confederate nationalism depends on limited proof.[28] Thus, while such feelings may have sustained some men, they offered little consolation to others, particularly as the war progressed. More importantly, one must be careful to understand what "country" meant to these men. It was often something other than a nation.

The absence of nationalism does not preclude the existence of other unifying factors—factors that, although different for each state and even for regions within states, nevertheless gave Southern citizens and soldiers common ground upon which to begin and sustain a struggle against the Union. Southern patriotism did not necessarily depend upon embracing the new nation. It found its source and its strength at levels below the nation, in places where loyalty and duty had always existed.

The Latin root of *patriotism* is *patriae*, which literally means home, native land, or native city. It has come to mean one's country, but *country* can likewise have many meanings, particularly in the nineteenth-century antebellum South. One meaning was clearly loyalty or allegiance to one's state. In April 1861, Bishop Alonzo Potter of the Protestant Episcopal Diocese of Pennsylvania circulated a war prayer to the clergy throughout his diocese. The prayer asked God to come to the country's aid in the face of impending Civil War; specifically, it asked that God "have pity on our brethren who are in arms against the constituted authorities of the land, and show them the error of their ways." Potter's prayer found its way South, and in May 1861 the prayer, selected editorials from the *Pennsylvania Church Journal,* and several Southern responses appeared in an Alabama pamphlet. The "hastily prepared pamphlet" was put forth "with a sincere desire that it may tend in some measure—however small—to the promotion of truth and justice, the correction of error, and the renewal of charity." Within the pamphlet was the response of W. T. Walthall of Mobile, Alabama, to Bishop Potter's prayer. On at least one level, Walthall explained the nature of Southern patriotism: allegiance to state.[29]

Walthall agreed with Potter that all power flowed from God. "Whether republican or monarchial," he wrote, power "exists *jure divino,* and that allegiance is a religious obligation." But there the agreement ended. Walthall insisted that Potter had misunderstood the conflict between North and South. The only question was state authority against federal authority. Southerners, he insisted, were "as true and loyal in our allegiance as you are, but we know no other allegiance than that due to the sovereign state, and such as the state authorizes us to yield to any central or federal authority." The Confederacy was a recognized central authority only because the true source of duty, the state, had acquiesced to that recognition. This was hardly the fervor necessary to build and sustain Confederate nationalism. The sense of "nationalism" or collective will ran to a smaller political subdivision. More importantly, love of state alone was not the source of the allegiance: duty by "divine and human law" was the source of the allegiance. This duty overcame any "traditional love" which they (Southerners) had been taught to entertain for the Union.[30] Thus, while a common belief may not have existed on a national level, the foundation for such a sentiment existed at the state level. The key was to keep the states on the same course, a job that would prove problematic as the war progressed and hardship fell disproportionately upon states. Because soldiers were recruited and enlisted by state, a state's deviation from the shared course could and did undermine the Confederacy's ability to keep men from those states in the army. Just as important, states themselves would have a difficult time sustaining a sense of shared commitment or belief as portions of states and certain classes suffered more intensely than others.

At the outset of the war there is ample evidence, particularly on the part of Confederate officers, that this duty to state overrode any duty to the Union, including the oath many had sworn upon accepting their commissions in the U.S. Army. Robert E. Lee declined not only to serve in the U.S. Army but to be its commander. He could not take up arms against his native Virginia. Among the enlisted ranks one can find this same sentiment. Perhaps more significantly, Southern soldiers came to realize that the key to protecting their states lay in fighting for the Confederate army and winning the war. For some, this became even clearer as the Union army began to invade portions of the South.[31] However, desertion was not an elite or officer phenomenon. While allegiance to one's state may clearly have motivated many officers and some soldiers, most soldiers looked to something more concrete.

The real root of patriotism is "home." Home is local; it is virtually the lowest level of allegiance, and yet in the South it may have been the most important element for the common soldiers. Although some men did feel a sense of nation and more perhaps clung to an allegiance to their native states, what really motivated Southern soldiers was home, community, and to a much greater extent, family. It was the defense of home, fireside, wife, and children that had real meaning for these men. The key for the Confederacy was to translate this sense of local allegiance into a larger commitment to the cause. The importance of this task did not go unnoticed among Southerners. In an article for the *Mobile Daily Tribune* entitled simply "Our Cause," an anonymous writer tied the obedience to state authority to the protection of home and family and specifically identified this connection as the motivating drive of the Southern soldier. In yet another

Southern response to Bishop Potter's circular, the writer referred to a sermon recently preached in a Mobile church in which the clergyman renounced as wicked those who would preach war. But, continued the writer, once called upon by the proper authorities (the state), "taking up arms for the defense of our homes, for the defense of our altars, for the preservation of our civilization from being converted to barbarism, for the protection of our children and the helpless race which is equally dependent on us," Southern men would answer the call. Once at war, the soldier, "thus armed in the panoply of conscientious principle and conviction of duty would be most likely to prove himself the true hero on the battlefield."[32]

In effect, the state, the highest constituted political authority, called upon Southern men to join the cause, not expressly for the Confederacy, or for that matter the state itself, but to protect their local and personal interests. Even references to the protection of "our civilization" and the "helpless race" could be translated into local concerns. As clergymen preached from the pulpit in support of obedience to state authority, they continued to predicate that obedience on the need to protect mothers, wives, and children from subjugation and even death.[33] Not only did the Confederacy lack a true sense of nationalism, but its people realized this problem. Although "state" had a more tangible pull on all people, for the vast majority of the men who would make up the Confederate army, the true allegiance was to home in a narrow sense. People saw themselves as citizens of their own backyards. What initially bonded men to the cause was a common hostility toward the Union, not an allegiance to nation or state. Many soldiers actually understood "country" as land, or earth, and knew only their own. Far from running from nation downward, allegiance ran out from locality. As one South Carolina soldier put it, "I go first for Greenville, then for Greenville District, the up-country, then for South Carolina, then for the South, then for the United States, and after that I don't go for anything."[34] Had he thought more carefully, he would have started with his own home. Significantly, the Confederacy does not appear in his list of loyalties.

However, despite allegiance at the local level, that loyalty could be the glue that bound men from many states together into a cohesive fighting force and sustained them as the conflict dragged on. In a strange way, localism became Confederate nationalism. Patriotism was literally love and concern for home, and therein lies the key. Everyone in the South could identify with a sense of home. Although "place" may have been different depending on where one was from, the notion of place was almost universal. The same could be said of wife and family. One soldier did not have to know anything about the family of another, but he understood the sacred place that home and family occupied. Thus, men from all over the South could join and sustain an effort that at its core was dedicated to protecting each man's personal sanctuary by driving the invaders away. Because regiments were recruited at the county or district level, units were initially made up of men who had a common understanding of what they were protecting. They could in turn join regiments, brigades, and divisions with men from other states who were likewise trying to protect their homes. It did not matter that everyone's home was different; the goal was the same. Thus a collective commitment did exist, one shared by both civilians and soldiers, that saw the real cause as one grounded in protecting personal ground. The beauty of the attachment to locality was that it could be articulated in vague and broad terms. Soldiers frequently referred to the defense of Southern soil and of the South. On its face it speaks to the defense of a large area, of the totality of the Confederacy, but beneath the statement is an implicit understanding that the soil I am defending is "mine."

Not only did Southern soldiers seem to universally understand the concept of home, but from top to bottom they understood that their homes were at stake in the struggle. Forget notions of protecting slavery or of independence; at a very real level the war was about survival. In the early years of the war, Gen. P. G. T. Beauregard knew what the war was about. Glory and politics were not the issue. "We are fighting . . . for our homes, firesides and liberties," he wrote shortly after First Manassas. Gen. Richard Ewell was even more pragmatic: "By taking the side of the South I forfeited a handsome position, fine pay and the earnings of twenty years of hard service." He did so not out of any notion of chivalry or political purpose but for family and community. "Our soil is invaded," he wrote in 1862, "& there is nothing to be done but what we do."[35]

Invasion and soil: these have been powerful motivators as far back as ancient Greece, where yeoman farmer hoplites fought in tight phalanxes in defense of their homes and farms. For the Confederacy, defense of home proved an equally powerful unifying force, at least in the beginning. Gov. Harris Flanagin of Arkansas tried to explain this to Jefferson Davis during the war. "Soldiers do not enter the service to maintain the Southern Confederacy alone," he wrote, "but also to protect their property and defend their homes."[36] Flanagin probably gave the Confederacy too much credit for being a motivating force. Not only would soldiers' letters reflect the desire to protect home and family, but as the war began this need to protect something personal, not some ephemeral sense of nation, would be the justification for stepping forward to fight. From Tennessee came the headline "To the People of Tennessee. Your Homes Are in Danger— Rouse You to the Conflict." The circular appeared in late May 1861 as an "extra" in the *Union and American*. It was signed by the editors of the *Republican Banner, Union and American, Christian Advocate, Nashville Gazetteer, Tennessee Baptist, Daily Nashville Patriot*, and *Banner of Peace*. They called for "every brave man now to defend his home . . . and every true woman to give up her husbands and sons." The circular closed by asking people to adopt certain war measures at a session on June 8, 1861, and in all capitals at the bottom was printed, "READ AND HAND TO YOUR NEIGHBOR." From the inception of the war the message was clear: the duty to step forward may have come from an allegiance to one's state, but its source was much higher. The religious periodicals support the idea that the duty to render obedience to the constituted authority came from God. The goal or purpose, however, was local. Protect your homes.[37]

As evidenced by some of the correspondence from Confederate soldiers and officials, the local nature of soldier loyalty and the need to protect and defend actually created a form of unity that was more concrete and definable than its Northern counterpart. We fight for "matters real and tangible . . . our property and our homes," wrote one Texas private. John Jones, a clerk in the Confederate War Department, echoed this sentiment in 1863 when he acknowledged that "our men must prevail in combat, or lose their property, country, freedom, everything." Even the Union realized what was at stake. "They [Confederates] are animated by passion and hatred against invaders . . . it makes no difference whether the cause is just or not. You can get up an amount of enthusiasm that nothing else will excite."[38] In 1861 Edwin Bass of south Georgia spoke plainly to his mother and sisters about what was at stake and why he answered the call. The South was threatened with "destruction by an inveterate enemy that is willing to show no regard for humanity or the rights of our section." Defense of home, not the cause of the Confederacy; Bass referred to "section," not nation.[39] With a government barely four months old and destined to have to do things that would alienate rather than ingratiate its citizens to its cause, the Confederacy entered the Civil War with soldiers who possessed a unity of purpose perhaps stronger than anything a sense of nation could have provided: survival, the most basic of instincts.

Into the war went the Confederacy, its sense of collective commitment predicated not on a bond between citizens and a nation but on a unity tethered to a foundation at home, on lines running to thousands of different places, all of which seemed to depend on a collective effort to protect. Not only was the source of unity local, but the South used local and community institutions to drive the message home, including churches and their clergy. But the ties that bind can also divide. Home brought men into the service, but in order for it to sustain them, to keep them fighting, the instrument they were all a part of would have to demonstrate that it could repel the invaders and protect a man's soil. Thus, Southern patriotism, nationalism—whatever name one wishes to assign to the Confederacy's glue—depended on success. Keeping the army in the field meant keeping the Union out of the South. Given the size of the Confederacy and the Union's ability to put large armies into all parts of it, this would be no easy task. The farther the Union penetrated into the South, the more it put the Southern army at risk. Southern soldiers could lose their attachment to the Confederacy if they began to believe that the Confederacy could not repel the invaders and that as individuals they were better able to protect their small part of Southern soil by returning to it. Once the government proved unable to keep the Union out, soldiers became susceptible to a variety of factors that weakened their resolve. The hardships of life as a soldier, poor food, disease, and other factors would start to weigh on these men. The safety of those at home no doubt loomed largest, and most disturbing would be not only the presence of the Union army but the inability of the government to protect and provide for their families while they were away. The threat to home and fireside from the Union army was in a sense imaginary. This does not suggest that the Union army's presence in the South did not adversely affect the civilian population. The mere fact that armies live off the land is by itself damaging, as middle Tennessee, northern Georgia, and western Mississippi discovered at various points in the war.[40] But the real threat came from the Confederate government's inability to protect Confederate civilians, not from Union invasion, but from starvation, from each other, and from the Confederate army.

At a basic level, government's job is to protect citizens and their property. Prior to the American Revolution, colonials saw their relationship to the English king as contractual. They had performed certain duties and in turn could look to the Crown to treat them fairly. The concept that government was a contract between rulers and people underwent a radical renovation in the American Revolution. Gone was the notion of a contract between people and rulers; instead, the people agreed among themselves to the formation of government. Like the notion of government, the concept of "contract" was Lockean. Governments had no rights, merely duties. Citizen obedience to government, and by implication its institutions, was by consent.[41] One of the arguments that recurred during the crisis period leading to the war was that the U.S. government not only failed to protect Southern property but actually threatened it by limiting the spread of slavery. That threat in turn created a legal justification for secession.[42] In effect, the South withdrew its consent.

But consent as a basis for Southern loyalty to Confederate institutions proved problematic. The notion that individual citizens had consented to Confederate rule began on shaky ground, as both the government and its leaders were chosen by the South's elite with no popular ratification by its citizens.[43] However, our Mobile, Alabamian, Mr. Walthall, had to some degree underestimated the degree to which many Southerners had learned the lessons they had been taught as former members of the Union. While the "love" may have diminished, or at least been strained, by the rhetoric of the 1850s, the underlying beliefs that formed the basis of the old Union remained a part of the Southern psyche. Government was still a matter of consent. Service in the Confederate military would likewise be a matter of consent. That consent would be conditional. Whether one called it a contract, like that characteristic of colonial soldiers, or a promise, Southern soldiers relied upon the representations of the Confederacy, its state governments, and the elites for whom many perceived they were fighting. Those representations went to the core of government's basic duty to protect persons and their property. In this case, the protection of persons translated into the protection of soldiers' families while they were away at war. If the Confederacy or its power-wielding planter class failed to honor their agreement or keep their promise, the consent to serve and fight could be withdrawn.

The promise was not merely implied; it was explicit. Its earliest expression came from a man who would ultimately withdraw his state's consent to be ruled, Gov. Joe Brown of Georgia. In 1861 Brown proudly claimed that "the government of our state protects their [yeomen] lives, their families and their property. . . . Every dollar the wealthy slaveholder has made may be taken by the Government of the state, if need be, to protects the rights and liberties of all." Brown believed without hesitation that he could call upon all of Georgia's citizens and that they "would come down like an avalanche and swarm around the flag of Georgia."[44]

Brown's statement stands as one of the clearest expressions of the promise made at or near the time the war began. Evidence of the promise would come out as the war continued, and there seems to be little doubt that the government and the rich promised to look after the soldiers' families. Joel Chandler Harris's stories of his Georgia childhood tell of the promise made to soldiers, the breach, and their reaction. In the course of Harris's boyhood adventures during the war, a Mr. Pruitt poses a question to him:

> Now, then, what do you call the fellers what jines the army arter they been told that their familes'll be took keer of an' provided fer by the rich folks at home; an then, arter they been in a right smart whet, they gits word that their wives an' children is lookin starvation in the face, a' stedder gittin better it gets wuss, an' bimeby they breaks loose an' comes home . . . they goes off expectin' their wives'll be took keer of, an' they comes home an fines 'em in the last stages. What sorter fellers do you call them?[45]

Were these men deserters? Probably so. But as the war progressed, soldiers, citizens, and government officials would not only acknowledge the existence of the promise but would recognize that in many respects it was broken.

To keep its promise, the Confederacy would have to succeed in establishing a nation in a purely structural sense. Although engendering a corporate will might have been beyond the reach of any nation as new as the Confederacy, it could still act like a nation and in the process provide the necessary administrative structure to marshal resources and redistribute the necessities of life to civilians and soldiers alike. Confederate nationalism could serve as a cohesive force in a purely structural sense. In order to succeed, the states would either have to allow the central government to exercise powers greater than would be allowed in peacetime by a confederacy, or, if not, the states themselves would have to step up and carry the burden of waging war, including the essential role of protecting the home front when the South's men went to war.

On its face, the Confederate Constitution—both the provisional and permanent versions—provided all the legal authority necessary to impose a national will and centralized control upon the war effort. The Confederate Congress had the power to tax, regulate commerce, raise armies, coin money, and control dissent. The challenge for the Confederate government was to provide for the army without depriving those at home with the basic staples needed for survival. Scarcity of necessaries like corn, meat, and salt plagued the Confederacy throughout the war.[46] The problem would come with application. The undercurrent of states' rights would either frustrate Confederate efforts to wage war, engender ill will among the citizenry, or both. The distinction between state and federal authority that Walthall argued lay at the core of the North-South conflict would in turn plague the Confederacy. Ultimately the responsibility for protecting soldiers' homes and families would fall on the states, and Joe Brown's promise seemed to assume this, as he stated, "the government of our state protects . . ." Again, if nationalism were to operate on the will of the Confederate soldier, it would come from a more local source.

The wealth and resources that the South needed to keep the Confederacy's promise to its soldiers lay with its elite planter class. Those with the most to gain and everything to lose would have to demonstrate a collective will at home that matched the commitment of the soldiers in the field. The task was simple: prevent those left at home from starving. The army took men out of small farm-based, semi-subsistence households. Even without acute tragedy or natural disaster, many soldiers' families would begin to suffer within a year of their men's departure, because despite all their efforts, there were just some jobs women could not perform, planting and harvesting being the two most important. To prevent these families from starving, two things would be required of the planter class: a shift from cotton-based agriculture to grain-based farming and a willingness to share their wealth and the fruits of the harvest with those now incapable of providing for their loved ones. Just as colonial and provincial soldiers refused to remain in the army when the contractual provisions of their service were not honored, Confederate soldiers were at risk to desert if the government and planter class did not honor their obligations.[47]

As the smoke cleared over Fort Sumter on April 12, 1861, America plunged headlong into a conflict that for fifteen years had been building between North and South. Although blood had spilled on occasion, the antebellum struggle had been waged in courtrooms, legislatures, meeting halls, and myriad other venues where the issues of section, expansion, and slavery played out. The struggle over the next four years would be waged on fields, fought with weapons by men on both sides willing to make the ultimate sacrifice. The loss of life would be staggering, and the struggle would test the collective will of both the old Union and its fledgling adversary, the Confederacy.

3. INTO THE BREACH, 1861

If you prick us, do we not bleed . . .
And if you wrong us, shall we not revenge.
Shakespeare, *Merchant of Venice*

Cry Havoc! Let loose the dogs of war.
Shakespeare, *Julius Caesar*

On April 12, 1861, arguments over why the South seceded, which side was in the wrong, or whose conduct led to violence all became irrelevant. America, North and South, had loosed war on the land. As the smoke cleared over Fort Sumter, few people understood what war meant. They certainly could not or did not foresee what was about to transpire. One of the realities of the disunion was that most of the military infrastructure remained with the North. Southern officers resigned their commissions to fight with the Confederacy. The military installations were Union and had to be seized unless they were abandoned. The navy was exclusively Union. In short, to sustain secession the Confederacy would have to build an army from the ground up.

At the outset of the war the Confederacy made a fundamental decision as to how it would wage war, a decision that would make desertion a possibility, if not a problem. Like their Revolutionary forefathers, Confederate leadership rejected the option of fighting a guerrilla war and instead chose to confront the North with a conventional army. It would build an army around its small but talented group of West Point officers. In addition to Robert E. Lee, James Longstreet, and Thomas Jackson, the South counted among its members' younger officers, men whose West Point training was still fresh and who looked at war as a conflict among organized armies with traditional military discipline where victory would be won on the battlefield between armies that openly confronted one another. The process of building an army actually began before Sumter, in February 1861, with the creation of the War Department and the organization of a general staff. The Confederate Articles of War followed on March 6, 1861.[1]

Thus although the Confederacy would have to build an army, before war had even been declared the groundwork for waging war had been laid.

While the Confederacy scrambled to establish the rudimentary structure of government, the army prepared for war. Desertion had not reared its head, and when it did there would be some debate as to how to define the offense. As was the case for so much of the American military's nineteenth-century experience, the crime of desertion had its roots in eighteenth-century regulations. The British Articles of War of 1765 addressed desertion but did not really define the crime. All officers or soldiers who received pay or had been duly enlisted in the service could be put to death if found guilty of desertion. Although the distinction between absence without leave and desertion was unclear, noncommissioned officers or soldiers who "absented" themselves from their commands and were convicted could be punished as the court-martial saw fit. But when did absence become desertion? Clearly it was a question of degree and intent. No noncommissioned officer or soldier could enlist in another unit without a regular discharge, and anyone who knowingly did so would be charged or reputed as a deserter and punished accordingly. Finally, any officer or solider convicted of having persuaded others to desert would be punished as deemed appropriate by the court-martial.[2]

In an army that had no qualms about punishing soldiers severely, the failure to define exactly what constituted desertion did not create a problem. Desertion was what the army decided it would be. A British soldier, while perhaps no more proficient than the Confederate soldier a century later, had no misconceptions about his rights and what he could expect from his superiors. He knew that his officers, men of a different social class, maintained discipline with an iron hand. Leniency was not something to expect; it could only be hoped for. However, these same ambiguities within Confederate military regulations would create discipline problems that the British army had never imagined. Those ambiguities would not only hinder the ability to convict deserters but also influence the severity of the punishment.

The rules and regulations of the Confederate army mirrored those of the British. Article 20 of the "Act for Establishing Rules and Articles for the Government of the Armies of the Confederate States" stated that any soldier or officer receiving pay or duly enlisted in the service would suffer death if convicted of desertion. Article 21 made it a crime to absent oneself from one's unit but left both the punishment and the offense up to the discretion of the court-martial. Article 22 made it desertion to join another unit, and Article 23 made it a crime for any soldier to induce another to desert.[3] The decision to fight a traditional war with a traditional army brought traditional regulations. However, the application of these regulations would prove difficult, because a citizen army would resist the rigidity of formal military regulations, and an officer corps, even though predominantly professional, would still hesitate to severely punish desertion, particularly early in the war. Officers with no professional training, men who led in civilian life and were accustomed to leading by deference, would find it even more difficult to impose military discipline.[4]

Defining desertion, establishing guidelines for controlling it, and imposing penalties only partially addressed the problem. To combat desertion if and when it occurred required a police force. The entity charged with maintaining order and discipline in the Confederate army would be the provost guard. Legally, the Confederate Articles of War provided everything necessary to establish the Confederate provost. Eventually the Confederacy would have a divisional and corps provost guard and a headquarters provost guard with the Army of Northern Virginia. However, the discipline problems that arose in Richmond as that city became the central receiving depot for thousands of new troops made it imperative that a military police force maintain discipline. More importantly, all of northern Virginia became an active war zone as both armies faced off near the two national capitals, and to meet the increased need for security and discipline a brigade-level provost guard existed in the Confederate army before First Manassas.[5]

The undisciplined nature of the volunteer soldier, both North and South, required an effective provost guard. Although drill and training would make Civil War armies effective killing instruments, many young men who knew little discipline prior to war found it difficult to embrace the rigidity of army life. Even Robert E. Lee, perhaps one of the most disciplined soldiers in American history based on his West Point record alone, admitted, "I could always rely on my army for fighting, but its discipline was poor." Thus the entity charged with enforcing discipline, including desertion regulations, faced a daunting task from the start. Its job became more difficult for several reasons peculiar to the war and the Confederacy's unique needs. First, what began as a military police unit would eventually have both military and civilian jurisdiction. Because the war was fought in the South, the need to control the conduct of civilians as well as soldiers was important and became more so as the Union pushed deeper into the Confederacy. As a result, the provost guard found its jobs increasing in number and diversity. Second, the Confederacy had to defend a vast area. In time the various district commands spread as far as Texas and became virtually their own governments. Keeping these large areas patrolled demanded more men, something that would plague every aspect of the Confederate military, including the provost. Finally, the Confederacy chose not to create a separate provost guard; it filled the ranks of the provost guard by detailing officers and men for such duties for extended periods of time. Often these men were chosen because of an illness or wound that made normal military service impossible. Units employed as a provost guard seldom spent long periods of time performing their police functions and enjoyed little of the continuity desired in other military units.[6] To the degree that desertion would damage the Confederate cause, that damage would be lessened or compounded by the proficiency of the provost guard.

As the war began, both sides hastened to put armies in the field for a conflict that neither thought would last longer than a year. Enlistments in the Confederate army were initially for one year, and young men across the South answered the call. As one would expect from a true "national" government, the Confederacy appealed not only to its native sons but to a small but significant immigrant population. Advertisements appeared calling on Irishmen to help fight against "our enemy," one that threatens more of a tyranny than their Revolutionary forefathers fought against. The "cause" even drew men from the North, as reports came in of two hundred Illinoisans crossing the river near Paducah, Kentucky, to join the Confederate army.[7] With war fever raging and men rallying to the flag, Southern patriotism from both soldiers and civilians ran high. From Richmond, J. B. Jones, a clerk in the Confederate War Department, marveled at the contributions of clothing and other provisions that flowed into the city. He estimated that at least twenty thousand dollars' worth came into Richmond each day. "Never was there such a patriotic people as ours," he wrote on October 9, 1861. Soldiers expressed the same zeal for the conflict. W. D. Wynne, a private in the Army of Northern Virginia, wrote his sister in September 1861. Upset that she had not written, he asked, "Do you think that because I am so far from home that I have no anxiety to hear from all of you? Home is as dear to me as ever," he insisted, "but do not think for one moment I would trade my present mode of living (though hard it be) for all that home could give. I have willingly sacrificed all this for my country's honor and come what will I have a heart to bring myself through all." Clearly, some sense of a shared commitment existed.[8] For some soldiers who eagerly answered the call, the Confederate cause was irrelevant;

they had priorities of their own. Pvt. C. C. Taylor wrote his father in July 1861, telling him it was unlikely they would ever meet again. They had apparently fallen out, but Taylor asked his father to forgive and forget, adding, "My mind is made up to be in the front rank if we ever get into a fight and there to make my mark if my heavenly father spares my life." Taylor had reasons for going to war that transcended cause and country.[9]

Perhaps more troublesome to Taylor than his relationship with his father was the realization that some Southern men had chosen not only to reject the Confederacy but to fight for the Union. Writing from Sewell Mountain in October 1861, Taylor told his father that his unit was almost in a fight and that they were opposed by Virginians, Tennesseans, and Kentuckians. He did not see how these men could possibly fight as well for the Union as they could for the Confederacy.[10] But Taylor's observations were important, because the signs were there early. Despite the clear support, indications of disunity nevertheless emerged. Mrs. Charles Besser wrote her husband from Enterprise, Mississippi, in June 1861 to describe the tremendous excitement and constant raising of companies of soldiers. But amid all the excitement came a sobering reality: "The misfortune here is there is too many home companies." In other words, men were willing to join, but not for Confederate service. R. B. Hardman wrote his brother from San Patricio, Texas, in August 1861. Hardman called the country the "coldest place for patriotism." From what he could tell not one single regiment had mustered from the county, and Hardman believed it was the only place in Texas like it. From New Orleans and St. Louis came word that units mustered from Mississippi refused to either serve in the Confederate army or to honor their twelve-month commitment. In Huntsville, Alabama, James Thrower observed the same sentiment Hardman saw in Texas: abolitionists openly resisting the Confederacy, local citizens fighting with soldiers, and the civilian population selling goods to soldiers for three times their value. Back in Mississippi, a Wilkinson County man, Jesse Ogden, wrote Gov. John Pettus complaining of slackers unwilling to step up for the cause in his neighborhood. John Dickerson sought Pettus's assistance with a volunteer company for citizen vigilance to put down disloyalty in the Fair River, Missouri, area: clear signs of unwillingness to join the fight and foreboding of things to come.[11]

Somewhat obscured by the avid turnout and expressions of patriotism was the reality that the Confederacy had problems raising troops from the beginning of the conflict.[12] An exchange between Confederate secretary of state Leroy P. Walker and Louisiana governor Thomas Moore shows how difficult it was to

INTO THE BREACH

raise an army as well as the tenuous connections among citizens, states, and the national government. Walker wrote Moore in late June 1861 regarding the immediate need for two regiments for duty at Corinth to protect the Mississippi Valley. His letter expressed confidence in Confederate success but was tempered with what he termed the "uncertainties of war." In an effort to cover all possible needs, the Confederacy was looking to raise a reserve army of thirty thousand men, and Walker wanted Moore to provide 10 percent from Louisiana. The complete exchange is not intact, but in mid-July Walker wrote Moore again, apparently in response to a letter Moore had sent on July 6. Walker began by applauding Louisiana's patriotism. It seems that he had questioned the state's commitment, and Moore had called the secretary on this point of honor. Walker admitted that troops were slow in coming. With the Union in Virginia on the eve of First Manassas, neither Virginia nor the Confederate government could assemble sufficient troops to meet the challenge. Walker insisted that he need not "stimulate any Southern functionary by belabored appeals to his patriotism, to make extraordinary exertions. The occasion itself is a most extraordinary one. It is a common cause and we have to fight a common enemy." By August the Confederacy was pressing the governors to direct their state quartermasters to requisition clothing and other provisions to meet the demands and needs of the soldiers. A war that had been expected to end quickly now appeared to be continuing, at least through the winter. [13]

The Walker-Moore exchange is revealing in several ways. First, it is clear that a thriving voluntary commitment to the cause did not exist among the entire Confederate citizenry. Whatever was driving men to enlist and women to support them, it did not rise to the level of a collective state of mind that motivated the large majority and inspired all of the Confederacy's citizens. Even with war a reality, people were hesitant to step up. A crisis that should have required no explanation or need to invoke patriotic feeling was requiring both. In an emotional sense, the Confederacy did not exert a strong sense of nationalism upon its members, either individuals or states. As a nation it was also struggling to perform one of the most vital ministerial functions associated with a government preparing for war: raising an army to defend its borders. This struggle would lead to one of the most controversial and possibly divisive decisions the national government would make: conscription. The binding concepts of home and land, while appealing to some to join the larger cause, compelled others to limit the extent of their military commitment to serving locally, or not at all. While it is unfair and historically inaccurate to measure the level of commitment to the cause of those who did join by the diminished commitment of those who would not, the unwillingness of the total population to embrace the cause and crisis over time could only undermine the resolve of those who committed early.

The need to compel patriotism clearly drove conscription, and that need was manifest in the inability to rally men to the military. South Carolina, the birthplace of the secession movement and the first state to act, fell short of the mark when political action required military force. Conscription came early in 1862, and former senator James Chestnut of South Carolina placed the blame for its imposition on the inability to draw volunteers in 1861. That inability stemmed directly from the force within Southern society that was to be its most important unifying element: home. Rather than draw men to the bigger cause, it retarded enlistment, and when home combined with other elements of civilian life that forced men to choose, they chose to stay home.

By January 1, 1862, 27,362 South Carolinians had joined the Confederate service. Of that number, 7,111 had joined for the war, the remainder for shorter periods. Confederate enlistment had severely crippled the state's ability to maintain a home militia. With an additional 5,000 men organized into sixty-four companies, South Carolina had still produced only half of its men eligible for military service by the end of 1861. By February 1862 that number increased only slightly to just over 30,000. Chestnut was adamant that the lack of South Carolinians in the service was not the state's fault. Gen. William Hardee had pursued recruits vigorously, but Chestnut had to admit that "while the men were in the country, the spirit was wanting. Very few volunteered and it became necessary to resort to a draft." Chestnut tried to explain to the Confederate government why voluntary enlistment lagged so badly. He insisted it was not from a lack of patriotism, yet his explanation suggests that patriotism, or dedication to home, and self-interest were exactly what crippled enlistment. He believed that the "time of the call was unpropitious to the agricultural interest, [and] the country to which they were ordered was supposed to be unhealthy at that season. The activity and love of ease and convenience, and the desire to pursue ordinary vocations had their full influence on those that remained."[14]

The call for troops came at planting and would continue through harvest. As other soldiers would attest from firsthand experience, as fall turned to winter and the weather likewise turned, the places where the Confederacy marshaled its forces, particularly northern Virginia, posed health hazards directly tied to the difference in climate. These men had not deserted per se; they simply refused to join. But, when the draft came in 1862, it would draw more men into the service than those who allowed themselves to be drafted. Many, faced with the inevitability of military service, chose to volunteer at the last hour. These men, though not technically conscripts, were also not "pure volunteers." Their commitment to the Confederacy, and thus its army, had already been tested and found wanting.

Compounding the signs of discord were early indications of hardship. In the summer of 1861, Governor Pettus was already receiving indications that enlistment of soldiers was working a hardship on families in Mississippi. G. W. Smith of Tishomingo County wrote seeking assistance for destitute families of volunteers. John Johnson pled with Pettus to return his son from service because his parents in Neshoba County needed him at home. From Winston County, Mrs. W. H. C. Lane asked Pettus to release her husband from duty to return home where he was "so desperately needed." Pvt. I. L. Walton of the Tenth Mississippi Infantry wrote Pettus on August 12 from Fort McRee, Florida, seeking a discharge. Walton had left behind in Arkansas a mother and sister who were completely dependent on him for support. By the end of the summer some entire units were requesting they be returned to Mississippi. Fifty-eight members of the Pontotoc Dragoons petitioned Pettus on August 30 to ask that their unit be reassigned from Tennessee to Mississippi.[15]

The war had not begun in earnest, and key elements of Confederate unity were already beginning to unravel. Mississippi's unrest demonstrated a reality that would characterize the war in the South. Different regions experienced the war differently at different times. Hardship would not really strike Georgia, for example, until late 1862 and 1863. Yet it seems clear that in some parts of Mississippi the brief absence of soldiers had already begun to undermine local family and community. The unifying concept within the Confederacy was protection of home and fireside, and soldiers and citizens alike in Mississippi were demanding that they or their loved ones return to Mississippi for that very reason. The pleas that began in 1861 would not abate until after the fall of Vicksburg in 1863. At a minimum, these requests put pressure on the government to step up and make good on Joe Brown's boast that every planter dollar would be used to care for the soldiers' families.[16]

In parts of Alabama the situation was much the same. The picture in Pike County, in the southeast corner of the state, was bleak. Maj. William Moxley left in July 1861 with the Eighth Alabama. In late November his brother wrote to tell him how much life in the county had changed in just a short time. There was no money to be had. People were taking corn to Greenville to sell it for salt, but without cash, bartering was the best that could be hoped for. Emily, William's wife, painted an even darker image. Even though little fighting had been done, poor soldiers were coming home corpses. The Pike County company had departed in September, leaving Emily with no brothers and no husband. With no men in the county and her husband gone, Emily could find very little male support, and she was having a difficult time getting along without it. By Christmas 1861 she had no meat, no money, and no salt. William's situation was no better. He described a picture that would become all too typical. Far from home and in a climate to which they were unaccustomed, soldiers were succumbing to illness. William also saw signs that both citizens and officers were using the war to speculate, making necessities that much more difficult to come by. As in part of Mississippi, destitution came to parts of southeast Alabama before anyone was prepared.[17]

North Alabama fared no better. James Thrower had described the early signs of trouble in the mountain region of Alabama, and this area, already predisposed to dissent, was suffering by early winter 1861. In a letter from Huntsville in November 1861, the Mason family wrote their son and described the situation at home. Northern Alabama was already getting bad, and there was no cash in these "Lincoln Times." "Unless something is done for the people," they added, "many, very many will have to suffer and some will suffer intensely and I do not know what the people are to do about taxes." Children were dying from diphtheria, and a woman named Sally Brown lost four of hers in three weeks. "In these times of war it seems sickness sweeps off those who the sword has spared." The Masons felt for all families who were suffering and expressed a heartfelt gratitude for those willing to lay their lives down in defense of "our homes, families and firesides."[18] The question the Mason letter begs is, how long would men be willing to lay down their lives when their families suffered and their children died at home? Serving in the Fourteenth Alabama in northern Virginia, just a mile from the Potomac River, Thrower admitted that he and others knew it was rough at home. To make matters worse, it was hard in Virginia. He warned his brother Sterling that he was sorry to hear that their brother Ben had joined a company forming in Auburn. James hoped Ben did not come North because he did not think Ben's health would stand the cold climate. It was hard at home and hard at the front, and the fighting had not begun in earnest.[19]

Although it was hardly cause for concern or a sign of the epidemic that would come, deserters began to appear in 1861. While few in number, in some instances these early departures signaled later trends. For example, Alabama's early desertion came from men who resided in its northern towns and counties, Huntsville and Scottsboro, places where Confederate sentiment had been weak when the war began. Mississippians stationed in Kentucky had begun to desert, and George M. Mosley, commander of the First Mississippi Volunteers, transmitted a list of deserters from his unit. Mosley's men had deserted from the First Mississippi to the Walker Reserves, a home guard unit, and he forwarded their addresses and physical descriptions to Governor Pettus. Mississippi officers in Virginia had similar problems, one reporting the desertion of a man from the Nineteenth Mississippi encampment in Richmond. On December 22, 1861, Pvt. Michael Welch, identified only as being in the "57th" from Wurtz County, was admitted to the hospital. On Christmas Day he deserted—the first man who took advantage of injury or sickness to desert a hospital of the Confederate Army of Tennessee.[20]

The volume of the early desertions could hardly be deemed significant, but the fact that it began before the real horror of war on the battlefield had occurred is significant. It indicates that in certain regions of the South, home and fireside were in danger, not from the North, but from the absence of men. Either the government had not provided for soldiers' families or the men did not believe the relief was adequate. It seems that no state's troops were immune. Louisiana had to address the desertion problem in earnest by the fall of 1861 as officers received specific instructions on the arrest of men deserting in and around Fort Livingston. Three Texans were shot in early December of that year near Fort Gibson. South Carolina troops were already demonstrating the problem inherent in keeping in the service solders who lived so close to where they served. The *Charleston Mercury* reported that two men had deserted from positions in and around Charleston. One, a native of Prussia, was originally a seaman. He had deserted his artillery company assigned to the newly captured Fort Sumter on August 5, 1861. A second man, serving in an infantry company on Sullivan Island, apparently deserted to try to get aboard one of the numerous privateers leaving the harbor at the time or to find a place in another volunteer company. At the time these incidents were hardly cause for concern, but the problem persisted among South Carolinians. An order from Gen. John Pemberton directed to brigade and regimental commanders in December 1861 sought to deal with the problem of men leaving picket duty. It directed all commanders to have any man leaving his picket tried for deserting his post and "made an example of." Not even proud Virginia was immune from these incidents of early flight. Amid cries of "War, War, War," Virginia newspapers reported isolated cases of desertion, such as Benjamin Akers, a private in a company from Lynchburg who was arrested for desertion in Petersburg in July 1861.[21]

Lt. William Crutcher enlisted in the Second Mississippi in 1861 from his home in Vicksburg. Stationed with the Army of Northern Virginia, he corresponded frequently with his wife, Emily. Their letters in December 1861 reveal the problem the Confederacy would have keeping its army in the field. With national unity so closely tied to the protection of local interests, victory was essential. Not just victory where a soldier like Crutcher served, but victory in the parts of the Confederacy where home lay. From Richmond, Will expressed his sorrow at their separation and his hope that the war would not last long. At that point in the war Crutcher believed a Northern invasion of Vicksburg was unlikely. If and when the Union came, he believed the Mississippi would run red with blood and that if the North were to reach Vicksburg they should "sack and destroy [the city] before Yankee hands shall contaminate a single item of Southern Property." Crutcher condemned Jefferson Davis for showing no concern for the cotton states. If Davis were really concerned, Crutcher believed, he would send an army to guard against invasion. With the Confederacy oblivious to the threat to Mississippi, Crutcher told Emily exactly how he felt:

> When Columbus [Missouri] falls and the day is just in that vicinity, you may expect to see me come home on the double quick. I have much to provide for and protect in Vicksburg, in fact all that I have in this world is sheltered by the seven hills of the city and tho I flatter myself in being a soldier obedient to all lawful superiors, I have no idea of my wife being left unprotected so long as I can handle a rifle—I would hate to desert, hate to have the stigma sticking to me and those after me who would bear my name, but I am human, and if die I must I will die where I know my efforts have at least been directed to the preservation of the dearest property I possess on earth.[22]

Crutcher's words spelled out the Confederate dilemma for both soldier and country. With few of the emotional ties that gave rise to a sense of nationalism, the Confederacy depended on allegiance to state and the almost universal feeling on the part of its soldiers to protect home, family, and property. However, each soldier's willingness to place himself and his efforts where the nation felt they were most needed was easily undermined if the Confederacy's sense of priority differed from that of its soldiers. The situation worsened where soldiers felt their homes and firesides were subordinated and, as a result, left unprotected. Dedication to military service remained strong so long as the military proved capable of protecting home. Desertion was a very real option—undesirable, but preferable to the alternative. In the end, if a man was going to die, he would die at home trying to do what his "nation" or state either would not or could not do: preserve "the dearest property I have on earth."

Crutcher was an officer, and despite his beliefs, he and his wife knew that abandonment of duty was probably not an option for him. Emily's replies reflect the resolve many historians find within the Confederacy. She assures him that "she has the noblest husband in the Southern Confederacy." He in turn knew that for him desertion was not an option, at least not in 1861. But for others, and perhaps even for Crutcher further down the road, the Southern cause might lose so much of its luster that deserting no longer presented a moral conflict. Crutcher could already see aspects of war that might drive men home. He had seventeen men in the hospital, sick from the steady movement and "weather such that a majority of us Southerners are not accustom." Sickness could weaken resolve, and hospitals would provide opportunity. As warfare became more deadly and home more alluring, Will admitted to Emily that "when a man wants to see his wife so badly—desertion is almost a justifiable crime." But, as he concluded his Christmas message home, he acknowledged that as a soldier he belonged at the front. "Sick men and cowards go home. I came to the war for the purpose of fighting for my wife and I can't desert her cause under any circumstances."[23] Strong words, perhaps even true, but if Crutcher could not envision the circumstances where he might desert, a possibility one must doubt given his earlier sentiments, other men in the army could and would. It was still 1861, and the war was young.

Will spoke for many men in his urge to return home, his fear of his family's struggling too far away for him to help, himself sick and suffering in a climate that was clearly not shared by most Southerners. Emily shed light on just how bad things could be. It was clear that her situation had not escalated to a critical level. But consistent with the letters pouring into Governor Pettus's office in 1861, for poorer men the times were already getting hard. In her last letter of the year, Emily told Will of the surrender of 905 Confederate soldiers in Missouri. The war no longer "excited her," and she found it disgraceful that so many men surrendered before one of them was killed. Turning to matters at home, she described the wife of a poor soldier and how her husband's pay was inadequate to meet her needs. Emily and Will's mother had tried to care for the young woman. Everyone in Vicksburg seemed dedicated to working for the soldiers, and Emily was trying to do her part. She wanted to see Will, but she deferred to his judgment. As 1861 closed the Southern people were beginning to feel the weight of the Confederacy's struggle for independence. In 1862 the war at the front would begin in earnest, but the war at home had already begun. Winning in Tennessee and Virginia would require keeping men in the field and throwing back the Union. Winning at home would demand that the Confederacy keep its promise. Neither would prove easy.

In the summer of 1861 it had seemed that it would be easy. The early stages of combat yielded impressive Confederate victories at Manassas and Wilson's Creek. More importantly, the South's upper class appeared to be rallying and closing ranks, showing signs of keeping the promise Joe Brown had so clearly articulated. In what the *West Baton Rouge Gazette and Comet* deemed a "Patriotic Move in West Baton Rouge," planters in West Baton Rouge Parish had organized a Confederate League in late June 1861. Some of its members had signed an agreement to deliver hogsheads, sugar, molasses, and corn to the Confederate government at market price and accept 8 percent Confederate bonds as payment.[24]

Even Mother Nature seemed to smile upon the Confederate cause. From Georgia to Texas came news of fair weather and bountiful crops. "What a glorious Fourth of July was yesterday," wrote a *Richmond Dispatch* reporter from Tuskegee, Alabama. "The merciful heavens celebrated it by sending down the most gentle and refreshing showers I have ever beheld." The ground had been completely soaked, and the farmers were "cheerful and happy." The forward corn was now safe, and in language somewhat akin to the nineteenth-century notion that rain would follow the plow, the writer expressed no doubt "of the universality of this rain in the Southern Confederacy." Even if it were not to rain another drop on the corn, the wheat alone, boasted the writer, was enough to feed the cotton states and the army. A letter from Albany, Georgia, dated July 6, 1861, echoed the Alabama optimism. "We shall in this section make plenty of corn to feed everything in this country, and to feed the army for twelve months." The wheat crop in northern Georgia apparently had "abundance to spare. With plenty of provisions and soldiers we can whip old Abe and his abolition band."[25]

But despite fair weather, internal schisms began to appear as 1861 came to a close, not so much among people but among the states. A dispute surfaced between Georgia and Tennessee over the planting of cotton versus food crops.

A Georgia editor commented on a resolution by the Tennessee legislature which recommended that the whole force of the South turn from planting cotton to producing food provisions. The editor argued that cotton was Georgia's only staple and that it could not compete with Tennessee and other states in the production of grain, nor could it sell at their prices. The substitution of grain, a short-term crop, would leave a vast amount of labor, both slave and animal, unemployed for a great portion of the year. Besides, the editor argued, cotton was the key to leveraging England.[26]

The debate is significant, but even more significant was the language. With the state as the highest unit of loyalty among Southerners, discord in the political arena could not bode well for soldiers or civilians who would soon find their resolve tested. The notion that Georgia was "competing" with other states and that its own economic well-being would be an overriding factor in a debate over the soundest policy toward winning the war undermined efforts to bring the South together. The hope that climate, pursuits, and institutions would bind the Confederacy together seemed dashed as the Georgia-Tennessee exchange evidenced differences in climate that altered the nature of agricultural pursuits and in turn displayed the disparate reliance upon the South's most sacred institution. Was this a precursor to military desertion? Probably not. Was it a sign that citizen allegiance to the most important political subdivision, the state, might conflict with Confederate goals? Clearly. Perhaps most important for the military was the debate over crop distribution and tax in kind. Each issue had a direct affect on the Confederacy's ability to feed both its army and its civilian population. That debate would come to affect desertion as the Confederacy moved out of the preliminary stages of the war and into 1862, when the war would escalate at home, abroad, and on the battlefield.

On December 21, 1861, the Confederate Congress passed "An Act for the Protection of the Frontier of the State of Texas." It called for the creation of a Confederate regiment to be sent to the Texas frontier, not to fight the Yankees but to protect the civilian population from an even greater threat: Indians.[27] The act was significant for several reasons. First, it acknowledged that domestic security was the responsibility of the Confederate government and that the government had moved to meet its obligations. Second, it recognized that the requirements of Confederate military service had hindered Texas's ability to protect its own borders. Finally, it demonstrated a key aspect of the Confederacy: different parts had different needs. Protecting home and fireside would be more complicated than simply preventing Union incursion. In essence it recognized that the Confederacy faced war on more than one front and from more than one adversary. Texans far from home fighting for the Confederacy would look to see that home was protected from this unique threat. As the war progressed, Indian raids would become increasingly problematic for the Confederacy and its need to keep an army in the field.

The legislation to protect Texas reflected the Confederate government's attempt to keep its army intact by making provision for the protection of homes and families on the frontier. However, by this point it was becoming clear that the Confederacy's resources were already stretched and that the protection of one area might result in the exposure of another. More importantly, those states left exposed would take matters into their own hands and begin to provide for their own protection. In the process of articulating the argument for keeping men at home in a state army, the state governments foreshadowed the exodus to come, as neither state nor Confederate governments could adequately provide for and protect those at home. The argument the states used in 1861 to withhold troops from Confederate service for home protection would sound very much like that used by individual soldiers who withdrew from military service as the war dragged on. The most outspoken man on the issue in December 1861 was Gov. Joe Brown of Georgia.

In a special message to the Georgia legislature on December 5, 1861, Brown explained the situation on the Georgia coast. Using an exchange of correspondence with the Confederate secretary of war, Brown laid bare the conflict between Confederate priorities and those of the state and the extent to which a state, in this case Georgia, would allow the Confederacy to make decisions about how war resources would be prioritized. According to Brown, he had done everything he could to induce the Confederate government to increase the forces along Georgia's coast before he took steps to bolster those defenses with state troops. Brown was adamant that the Confederate government was not guilty of any "wilful neglect," since the Confederacy was using the means and forces at its command "in such a manner, and at such places as will best promote the general good." But from their vantage point in Virginia they thought that the "greater necessity for the troops and reserves at their command, [belonged] at other points." As a result, Georgia's coastline was left inadequately defended.[28] The problem now was that the Confederacy needed the soldiers whom Brown had enlisted in the state service.

Brown had waited as long as possible before acting. By September 1861 newspapers all over the North proclaimed the strength of the Union fleet and declared that Georgia would be invaded from the sea. Quoting directly from the Confederate Constitution regarding the authority of a state to engage in war "when actually invaded or in such imminent danger as will not admit of delay," Brown stated that the people of the coast continually called for protection. Had he delayed and waited for Confederate help that might never have come, he argued, the verdict of every Georgia patriot would have been "one of universal condemnation." The Union's invasion of the Georgia coast vindicated the governor's decision. However, the Confederacy's need for troops notwithstanding, some members of the Georgia legislature wanted to disband the Georgia coastal defense force, or transfer it and the expense of maintaining it to the Confederacy. Brown objected, and his rationale underlined the duel nature of patriotism as a binding national force in the Confederacy, a force that could either draw people to embrace the cause or lead them to reject the nation.

Brown had promised at the outset of war that every dollar of the planters' money would be used for the protection of Georgia and her citizens. Now he needed $5 million to support his coastal force, and the legislature—of which some members were wealthy planters—was balking at the price tag. For Brown it was simple math. Georgia had property worth $700 million and faced the prospect of a Union invasion. If the state was lost, then so was its property. How could anyone refuse to spend a smaller sum to protect the larger? If troops were transferred, the Confederacy would pay the expense and then pass it back through to the states, including Georgia. If the troops were disbanded, Savannah and the coast would fall and the loss would be ten times the proposed expense of supplying the force. Brown stated flatly that Virginia, Louisiana, Tennessee, North and South Carolina, and "probably other states" had all formed and financed state troops for local protection, and no one in those states complained. Tennessee had spent $5 million in six months with no resistance from the legislature. To Brown this was an aspect of the "promise," and the wealthy needed to step up and allow Georgia to protect her own citizens and soil.[29]

Patriae, patriotism, and home were key themes in drawing men to fight, Brown argued, and equally vital if they were to be expected to stay. As far as Brown was concerned, all the property and money in the state "is as nothing compared to the principles involved." The men on Georgia's coast had volunteered as "state" troops, not Confederate soldiers. It was not a part of their contract that they could be transferred to the service of the Confederacy, and the state had no right to do so without their consent. These men "are not cattle to be bought and sold in the market," Brown insisted. "They [are] brave, generous, high-toned freemen, who have left their homes at the call of their state, and are now undergoing all the fatigues and hardships of camp life for her defense—. While they are brave enough to defend their rights," he continued, "they are intelligent enough to understand them; and we are greatly mistaken if we suppose they will submit to a change in their present organization, or to an act of injustice to those who have their confidence, and who have been legally appointed to command them."[30]

It is unclear if he realized it at the time, but Brown had defined the Southern soldier, regardless of where he served, or in which army. Whether from the mountains, piney woods, black belt, or frontier, these soldiers understood their rights and obligations as well as the obligations their government owed to them. In Brown's words, the government would be "greatly mistaken" if it thought it could mistreat these men and not have them know it and respond accordingly. As the war progressed, mistreatment, or breach, would become a matter of interpretation. Conduct the army saw as necessary would be onerous to soldiers and their families. The government's inability to provide for families and protect home would become a breach of the promise. Brown understood what was at risk. His description of Georgia soldiers is replete with the symbols of Confederate nationalism and patriotism. These men were not poor soldiers, and they were certainly not slaves. They were "freemen," members of the highest class regardless of wealth, first among equals in every white man's "best government," concepts that lay at the heart of Southern Herrenvolk democracy. They had left their homes to protect the collective "soil" and suffered the lot of a soldier to do so. Although they were brave and patriotic, both qualities had limits. Brown's immediate concern, changing unit organization without consent, would cause some desertion later. His larger concern—that soldiers would perceive injustice or a lack of support and react accordingly—would prove more damaging, and in Will Crutcher's words, desertion would become a "justifiable crime."

Brown's message summarized what had happened to the Confederacy during the first year of the war. A section trying to become a nation had begun to lose even its sectional cohesion. Including Georgia, Brown identified at least six states, more than half the Confederacy, that had formed state armies. A seventh state, Alabama, omitted from Brown's list, not only had a state militia but had further divided it into "classes" based on where its units were mustered and whether state law would allow them to be taken beyond the state or county. A nation that entered the war with citizens lacking a true emotional attachment commonly associated with nationalism had failed in a structural sense to exert national control over its human military resources. The Confederacy had competing armies, one controlled by its president, Jefferson Davis, the other by its coordinate executives, the state governors. In some instances, like South Carolina, only half the eligible males had enlisted by the end of the year, and the other half were not inclined to serve locally, a fact confirmed by Chestnut's comment that Confederate enlistment had hurt the state guard. In many places men were unwilling to leave the state to serve, a sign that patriotism had its limits and that those limits were defined by state or county borders.[31]

Understanding Confederate desertion is more difficult because it is easy to find men who professed not only an undying loyalty but a loyalty to something larger than home. In his memoirs, written in 1882, Carlton McCarthy, a private in the artillery of the Second Corps, Army of Northern Virginia, professed an almost spiritual explanation for why men fought. It is possible that some of his sentiments were a product of the postwar struggle in the South. He claimed that "the principles for which the Confederate soldier fought, and in defense of which he died, are to-day the harmony of this country." When explaining these principles, he wrote: "It is not fair to demand a reason for actions above reason. The heart is greater than the mind. No man can exactly define the cause for which the Confederate soldier fought. He was above human law, secure in his own rectitude of purpose, accountable to God only, having assumed for himself a 'nationality,' which he was minded to defend with his life and property, and therefore pledged his sacred honor."[32]

McCarthy felt this way personally, and he purported to speak for "the Confederate soldier," yet it is clear that he did not speak for everyone. Many men felt accountable not only to human law but to duties and obligations far below God. Those who volunteered may have lacked formal education, but they were not stupid. As war tested their loyalty, these existing conflicts would not go unnoticed, and neither would some of the inequities of allowing some men to serve instate while others suffered, fought, and died far from home. The year 1861 saw very little desertion, but as Colonel Woodbury suggested, desertion is a gradual process, and the process had begun before the effects were noticed or felt.

A week into the new year, James Thrower was "still sick" and many of his comrades were dying in the hospital. Writing from Shelbyville, Tennessee, on January 18, George Athey was cold and his pants and shoes had already worn out. "I have been troubled very badly lately," he wrote his mother. "I am heare and my mind is wit you and home I wish the waire would stop fur I cant live in any pease attal heire."[1] Far from home, ill equipped, and lonely, men watched as disease was killing men whom the sword had not yet had an opportunity to reach. That would soon change. The war in the West was about to get under way.

In February 1862 Grant seized Forts Henry and Donelson and drove south down the Tennessee River, where the first great slaughter of the war would take place at Shiloh. At the same time, David Farragut moved up the Mississippi and seized New Orleans. By the spring of 1862 portions of four Confederate states had fallen to Union forces. As the Union moved into the South it threatened "home" and in some cases subsumed it. To meet the challenge, the Confederate civilian and military leadership began to exert a "national" authority. But efforts to act as a cohesive unit would have the effect of tearing away at the tenuous connections that bound Southerners together. Confederate war measures would create problems that would not only drive desertion but would combine with it to create problems that the Confederacy would deal with for the remainder of the war. By February 1862 it became clear that some men were unwilling to stay in the service. For a nation already undermanned, that would be unacceptable. In the West, one region had already begun to slip into chaos.

The early signs of Confederate desertion came from two places: North and West. The former source came from prisons. As the warfare intensified in the spring and early summer of 1862, Union prison officials and camp commandants began to notice that an increasing number of Confederate soldiers simply did not want to return South. Although a prisoner exchange system was in place,

Confederate soldiers did not want to be exchanged. Instead, they expressed a willingness to swear an oath of allegiance to the Union and go home or remain in the North. More importantly, some men were not prisoners but claimed to be deserters, and for them, returning South meant punishment and possibly death. There are no data to identify the extent of the problem in 1862, but the increased correspondence between prison officials, Secretary of War Edwin Stanton, and Commissary General of Prisoners William Hoffman indicates that Confederate desertion had reached sizable enough proportions to create administrative problems for the Union army.[2]

One of the interesting dilemmas lay in trying to distinguish prisoners from deserters. Technically, both were deserters. In the nineteenth century it was almost universally believed that capture did not take one out of the army. Therefore, prisoners seeking to take the oath of allegiance to the Union appeared to be deserting as much as men who claimed to have deserted and sought to take the oath. The only problem was that prisoners had not technically left the Confederate army voluntarily. Their status as prisoners was involuntary, and thereafter they sought to make their separation from the Confederate army permanent. Deserters, to the extent that they could prove they had deserted, had voluntarily found their way into Union lines. The danger lay in releasing either classification of men and having them return to the Confederate service outside the parameters of the exchange program that went into effect in May 1862.[3]

Although the early signs of desertion appeared from Northern prison camps, the source of that desertion can be traced further south, to Tennessee. Grant's early success along the Cumberland and Tennessee rivers had the effect of opening up a portion of western and middle Tennessee to Union control and enabling Lincoln to appoint Andrew Johnson as the state's military governor. Johnson's goal was to bring Tennessee back into the Union as quickly as possible, and part of that process involved bringing Tennessee Confederate soldiers home. Again, accurate numbers for 1862 are lacking, but the volume was large enough that Johnson appointed two commissioners to tour Union prison camps, interview soldiers, and pass muster on their applications to swear the oath. The job eventually fell exclusively on Judge William Campbell, and the travel involved ultimately exhausted him. This alone suggests that the desertion problem had already escalated, and it provides an excellent opportunity to examine the question of harm to the Confederate war effort.[4]

Many Tennesseans believed the Union invasion in early 1862 would not last. In reality, the Union army had arrived for good. After early 1862, the majority of middle Tennessee would remain under Union control except for a stretch from fall 1862 until early summer 1863. Not only had the Union come, but the invasion brought to the state two great armies that, in living off the land, devastated the region. While the Union army contributed significantly to the ruin, it did not act alone. In early 1862, retreating Confederates destroyed vital infrastructure such as railroads, bridges, buildings, and warehoused supplies. In time, Tennessee residents came to dread the "friendly" visits of Confederate soldiers. The observations of both Union and Confederate soldiers confirmed the nature and extent of the devastation: broken fences, depleted corn and hay, and the total absence of any horses the latter would have fed. A Confederate soldier passing through Bedford and Rutherford counties in late 1862 admitted that "the country wears the most desolate appearance that I have ever seen anywhere, there is not a stalk of corn or a blade of wheat anywhere." Even Gen. Kirby Smith could not hide his despair. In a letter to his wife in June 1862 he described farms and houses sacked and property seized. "My heart bleeds for them and I feel powerless to help," he wrote. Smith offered a harsh appraisal for a region known for its prolific wheat and corn agriculture, as well as a stark admission that the Confederacy seemed incapable of alleviating the suffering.[5]

Western Tennessee fared no better. Like the middle part of the state, it fell early to the Union invasion down the Mississippi. Memphis succumbed to the Union army on June 6, 1862. The skies filled with dark clouds as citizens and Confederate soldiers burned cotton to prevent it from falling into Union hands. They also destroyed huge stores of sugar and molasses. The total estimate of property destroyed was in the neighborhood of $129 million. Granted, the Union did not seize these supplies as they did in Nashville, but then neither would they benefit the Confederate military or civilian population. Initially the Union occupation served as a nuisance, its effects confined to Memphis itself, but in time the occupation began to affect morale, and in the surrounding rural areas citizens soon found themselves on short rations.[6]

Thus, portions of Tennessee fell early. Isham G. Harris, the Confederate governor of Tennessee, realized that defeat carried serious ramifications. In February 1862 he tried to use the Union victories at Forts Donelson and Henry as a tool to motivate enlistment and encourage dedication to the cause. In an official proclamation he described the early defeats and then called on every able-bodied man, regardless of age, to enlist for the duration of the war:

DESERTION IN THE HEARTLAND

I appeal. Go cheer your brethren already there. Your native land now calls upon you—you have only waited until you were needed. The Confederate government calls upon me to raise 32 regiments. You will be armed. Come, then. It is for your independence, your homes, your wives your children and Tennessee you are to fight. Who will, who can remain idly at home? Will you stand still and let others pour out their blood for your safety? Patriotism and manhood will cry alike against you. Forbid it (subjugation by the North) sons of Tennessee. Forbid it men on the plains and of the mountains.[7]

In language reminiscent of Georgia governor Joe Brown's plea in 1861, Harris cried out for these men to protect home and fireside. But this was 1862, and recruitment was a much tougher sell.

The extent of the military failure cannot be underestimated. Middle Tennessee proved disastrous for Confederate supply and logistics. The powder mills on the Cumberland were gone, as was the great western iron belt. A region expected to supply the Confederacy with corn and livestock became incapable of feeding itself. Tons of supplies at Nashville fell into Union hands. Militarily, one-third of Albert Sidney Johnston's army had been lost at the inland forts and at Mill Springs. Eighty-three pieces of artillery were lost at Fort Donelson, as were more than twenty thousand small arms. No Confederate army remained on the western front, as two separate detachments, one under Beauregard and the other under Johnston, fled south into Mississippi. Memphis was a devastating loss. It was the Confederacy's fifth-largest city. Lying along the Mississippi River, it served as the water terminus for the Memphis & Charleston Railroad. Although the loss of Corinth effectively severed the railroad, Corinth might not have been lost, or could have been retaken, but for the loss of Memphis.[8]

To the extent that Confederate efforts in 1861 had succeeded in rallying Tennesseans to the cause, these early failures in 1862 served to undermine the very core of Confederate unity: defense of home. Not only had Memphis been lost, but there were those in the Confederacy who believed that the Confederacy and Jefferson Davis had not tried to save the city. James Lusk Alcorn, a Mississippi Whig and one of Davis's most outspoken critics, resigned his commission as a general in command of a brigade and returned home. In an address to the Mississippi House of Representatives, he attacked Davis for treating the Mississippi Valley as a second-rate front. Admittedly, Alcorn hated Davis for passing him over for several military appointments, and as a Whig he had been less than enthusiastic about secession in the first place. But whether or not Alcorn was correct about Davis's intentions, he echoed the beliefs of soldiers who saw their homes and firesides relegated in importance. Will Crutcher's prophecy in late 1861 would come to haunt the Confederacy: the loss of home might well make desertion a "justifiable crime."[9]

Andrew Johnson wasted no time in exploiting the opportunity. In a sense, Tennessee served as an example of what the Confederacy faced and how desertion could hurt. First, the mere existence of the prisoner exchange program indicated that the South contemplated getting soldiers back into the service, and desertion or oath swearing by pows clearly undermined that effort. Those men taken prisoner in early 1862 might not be returning, at least not all of them. More importantly, the presence at home of these oath-swearing deserters would symbolize their rejection of the Confederate cause. At home these men could care for their families, and many Tennesseans would come to see the Confederate war effort as something that no longer concerned them. By late 1862 that would be the case. R. B. Hardman, who lamented the poor turnout from San Patrico, Texas, in 1861, had joined the army and in 1862 found himself in Tennessee. In November he wrote home to his mother indicating his unit was headed to middle Tennessee the next day and that he was not looking forward to the move. As a Confederate soldier he would find himself among a civilian population that looked upon the war as "a quarrel in which they were not particularly interested."[10] Thus to the extent that desertion allowed soldiers to return home to Tennessee, it not only served as a reminder that the Confederacy had failed to protect home and fireside but also allowed the civilian population the luxury of removing themselves from the war, an act that severely hurt the efforts of a nation trying to establish itself. In fact, the loss of territory did not go unnoticed by foreign powers. Ambassador to Great Britain James Mason had the unfortunate task of trying to convince British officials that the Confederacy was viable. The loss of Tennessee made that a more difficult sell, and Johnson's efforts to bring deserters and pows home made the task of holding onto Tennessee much more difficult.

Johnson's job became easier because Tennessee also provided some of the earliest evidence that the "promise" by the wealthy to provide for the poor soldiers' families had been broken, and with it the underlying contract between soldier and nation. The proof came in the spring of 1862. The most conspicuous victim of the Union invasion and the war itself was the family. When most Tennesseans marched off to war they left behind a family that by virtue of their absence became more vulnerable and weakened. This reality did not escape those who left. Henry Yeatman flatly told his wife, "I am pulled between two inclinations, most unpleasantly. The first and strongest is to stay near you my precious wife & my little daughter. The other is to go & do my part as a soldier. . . . I can't make up my mind to leave & yet I feel dissatisfied with myself." Like many other parts of the South, Tennessee society existed within a paternalistic framework that recognized the existence and role of their aristocracy. While some citizens chafed at the class distinctions, it had its benefits, including assistance to the poor. In exchange for these paternalistic benefits the yeoman and lower classes demonstrated a willingness to defer to their richer neighbors. When it came time to go to war, many of these men saw the promise by the rich to protect home and family in their absence as a mere extension of the assistance they had been accustomed to receiving during peacetime. Thus the promise was supported by a history of assistance. In peacetime one merely had to show that he was hardworking and making an honest effort to succeed in order to effectively appeal to the good graces of the wealthy.[11] Surely, going to war on behalf of the Confederacy, a war that clearly benefited the aristocracy, went far beyond deference and would be more than enough of a sacrifice to encourage the rich to provide for soldiers' families in their absence. But they did not; and as Joe Brown stated in December 1861, these men were not cattle and they were not stupid. They knew the promise had not been kept and reacted accordingly.

It did not take a lawyer to interpret the breach, but the earliest signs nevertheless came from one. Louisville attorney Curran Pope could see the signs in April 1862. In a letter to Andrew Johnson, Pope wrote that the rich in Tennessee and "elsewhere who stimulated volunteering are not true to their lavish promises they made in regard to the families of the soldier." Pope suggested that the broken promise could be an invaluable tool toward undermining the Confederacy's ability to continue the fight, particularly in light of the wealthy's reaction to the wavering will of the poor, a reaction that began to take the form of threats as the soldiers and their families objected to the wealthy's failure to provide the support they promised.[12]

Broken promises and Union occupation provided all Johnson needed to begin using desertion as a tool of war, and the opportunity came almost immediately after he became military governor. On March 8, 1862, Nathan T. Allman, a forty-two-year-old captain from Stewart County, Tennessee, wrote Johnson from the confines of Camp Chase, Ohio. Claiming he had always been for the Union, Allman was willing to swear the oath. He had tried to resign his commission, but the Confederate government refused to accept his resignation. Now, however, the Confederacy's wishes no longer mattered. Allman's home lay within Union lines, and he could swear the oath and return home without fear of recapture. Similar letters came from men at Camp Butler, Camp Douglas, Camp Morton, and Johnson's Island. One came from Robert G. Bails, who, speaking for himself and "nineteen or twenty other men," bluntly asked Johnson, "why keep us here when those who stand in such want of our support, I mean now our families—need us so much." Bails came from Hickman County, and his comrades were from Hickman, Maury, Lawrence, and Lewis counties in middle Tennessee. To Johnson the harm to the Confederacy and benefit to the Union were obvious. The men could return home and fend for themselves. The Union would not have to feed or guard them, and the Confederacy would lose soldiers it was counting on being exchanged.[13] C. C. Taylor, the young man from Texas who joined after he and his father had a falling out and who swore to get on the front ranks and die if need be, had managed to survive into the autumn of 1862. If his observations were accurate, oath swearing was having an effect. Apparently engaged in a "big fight" near Corinth and captured, Taylor wrote his father after his exchange. He estimated that if the number of prisoners taken at Fort Donelson was added to those taken around Corinth, the Confederacy had between eight and nine thousand soldiers taken as POWs. Of that number, a thousand died in prison, two to three hundred escaped, and "500 took the oath of allegiance to the federal government. A majority of these were Tennesseans."[14]

This early activity clearly shows desertion's harmful effects. Not only did it deplete the army and cause unrest among the soldiers, but it served as a means to alleviate suffering at home, thereby using the notion of home to further distance Confederate citizens from the cause. It also demonstrated a key component of the Union program to induce desertion. Confederate loss of territory not only put the civilian population under Union control, thereby causing concern among her soldiers, but made it possible for men who were predisposed to desert to return home safely. From Johnson's perspective there was a larger component to using oath swearing and desertion. Johnson's goal was the wartime reconstruction of Tennessee. He wanted Tennessee to elect a state legislature as quickly as possible, and using Tennessee soldiers who no longer felt a strong tie to the Confederacy seemed ideal. In early 1862 the Union controlled only about one-fifth of the state, and elections could not take place until the chaos in places like middle Tennessee had subsided. Men from these local communities would not only strengthen their own families but would begin to provide badly needed community support. Rumors in Kentucky of bands of Confederate irregulars had begun to filter back to Tennessee, including stories of civilians being killed. About the same time, similar bands had begun to make their presence felt in the area, and soldiers returning home could provide essential local security. As the soldiers returned, having already sworn the oath and deserted not only the military but the Confederate cause as well, they would serve as examples to the civilian population to do likewise.[15] Thus, in Johnson's hands, desertion had become a tool to not only undermine the Confederate military but to further the Union war effort by reclaiming territory politically as well as physically.

From June 1862 until late summer, Union officials struggled with how to most effectively ensure the loyalty of men swearing the oath. They understood the distinction between pure deserters and those who wished to desert from prison. However, at that juncture they were willing to take a chance, and in late August Johnson got authority from the War Department and the Commissary General's Office to proceed with prisoner releases. Lists of deserter oath takers would not be available until July and August 1863, when the Union army finalized its procedure and began to keep accurate records. However, Johnson's 1862 correspondence reveals a significant backlog of requests from Northern prisons that provided more than enough work for his POW commissioners. As Johnson had hoped, the oath-swearing fever quickly spread from military deserters to civilians. Amid the flood of soldier requests came a petition from thirty-two men held in a Nashville prison who claimed to be political prisoners unjustly held as secessionist sympathizers. Johnson combined the release of soldiers with the deft freeing of civilian leaders. A good example is that while he tried to seed middle Tennessee with rehabilitated soldiers, he released William G. Harding, the owner of a large plantation and a civilian leader in the area. Judge Campbell's work at prisons in Ohio, Indiana, and Illinois began to show results, and Tennesseans were deserting and returning home. The investigative duties began to take their toll, however, and Campbell succumbed to sickness. He had traveled alone to the various Northern prisons and by the early winter of 1862 was badly in need of rest.[16]

Johnson's authority to release Confederate POWs and deserters ended in November 1862. The complicated issues involved and the fear that men would swear the oath and then return to Confederate service outweighed Johnson's political and military goals. Eventually, only military district commanders would have authority to release deserters, and the release of Confederate POWs would be at the sole discretion of the Commissary General's Office and the War Department. Johnson would find a loophole in 1863 that enabled him to continue to undermine the Confederate war effort, but he would never again have the wide latitude he enjoyed in 1862. However, that does not lessen the significance of what occurred in Tennessee during 1862. In a letter to his parents on June 29, 1862, Capt. Jason Hall of the Ninth Tennessee Infantry tried to encourage people at home to keep the faith. More than an encouraging sermon, however, the letter is significant as evidence of what the soldiers knew was happening at home. Writing from Tupelo, Mississippi, Hall had not seen anyone at home since the abandonment of Corinth. He knew the Union occupied large portions of middle Tennessee and told his family to "be patient. Before next fall there will not be a Yankee in our state. We are anxious that our friends should under no circumstances take the oath of allegiance to the fed Gov." But people were taking the oath, and many were taking it because their fathers, sons, brothers, and husbands serving in the army were also taking the oath and coming home. Although Hall claimed that the army had seen "gainers rather than losers by desertions" and believed that only bad soldiers left, this was hardly the reality across the board. Johnson's efforts were clearly weighing on the men in Mississippi and making them even more restless to be led back into Tennessee. Johnson had found a way to use desertion and oath swearing as a weapon in Tennessee, and although he lost direct control over the instrument, the Union military would continue to chip away at Confederate unity, both in the army and at home.[17] These efforts, combined with the Confederacy's approach to the trans-Mississippi, would hurt the South and drive desertion. Within a short time, the failure to adequately defend Memphis would begin to have a domino effect. Arkansas would begin to feel abandoned, and the problems that started in the Volunteer state would find it a quick jump across the Mississippi River.[18]

Arkansas, like Tennessee, seceded after the conflict began in 1861. By spring 1862 the twin specters of unrest and disorder had visited themselves upon the land, and desertion played a prominent role in both problems. The state of affairs in Arkansas, vividly described by Brig. Gen. Thomas Hindman when he arrived in late spring 1862, showed a state in turmoil. Five thousand Union troops were at Fort Scott, and with their assistance, Indians were collecting on the Arkansas border. Union cavalry roamed through upper Arkansas, burning homes, plundering, and stealing livestock and slaves. Loyal men had been murdered, and the weak were swearing the oath of allegiance to the Union.

In the process the Union was spreading Northern propaganda throughout the region. Equally injurious were the bands of stragglers, men Hindman identified as from "distant commands," who with loyal Unionists "traversed the country, armed and lawless, robbing the people of their property under pretense of impressing it for the Confederate service." The previous year's crop had been short, and the crop in upper Arkansas had failed completely. Government no longer functioned, extortion ran rampant, threatening the poor with actual starvation, and to add insult to injury, on his way out of the state the governor condemned the withdrawal of troops from the state and threatened to secede from the Confederacy.[19] Hindman's report came in late May, but clearly this set of circumstances did not arise in one month. What is most telling is that the state of affairs in Arkansas in late spring 1862 would serve as a precursor for the plague that would eventually descend on the entire Confederacy. Desertion, while hardly the sole problem, figured prominently in the deteriorating situation in Arkansas. While the presence of Union troops, threats from Indians, and crop failures clearly posed serious problems and caused real harm, desertion hurt in a unique way, damaging not only the army but the civilian population as well.

A fifth column is a clandestine subversive organization working within a country to further an invading enemy's military and political aims.[20] Although the term did not exist until 1936, when Spanish nationalist general Emilio Mola Vidal applied it to a group of rebel sympathizers inside Madrid, conceptually it was present long before the twentieth century. Perhaps one of the most damaging effects of desertion on the Confederate war effort was the way in which Confederate deserters became a Union fifth column. The definition suggests that a fifth column works in knowing concert with an invading army, but that does not necessarily have to be the case. Conscious collaboration with the Union by guerrilla groups does not appear to have occurred with great frequency in the South, but no one can deny that the activities of deserter pockets, or bands such as the one Hindman described in Arkansas, furthered Union war and political aims. A nation whose soldiers' sense of loyalty was grounded in the protection of home and fireside could not guarantee victory over the Union army or stop Indian raids. But deserters did more than just deplete the army in "distant" places like Tennessee and Virginia. Some men managed to get back to Arkansas. Upon returning, rather than protect the home population, as Andrew Johnson and Curran Pope had suggested, many of these men actually preyed upon the civilian population. It was bad enough that they took from those they were supposed to be protecting, but to do so under the guise of being officially connected to the Confederate service served only to compound the harm.

The Union had already recognized a benefit in bringing Confederate soldiers back home. By threatening the homes of both civilians and soldiers, deserters created a conflict in duty among those who remained. It was one thing for a man to stay at war knowing the enemy was threatening his home, but to endure the hardships of war and camp life and learn that other men—men who should be with you—had not only deserted but were harming your home would prove unbearable for some. The Union's war aim was to crush the Southern army by any possible means. Its political aim was to reunite the nation. By their actions, deserters in Arkansas helped the Union accomplish both goals. The situation was severe enough by June 1862 that Hindman had to address the problem. He issued a general order forbidding the taking of any private property without express authority from his headquarters, "exhibited and read" to the owner prior to impressment, unless the owner had absented himself in order to avoid lawful impressment. Hindman authorized Confederate officers, soldiers, and civilians to resist any unlawful impressment and declared that such men were robbers and marauders and would be put to death without hesitation. [21]

It is tempting to assume that desertion took only the weak, but that does not seem to be the case. Junius Newport Bragg, a surgeon in the Eleventh Arkansas Infantry, wrote his girlfriend, who later became his wife, for most of the war. In January 1862 he reported the desertion of a man from picket duty while the unit was encamped at New Madrid, Missouri. Not only did the man desert, but like many Tennesseans were beginning to do, he went over to the Union. Bragg was obviously hurt by the man's defection. He was not only a friend but "a favorite with everyone and stood high as a soldier." His motive: "a desire of seeing his sweetheart who lives in the state of Pennsylvania." [22]

It was more than just deserters from "afar"; Hindman had severe problems keeping his own Arkansas troops from deserting. Four regiments of cavalry deserted when he had them dismounted in order to save corn. When he arrived to take command in Arkansas, the men had not been paid. Hindman took $400,000 in funds due for the Confederate tax and tried to pay his soldiers. As he put it, "the unavoidable delay in doing so . . . occasioned many to desert. In a word, desertions took place upon every conceivable pretext." Hindman described frequent arrests, but in most cases the men were released. Forgiveness was extended for a variety of reasons. Some men were just too ignorant to understand what they had done. Others were driven to desert by "wives and children suffering for food." Hindman also recognized that his military organizations were not sanctioned and admitted that he shrank from inflicting the death penalty. However, like George Washington and Nathanael Greene in America's eighteenth-century wars, Hindman came to understand that leniency "brought forth evil fruits." If these men were not executed, the desertions would increase. As Hindman put it, "mercy was mistaken for timidity." Hindman's command seemingly dwindled to nothing. Desertions killed the ability to recruit. At one point, Hindman received word from a Colonel Nelson that the men had conspired to disband and go home. A regular organization for that purpose was created with an official badge that enabled members to recognize one another. A few hours after Nelson discovered the conspiracy, a signal gun fired in the camp of an Arkansas regiment and sixty men, led by two lieutenants, deliberately marched away with their arms and accoutrements. Orders to arrest them were ignored.[23]

Hindman's experience and hesitancy to severely punish desertion was consistent with the general approach to desertion in the Confederate army. During 1861, court-martial for desertion had been virtually nonexistent. Granted, desertion had yet to emerge as a major problem, but the limited evidence suggests it was a bigger problem than is evidenced by the paltry attention it received from the military justice system. There were forty-one courts-martial for desertion in 1861, and not one convicted soldier was shot, at least not as a result of the official process. This does not mean that men were not executed in drumhead-type proceedings, such as the three men whom George Griscom of the Ninth Texas described as being shot in December 1861. In that instance only one of the unfortunate three was identified by name, Eli Smith. But the only Eli Smith who appears in the court-martial records for the Confederate army belonged to the Thirty-seventh Virginia Cavalry, and he was tried in 1864 and sentenced to confinement and rations of bread and water. In 1862 the reported court-martial proceedings increased dramatically compared to 1861. That year 496 men were tried for desertion, but consistent with the leniency that prevailed in Hindman's Arkansas, only 37 were executed.[24]

In Arkansas the leniency came to an end. Hindman not only forced men into the service but forced them to stay. Those who did not stay he shot. Within a short time he had ten men tried and shot for desertion. Several members of the Thirty-eighth Arkansas Infantry who served in Arkansas were shot in the latter days of Hindman's command. "These summary measures had the desired effect," he wrote. "The spirit of desertion was crushed." Using his own provost guard, Hindman put a marshal in every county. He centralized these "county" marshals with a provost-marshal general. By doing so he stopped extortion, which in his words "tortured soldiers into deserting by starving their wives and children." His marshals also effectively arrested stragglers, deserters, and traitors. Hindman claimed later that only traitors ever voiced opposition to martial law. He was satisfied that the situation made the remedy necessary.[25] The harm caused by desertion in this situation is clear. It forced the creation of a force to specifically address the problem. In a conflict where the Confederacy lacked human resources, men badly needed elsewhere had to remain in Arkansas to protect the state. Although desertion was clearly not the only problem, it acted in concert with others to create a situation where the only solution appeared to be the total restriction of the very rights the South had gone to war to preserve. Despite almost herculean efforts that included the imposition of martial law on June 30, 1862, contrary to Hindman's beliefs, he could not prevent the desertion problem from getting out of hand. Although his efforts clearly helped transform the situation in Arkansas for a short time, his stay was far too brief to make a difference. The cure proved more unpalatable than the disease, as many Southerners chafed under military law.

Did desertion hurt? In Arkansas during 1862 the answer would have to be "yes." The Union invasion of northern Arkansas eventually resulted in the destruction of civilian government. Into that void came not only the Union authorities but bands of irregulars, stragglers, and Confederate deserters. In the absence of government, speculators preyed upon those who remained. Desertion not only depleted distant armies but also infected Hindman's local forces. Perhaps more significantly, Hindman's efforts, even if temporarily successful, forced the Confederate government to draw a line in the sand as to how far it would be willing to go to combat the disorder and disarray, conditions to which deserters contributed even if they were not the sole cause. The government's limits not only began the demise of control in Arkansas but signaled how it would deal with similar problems in other Confederate states when desertion spread deeper into the South.

Across the Tennessee-Arkansas border, Mississippi was beginning to feel the same effects of the war. Although the indications were slow to come, they arose early in 1862 and found a focal point in the governor's office. One man warned Governor Pettus in January that if something was not done, the "money grasping knaves at home would deliver our state to Lincoln while they are delivering their

DESERTION IN THE HEARTLAND

souls to the devil." Slightly behind and not initially as noticeable as the declining economy, rising speculation, drought, and famine, desertion was nevertheless present. On January 1, Miss Wilkinson from Pearlington in Hancock County complained of deserters and marauders in her neighborhood. Home guards were demanding to know how to deal with traitors and anti-Southerners in their midst. Confederate soldiers were also becoming problematic, as Georgian cavalry near Corinth had stolen goods and forced citizens to appeal to the governor for relief.[26]

Part of Mississippi fell under Union control in 1862. With the fall of Memphis, the Confederate positions in parts of northern Mississippi became untenable and had to be surrendered, including the key railroad junction at Corinth. Although battles occurred at Corinth and Iuka that fall, Confederate political control of the area had slipped away before the summer of 1862. With his control over a portion of his state declining, Pettus struggled to keep Mississippi intact. The size and nature of this problem is revealed in the correspondence that flooded his office in 1862.

The variety of requests and complaints from citizens reveals the difficulty of maintaining peace, order, and prosperity in Mississippi. In the winter and spring of 1862, most people seemed preoccupied with the draft. Citizens wrote from counties across the state about the status of efforts to raise units and enroll men in the army. In some areas men were already trying to avoid the draft, while in places like Franklin County the necessary government infrastructure did not exist. Franklin County had no police board and therefore could not enroll anyone for the draft. In what would become a routine part of the draft, requests for exemptions flooded the governor's office. The requests ranged from trying to secure the release of physicians to men wanting themselves or their sons returned to look after what were described as "destitute" and "penniless" families. For those at the bottom end of the economic scale, the war had already taken its toll.[27]

The trend continued throughout 1862. The inequities of the draft, the need for home guards to protect people from stragglers and bushwhackers, and the general destitution in the state dominate the letters to the governor. By the end of 1862, conditions approaching famine prevailed in the Union-controlled areas of northern Mississippi. In the winter, writers repeatedly sought the governor's assistance in caring for the families of absent soldiers, many now starving or near starvation. At one point Ulysses Grant ordered his men to sell food to civilians to alleviate the suffering. There was simply not enough food and provisions to go around. Morale was declining, and men wanted to go home and take care of their families. Women in need of male help wrote asking what would become of them if all the men were taken away.[28] For men whose wives could not subsist on eleven dollars per month, desertion was becoming a real option.

In March 1862, J. W. Ward, an officer in a Mississippi unit, wrote to his parents about how economically stretched his men had become. He could not understand why the Confederate army would make men who earned only eleven dollars a month pay twenty dollars for something as basic as their uniforms. He felt the government should give the men their uniforms, and he knew the men would remember such a gesture in these "troubled times."[29] By December the situation was even worse, both at home and on the war front. The evidence available for 1862 indicates that many Mississippi troops resisted the urge to desert. Not all did, however, and the question remained: How long would men continue to fight?

No single letter coming into Pettus's office in the second half of 1862 stands out. Collectively they show a state slipping into despair punctuated by lawlessness. The chaotic nature of life in Mississippi is important for this story because it hints that desertion was the cause of the chaos and lawlessness, that the chaos itself had begun to drive desertion, or both.

In late October or early November, Pettus received two anonymous letters, both dated October 28. One was from De Soto County, the other from Hancock County. The writer from De Soto County did not live there, but he wrote on behalf of his brother's widow. His letter was more than a simple request for the governor to take care of the women and children. It made an earnest plea to protect the women and children from what the writer described as "partisan warfare." Men he called "partisan rangers" appeared to be made up of conscripts who refused to report or who had reported and since left. Not only were these men engaging in irregular activities—activities that placed women and children in peril—but the knowledge that they were conscripts could only dampen the spirits of those fighting in Virginia and other places who needed the infusion of manpower. The situation "is just cause for complaint by their comrades in arms who are periling their lives in defense of their country."

The news from Hancock County was just as alarming. The writer described the lower Mississippi counties as abandoned to the enemy, with women and children left to deal with the Union occupation. The livestock that remained after the Union army passed through had been driven off by the Confederate army. The writer was too old to join the service, but he had four sons fighting in the upper Confederacy, one of whom was dead already. He was born in South Carolina and claimed to be a "Southern" man. His father fought in Mexico and his grandfather in the Revolution. He stated that if "he could he would fight now, but he can't." He implored Pettus to have the government do something to alter the present management of the war. Without some change, he conceded, "we fall." More importantly, he assured Pettus that common soldiers knew more about what was going on than the officers. He lived on a "public way" and got the news from those who traveled by his home. He reported that thirty-five members of a disbanded military unit came by and swore to him that they would never leave their farms and families to the enemy.[30]

Indications came from the military in June 1862 that Mississippi was beginning to feel the effects of some desertion, possibly causing the problems of which these two men complained. General Beauregard telegraphed Pettus and indicated that all soldiers who were not officially provided with sick leave or furloughs had to be considered deserters.[31] Beauregard's message signaled two things. First, desertion had begun in 1862. Second, the fact that he contacted Pettus indicated that men who deserted from the front were finding their way home, since soldiers who were legally returning home would have sick leave or furlough documents in their possession. Those found in Mississippi with neither document would be presumed to have deserted. As the letters from Mississippi indicated, however, apprehending such men would be no easy task. Those fortunate enough to have made it back home would be unwilling to leave to fight in a state where the people seemed less like kinfolk and more like strangers.

Pvt. Hugh A. McLaurin of the Seventh Mississippi was one of many who left Mississippi to fight. Eventually he and his unit joined the Army of Tennessee and fought in the bloodbath at the Battle of Stones River between December 31, 1862, and January 2, 1863. He obviously missed his family and wanted to hear from home "worse than you ever seen a boy." His unit had taken a circuitous route to central Tennessee, having marched all the way to Knoxville before reaching Murfreesboro in early December 1862. The march enabled McLaurin to get a sense of the people, and his observations reveal just how difficult a task the Confederacy faced in trying to unite Southerners. McLaurin felt that the "people were different" in Tennessee. He told his father that he became so incensed with one man that "if he sees the man after the war he will whip him or the man will whip him." Strong words, probably just a disagreement, but the perception of difference is important to the desertion story. Each state would suffer; several already had. Men out of the state had a difficult enough time rationalizing their absence when they knew that those at home suffered. When it appeared they were fighting for people they could not or did not culturally identify with, it made the job harder and the pull from home more difficult to resist. Hugh McLaurin was one of many to realize that the "South" was not home. Mississippi was home.

Unfortunately, McLaurin did not get long to ponder the cultural disparity between himself and the citizens of the state where he was then fighting. He had come to war with Frank, either a friend or a brother. Frank got sick in Knoxville, and by the time they arrived in Murfreesboro he was dead from fever. Hugh's attempts to find him adequate shelter and food proved futile; in the end he got him a coffin, found a "couple of negroes" to dig a grave, and laid Frank to rest. McLaurin blamed himself for Frank's death—yet another burden that weighed on him and soldiers like him, and a burden that must have weighed a little heavier in late December when he watched as a soldier was shot for desertion. The incident appears to have made an even greater impression because the man asked the officers if they would give his body to his wife so she could take it home and bury him. They agreed to do so.[32]

McLaurin was not the only one to sense the difference in Tennessee. In March 1862 an article appeared in the *Daily Advocate*, a Louisiana paper, that expressly questioned the patriotism of the people of Tennessee. Although admitting that Governor Harris was a "tried and noble man," the article asked, "but what of his constituents?" Prior to the fall of Forts Donelson and Henry, Gen. Gideon Pillow had sent the governor and the legislature a request for assistance. The article claimed that a state capable of giving 60,000 gave none. "Has Tennessee as many men under arms as Louisiana?" Louisiana had a 40,000-man voting population and 40,000 men under arms.[33] The article appeared two weeks after Andrew Johnson became military governor and placed blame for the fall of the forts on the Cumberland and Tennessee rivers at the feet of the people, not the army. To the extent that Louisiana would become aware of Johnson's efforts to induce soldiers to take the oath, the sentiments in Louisiana that a sister state had failed to carry its weight would only grow stronger.

No state seemed immune. The same alienation that McLaurin felt as a Mississippi boy among Tennessee civilians was felt by Thomas W. Peebles, an Alabama boy, among McLaurin's "people" in Mississippi. Alabama had escaped Union incursion but not the suffering that came with the war. The first year of the war had seen Alabama's civilian population begin to hurt, and her soldiers away from home, fighting in Mississippi, struggled there with the same conflicts that men like McLaurin struggled with in Tennessee. But while McLaurin's sentiments about Tennesseans were more generalized, Peebles pointed to specific examples. If one considers that the South was at war for its survival, some of what Peebles saw and experienced undermined any notion of a collective will and unified support for the war and the men fighting the battles.

Peebles served in the Thirty-fifth Alabama, Buford's Regiment of Loring's Division. His family and home were in northern Alabama, a region torn by ideological conflict and strong Unionist sentiment. Peebles must have fought at Shiloh and survived, because in May 1862 he lay in a hospital bed recovering from the mumps. Despite his illness and the tactical defeat at Shiloh, Peebles seemed very optimistic. He never regretted his decision to enlist and claimed that if the war "lasts a hundred years I expect to be a soldier boy for the rest of my life." Some men were already complaining and grumbling, he admitted, but not him. By July 1862 his unit and the rest of the Confederate army defending Corinth had been forced to abandon the city and had retreated to Vicksburg. The journey had been both enlightening and disappointing. Now he could not wait to get back to Alabama. The retreat had taken him and his comrades through Tishomingo and Itawamba counties in Mississippi. Peebles said no one "could find a place where soldiers had been treated so badly. Could not get a drink of water in either county. Along the Corinth-Tupelo Road, farmers had removed the buckets from their wells so that soldiers could not get a drink. One old farmer near Vicksburg said he would rather the hogs have his vegetables than the soldiers."[34] If a collective will to wage war existed in the South, Peebles did not see it in Mississippi.

While Tennessee, Arkansas, and northern Mississippi experienced Union invasion from the north that disrupted the social structure, undermined loyalty, and drove desertion, Louisiana felt the push of invasion from the south up the Mississippi River. Despite the difference in the avenue of invasion, the loss of territory and the subsequent threat to home and fireside affected Louisiana as much as it did its neighbors. Even before Farragut's invasion, Louisiana citizens saw the threat. Perhaps more significant, prior to the fall of New Orleans evidence of the broken promise Curran Pope identified in Tennessee also existed in Louisiana.

E. W. Halsey, personal secretary to Louisiana's governor, Thomas Moore, penned a lengthy note to his superior in March 1862. Rumors of "difficulties" in

New Orleans had chilled enlistment. People were "afraid of the Lincolnite 'fire' in the rear." The threat of invasion had brought out the weakness in men, who complained of government efforts to protect private property and were ready to "hoist the federal flag and take Lincoln's oath as soon as a yankee gunboat steams down to Baton Rouge." Halsey saw trouble brewing. He knew that conscription was a reality and that men had not been willing to volunteer, but like Pope in Tennessee, he placed the blame at the feet of the wealthy. Halsey claimed to have never doubted the Confederacy's ultimate success. "We could lose half our country but that don't whip us. We may be driven to the swamps and mountains and still win." The problem, in Halsey's mind, lay with the property holders. "Although taxed and liable for future tax, they don't come up to their work," he told Moore. Halsey saw this as a call upon Joe Brown's claim that the last dollar of planter money would be used to support the poor soldiers' families, a promise that in Halsey's view was in dire need of reaffirmation:

> Thousands of poor men would go to the army if their rich neighbors would guarantee the protection and support of their families. And if they have just enough to support their families without the aid of their neighbors, it is hard for them to give up their all for that purpose when their neighbors do not contribute in the same proportion. This war ought to press equally on all shoulders. The wealthy cannot take their share of the hardships of a poor volunteer's life. If the representations of the five hundred millions of property will come up to scratch there will be no trouble about getting our quota of volunteers. In all wars and revolutions poor men and boys always do more than their share.[35]

Halsey had identified the problem: the "five hundred millions of property" had not lived up to their "representations." A promise had been broken. He also touched on another reality: the poor always do most of the work. All one had to do was look at America's prior wars and revolutions: in the Seven Years' War and the American Revolution, wars were fought by armies of poor, or in Halsey's words, men who could not go to war and still support their families. The South went to war in the nineteenth century with soldiers clinging to an eighteenth-century mentality. The same problem faced by Washington, Dinwiddie, Shirley, and Greene confronted Lee, Bragg, Davis, and Moore: raising and maintaining an army of farmers. Regardless of how professionalized these men had become in the ways of war, a fact attested to by their performance in battle, the lodestone of home would continue to pull. It would be a pull that seemed to increase as those in the field realized that home was not being provided for or protected.

Louisiana provides an excellent example of how historical interpretation differs from contemporary perspective. It is a common perception that the fall of Vicksburg and Port Hudson severed the trans-Mississippi from the eastern part of the Confederacy. While that may be true, to those living in Louisiana in 1862 the state had already been severed with far-reaching ramifications.

In June 1862, Moore tried to explain to Jefferson Davis just how severe the situation had become. Moore admitted he could not organize, equip, and subsist an army in Louisiana. He simply did not have the means. "Our legislature did not anticipate nor provide for the stupendous calamity that has deprived us of our metropolis (New Orleans), severed the state and rendered all the banks of our navigable rivers for a distance of some 2000 miles, vulnerable by the enemies armed vessels." As far as Moore was concerned, Louisiana was cut off in June 1862. Not only was it cut off from the rest of the Confederacy, but it had become vulnerable. "With a voting population of 50,000, thirty regiments have been raised for Confederate service and are now employed outside this state. We have no arms left us but shotguns and no ammunition except small quantities, mostly in private hands. All means of subsistence, except such as are produced here are only obtained at an enormous cost by land and carriage or at great risk by water." Moore had no way to defend the state, and feeding the people was becoming difficult. He told Davis that the only resource the state had was "hand loomed cards," and those were both rare and expensive, often selling for thirty times their value. [36]

More problematic than physical hardship was the effect on citizens' morale. Moore explained that the "hardships had disheartened some of our citizens and demoralized the rest." Most people had begun to feel insecure in both their person and property, and worse, "dormant disloyalty has [surfaced] with the disaster that brings our enemy so near . . . the murmurs of the suffering mingle with the complaints of the many, the taunts of the disorganizers and whispered treason of the tories." Moore conceded that the incidents of treason remained small but stressed that it required "sleepless vigilance and some severity" to contain. Given time, the tories would apprise the Union of the unrest and it would eventually realize the disaffection and take advantage of the situation by pushing its invasion further inland. Moore understood that men could not be taken from the Army of Northern Virginia or the Army of Tennessee, but he wanted Davis to allow men recently conscripted for Confederate service to remain in Louisiana. However, he would need arms and materials to equip the local army. In Moore's estimation, this drastic measure was necessary to restore public confidence. It would allow men already in the field, far removed from their homes and families, to render more "efficient" service because they knew that protection had been provided for their homes and families. "The feeling prevails from throughout the state that no men or arms should be spared for distant service until the yet uninvaded part of the state is guarded against marauders." Moore went on to explain that many plantations "have only a single white male, and some have none." The fall of New Orleans and the surrounding counties had crushed his ability to draft soldiers. Conscripts could not be expected from the southern part of the state in and around New Orleans, and the Confederate government needed to reduce its demand for soldiers to take into account the loss of territory in Louisiana.[37]

Moore's appraisal of the situation in Louisiana seems accurate. Sugar plantation owners from the area around New Orleans wrote the governor in July 1862, desperately seeking his assistance. Although they understood that war necessitated rules governing trade with belligerents, they had to be able to trade in New Orleans even if it was Union-occupied. The trade exclusions were breaking them. One man had not sold his crop in over a year and was going broke, and if he slipped any further into debt he could not maintain his slaves, who would then become restless. During the same period, Moore began signing promissory notes to private banks on behalf of the state to secure funds needed to purchase arms. He had to have troops, but without arms he could not raise an army.

Even if an army could be raised, there was no assurance it could be kept in the field. Gen. Mansfield Lovell wrote the Confederate secretary of war, George Randolph, reciting the events that led up to the abandonment of a Confederate fort on Bayou Grand Caillow. Disgruntled with service, the men ignored his orders, disbanded, and returned to New Orleans and Union jurisdiction. Lovell did not call it desertion, but he demanded that the officers in charge be punished. His analysis of the situation was harsh. As he saw things, Louisiana had two classes of people: the rich, concerned with their property and not eager to resist Union encroachment without assistance from the Confederate army; and the poor, commonly called Arcadians, on whom "there is not the slightest dependence to be placed." Without troops, Lovell could not hold his jurisdiction. To make matters worse, the problems Hindman encountered in Arkansas had found their way to Louisiana. Governor Moore wrote Hindman in June 1862 to protest the impressment of property by men clearly not authorized to do so. He did not call them deserters, but clearly they were not part of the army and were armed. Moore specifically complained of a Captain Taylor from

Texas. When asked by a citizen to show his authority, Taylor replied, "What a Texan always carries—a Bowie knife and pistols." The robbers and marauders Hindman battled in Arkansas had found their way further south.[38]

While desertion had not reached epidemic proportions in Louisiana, the signs began to show. Two men were tried for desertion in late 1862 on the grounds that having availed themselves of the rights and privileges of citizenship, they refused to serve in the military and joined the Yankees. Tried in St. James Parish under Article 20 of the Articles of War, both men pled not guilty. The trial transcript contained the testimony of the captain of the St. James militia, who said the two men were able but refused to drill. The Articles of War technically did not apply to the militia. The allegations against the defendants— Fulgence Gregoine and Jacques Gregoine Jr.—stated that as members of the beat they had been regularly notified of militia drill and never attended. There is no indication that the militia was "called up" or that the men had otherwise entered the military service of Louisiana or the Confederacy. Most of the trial record reflected an attempt to convict both men based on their poor reputation in the community and shows the degree to which fear had taken hold. The need to maintain order in the face of Northern invasion took precedence over fairness.[39] In the process, desertion had taken on an expanded definition and found its way from the military into the civilian sphere.

By the close of 1862, E. W. Halsey conceded that this was "indeed the winter of discontent." Foreign intervention appeared unlikely, but he hoped that by the end of 1863 Northern capitalists would grow weary of the war. In a letter to Louisiana secretary of state P. D. Hardy, Halsey passed along a copy of General Order no. 82 from the office of the Confederate adjutant general and inspector dated November 3, 1862. The order contained a copy of the Confederate act to extend twelve-month enlistments to three years. Clearly the Confederacy had to do something to ensure the integrity of its army, but by forcing men to stay who believed their service was contractually over after one year, the government ran the risk of losing them anyway. Hardy also passed along more troubling news: a list of cases pending before a court-martial in Thibedeaux Parish dated October 23, 1862, three of which involved men who had either deserted or were AWOL. On December 9, a six-and-a-half-page list of deserters was sent to the governor. It called for a thirty-dollar reward for the arrest of any of the men. Most were from the Eighteenth and Thirty-third Louisiana, 150 men total. Both units were in the Army of Tennessee and had fought at Shiloh in April. The occupations of most deserters were predictable: "farmer" and "planter."[40]

As the situation in Louisiana showed, conscription had the potential to either prevent or drive desertion. But by 1862 it was clear to Confederate officials that manpower mobilization could not depend on volunteers alone. As James Chestnut had pointed out, not all men were volunteering, and the problem existed across the Confederacy. William Hinson, a farmer from Carroll County, Arkansas, told his father bluntly, "They have all the regiments they need. For my part, I can't leave my family until I make a crop." From Gonzalez in southeastern Texas, a man wrote his mother that people there were "very backward about volunteering I have heard different persons say they would not leave the state to fight." Not only did men refuse to leave, but their staying made it more difficult for those who had joined. Writing to her cousin Lizzie, a Texas woman said that only old men remained in her county, and she "felt it right mean" that the boys in her cousin's county not only shirked their military duty but wrote to those in the field of the pleasures at home.[41]

It is difficult to measure just how much conscription intensified the struggle between home and military duty. What seems clear, however, is that as Governor Harris pointed out in Tennessee, many men had not joined the army in 1861. Harris gave them the benefit of the doubt, choosing to believe that they had only waited until they were needed. While that may be true, the reality was that whether or not they were needed at the front, they were clearly needed at home. The Confederate Conscription Act of 1862 took away any discretion. Now it was join or be drafted. Volunteering offered the opportunity to serve within a community-based unit and avoid the stigma that accompanied being a conscript, but it now took on an element of coercion for those who could not afford to have the man of the house go to war.

In March 1862, Lizzie Scott Neblett prepared to send her husband, William, to war. As he made ready to leave their home in Grimes County, Texas, Lizzie wrote her cousin of the anguish they felt. "These are times that try men's souls, and women, for if my soul is not surely tried then I do not know anything about it [the war]." William would soon be "leaving me and his babies to set himself up as a target for the abominable yankees to shoot at." Then she touched the heart of the dilemma, that he was anxious about leaving and knew he left without fully providing for her. Although Lizzie did not believe she would starve, she knew that she would "indeed be alone." Her situation repeated itself hundreds of times in the county. Moses Noble of Hays County, Texas, volunteered in March 1862 to avoid being drafted. Just like William Neblett, he left a wife uncertain as to how she would survive in his absence, an uncertainty he must have shared.[42]

The pleas for exemptions that poured into the offices of the Texas governor and adjutant general told the story of where loyalty lay. Like Tennessee, Texas showed how the diversity that dominated the South undermined its war effort and how conscription, designed to bolster the ranks, would actually deplete them. Conscription was designed to help defend the Confederacy, but by February 1862 most men were concerned with defending home and did not equate the two. William Morris, a resident of the Texas coast, wrote Gov. Francis Lubbock demanding exemptions for employees of the Texas & New Orleans Railroad, telling him to "come down here or some other point on the coast and stick your flag down and ask for 20,000 Texans to rally for the defense of Texas and Liberty." One blast from Lubbock's "horn" would do more to rouse Texans than forty blasts from a foreign (i.e., Confederate) one. The same plea came from Colorado County further inland; men seeking exemptions were unable to leave families without their starving. Though they would gladly defend the state, they could not leave.[43]

It was more than just the local nature of loyalty; it was the local nature of need. Some county populations in Texas had been misrepresented in the draft. In 1861, Bee County in southeastern Texas had only 150 people and had already raised fifteen companies. The companies must have been small, because by nineteenth-century standards fifteen companies would have taken everyone. But the 1861 muster took so many men that a draft would leave no one remaining. The chief justice of the Bee County Court asked frankly, "Is it just and right that a draft should be sent upon us as is talked of, after nearly all of the force that can possibly be spared and take care of the families, even say nothing about taking care of property? We have more men in the field than we can well spare."[44]

Conscription revealed more than local need; it accentuated the unique problems of certain portions of the South and the unique nature of the pull that would come from home. Twenty-one men from Bandera County, Texas, wrote Governor Lubbock asking for exemptions. Situated on the westernmost frontier of Texas, just northwest of San Antonio, the Bandera County still suffered from Indian raids. Most of the men had joined the service in 1861. "We are a poor and hard working population whose families depend on them for their daily support," the men wrote. "A draft now would be the equivalent of an order to break the county up and our families cast on the charities of the state." The same plea came from Medina County, where a drought had delayed planting and Indian raids remained a problem. The county could not withstand a draft without being drawn into destitution.[45] Problems with Indians were rare throughout most of the South, but in Texas the situation was critical on its western frontiers. The Confederacy seemed to recognize this fact when it passed the legislation in December 1861 to raise a force to patrol the frontier. However, the unit had either not gotten to full force by spring 1862, had been formed but proved ineffective, or, if effective, was inadequate by itself to combat the problem. For many of these people the "Yankees" were a concept. Many had never met one and did not fear invasion from them. Indians, however, were a known enemy. The draft now threatened to compel men to leave their homes and families vulnerable to a formidable foe, who, unlike the Union, would lay their communities to waste and slaughter their loved ones. For men who joined under the threat of a draft, "volunteering" was tantamount to compulsion. Whether such volunteers would remain in the army depended on how well the Confederacy protected home and fireside.

The draft brought out one other aspect of the war in Texas: evidence that the promise that home would be provided for had been made and understood across the South. In 1862 the community of Long Point had done like most of their neighbors and submitted exemption requests to the governor's office. Lubbock acknowledged receipt of the requests in July of that year, indicating that they would be given "all consideration." Sallie Lauderdale felt unsatisfied with the status of the requests and wrote the Texas adjutant general, J. Y. Dasheil, to emphasize the importance of the exemptions. Her letter purported to speak for "the Ladies of Yequa Bottom Long Point" and clearly articulated her beliefs as to why the war was being fought and what she should expect from the government: "Our understanding has been that the war was for the protection of the women and children, the homes and firesides of the Confederacy. But we are not able to appreciate the promise, when every physician and overseer is taken away, leaving us in the hands of our restless negros and without assistance and medical aid in the hour of distress and sickness."[46] Sallie followed this letter up with another one stating that without a physician "we dwell in an unhealthy country and our condition could hardly be made more hapless by the presence of the invader."[47] Parts of Tennessee, Arkansas, Louisiana, and Mississippi would be hungry by the end of 1862, and portions of Texas harbored the same fears. Sallie Lauderdale did not seem to fear going hungry; for her and those in her community death stalked from elsewhere, the very land itself. But she understood that the Confederacy promised that home and fireside would be protected, and part of that promise for her was not just that men went away to war but that provisions would be made for those at home, even if it meant leaving men at home, most importantly doctors. Whereas Curran Pope believed that the Confederacy and its wealthy had already broken their promise, Lauderdale seemed to imply that a breach was imminent and that the draft was the instrument that would make it complete.

Across the South, men who had not joined in 1861 felt compelled to enlist in 1862 as the draft threatened every man between seventeen and forty-five years of age. Virtually all units in northern Georgia mustered out in the spring of 1862. Men in communities where slavery and plantation farming were either nonexistent or mattered little left only when conscription forced them to volunteer or be drafted. On February 11, 1862, Governor Moore of Louisiana issued a decree disbanding all present volunteer companies, effective April 15. He indicated that volunteers would be accepted and new companies formed until March 15, 1862, but afterward only by consent of the commander in chief; none, however, would be received into a volunteer unit after March 15, 1862, without consent of the major general. Moore's decree came in response to a letter from Secretary of War Judah Benjamin of February 2, 1862, which claimed that Louisiana still "owed" an additional 7,754 volunteers and asked Moore for five regiments. Moore authorized the use of a fifty-dollar bounty, but the regiments had to be in the field by March 15, 1862.[48]

Just as important as those unwilling to go were those in the service who were not all willing to stay. By February 1862, reenlistment had become a popular topic in the camps. L. B. Fielder, stationed near Norfolk, Virginia, flatly told his sister he would not reenlist. He would come home. He had not seen combat and most likely would not see any. He told his sister his mind was made up but that he still wanted to hear from her.[49] Some of the trouble in Arkansas also related directly to conscription. Junius Bragg complained that the poor soldiers were not even allowed the privilege of volunteering again. Bragg boasted that as soon as his enlistment expired there would not be enough men and cannons to keep him from going home and staying if he felt it was "proper" to do so. The notion of being forced to reenlist for three more years was not part of the "engagement" between himself and the government, and he felt the government was powerless to change his understanding. He told his girlfriend, "I do not care for forty Conscription laws, so long as I am brave, truthful and upright in your sight, the edicts of our booby congress have no weight with me." Of greater concern was the fact that Bragg believed the Eleventh Arkansas would mutiny if they were not at least furloughed home as soon as their term expired so they could see their families.[50]

Louisianans proved just as resistant. Men who had enlisted for a year were being told that they were committed for the duration of the war. But while the Confederacy insisted on holding them, Louisiana authorities tended to abide by the letter of the law. Administratively unable to handle the task of drafting men, the Confederacy saw valuable soldiers leave the service with the blessing of state authorities. Governor Moore, who released all one-year men in February 1862, explained to General Beauregard in June 1862 why he had released men who had been drafted: "The law is the law, we kept them 15 months, three months beyond their enlistment." Besides, Moore had no guns, no tents, and no stores.[51]

The decision to draft represented one of the Confederacy's earliest and most definitive statements of national action. It would also become its most controversial step and in the end would fuel desertion. To the extent that the lower and yeoman classes had failed to recognize the notable absence of many of their richer neighbors, the Conscription Act removed any doubt that the rich would expect the poor to fight. In addition to a hefty number of exemptions based upon occupations deemed crucial to the operation of the government and home front, the act contained an exemption for Southerners who owned twenty or more slaves. However, it would not be just conscripts who would desert.

Woodbury claimed in his 1920 study that desertion is a gradual process. It creeps up, and signs exist that it is coming. Such was the case in the Confederacy. But what were the signs? The numbers simply do not show that desertion was a major problem or that it hurt. Yet the non-quantitative data suggest that both were the case, even in 1862.

One of the more subtle but nevertheless telling signs came from a record from General Hospital Franklin & El Paso, Texas. Dated June and July 1862, the record was a list of men who had been admitted to the hospital. It appeared on a preprinted form that included columns for admission date, discharge date, nature of injury or disease, and whether or not the patient had deserted. The form for those months did not identify anyone as having deserted.[52] It is significant, however, that the form contemplated that desertion could occur from the hospital. Perhaps it was a preprinted Union form adopted by the Confederate army. In any case, it would prove prophetic. Both of the Confederacy's two main armies would see a significant number of soldiers desert from the relatively unguarded confines of hospitals.

From Texas came a more ominous sign of desertion in 1862. On April 17, Col. H. E. McCullough, the Confederate commander of the military subdistrict of the Rio Grande, wrote to Mexican general Don Santiago Vidaurri, the governor of the free and sovereign state of Nueva León and Coahuila, to complain that he had been "officially informed" that soldiers were deserting from his forces on his side of the Rio Grande and taking refuge in Matamoras, Mexico. The desertion was bad enough, but McCullough had word that the Confederate deserters were being "subsisted by the consul of the United States, with the knowledge of the military commander of Matamoras." The information indicated that there were now many Americans in Matamoras, some of them armed, who "are declared enemies of the Confederate States, who are doing everything which is possible to poison the minds of the officers and citizens against us, and to stimulate them to commit bad acts against our country and its citizens." McCullough claimed to have an abundance of evidence suggesting that to the U.S. consulate was inducing Confederate soldiers to desert. He wanted the Mexican government to take steps to stop the inducement and the hostile actions of those on the Mexican side.[53]

McCullough's problem reflects the degree to which the Union had begun to use desertion as a weapon of war. Just as occupied Tennessee offered safety for Confederate deserters and oath takers, Mexico offered the same benefits along the Confederacy's southern border. Like the fifth column that had begun to appear in Arkansas and Mississippi, Mexico offered a safe haven from which to operate in and out of Confederate Texas. Not only was desertion occurring in 1862, but the evidence suggests that it hurt in southern Texas. Even if the numbers do not exist to demonstrate a widespread exodus across the Rio Grande, McCullough felt the problem significant enough to invoke the aid of the Mexican authorities. It was probably his only avenue for potential relief, because he was not going to receive the cooperation of the U.S. consulate. Time would tell if Mexico would be willing to jeopardize its relationship with the U.S. government to protect a nation that had yet to prove it could survive.

With Andrew Johnson working diligently in Tennessee to encourage desertion in and out of prison, and with the North developing a policy to induce desertion, the prisoner exchange program became all the more important to the Confederacy. Getting men back into the army would be crucial. However, simply because a soldier was exchanged did not mean he would be returning to Confederate service, as Gen. Braxton Bragg concluded in 1862.

In September 1862, Bragg took matters into his own hands. He issued an order that reflected both the degree to which desertion may have begun to hurt and the need to expand its definition. Technically, desertion is leaving the army with the subjective intent to not return. Bragg's order, however, made straggling tantamount to desertion. Straggling literally means falling behind, but Bragg believed that men straggled so that they would be captured. With the exchange system in place, they hoped to get paroled and then return home. For those who were captured, whether legitimately or not, Bragg's order went one step further and refused to allow them to return home once they were paroled. They could remain in camp until they were exchanged.[54]

Despite having a reputation among his peers that was far from favorable, Bragg understood something that his superiors, peers, and colleagues did not: the Confederacy had an army of farmers. Whether or not he understood the connection to the desertion problems of his eighteenth-century predecessors, Bragg knew that these men were fighting at home, that they would were being drawn back there, and that he had to take immediate steps to close off the avenues of departure. Straggling offered the opportunity to escape military duty without suffering the legal consequences by using the exchange policy. The difficulty of getting parolees to return to duty had already become apparent. Attempts in Mississippi had proved futile. The situation became so bad that orders were issued to officers to go to the towns and counties and pick up men on parole. Those refusing to return would be treated as deserters.[55] Bragg's foresight would be validated again in 1863, as the Confederacy called men paroled at Vicksburg back to "parole camps" after they had been exchanged and found the response less than enthusiastic.

Bragg's foresight extended beyond straggling to another area that would come to haunt the Confederacy: hospitals. Hospital furloughs were part of the recuperation process. The Confederate adjutant and inspector general had issued an order in September 1862 providing for disability furloughs for both soldiers and officers that allowed them to go home and convalesce. A report from the Confederate Congress in 1862 strongly supported this practice and indicated that convalescent leave was crucial to a full recovery.[56] Bragg felt otherwise. Although his order was not issued until January 1863, his experience in 1862 led him to believe that hospital furloughs were just another avenue through which men were deserting. In language that reflected the severity of the problem, Bragg suspended hospital furloughs, "owing to the great abuse practiced by the general hospital in granting furloughs . . . the authority to grant such furloughs is suspended until further orders, that a thorough inspection and report may be made. No army can exist under a system so applied."[57]

Once again, although his move was unpopular, Bragg understood that hospitals were an avenue of potential or actual desertion. As with his straggling and exchange procedures, events of 1863 would validate Bragg's apprehensions and his efforts to stop desertion. Just as important, the fact that he had to take these steps shows how desertion hurt. Samuel Stout's hospital records do not reflect the number of men leaving the hospital in 1862, nor do they show how many men had taken advantage of the furlough policy. Bragg clearly sensed the need to do something and either felt the numbers were already greater than he could tolerate or saw the potential for the problem to escalate. Despite trying to curb desertion from the hospitals, there was a strong likelihood that Bragg's policy would result in losing soldiers anyway. One of the medical benefits of a hospital furlough was the ability to get men away from other sick men. Those fortunate enough to survive their wounds or sickness had to also survive their time in the hospital, and that was not always an easy task. Anyone trying to help the sick likewise ran the risk of dying. No example better illustrates the dangers of Civil War hospitals than an incident in Atlanta in which a South Carolina woman came to the fairground hospital to care for her injured husband. He could barely move, and in trying to make his situation more bearable, she ushered in her own death:

> It was a bad scene! In the fairgrounds hospital lay a poor soldier, too badly hurt to turn himself upon his bunk. His wife leaving home and little children in South Carolina, had come, as swiftly as love could bring her, to his side, to nurse and comfort him. Yesterday she reached him—anxiety, toil and trouble proved too much for her delicate nature. Today she was a corpse by the side of her husband. Her lifeless form lay in the midst of strangers.[58]

This brief account leaves many questions unanswered. Did the journey kill her? Did she contract something in the hospital? Did she simply die from the hardship of seeing her husband in such a state? The point is that hospitals were dangerous places, and the 1862 Confederate Senate report reached the same conclusion. The fact that men used hospitals and the furloughs they granted to escape the service forced Bragg to restrict what seemed to be an essential component of rehabilitation. Any soldier witnessing the plight of the South Carolina woman might be encouraged to desert, whether with a furlough or just by walking away. Desertion had forced some hard choices on Confederate leadership, as any decision seemed to yield an unpleasant and damaging consequence.

Bragg's observations were either shared by the civilian authorities or managed somehow to trickle up. As Bragg moved to curb desertion in the Army of Tennessee, Confederate legislators took steps to limit the damage done by desertion. Like Bragg's military orders, the proposed laws began to broaden the definition of desertion, placing conduct that technically did not rise to the level of desertion on the same plane as leaving the service with the intent to never return. In August 1862 a Senate resolution went to the floor that allowed the army to arrest officers who were AWOL and treat them as deserters.[59] Three months later, Jefferson Davis wrote a letter to the governors of all the Confederate states in which he emphasized the Union defeats inflicted by the Confederate armies but asked the governors to join him in accomplishing several important tasks. One of the more pressing tasks was to see that all officers and men presently AWOL, or temporarily discharged but now "able again," be returned to their units. The latter would seem to refer to men sent home on hospital furlough who had not returned, proof that Bragg may have been correct. Not only were men deserting, but Davis's second request hinted at the reason why. He asked the governors to encourage their various state legislatures to pass laws to curb or eliminate extortion (the selling of necessary goods at exorbitant prices). Davis called the extorters "worse enemies of the Confederacy than if found in arms among the invading forces." Both the armies in the field and the soldiers' families at home were prey to such men, and Davis believed that "only through state action" could the practice be repressed.[60]

Local data and isolated incidents seem to justify the level of concern expressed by Bragg, Davis, and others in the West. Andrew Johnson's efforts to bring Tennessee soldiers back home by offering the oath of allegiance had spread, like desertion itself, to men from other states. On October 1, 1862, a story entitled "Traitor to the Confederacy" appeared in the *Montgomery Weekly Advertiser*. The article printed a letter from the officers of the First Alabama, Army of Tennessee, to Lt. Samuel B. Moore that had been hand-delivered to Moore upon his release from the Union prison at Johnson's Island. Moore had sworn the oath of allegiance and was headed home. The letter, signed by thirty-nine officers of the First Alabama, expressed how "mortified" his comrades were with his action, an action they claimed to be desertion from the Confederate army. Educated in Pennsylvania, Moore had gone South before the war and enlisted when the conflict began. He claimed that he had sworn the

DESERTION IN THE HEARTLAND

oath of allegiance because his parents were ill and he was needed at home. His comrades branded him a "renegade and a morally perjured man." It is unclear where Moore was from, but he felt needed at home. To make matters worse, on November 19, 1862, a long list appeared in the paper of men from the First Alabama who had died in prison. Men leaving prison were deserters, and those who would never leave bore a morbid witness to the abandonment of cause and comrades.[61]

Lieutenant Moore was not the only man needed at home, however, as problems that surfaced in Arkansas, Tennessee, and Mississippi seemed to have spread into Alabama. At the bottom of the page of the same newspaper where the Moore letter was reprinted was a note about a band of renegades ranging through Madison County, Alabama, on the Alabama-Tennessee border. The group, which claimed to be "partisan rangers" but was not part of the Confederate army, indiscriminately seized horses, mules, and anything else they could find. Men who should have been, or perhaps had been, in the Confederate army were preying upon the very people whom Madison County soldiers had gone to war to protect.[62]

Events at the end of 1862 provide an eerie confirmation of what Hindman had suggested in Arkansas, what Bragg saw in Tennessee, and what Washington and Greene had learned during the Seven Years' War and the American Revolution: leniency breeds desertion. In South Carolina the state government adopted Confederate army regulations for use in the state militia. Article 6 of those regulations stated that men liable for service who defaulted would be subject to punishment "short of death."[63] People refused to call it desertion and were hesitant to execute soldiers. By the end of 1862 even the civilian population, including the Southern newspapers, had picked up on the desertion problem and the Confederate army's inability to deal with men harshly. In December 1862 an editorial in the *Montgomery Weekly Advertiser* entitled "Desertion from Our Army" referred to the mistaken policy of leniency taken by officers in the first eighteen months of the war. Men convicted of desertion were not being punished as required by the articles of war. Deserters were routinely placed under house arrest and returned to duty. As a result, "if unchecked, [desertion] threatens to demoralize the army to an alarming extent." The editor believed that deserters should be shot and claimed that the desertion problem had reached "alarming numbers" by the end of 1862. The editorial referred to a man named Cain, shot for desertion in Virginia, whose last words were, "If the law under which I am shot had been faithfully executed during the last 18 months, I should today be a faithful soldier in the ranks." Bragg is identified in the article as having issued an order of amnesty to induce men to return and stating that thereafter any man deserting would be shot. It was his hope that such measures would ensure far less desertion than in the last six months.[64]

Bragg's move toward a harsher policy coincided with the Confederate adjutant general's efforts to address desertion. On November 27, 1862, Samuel Cooper's office issued General Order no. 96, telling all men absent from their commands to return at once or be treated as deserters. Men not returning would be put on a list along with conscripts who had failed to appear. Officers not returning would be stricken from the rolls and reenlisted as privates. Once the lists were compiled, they would be published in newspapers throughout the South.[65] Desertion had begun to hurt, and 1862 revealed that there was more than one way out of the army. The Confederacy had also come to the conclusion that a "national" problem required a local solution and the zealous efforts of the states. Men were leaving, and the fact that Davis looked to state governors to help return them indicated that they were going home.

By the end of 1862, desertion was probably not the Confederacy's most severe problem. Shortages of food, salt, clothing, medicine, and physicians plagued both citizens and soldiers. The absence of a male workforce had already brought hardship to many states. In Texas, organized resistance to the draft had sprung up in the northern counties of Wise, Denton, Grayson, and Cook. Men were encouraged to avoid the draft and, if drafted, to desert when battle began. The group cut across class lines and apparently had secret handshakes, signs, and passwords.[66]

If desertion was a disease, it was beginning to spread into a body that was already weakened and had yet to feel the full brunt of war. It had begun to spread out of the army and into the civilian population. Both soldiers and civilians had begun to believe that the Confederacy had reneged on a promise by the state that lay at the heart of the common man's commitment to leave home and fight: to take care of those at home. The states were trying. Alabama's Soldier Relief Records show the government mobilizing the program in late 1861 and providing aid throughout 1862. However, it was not enough. To provide aid, one must have the resources. People could not eat money, and even if they could, Confederate currency had become unpalatable. Aid meant food, and food was clearly a problem. South Carolina newspapers insisted that the reduction of cotton crops would be one of the "grandest features of the war." One paper called upon safety commissioners to canvas the various districts of the state and destroy cotton crops of anyone disregarding the common interest.[67] A Georgia paper printed a citizen resolution from Greensboro, Georgia, that painted an even bleaker outlook. In resolving to devote all their energies to the production of food, the citizens conceded that

> *The crop of provisions raised by us does not supply the demand in even ordinary times and will be still more inadequate to the increased demand produced by a state of war, the consumption of the army being greater than that of the same number of men and horses at home, and the losses in transportation and by the enemy greatly increasing the quantity needed and the number of producers being greatly diminished by the transfer of scores of thousands of horses and hundreds of thousands of men from agriculture to war. . . . [T]he great graineries of the North are closed. . . . [S]upply is further diminished by the loss of parts of Mississippi, Kentucky, Virginia, North Carolina, South Carolina, Georgia, Alabama, Tennessee, Arkansas and Texas. . . . [T]he seasons in our climate are so uncertain that, if the whole country were planted in cereals, we might still fail to produce enough to supply the demand. . . . [T]he skill of our officers and valor of our troops is of no avail without bread.[68]*

The citizens acknowledged that if the South could not change its agricultural practices it was doomed to defeat by an enemy using almost no effort. Failure to change would be "National Suicide." The government and the wealthy had promised that home would be provided for. The signs in 1862 were that it was not—and some believed it could not be—adequately supported.

However, the many problems that had begun to interact with desertion were not restricted to the western Confederacy. Virginia, where two great armies struggled within one hundred miles of each national capital, could not escape the ravages of war, nor could the vaunted Army of Northern Virginia escape the disease of desertion.

5. DESERTION IN THE EAST AND THE FOLLY OF LENIENCY, 1862

On April 2, 1862, Ms. N. L. Beckley wrote her cousin Lizzie from war-torn Virginia. Several weeks before, Lizzie had prepared her husband to go off to war from their home in Texas, a place so far away from Virginia that it must have seemed like another world to Ms. Beckley. Lizzie had struggled to accept the fact that her husband had to leave and set himself up as "a target to the Yankees." But as close as the war must have felt to Lizzie, her cousin made it clear that Texas did not know war yet. "You do not know the heart rending trials I have undergone. Oh Lizzie war is awful, but you feel it not as we do—our homes invaded, crops taken, negroes taking refuge, constantly passing, homeless, and we know not how soon we may be driven off." By the spring of 1862, Virginia planters had threatened to burn everything and take their slaves south if the Union reached Richmond. The early rains had made planting impossible, and with all the men gone Ms. Beckley did not know how they could make a crop.[1]

Eventually Lizzie would know the hardships of war, as not even Texas would escape unscathed. But despite the importance of the western theater, for most of the war all eyes focused on Virginia. With its capital less than one hundred miles from Washington DC and its borders touching Pennsylvania, Ohio, Maryland, and Kentucky, Virginia became the focal point of the war. Lee's Army of Northern Virginia would struggle with the Union's massive Army of the Potomac, a conflict that would be exclusively a Virginia contest as Lee's army left the state only twice during the war. In time the Army of Northern Virginia would become a symbol of the Confederate nation, just as its Revolutionary War predecessor, the Continental army, had become the symbol of the fledgling United States. Likewise, Lee would come to be seen by many Southerners as the George Washington of the Confederacy.[2] For all of its accomplishments, the presence of the Army of Northern Virginia brought with it all the hardships of war. As Ms. Beckley attested, the invader had come to Virginia. That Lee's army performed well, even brilliantly, did not alter the fact that two great armies faced off against one another and brought all the destruction that resulted when armies lived off the land.

There are several reasons why Lee and the Army of Northern Virginia avoided the desertion issue until mid- to late 1863. First, from June 1862 until September 1863 the army was either fighting and winning or basking in the glow of victory. Morale remained high among those in the army because the war, at least for them, went well. Instances like Antietam, where the losses were severe and the outcome could be construed as a draw at best, were followed up by Fredericksburg, where victory was never clearer and the losses low. Most of the historical literature that addresses the Army of Northern Virginia during this period focuses on its battlefield exploits. Lee's own reports and correspondence contribute to the perception that the Army of Northern Virginia enjoyed immunity from desertion. His wartime papers contain no mention of desertion by name until the middle of 1863. Likewise, the *Official Records* contain little from Lee on "desertion" by name from the Confederate perspective until 1863.[3] While the problem may not appear in Lee's writings or other "official records," it was nevertheless there, as were the causes at home that had begun to drive desertion among troops from other parts of the Confederacy.

Lee does not describe desertion per se in 1862, but his correspondence clearly reveals that the problem was surfacing, regardless of what he chose to call it. Georgia soldiers complained that furloughs had become difficult to obtain in the spring of 1862. On March 21, 1862, several months before Lee assumed command, Adj. Gen. Samuel Cooper issued General Order no. 16, which revoked all furloughs except for men on medical leave. He cited "the necessities of service with the enemy pressing on all sides" as the justification.[4] The *Staunton Spectator* reprinted the order and with it an urgent call for all men to return. The plea carried what had now become the standard rallying cry: "We appeal to them in the name of all they hold sacred—country, home, wives, children, friends, altars, and firesides—hasten at once to the field."[5] By May 1862 they were still not coming in fast enough. That month the adjutant general's office issued Special Order no. 107, directing men who were "absent" from their commands to return. It ordered the commanding general of the Department of Henrico to arrest such men, and if they disregarded the arrest they would then be listed as deserters. The intent was sound, but it continued to treat men as absent, deeming them deserters only if they defied arrest.[6]

The restriction on furloughs was intentional, and after the Seven Days' campaign Lee moved to enforce the order and plug any administrative gaps that might otherwise allow men to slip away. "I have been obliged to issue an order that no applications for furloughs will be considered except on a surgeons certificate of disability," Lee explained to Secretary of War Randolph. "If this order can be evaded by application to the War Department dissatisfaction will be created by those who have been refused. I know you understand the condition of the army, and believe it is only necessary to call your attention to the injurious effects of this course to have it remedied. I regard the subject as one of immediate importance to the efficiency of the army."[7]

Certainly one could justify the furlough restriction as necessary for Lee's Manassas campaign planned for late summer. With men on furlough it would be difficult for them to catch up to an army on the move. However, another explanation, and the more likely one, is that Lee saw the potential for men to return home on furlough and not come back. Language that refers to the "injurious effects of this course" seems to be talking about the effort to circumvent his authority by going directly to the War Department. However, it is clear that non-hospital-related furloughs were to be avoided at all costs. The order suggests that Lee feared a legal leave of absence might well become a permanent condition. He spoke of the "condition of the army" as if its stability were somehow precarious in late June 1862. He instituted strong disciplinary measures almost immediately upon taking command, and among the many vices he sought to abate was unauthorized absence. The discomfort that came with camp life caused soldiers to long for the comforts of home. As the summer and fall campaign season began to wind down both armies went into camp, and the level of discomfort threatened to increase as the weather made life outdoors even more inhospitable. If a man left such a situation and tasted the comforts of home even briefly, he might not return. Stopping furloughs would definitely prevent any confusion about men legally absent and those AWOL. Anyone not on a hospital furlough would be deemed AWOL. In time, hospital furloughs in the East would disappear just as they had in the West, but nonmedical releases had been cut off.[8] Events in 1862 not only gave credence to Lee's concerns about keeping the army intact but make it clear that desertion and absenteeism drove his policy decisions.

The second indication from Lee that desertion might become a problem came in a more subtle form in the summer of 1862. Gen. George McClellan's Peninsula campaign may have failed to capture Richmond, but it brought certain portions of eastern Virginia under Union occupation, even if only briefly. On July 21, 1862, Lee wrote McClellan to complain that Confederate civilians "engaged in peaceful avocations" had been arrested and imprisoned because they refused to take the oath of allegiance to the United States. Others had been compelled by duress to swear on oath not to take up arms against the United States. One hundred of these oath takers had recently been released from Fort Monroe. Lee insisted that the Confederacy refused to admit the authority of the United States to arrest its citizens and extort from them their parole not to render military service to the Confederacy under the threat of punishment should they do so and fall into Union hands. Secretary of War Randolph took the position that the oaths would not be binding and that such persons would still be held to military service. Lee threatened retaliation if the Union tried to punish these people.[9]

The debate over oath swearing depicted in Lee's letter came sixteen months before Lincoln's Proclamation of Amnesty in December 1863, which offered Southern civilians the chance to come back to the Union. The oath swearing that occurred in 1862 was tied to the Union's use of desertion as a tool of war. In Tennessee, Andrew Johnson was using the oath to bring both soldiers and civilians back into the Union. The oath not to bear arms actually contained language about being properly exchanged. Regardless of what the Confederacy claimed insofar as the oath's being ineffectual, the citizens who took it voluntarily or under duress found themselves in a precarious situation. If they adopted the Confederate policy that the oath was involuntary and therefore of no consequence, that might not shield them from retribution by the Union army if they did join the service and were captured. On the other hand, if they were called to service by the Confederacy and failed to appear on the ground that they had sworn the oath to the Union, the Confederate government and military would treat them as deserters. The mere use of desertion and oath taking placed Confederate citizens in a position where responding to their nation's call to arms presented risks beyond those normally associated with military service.

Not only did Lee see the early signs of desertion within his army and state, but he knew that the war was beginning to cause the same problems in the East that the Confederacy experienced in the West. By August 1862 the Army of Northern Virginia boasted regiments from almost every Confederate state except Arkansas. By the Battle of Gettysburg, in July 1863, Arkansas would be represented, but Virginia contributed the majority of the army's troops. Over the course of the war North Carolina supplied more soldiers to the Confederate cause than any other state, but in August 1862 it was fourth behind Georgia and South Carolina in the number of regiments in the Army of Northern Virginia. Nonetheless, the ability to protect the homes and firesides in Virginia and the Carolinas would prove crucial to maintaining the army in the field. During the American Revolution, Nathanael Greene had watched as desertion stripped his North Carolinians from the ranks. Lee and the Confederacy could ill afford the same experience during the second revolution. Virginia would be the chessboard of the eastern theater. Her native sons would therefore fight at home, and the temptation and ability to escape would beckon soldiers throughout the war. However, at least they were home. Fighting in Virginia to protect Virginians made sense. For men in the Army of Northern Virginia who hailed from places outside Virginia that were also threatened by the Union, the temptation to desert would also be there. For these men the argument to stay in the army would not seem as compelling. [10]

On August 8, 1862, a day before Jackson's stunning victory at Cedar Mountain that began the Manassas campaign, Lee responded to a letter from North Carolina governor Henry T. Clark. Clark had written Lee on August 4 regarding his concern over the Union occupation of portions of North Carolina's coastline and the harm that an invading army might cause. Lee empathized with Clark. "I have been an eye witness of the outrages and depredations upon private property committed by the enemy in this state," he wrote, "and can fully appreciate what you say of injuries sustained by the people of North Carolina." But then Lee set forth the problem: "It is impossible with the means at our command, to pursue the policy of concentrating our forces to protect important points and baffle the principal efforts of our enemy, and at the same time extend all the protection we desire to give to every district." The overriding theme of the Confederate war effort comes through in the words of its most respected warrior. There simply were not enough resources, military or otherwise, to provide for everyone and every contingency. To keep his army in the field. Lee would have to convince his soldiers of what he told Clark: "The safety of the whole state of North Carolina, as well as of Virginia, depends in a measure upon the result of the enemy's efforts in this quarter [Virginia], which if successful, would make your state the theater of hostilities far more injurious and destructive to your citizens than anything they have yet been called upon to suffer."[11] A nation that held its citizens and its army together on the ancient notion of *patriae* had to be able to convince its soldiers and civilians that the best way to protect home in the long run was to fight in a venue that for most was far from home.

In theory, Lee's argument had merit. In the West, Union victory and Confederate defeat had opened up portions of the South, and the injury and destruction in places like Tennessee and northern Mississippi were severe. The argument that "things could be worse" had very little effect on men who knew only that at their homes it was "bad right now." Even if successful, the Confederacy's war plan left portions of the South at the mercy of the Union army. Governor Brown saw the conflict in 1861 and was unwilling to let Georgians go to Virginia. Governor Moore also understood the difficulty of protecting home from far away, and his pleas to Jefferson Davis to allow conscripts to stay in Louisiana reflected a belief that not only were the men needed there but that if there was a sense that Louisiana was not being physically protected by men stationed in the state, those serving in Tennessee and Virginia might not be willing to stay. As the Union demonstrated the ability to fight the Confederacy's major armies and still invade other portions of the South, Lee's argument that victory in Virginia was saving other parts of the South would become much less tenable. What would make it even harder to sell would be the knowledge of those in Virginia that conditions in that state threatened home and family. If Virginians became uneasy over the safety of their homes and loved ones, the effect on those who left families in Georgia, Alabama, Tennessee, and the trans-Mississippi would be equally damaging.

Signs that Virginia's home front was withering from the war came from both the top and bottom of society. From the top, Gov. John Letcher surveyed the landscape and realized that his state was already feeling the effects of a war that had really just gotten started militarily. In addition, like officials and citizens in other parts of the Confederacy, Letcher saw that conscription threatened to undermine morale. In May 1862 he addressed the Virginia Senate and complained that "multitudes have been released from military service who have no just claim to exemption." Exemption applicants were allowed to choose their own physicians for medical discharges, which injected bias into the process. Physicians received fees for doing physical examinations, which had become a side business for some. Letcher seemed to imply that the more exemptions a physician granted, the more applicants he would receive.[12] By September, the problem in Virginia had gone beyond the inequities of the draft. Salt, that most precious of nineteenth-century commodities, had quickly run out. People were already suffering because the present supply was inadequate and the future prospects looked even bleaker. People across the state complained that the limited supply had given rise to exorbitant prices, prices so high that the average citizen could no longer afford to buy salt. Soldiers' families were hit particularly hard. Letcher saw the discrepancy between what these men were paid and what their monthly salary was expected to provide. Virginians were no different from any other soldiers in the Confederacy. A large number of these men were heads of families, mostly poor men, dependent on their own labor to make a living. "They have cheerfully left their homes and families to engage in the service of their country. Since they entered the service prices have run up to fabulous amounts for every article that enters into domestic use." A soldier's monthly pay would not buy most necessities. Letcher believed it should be the government's policy "to care for those who are fighting this battle for Southern Independence, and whose noble deeds are furnishing the material for a history."[13]

The problem was not just scarcity but also the willingness of some to take advantage of the situation. "A reckless spirit for money making seems to have taken the entire possession of the public mind," Letcher said. "The ledger is the bible and gold is the God." Extortioners acted with total disregard to the plight of the needy, and Letcher knew that such a practice, if unchecked, would kill the spirit of the fighting man. "What must be the feelings of a man who is fighting the battles of the country, surrendering all the endearments of home, submitting to all the sufferings and sacrifices of camp life and active military duty, when he (receiving only $11.00 a month) is informed that a pack of salt costs $50.00, or a pair of ladies shoes costs $16.00, with everything else in proportion?" Unless he was a man of means, such a soldier would have to feel that while he was defending his country his family suffered, unable to acquire basic necessities. "With what heart can he fight our battles under such circumstances?"[14]

In a sense it was a rhetorical question, but the answer apparent to all was that many soldiers could not and would not continue to fight under such circumstances. Surviving camp life proved difficult enough. By September 15 the Army of Northern Virginia had pushed McClellan away from Richmond and driven north, winning a small battle at Cedar Mountain and a major victory at Manassas. Two days after Letcher's address it would face off against the Army of the Potomac in an epic struggle for its own survival at Antietam. Several thousand would never leave Maryland, and thousands more left wounded, destined to either die later or suffer in Confederate hospitals. Their sacrifice was real, and the government's inability to care for their families at home would begin to weigh on Lee's soldiers. Letcher had come to grips with the same problem Lee observed: the swearing of oaths to the "Lincoln government." Letcher proposed that amnesty be offered to people who had taken the oath of allegiance to the United States because their "portion of the state has been overrun." Amnesty would be conditional, based upon the guilty party's manifestation of fealty to the Commonwealth, a loyalty that had to be shown by "works." How one demonstrated such loyalty was not explained.[15]

Virginia's citizenry ran the full spectrum of Southern class, from the planters who threatened to take their slaves and go south, to a family of what one Union cavalryman called "poor white trash." Shoeless, dirty, destitute, and hungry, the Culpeper County family seemed totally unconcerned with the war, showing little interest in anything outside their little homestead and few livestock. But they cared. All Virginians cared one way or the other. The state was occupied, and the presence of two armies made life in Virginia difficult. Margaret Preston of Lexington had come to "loathe the word war" by 1862. Schools and stores had closed, and goods were either unavailable or, as Letcher pointed out, going for ridiculously high prices. Preston had dressed her baby in a calico dress she made from the lining of an old dressing gown. Lucy Johnson of Fauquier County claimed she was "reduced to a bacon bone." The Union army had overrun her home, destroying what they could not carry off, and her servants and family were ill. In the summer of 1862 Culpeper County also felt the presence of war. One farmer was said to have lost "all he had" to John Pope's army, including all of his livestock. Some men lost even more. Samuel Luckett and Rufus Humpheries, twenty-two-year-old lieutenants in the Thirteenth Virginia, both had homes in Culpeper County, and both fell in the cornfield at the Battle of Cedar Mountain. In short, sacrifice was apparent everywhere. For some it seemed like too much. Even prior to Manassas, Lee's army seems to be straggling, and Jackson had three men shot for desertion on August 19, 1862. Lee's no-furlough policy would continue into the winter of 1862. Some thought it was unfair, as the physical discomforts of camp made army life that much more difficult to bear. Virginians longed to return home, and some, like those in the Seventh Virginia, were lucky enough to camp in Culpeper County. But even among units camped close to home, just being nearby was not enough. It was too close and men deserted as early as fall 1862. Some were not so fortunate, since their homes lay in Texas, Alabama, and Mississippi. Many men had not seen home in over a year, and Lee's policy made matters worse.[16]

The experiences in Culpeper County mirrored those of other northern Virginia counties in 1862. Union policies toward civilians seem to have hardened.

Given the problems with a lack of provisions and the willingness of Virginians to extort from their fellow citizens, the situation was difficult for men in the service to accept. Events in 1862 justified Lee's strict approach. In the winter of 1861–62 the Confederate government handed out furloughs to men for reenlisting for three years. Not everyone received a furlough, and those who did not began to "run the blockade." Thus, giving furloughs drove desertion, because those who did not receive them felt entitled to leave the army on their own. Discipline was lax, punishment, consistent with the rest of the Confederacy, was light, and men left with impunity. The inability of the Confederate officer corps to enforce discipline only made matters worse. Men going home in 1862, whether intending to return or not, found a sympathetic ear in many officers. Some even encouraged continued absenteeism. The need to provide for those at home still carried weight and counted as a mitigating factor among soldiers and their commanders. As winter 1862 approached many men expected the same leniency that had dominated the army in the winter of 1861–62. With battle behind them, men expected a reprieve, and feeling they were less needed at the front, many left with or without a furlough.[17] Again, the specter of America's eighteenth-century armies raised its head.

What must have seemed perplexing for Confederate government and military leaders was the inability to balance the equities. It seemed as if either choice begot the same result. Too many furloughs exposed the army to mass absenteeism and perhaps mass desertion. No furloughs had the equally negative effect of causing men to take what they believed was a right whether the army was willing to acknowledge it or not. A selective furlough policy created inequities, with some men willing to take unauthorized leave if they felt they had been passed over unfairly. Adding fuel to the fire, early Confederate policy had treated desertion and absenteeism with a soft hand. Jackson's executions in August 1862 were as rare as Hindman's had been in 1862 Arkansas. Fines, temporary incarceration, or other camp punishment was but a small price to pay for a few days home, or perhaps the chance to stay home forever. Thus, in the Army of Northern Virginia, the bad habits formed in 1861 and 1862 carried over into late 1862.

There is no broad study of desertion among Virginia soldiers in the Army of Northern Virginia or of the army itself. However, the studies of smaller units and the more general observations of Confederate commanders led to the conclusion that desertion in 1862 claimed a significant number of soldiers, making it the worst year of the war for some units. A study of ten Virginia regiments, representing four regions of the state, reveals how serious the desertion problem had become in 1862. Of the ten regiments, half had more deserters in 1862 than in any other year of the war. For several regiments the problem was extreme. The Fifth Virginia reported 210 deserters in 1862, almost 60 percent of its 352 total for the war. That represents slightly more than 10 percent of its total enlistment of 2,010. The numbers for the Thirty-third Virginia were even more severe. Two hundred thirty-five men deserted in 1862, again more than 60 percent of its desertion for the war. But the total enlistment was only 1,382, making its 1862 desertion numbers 17 percent of its total enlistment for the war. The desertion figures as a percentage of the whole would have been significantly higher for 1862.[18] The units of high desertion from the Shenandoah Valley were not only in Jackson's Corps, or "wing" as it was identified at that time, but were part of the famous Stonewall Brigade, renowned for its courage and fighting ability. Perhaps this explains why Jackson shot three deserters in August 1862. If the pride of his corps would desert, anyone would. To Jackson's credit, he understood the necessity of a strong deterrent. He may have just grown weary of trying to distinguish a straggler from a deserter. Straggling had reduced his force at Kernstown in March 1862 by roughly fifteen hundred men, one-third of his force. Whether soldiers intended to leave forever or not, such men were not there when it counted.[19]

Jackson's was not the only corps to suffer. James Longstreet, Lee's other corps commander, also felt the weakening effects of desertion. In June 1862, as Lee prepared to launch his campaign to break the siege of Richmond, Longstreet took stock of his corps. Commanding what was then the right wing of the army, he observed that he had twenty-four Old Dominion regiments, with 32,000 Virginians in his wing. However, of that number he commanded only about 20,000. Of the 12,000 not present for duty, about 7,000 were absent.[20] If the remainder—about 5,000—were either sick or wounded, absenteeism stood as the greatest single cause for the depletion of his total numbers. The last battle prior to the Seven Days' campaign was at Fair Oaks on May 30, 1862. Thus, even given a pattern where men and officers found it acceptable to disappear after a fight and return later, a significant number had not returned. Longstreet's numbers are estimates, but they reflect a severe problem keeping men in the army on the eve of the largest fight in the eastern theater at that point in the war. Gen. Harry Heth, then a brigade commander, saw what Longstreet felt, and in June 1862 he issued a directive addressed "To Whom It May Concern." Heth gave notice to all men between eighteen and thirty-five in ten Virginia counties who were subject to the conscription law and had either never reported or, as Longstreet indicated, had joined the service and deserted. He gave such men five days to report or be subject to execution as deserters. The office of the adjutant and inspector general followed up Heth's directive with General Order no. 43, which authorized all Virginia sheriffs, deputy sheriffs, and constables to arrest deserters. Thirty dollars would be paid for each man delivered to his unit, fifteen dollars for men captured and held in jail. There is no indication that anyone returned, however, and the concerns that Longstreet had voiced in June continued as many people refused to recognize what Heth and Cooper tried to address.

Straggling and desertion were essentially the same in that they depleted the army of manpower. Almost three months later, in the aftermath of Antietam, Gen. D. H. Hill remarked that stragglers were cowards and thieves, "lost to all sense of shame." Lee struggled with the problem, but he refused to recognize that the straggler was always a potential, if not an actual, deserter. He had to concede that straggling may have cost him a shot at victory at Antietam because many men never crossed the river into Maryland.[21] Soldiers' tendency to absent themselves and officers' willingness to overlook that conduct, even if it did not rise to the level of desertion, laid the groundwork for desertion later in the war. If the Confederate army could not see the signs in Longstreet's observations, they should have been able to see the symptoms in other places, not the least of which was the Army of Northern Virginia court-martial proceedings that began in August 1862.

In the wake of Antietam, Lee insisted on sterner measures for straggling, even if he could not admit to himself or others that it had become a form of desertion. He had, however, begun to accept the fact that even if straggling was not an attempt to leave the army permanently, it was not a post-combat problem but had risen to the level of deserting in the face of the enemy. The 1862 court-martial records of the Army of Northern Virginia have a great deal to say about straggling and desertion. Straggling sometimes lasted months, and not only did desertion occur in 1862, but the attitude of leniency and sympathetic understanding among Confederate officers permeated the judicial system. Even when conduct seemed to rise to a level that merited death, leniency could be found somewhere higher up the chain of command. The first reported cases demonstrate why absenteeism proved so difficult to control. Punishment was either minimal or nonexistent. Pvt. Lewis Harcum left camp without permission on August 4, 1862, was gone for more than twelve hours; he pled guilty to being

AWOL and received seven days' confinement. Pvt. E. M. Ezekiel of the Forty-sixth Virginia Infantry left on August 17 and returned a day later. Although he was found guilty of being AWOL, the court determined he should be acquitted, "believing the punishment he has already suffered sufficient for the offense." James J. Martin left on August 6 and returned two days later. His sentence was likewise commuted on the ground that he had served enough time already. Cpl. Lafayette W. Banks left on August 3 and returned two days later only after a detachment was sent to apprehend him. Found guilty of being AWOL, he was reduced in rank to private, having been dealt with leniently "on account of extenuating circumstances."[22]

One could argue that the four men tried for absences that did not go beyond two days deserved lenient treatment. However, Banks did not return until after the army took steps to apprehend him. The findings do not indicate the nature of his "extenuating circumstances," but it could be argued that he did not intend to return voluntarily. For an army struggling to maintain its strength, the court-martial of William Callum illustrates how the army and its officers contributed to the problem. Callum, a private in the Twenty-sixth Virginia Infantry, left his camp on May 6, 1862, while on the march from Gloucester Point. Thereafter he remained within the enemy's lines and did not rejoin his company until he was brought to Richmond by a detachment of Confederate cavalry. Callum was found guilty of being AWOL, his charge was reduced from desertion to unauthorized leave, and he was sentenced to sixty days' hard labor with a twelve-pound ball and chain attached to his leg and ordered to forfeit two months' pay. Callum's sentence reflects another grant of leniency based on extenuating circumstances. Callum was found within enemy lines and was returned under guard. Reducing the charge to unauthorized leave ignored the facts. Callum's conduct evidenced all of the requirements of traditional desertion. Although intent may be difficult to read, removing one's self into enemy lines could at least be construed as intending not to return. Perhaps his home was behind the Union lines, but in a strict military sense that does not excuse the conduct. However, it seems clear that "strict" military regulations were not being applied. For some, desertion had become a "justifiable offense."[23]

A clear trend of reducing desertion to unauthorized leave appears in 1862 court-martial proceedings, This is the case even when men were gone more than two months, secreted themselves behind enemy lines, or, most importantly, left in May 1862 and did not return until after the Seven Days' campaign in July. While not all cases involved desertion or unauthorized leave, those two offenses made up the majority of the docket, and the results are telling. Of the thirty-six cases tried in the August–September term, thirty were for desertion or unauthorized leave. Of that number, twelve men had been gone at least two months and had completely avoided all combat from May to the end of July. Of the seventeen trials for desertion, nine resulted in a finding of guilty of the lesser charge of unauthorized absence, despite the fact that several involved absences in excess of two months. In no instance was the death penalty inflicted. Those convicted of desertion routinely received periods of hard labor, were branded on the left hip with a "D," and in some cases were drummed out of the service. One man had his head shaved prior to being discharged. The harshest sentence fell on Pvt. William Haywood of the Twenty-fifth Virginia Infantry, who, like Callum, left on May 6, 1862, and was captured months later after the Seven Days' campaign. Haywood forfeited all pay, was placed in solitary confinement every two weeks for a day until he served eighty-four days of solitary, was put to work during that period at hard labor with a twelve-pound ball and chain on his ankle, and upon completion was branded with a "D" and drummed out of the service. Although his punishment was comparatively harsh, Haywood not only deserted but also persuaded others to do so. More than one-third of the deserters/absentees managed to avoid combat on the peninsula completely. An informal policy of leaving when one felt he was "not needed" resulted in men being gone when they were badly needed. The record shows an almost uniform policy of leniency, and in some instances it shows one man treated harshly and another virtually let go when the specification or description of the conduct is virtually identical.[24]

The Army of Northern Virginia court-martial reconvened on October 15, 1862, and tried thirty cases, of which twenty-six involved unauthorized absence or desertion. Of the six desertion cases, three verdicts were reduced to unauthorized absence. As of case 18, the record stopped reflecting the specific factual specifications, so it is impossible to tell how long these men were gone or whether that omission was intentional or not. However, through case 17, nine of the men had been gone from May until sometime in July, after the end of the Seven Days' campaign. One soldier, Pvt. James Brown of the Twenty-sixth Virginia Infantry, was gone from May 5 until October 1 and yet was found guilty only of unauthorized absence. Most of the sentences involved some form of hard labor, but the presence of leniency runs throughout the record, despite indications that men went home to places behind enemy lines or did not return until apprehended.[25]

The first two sessions in the list reflected proceedings from the headquarters of Gen. H. A. Wise and involved Virginia soldiers almost exclusively. Soldiers from the Forty-sixth and Twenty-sixth Virginia Infantry dominated the roll of defendants. In October 1862, a session at the headquarters of Gen. Junius Daniel ran contemporaneous with the session at Wise's headquarters. Daniel's men were North Carolinians, and of the twenty cases tried, nineteen were for desertion or unauthorized absence. The specifications were omitted, so the severity of the action and the duration of their absence remain unclear. However, some of these cases provide insight into this "culture of leniency," particularly that which benefited Pvt. L. B. Seymour of the Fiftieth North Carolina Troops. Seymour was convicted of desertion on October 10. His offense must have been particularly egregious, because his punishment was unusual. Whereas most men were put to hard labor for a set period of time, flogged a predetermined number of strokes, and perhaps branded with the letter "D," Seymour was sentenced to hard labor for the duration of the war, branded on the left hand, and directed to be flogged thirty-nine times every three months for the period of the war. A close examination of Seymour's case reveals that he was originally sentenced to death and the sentence was commuted. In view of what had been handed out for most of the sessions, the leniency was not surprising; what was surprising was the rationale.[26]

News of Seymour's death sentence found its way to W. S. Barton, the assistant adjutant general at headquarters in Richmond. Barton's letter to Cooper forwarded the entire list of 1862 court-martial proceedings but specifically addressed only one man, Seymour. Barton indicated that Article 20 of the Confederate Articles of War imposed death, or other punishment as by the sentence of the court-martial, to be inflicted upon any officer or man convicted of desertion. That portion of the law was clear on its face. However, Barton then added: "By the 'custom of war' as shown by the writers of England and America, and well established usage, the punishments of flogging, branding and hard labor, can be inflicted on deserters by courts martial, in lieu of death." In 1862 the Confederacy simply would not adhere to a standard policy of executing men. True, commanders like Hindman and Jackson resorted to execution and were technically within the letter of the law. Even Lee reputedly ordered a "ritual" execution in August 1862, although there is no evidence of any such order from his papers. Given the treatment of desertion and the sentences handed out as reflected in court-martial records, Barton's letter demonstrates a nation and an army that had not come to grips with their desertion problem. To avoid the full measure of the law, the government had found legal justification for softening the death sentence. In addition, Barton indicated that by law no more than fifty lashes could be administered for any one offense, and therefore the portion of Seymour's sentence that called for thirty-nine strokes every three months would be abated if the war lasted long enough for the flogging portion of his sentence to exceed the maximum allowable number of lashes.[27]

Aside from Seymour and Pvt. William Jordan of the Forty-third North Carolina, every charge of desertion was reduced to unauthorized absence. The court-martial proceedings convened in November and continued through January 1863. The defendants were predominantly Virginians or men from Virginia units. The leniency that characterized the earlier sessions continued. Of the ninety-four cases listed, sixty-four involved desertion and in only two instances were men sentenced to death. Pvt. Dan Kennedy of the Tenth Battalion of Virginia Artillery and Pvt. James Broderick of the Letcher Artillery were both sentenced to be shot. Kennedy's sentence was commuted to flogging, and Broderick represented the lone deserter actually sentenced and shot during the proceedings. His trial occurred in January 1863, and perhaps his sentence reflected a growing realization of the magnitude of the problem and the need for harsher remedies. In most cases the sentence involved flogging and detention, with the guilty party returning to the service. The cases that must have been more egregious resulted in the offender's expulsion from the army. But in a sense expulsion was exactly what the offender was seeking when he deserted. However, rather than allowing the sentence to send a message that the only way out other than honorable service was execution, the Confederate army consistently avoided the ultimate penalty.[28]

In light of the clear language in Article 20, Lee should not have had to ask Davis or anyone else in the government for "sterner" measures to combat his absentee problem. Desertion already carried the death penalty, and imposing it required construing the conduct in question as desertion and then acting within the clear parameters of the law. The problem was not legal or governmental, it was cultural. Men believed that certain conduct was "justifiable," and officers concurred. In the West, Bragg had moved to stop straggling by making it desertion, aware that stragglers took advantage of the parole system to get captured and go home. Lee saw the same conduct in the East. He did not need Davis to strengthen the law, but he did need his officers and courts to strictly enforce the law already in effect. Teaching men how to fight well was only half the task of turning civilians into soldiers. Soldiers needed to understand that discipline extended beyond the battlefield into every aspect of soldiering. Absenteeism and desertion demonstrated just how much of the civilian remained in Lee's soldiers. Despite the relationships that may have existed in peacetime, enlisted men and officers were not equals. If the common soldier believed he had a right to leave when he wanted, it was incumbent upon the officer corps to disabuse him of that belief. The fact that they actually condoned such conduct while it was taking place is evidenced by the equally difficult time they had punishing the conduct once it occurred.

Given the magnitude of the desertion/absentee problem in the Army of Northern Virginia in 1862, the court-martial records reflect another problem. The Confederate army had real problems apprehending most of the men that were leaving. In May 1862, reacting to the growing straggling and desertion problem, the provost guard became primarily responsible for the apprehension and return of deserters. In June divisional provost guards were created, and by September a corps-level provost guard had been established. From July through November 1862 the Confederate government actively enlisted the aid of anyone it thought could help. Conscription officers were given authority to arrest deserters, railroad officials were directed to scrutinize all passports to catch deserters, contractors employing conscripts were given authority to bring in deserters, and commandants of conscripts were told to post notices in newspapers across the Confederacy ordering absentees to return to their commands. Unable to deal with the problem at a national level, the government turned to the various states to curb the problem, a clear recognition that desertion was overwhelming the Confederacy's ability to handle it, even with the provost guard's active participation and an understanding of where men went for refuge once they deserted. While a deserter may have been easy to recognize traveling the roads without a pass, many deserters and stragglers found their way into a "safe harbor," the Virginia State Line. State troops existed in every state and offered a place for men to go after deserting the Confederate army. By September 1862 the problem had become significant enough for Governor Letcher to take steps to seal off this avenue of escape. In a letter to the Confederate attorney general, Letcher says that from the initial days of enlistment, every step had been taken to prevent deserters and stragglers from crossing the Virginia state line. Letcher was also doing everything possible to give Confederate officers whatever assistance they needed to discover deserters in the state service.[29]

From the estimates and court-marital records it seems that more men escaped detection than were found. As the court-martial proceedings were in session, an advertisement appeared in the *Montgomery Weekly Advertiser* listing sixty-three deserters from the Twelfth Alabama Infantry alone. Part of Gen. Robert Rodes's brigade of the Army of Northern Virginia, none of these Alabamians appeared in the court-martial records. So, although only Virginians and North Carolinians were being tried, they were not the only ones deserting. Desertion, even if called "absenteeism," was already disrupting the Army of Northern Virginia.[30]

Estimates are a problem because they tend to be viewed as exaggerations, even if they come from a source as well respected as James Longstreet. About the time the Army of Northern Virginia court-martial proceedings were beginning in earnest, a report appeared in several Southern newspapers quoting a "unnamed officer of high rank in the Confederate Army." The anonymous officer claimed that by the end of August 1862, seventy-five thousand men had deserted or were AWOL. Of that number roughly 5 percent were officers. The article claimed, perhaps correctly, that the South had the makings of the best army ever assembled and could not allow men to desert whenever they pleased. Excessive leniency was blamed for the problem. Shooting enlisted men was not enough; they also needed to shoot officers who deserted. Although the article did not specify which Confederate army was suffering so badly, some of the comments appear to be aimed at the Army of Northern Virginia. The piece claimed that when Bragg saw his army melting away from desertion he began shooting every man convicted by a court-martial, and that as a result his army had become "well disciplined."[31]

There was probably some truth to the article even if the numbers were high. There are no records to substantiate seventy-five thousand deserters or even AWOL soldiers. That number would have equaled the size of Lee's entire army. However, perhaps what is important is that to those charged with trying to keep the army together, it felt like that many. It is also significant that the paper perceived the same situation that Longstreet's estimates reflected: Lee's army had a desertion problem even if no one was willing to admit the extent of the situation. What was accurate, given the sentences handed down in 1862, was that leniency prevailed as a part of the military justice culture. Perhaps less accurate was the article's assumption that Bragg's army had become well disciplined. "Better disciplined" was probably more accurate. Bragg clearly recognized the problem even before Lee, but even the most stringent measures could not guarantee that desertion would be eliminated. Scattered notices in the newspapers showed that desertion was a problem in the late summer and fall of 1862, both from men taking advantage of furloughs and from those who just left without permission.[32] However, at least Bragg had taken concerted steps to address the problem.

Lee's order regarding furloughs had left open the option of hospital furloughs. Bragg had discovered that hospitals were yet another avenue out of the service, and the Army of Northern Virginia hospitals were apparently no different. With regular furloughs cut off or severely curtailed, soldiers in hospitals took advantage of one of the few ways to get home. Able to travel the roads and rails legally, men from places beyond Virginia found hospital furloughs an ideal ticket home, facilitated even further by a Confederate practice of segregating hospitalized soldiers by state and then sending them to hospitals within their respective states to recover. Signed in September 1862, "An Act to Better Provide for the Sick and Wounded of Army Hospitals" reflected a unique twist to the concept of states' rights. Predicated upon a belief that most problems that beset men in the hospital stemmed from mixing them up with soldiers from other states and scattering men from the same neighborhoods and regiments, the act sought to provide a remedy. Hospitals were designated by number and state, and a system was developed to transport men to their home states for recovery. Men unable to find a way home through normal military channels received not only a pass home but transportation provided by the medical arm of the army. The potential for abuse loomed large, and it would not be long before soldiers took full advantage.[33]

The records of the Virginia hospitals alone reveal the degree to which medical facilities became avenues of desertion. September 1862 began a twenty-three-month period that saw 5,895 patients desert, an average of 256 a month—more deserters than most Virginia units lost in a year. Again, the signs were there and were either overlooked or ignored. One medical officer in Virginia remarked that Georgia soldiers of all ranks "don't seem to have any just idea of the true character of the war. They all want furloughs to see their families, or if they get a cold, they must go home or never get well, and if there is a battle impending, they take diarrhea, rheumatism or something of the kind and some don't wait to get sick but run strait off." In one instance, 135 of the 330 men transferred from a hospital at Camp McDounough in Atlanta to one in Marietta, Georgia, only twenty miles away, deserted. While there are no hard statistics for 1862, Secretary of War Randolph estimated that only about one man in three furloughed from a hospital ever returned.[34]

The use of oaths to facilitate the desertion process had not surfaced in Virginia and the East to the same degree it had in the West, but taken together, Lee's and Letcher's concerns over oath swearing in late 1862 raised serious issues of internal control and national loyalty. Desertion and oath swearing were opposite sides of the same coin. In Northern prisons men were being encouraged to swear the oath and leave prison. Their comrades clearly saw such an act as desertion. Men who had already deserted swore the oath to gain sanctuary in the North or the opportunity to make their way home. Civilians, finding their homes and farms overrun, had likewise begun to swear the oath. Clearly the Confederate government saw oath swearing as military desertion, and the debates within state and Confederate assemblies showed that civilians were likewise categorized as deserters for taking the oath. As soon as they swore the oath they were renouncing the Confederate cause, but they did not really understand the effect of the oath at the time they swore allegiance to the Union. However, if and when they were called upon to render military service, they would be confronted with having to either join the Confederate army, and risk retribution from the Union if subsequently captured, or refuse, and be deemed deserters for not reporting to conscription camps. The definition of desertion was expanding and catching within its prohibitions people who had not yet joined the army but who ultimately could not go even if called.

That the Union would use oath swearing as the tip of the sword in inducing military desertion and civilian disloyalty only confirmed Southern fears manifest in late 1861. Those fears had come to fruition in 1862 and appeared among other places in an area that did not need anything further to divide its loyalties: North Carolina. In late 1861, an ordinance came out of a committee of the North Carolina legislature that pushed the issue of oaths to the forefront. Entitled "An Ordinance to Define and Punish Sedition, and to Prevent the Dangers Which May Arise from Persons Disaffected to the State," the act addressed the problem of internal dissension in North Carolina and specified punishments for a wide variety of crimes. Punishable under the ordinance were giving intelligence to the enemy, publishing or speaking out against the public defense, maliciously advising the people to resist the government of North Carolina or the Confederate States, and knowingly spreading false and dispiriting news. The two offenses that went to the heart of the desertion problem were persuading people "to return to a dependence on the Government of the United States" and "terrify[ing] and discourag[ing] the people from enlisting in the service of this state or the Confederate States." These prohibitions anticipated both the desertion problem and the Union's effort to use oath swearing to bring both soldiers and civilians back into the fold. The act appears well intentioned, and in many ways it addressed actual and potential problems. In its application, however, it went too far because in addition to creating a classification of crimes and limiting certain basic civil rights, it required North Carolinians to swear an oath to North Carolina and the Confederacy while renouncing any allegiance to the United States.[35]

The Honorable William Graham of Orange County spoke out against the ordinance in 1861, and his speech was subsequently printed and distributed in 1862. The heart of the speech reflected the problem that had plagued the Confederacy from the outset: the inability of the states to look beyond their own needs and to see how some of those needs should be subordinated to the preservation of the greater whole.

The debate over the sedition ordinance in North Carolina demonstrated this problem. Judge Graham's basic objections to the act were that it was really an action by the state to protect the Confederacy, something North Carolina should not and could not do. More importantly, the law vaguely established nine violations that were so poorly defined that it threatened to "produce neighborhood strife without end." Graham saw the aspects of the ordinance requiring people to swear out accusations against their neighbors as putting "the greatest temptations to malignant accusers." He touched upon a point that would come to fruition. The Confederacy had gone to great lengths to characterize the war as one between itself and a foreign power, but this ordinance turned the conflict into a civil and social war within the Confederacy, one in which "no man is to be trusted." In effect North Carolina recognized what people in Arkansas realized. There were limits to how far they would submit to government control. Taking away the very rights they were at war trying to win was going too far. However, some of what the ordinance tried to prevent would prove necessary. The committee report stated that the ordinance was needed to "rid the country of traitors of the heart." Graham begged to know, what made the North Carolina legislature the "searchers of hearts"? Was it not enough that thirty-five thousand North Carolinians, representing every county in the state, were in the Confederate army, and that men had left their homes and now "exposed their lives to the arms of the enemy and the pestilence of the camp and garrison"? Graham saw only that the citizenry was behind the war effort and that there was no shadow of disloyalty in the land. In his opinion, this ordinance would cause the very unrest it purported to stop.[36]

In December 1861 Graham was probably correct, but in 1862 many of the ills the ordinance sought to prevent or abate would come to fruition. North Carolina in 1862 would be a dangerous place, particularly the western Appalachian counties. The Confederacy needed the force of state law to achieve national aims. Lost in this debate and the "defensive posture" taken by members of the North Carolina legislature in late 1861 is that "confederacies" by definition act nationally through their various component parts, in this case the states. Confederate nationalism depended on states taking initiatives consistent with broader war aims. With Southerners so wedded to state and local loyalties, the war effort gained strength from a perception that the "state" supported the Confederacy. A state law that required supporting the national government and its armies could only serve to help alleviate any sense of conflict among soldier and civilians that existed between state and nation. Hard times require hard measures, and while Graham's observations about the vagueness and breadth of some of the crimes elaborated under the ordinance may well have rung true, 1862 would prove how necessary state support of national aims would be.

Unrest in North Carolina in 1862 found its epicenter in the Appalachian Mountains of the western part of the state. Unlike those of middle Tennessee, Mississippi, and Louisiana, the mountains of western North Carolina provided a buffer to the broad military efforts that characterized the war in other areas of the South. However, by 1862 the war had visited the nineteen counties of Appalachian North Carolina, and the people there not only felt its effects but resolved to take steps to prevent the situation from growing worse.[37] Robert E. Lee's response to Governor Clark in August 1862 only vaguely referenced the nature of the hardship North Carolinians had endured to that point.

The most pressing problem and the one from which all other problems stemmed was the lack of men left in the region. Mobilization for the war had sucked the mountains dry, and the people knew it. The depletion of the male population played directly into several other problems unique to the region. Since the military-age men were mostly subsistence and semi-subsistence farmers, their exodus had crippled the area's agricultural capacity. The region also bordered eastern Tennessee, not only home to an ardent Unionist population but the potential jumping-off point for a Union military invasion of the state. In early 1862 a Union invasion of eastern Tennessee had temporarily seized the Cumberland Gap, escalating fears that western North Carolina would follow. The presence of Unionists also meant armed conflict, and a strange form of guerrilla war developed along the border between eastern Tennessee and western North Carolina. Unionists from eastern Tennessee easily crossed into North Carolina. Many had fled into North Carolina early in the war because the Confederacy suppressed Unionism in the Knoxville area. Once in North Carolina these Tennessee exiles picked up where they left off, raiding back into Tennessee and causing unrest in North Carolina. The situation reached the point that North Carolinians demanded protection from the state, and Governor Clark ordered Robert B. Vance's regiment back from Knoxville to patrol the border.[38]

Notwithstanding Clark's efforts to shore up western North Carolina's sagging defenses, public opinion showed that at least among those still at home, the Confederacy's message that home is best protected by fighting abroad was not well received. The call for troops in 1861 left too many families without a male protector and much more vulnerable than they should have been. For those who remained, the best way to protect "home" was to stay there. This unwillingness to leave home initially applied not only to fighting in Virginia or in the West but extended to crossing into eastern Tennessee to suppress Unionist guerrillas. Quickly, however, guerrilla threats evolved into a fear of a Union invasion. In May 1862 a small Union force raided into Haywood County and forced the release of a Union man condemned to death. The incident was relatively minor, but it fanned fears of increased Union military activity in the region. Local North Carolinians were now no longer willing to leave, and some, like William Holland Thomas of Jackson County, expended considerable personal resources to raise a home defense. Into this mix then came conscription, and the Confederacy's attempt to act "nationally" not only backfired but actually drove desertion.[39]

Conscription was unpopular throughout the South, but nowhere more so than in its mountain regions. Only two North Carolinians voted against the Conscription Act, and both were from its western mountain region. Part of the resentment flowed from having already contributed so many soldiers. By April 1862 thirteen hundred men from North Carolina's mountain counties were enrolled, and eleven hundred were in active service. The soldiers' families were already suffering from crop shortages and other deprivations, and if the conscripts were taken there would be no one left to help provide for the civilians at home. In words very similar to Governor Letcher's, David Siler of Macon County, told his friend Gov. Zebulon Vance how important it was to leave men at home. Family councils in the mountain counties had met and decided who would stay and who would go. If the government did not allow men to stay, Siler warned, the consequences would be grave for both those at home and the men in the service. Men's ability to endure hardship and their loyalty to wives and children were well known. Siler told Vance that soldiers "can turn away from the graves of comrades and brothers firm in their resolve to die for the sake of objects coming to their recollections with thoughts of home. But what consolation or encouragement can come to a man's heart in an hour of trial from home where the helpless are perishing for want of his hand to provide?"[40] Using the protection of home as a motive to support the Confederate cause was beginning to have the reverse effect.

Even North Carolina's soldiers fighting in Virginia realized the importance of keeping men at home. Lt. George J. Huntley served in the Thirty-fourth North Carolina in 1862. Attached to Maj. Gen. A. P. Hill's division of Jackson's Corps, Huntley understood the conflict between home and the Confederacy. Camp life and "all of its train of evils" had taken its toll on him and his men by the spring of 1862. But someone had to do the fighting, and he thought it should be the young men. However, men with families should be allowed to stay home, because "someone had to stay."[41] The threat that conscription would take everyone brought a vicious backlash from North Carolina soldiers. A law designed to bring men into the service and strengthen the Confederacy's war-waging ability was threatening to deplete the army. Dissatisfied North Carolinians in Lee's army reacted almost immediately, claiming that regardless of the law, they were coming home as soon as their one-year enlistments expired. The reactions of some went beyond mere concern for home and reflected a contempt for the Confederacy and its leaders. Norm Harrold of Ashe County flatly told Jefferson Davis, "And now bastard President of a political abortion, farewell. 'Scalp hunter,' relic, pole, and chivalrous Confederates in crime, good-bye. Except it be in the army of the Union, you will not again see this conscript." Apparently Harrold never sent the letter, but his sentiments spoke volumes.[42] Not only did conscription threaten North Carolina's safety by draining manpower it could no longer spare, but in the process of acting like a nation, the Confederacy continued to undermine any national cohesion it had managed to engender. Particularly disturbing about Harrold's comments was his willingness to return to the Union rather than submit to Confederate conscription. The Union's desertion policy was taking shape in 1862, and a central component would be an oath to the United States. With North Carolinians already resisting Confederate efforts to create a nation, it did not bode well for the South that men were willing to return to the Union.

In 1862, desertion in North Carolina brought twin evils. First, it created bands of men with loyalty to no one but themselves. Some of these groups proved so formidable that local militias could not protect the area. In order to restore order and protect the civilian population from their own soldiers, Governor Vance had to enlist men for special units to police the mountains and subdue the roving bands. The Sixty-fourth North Carolina was one such unit, and its distasteful role of policing the mountains for deserters and bushwhackers led to atrocity in early 1863. One band of marauders that the Sixty-fourth pursued was led by John Kirk, a Unionist raider. On January 8, Kirk's unit, which consisted of Unionists and deserters, ransacked the town of Marshall, partially in an act of retaliation. In an effort to curb desertion among soldiers from that town, most of whom were former members of the Sixty-fourth, town officials had cut off county aid to families of the deserters. The raiders not only looted the town but harassed the wife and children of Col. Lawrence Allen, the commander of the Sixty-fourth North Carolina. Allen and his men pursed Kirk's band and arrested fifteen members. Thirteen of the prisoners were subsequently executed without trial in drumhead proceedings en route to Knoxville, where they were to have been given real trials. Governor Vance estimated that by the end of 1862 there were as many as twelve hundred deserters in the mountains of western North Carolina. In early 1863 he issued a proclamation that all men "illegally absent" should return to their units, or the state would use its full power and resources to apprehend and punish them. As North Carolina tried to curb desertion, men who were still in the army were forced to weigh the competing factors of getting home versus getting caught—and many were now willing to run the risk.[43]

Second, desertion's ill effects now reached far beyond the army into the heart of the civilian population. In his letter to Governor Clark in August 1862, Lee had insisted that protecting Virginia from Union incursion would keep North Carolina from becoming the next theater of war. However, desertion had made North Carolina a battlefield anyway, pitting neighbor against neighbor and threatening the very fabric of the community. In a sense the Confederacy was doing to itself what the Union could not—and in many cases would not—do. Atrocities by Union soldiers against Confederate civilians occurred rarely during the war,[44] but those perpetrated by Confederate deserters far exceeded anything people feared from Union troops. Unfortunately, 1862 was only the beginning. At stake was not only the Southern civilian's faith in the government but the ownership and use of precious resources such as food, livestock, and salt that were in such low supply and high demand.

Like most diseases, desertion did not discriminate; it affected the Confederacy's most respected army just as it had its lesser forces in the West. Having struck the army, it spread into the civilian population, moving from the war front to the home front. Contrary to popular belief today, it began long before 1863 and would become an epidemic long before the exodus around Petersburg in 1864 and 1865. Its progress was gradual in some places and rapid in others, but no matter how one chooses to identify its spread, desertion hurt the Confederacy in 1862.

Desertion depleted the Army of Northern Virginia of badly needed soldiers. Virtually every action the Confederate government and military took in terms of policy and discipline reflected the need to bring men into the service and keep them there. Furlough limitations, passports, and camp restrictions instituted by Lee in 1862 demonstrated a concerted effort to prevent men from leaving the army, even if legally and for just a short time. One can only conclude that Lee understood that authorized absences, even if short term, turned into longer, sometimes permanent departures. Thus one need only look to the nature and degree of the remedies to determine that the problem had already begun to hurt.

The year 1862 witnessed some of the most active campaigning of the war. Battle began in April and lasted until December. The period from the beginning of the Peninsula campaign until the end of the Seven Days' campaign saw almost continuous combat in two major theaters, the Virginia peninsula and the Shenandoah Valley. The respite following Malvern Hill lasted roughly a month, and beginning with Cedar Mountain the armies were fighting or moving to fight almost continuously until shortly after Antietam. The Confederacy was fighting hard and needed every man. The fact that one must rely on general estimates supports Robert Kean's observations that Samuel Cooper had no idea how many men he had in any army at any time. Even without an accurate count, Longstreet's observations were telling. Whether "temporarily absent" or gone for the war, almost a third of his corps was not in the field when Lee launched his offensive to push McClellan away from Richmond. What Longstreet experienced in late June 1862, others observed as the summer wore on. The straggling before and following Antietam is well documented. Lee went to Maryland with slightly over forty thousand effectives. His losses at Second Manassas attributed to his diminished force, but Longstreet's absentees in late June alone were equivalent to 80 percent of the 9,197 Confederate casualties at Manassas.[45] Three weeks after Manassas, an army that was outnumbered on its best day went into a fight in Maryland that was arguably the pivotal clash of the war in terms of the South's chances for foreign recognition and the opportunity to break Northern will, with thousands of able-bodied soldiers simply not there. Confederate apologists, both then and now, point to the fact that many of them came back, but whether or not they returned, they were not there when they were needed.[46] Debating issues of intent to remain gone or larger questions of abandoning the "cause" ignores the problem. At Antietam, seven to twelve thousand Confederate soldiers could have made a difference. Historians look at Antietam and evaluate what happened with the benefit of hindsight. Lee survived, and the return of the "stragglers" only strengthened his army, but as the battle unfolded no one knew if the army would survive. In great part Lee's fate rested in McClellan's hands, and the fact that McClellan blundered does not alter the reality that the absence of almost a division of soldiers hurt any chance the Confederacy may have had to win north of the Potomac. Distinguishing desertion from mere absence becomes an absurd exercise when absence, whether permanent or temporary, directly affects an army's ability to fight.

Desertion in 1862 became lost in a myriad of loosely defined conduct that did not rise to the level of leaving the service with the intent never to return. Straggling, skulking, lying out, bumming, and unauthorized absence all became "lesser included offenses of desertion." Army of Northern Virginia courts-martial in late 1862 routinely took desertion charges and reduced them to unauthorized absence. This occurred even when the absence lasted for months, spanned periods of heavy fighting, or ended only with the forcible apprehension and return of the culprit. Contrary to the belief at the time, soldiers did not wait until after battle to disappear. Many left before battle, often while the army was on the march in the summer and fall of 1862.

Not only had desertion spread from the army into the civilian population, but it had also become a state problem. In the summer of 1862, prior to Antietam, Secretary of War Randolph wrote several state governors lamenting that "our armies are so weakened by desertions and by the absence of offices and soldiers without leave, that we are unable to reap the fruits of our victories and to invade the territory of our enemies." He wanted the governors to use their state militias to arrest deserters and absentees. However, in the process of helping, Randolph insisted that the governors conceal the true extent of the problem from the enemy, although he admitted that to fight the evil required recognizing its existence. He just did not want the Union to know how bad the situation had become.[47] Some state governors got the message, while others tried and found the task too difficult because local resistance was too strong. In the case of Randolph County, Alabama, in December 1862, Gov. John Gill Shorter had to report that the county defied the Conscription Act and that an armed band forced the jailer to surrender his keys and free deserters who had been incarcerated. Shorter actually put the onus back on the Confederacy to provide troops to assist the state. Joe Brown faced a different problem in Georgia. He objected to using his local sheriffs and constables in instances where the Confederacy's enrolling officers wrongfully tried to detain a man as a deserter. Brown felt that in such an instance it was incumbent upon him as the state's chief executive to protect his citizen from the wrongful act of an enrolling officer.[48]

Shorter's problems and Brown's intervention on behalf of a deserter notwithstanding, even with a strengthened provost guard, deserters were running loose and the Confederacy needed help. Just as Governors Pettus and Moore were asked to address desertion in Mississippi and Louisiana, Letcher and Vance began to bring their respective state resources to bear on desertion by the fall and winter of 1862. For the Confederacy to survive the desertion problem, the states would have to take the lead. The soldiers may have been leaving Lee's army, but they were seeking refuge in Letcher's state service and in the North Carolina mountains. In 1861 the Confederate government had pressured the states for more troops, causing state leaders and citizens throughout the South to question the degree to which their interests diverged from those of the national government. In Louisiana, Moore resisted; in Georgia, Brown defied Richmond to protect Georgia's coastline. But by the end of 1862, desertion provided the justification for many Southern governors to do what they had been trying to do for more than a year: retain a portion of their state's male population at home for protection. Just as North Carolina had dedicated units like the Sixty-fourth North Carolina to apprehend deserters and control the unrest that came with pockets of deserters lying out in the mountains, other states would be required to dedicate men and resources to the problem.

Desertion would now take men from the Confederate service in two ways: the man who deserted and the man who would serve in some state or county unit to apprehend him. State intervention in the Confederate desertion problem would not only draw on local resources and deplete the pool of available men for Confederate service, but it would expose the conflict that Judge Graham raised in North Carolina over the sedition laws and test oaths: Are states legally obligated or permitted to take on responsibilities that were essentially "federal" in nature? The answer to that question, at least insofar as desertion was concerned, would come in 1863, and it would add fuel to an already burning fire. In November 1862, however, Governor Vance tried to help, using his discretion to have the state militia try to arrest deserters. However, he acknowledged that desertion was not a state common-law crime, nor was harboring a deserter. He earnestly requested that the North Carolina legislature take steps to make both desertion and aiding desertion state offenses.[49] The state legislature declined to act, and in 1863 the North Carolina judiciary would make both North Carolina and the Confederacy pay for that failure.

Desertion in the East during 1862 reacted with other problems as well. Extortion, inflation, scarcity, and conscription all created hardship at home. A nation whose recruitment tool centered on the protection of home and family saw both threatened, not only by the actual or potential incursion of the Union army but also by Confederate soldiers, many of them deserters living outside anyone's law. These men undermined both civilian confidence and the faith of those fighting in the field, creating the perception that protecting home required being there. The year 1862 revealed another aspect of the Confederate war effort and perhaps emphasizes why firm numbers on desertion are so difficult to obtain. Writing from home in late December 1862, Asbury Myers addressed the editor of the *Staunton Spectator* in an effort to correct a grave oversight. The December 16 edition of the paper had included Myers among a list of deserters from the Fifty-second Virginia. Myers did not believe his inclusion was intentional, but he lamented that it was the second time it had occurred. He enclosed a copy of a surgeon's certificate that indicated he was admitted on June 23, 1862, and had been hospitalized continuously from that point forward. Myers was ill, not wounded, and on November 16 he was furloughed to go home for sixty days. He was still on furlough in December when he wrote the editor.[50]

Myers's situation was not uncommon; it would happen to other men later in the war. It also reflects the questionable nature of Confederate statistics. Myers wrote the editor of the paper, but he should have written his regimental commander. Desertion reports were prepared at the army level and sent to newspapers, which printed only what they received and often ran the ads for several weeks, which may account for why Myers had seen his name before. Myers was absent from roll call, and no one knew why. No one had been able to verify his death or his wounding, and he was not listed as being on furlough, so the only other possibility was that he had deserted.

Myers's plight reflected an army which assumed that any man not otherwise accounted for had deserted. In retrospect, the assumption may have been correct. Desertion had already begun to hurt the army and the Confederacy as a whole. On the day Lee inflicted a severe defeat on the Army of the Potomac at Fredericksburg, a notice appeared in newspapers across the South. It contained a reprint of General Order no. 96, issued by the office of the adjutant general and inspector on November 27, 1862. It ordered all men absent from their commands to return without delay or be listed as deserters. Four days later an article appeared in the *Montgomery Weekly Advertiser* that provided some insight as to why so many men were absent. The short piece indicated that in some parts of Virginia the price of flour had risen to forty to fifty dollars per barrel. The wheat crop in Georgia had failed, and the corn supply would not last. The article argued that there was enough bread in Virginia, North Carolina, and eastern Tennessee for the whole Confederacy but that it was locked up in military stores.[51] Just how much food the South had available remains the subject of debate. Civilians clearly did not have enough to eat, and most men in Lee's army would have been surprised to learn that the military was hoarding all the food. Home was hurting, and the evidence from 1862 suggests that men were reacting to that suffering and going home.

Desertion in 1862 had clearly increased from the previous year. Part of the increase may be reflected in the way absence was treated. Conduct by which men left for periods of time in 1861–62 was condemned, even if leniently, in 1862–63. Whereas absence may have been felt only slightly at a time when most soldiers had yet to fire a round in anger, twelve months later the Confederate army had tasted combat. But if desertion in 1862 had yet to reach epidemic proportions, people should have seen the signs. In nature, large waves are seldom seen coming except to the extent that they are preceded by a rapid receding of water from the shoreline. As tidal waves approach, the water sometimes withdraws hundreds of yards, uncovering parts of the ocean that normally lie beneath the surf. In a sense this is what occurred in the Confederacy in 1862. As desertion began to pick up, it not only weakened the army but began to lay bare some of the Confederacy's weaknesses, problems that lay below the surface and out of sight. The wave was coming, and when it hit in 1863 it would start to wash away the Confederate war effort.

The end of 1862 brought more signs that the factors destined to undermine the cohesion of the army lay at home, not just in the hardships visited upon civilians but in the willingness of the state government to oppose the Confederacy and the failure of the elites to fulfill their obligations. Conscription had proved a failure. Even if it brought additional men into the service, it motivated those already serving to leave, and in many cases it hardened the resolve of men not in the service to resist. Conscription was said to have been "repudiated" in Georgia. One editor questioned how other states could be expected to honor the law if Georgia openly ignored its requirements. The army faced a "life or death" situation, and states' rights was now an impediment to Southern survival. "The right of the states existed as a substantial benefit only in time of peace," he wrote, "so too does the rights of individuals. In times of war our ease and happiness is given up and semblance of state sovereignty is merged in the general government, which is but the common agent of the states. If we do not succeed in founding a new government, our states rights will be swallowed up in the vortex of the ruin which awaits us." Georgia was not alone, as virtually every state saw strong resistance to the draft, and even South Carolina, the birthplace of secession, experienced violent resistance to conscription. The Confederacy was slowly collapsing under the weight of its own conceptual framework.[52]

With clear signs emerging in 1862 that the elites had failed to fulfill their promise to provide for soldiers' families, observers noted that part of the reason was the unwillingness to convert from cotton to food crops. Southern planters continued to be caught in "the monotonous round of growing more cotton to buy more Negroes to raise more cotton," stated a writer for the *Selma Morning Reporter* in November 1862. "This has been the height of ambition for the last half century, and such has been the force of habit, that many of our sturdy planters have settled down in the opinion that their mission is sufficiently fulfilled if they can only be permitted to continue this treadmill manner of passing away their existence."[53]

Without saying so, the article implied what most people already understood: the planter elite was far from fulfilling their wartime mission. The unwillingness of the rich to adapt to the exigencies of war made it virtually impossible for them to keep their promise to provide for soldiers' families. The demands of war had already overtaxed the states, and as they pulled away from Confederate efforts to wage war they sent a message that both citizens and soldiers understood. If the states felt no allegiance to the Confederacy, why should anyone else? Under less strenuous circumstances the unwillingness to support the efforts of the central government might have taken the form of a passive indifference, but as 1862 neared its end the times were those that tried everyone in the South, and the Confederacy could not allow its citizens to passively ignore its efforts.

As the Confederacy pushed its people harder it also continued to lose ground to the Union, which, although still not a military match for Lee in the East, moved with the deliberateness of a glacier in the West, slowly consuming portions of the South. As it did so it offered people who had passively rejected the Confederacy the opportunity to actively embrace the Union by swearing allegiance to their former country. Oath swearing presented a choice, one the Confederacy saw as damaging and attempted to downplay by emphasizing the coercion involved. In the fall of 1862, Kirby Smith took the same stance in Kentucky that Lee had taken in Virginia. In an order issued on September 4, Smith declared that oaths of allegiance had been coerced from Kentucky citizens binding them to oppose the Confederacy in all respects. As commander of the Confederate forces, he would not respect such oaths and would protect all citizens in the nonperformance of such forced oaths. "They are neither binding in law or in conscience."[54]

Although the Confederacy and its leaders wanted to believe that people swore the oath unwillingly, one must question the degree to which the oaths were coerced. Confederate citizens were losing faith in their government. Kentucky was not even a Confederate state. The Confederate invasion of the state in 1862 revealed the same lack of support for the cause that Lee encountered in Maryland. The larger problem, however, was that Kirby Smith's unwillingness to recognize the legitimacy of the oath was only half the equation. While oath swearing clearly exposed citizens and deserters to sanctions from both sides, some people in the South began to see a greater problem with the Union's use of oaths. Simply swearing the oath "from the teeth out" might sound acceptable, but some observers saw a far greater evil. That evil would surface in 1863 as the Union desertion policy and wartime reconstruction efforts placed the oath of allegiance at the forefront of the effort to win the hearts and minds of Confederate soldiers and civilians.

6. DESERTION, IDEOLOGY, AND THE INSIDIOUS BUSINESS OF OATHS, 1863

In the West, 1863 opened with battle as William Rosecrans and Braxton Bragg squared off at Stones River. In the East, both armies rested in winter quarters in the aftermath of Fredericksburg. In western Tennessee, Grant continued his efforts to solve the puzzle of Vicksburg. The war was far from over, and although the Confederacy continued to hold its own on the battlefield, the Union was applying pressure on all fronts, making it more difficult for the Confederacy to keep its home front safe and its army intact.

In the aftermath of Stones River, Pvt. W. L. Gammage, a soldier in Bragg's Army of Tennessee, wrote home to Texas. He described the fighting and then told his friend, "Remember one thing—the Fabian policy is our true policy, time wears out the federal army whilst it strengthens ours, and we by holding off can choose our own time to fight. Our troops are cheerful and hopeful as they ever were we have never yet despaired of the Confederacy—and never will."[1] It is difficult to find a statement both more incorrect and more portentous of the disaster that lay ahead. Fabian policy would indeed dominate in the West, but far from wearing out the Union army, it would embolden it. The strength such a policy drained would be that of the Confederate army and civilian population. While Gammage may not have despaired, and perhaps never did, others had and would. By withdrawing and allowing the Union to move into the South, the Confederacy opened the door for many of its own soldiers and civilians, a door that led to Union lines and an abandonment of the Confederate cause. It was a door many would pass through in 1863.

Desertion escalated dramatically in 1863, and a key component was Confederate soldiers' swearing an oath of allegiance to the United States. But as 1862 demonstrated, soldiers may have been deserting the army, but they were not the only ones deserting the "cause." Civilian renunciation of the Confederacy at home went hand in hand with military desertion. Just as soldiers could desert by merely leaving, civilians could vote with their conduct by refusing to join the service, failing to report if drafted, being unwilling to share what they had with neighbors, or selling goods at prices no one could afford. However, both soldiers and civilians also had the option to not only abandon the cause and their duty but to do so by actively embracing the United States government.

On January 13, 1863, a joint session of the Confederate Congress passed a resolution commending the people of Louisiana for refusing to take the oath of allegiance. Part of the resolution acknowledged that "the men and women behind enemy lines have resisted all appeals to pecuniary interest and refused, in spite of pains and penalties[,] to forswear their own government by taking the oath of allegiance to the United States."[2] On its face, the resolution served as an effort to bolster the civilian morale in a state slowly falling to the Union army. However, the act itself demonstrated that oath swearing hurt. More importantly, in areas under Union control the Confederacy seemed powerless to prevent the practice. Contrary to Kirby Smith's claim of protecting Kentucky citizens, he could not protect people in a state he did not control. Just as the Confederacy could not protect the Missourians hung in October 1862, it would be unable to protect Louisianans living in territory that fell under Union control. As 1863 began, Confederate civilians and soldiers had to make a choice. Swearing allegiance for convenience ("from the teeth out") would become more difficult. Confederate soldiers found to have violated their oath would be subject to death from Union authorities. If captured by the Confederate army, they were guilty of deserting to the enemy. But the damage caused by the oath process went deeper than creating a potentially irreconcilable conflict.[3]

One observer saw something more dangerous, and in February 1863 he put his thoughts to paper and in the process not only set forth the damaging effect of the Union oath of allegiance process but defined what was happening to the Confederacy, both at home and on the battlefield. On Thanksgiving Day in 1860, Rev. Benjamin Morgan Palmer, pastor of the First Presbyterian Church of New Orleans, had delivered what would become one of his most famous sermons, advocating Louisiana's secession from the Union. Palmer was a community leader and a well-known religious scholar of the nineteenth century. Like other religious figures in the South, he saw religious implications in secession and had lent the power and prestige of his position to the Confederacy's quest for independence. Two and a half years later the Confederacy was locked in a war for its very survival, and from the standpoint of those in Louisiana, and particularly its New Orleans citizens, the war was going badly. The city had been under Union occupation for almost a year, the Mississippi had fallen with the exception of the stretch between Port Hudson and Vicksburg, and Grant was working diligently to wrest the remaining two strongholds from the Confederacy. With Andrew Johnson continuing to work for the restoration of Tennessee, Louisiana was rapidly becoming Lincoln's second experiment in wartime reconstruction. Having advocated secession, Palmer took the opportunity to reflect on the state of the Confederacy in February 1863. In a letter to the Honorable John Perkins, chairman of the Louisiana state secession convention and Confederate senator from Louisiana, Palmer addressed the problem the Union created with the oath of allegiance. His letter is a treatise on oath swearing, and in the course of his correspondence he touches upon the conditions of the Confederacy that made oath taking so prevalent. In the process he also showed an ignorance of how the Southern people conceptualized their new nation, a notion based far more on secular political theory than any sense of religious duty.

Palmer began with a note of approval for the joint resolution that praised Louisiana citizens for resisting the oath. He pointed to the language in the resolution which acknowledged that certain people in Louisiana had been "duped" into swearing the oath. As Palmer saw the situation, there were two classes of people taking the oath. There were those whom he claimed had always been traitors: men and women who had never supported secession and were prepared to align with the enemy as soon as it appeared. Within this category Palmer included people who had never cared one way or the other and those who valued only financial gain and would do whatever was necessary to secure their own economic well-being. The second class of oath takers included those whose hearts were still loyal to the Confederacy but who had taken the oath under "constraint." Palmer believed these otherwise loyal citizens thought the oath could be taken "salva fide," excepting their loyalty to the Confederacy. In common jargon, it was sworn "from the teeth out" with no intention to honor the oath.[4]

Palmer believed loyal Confederates were "under a very peculiar pressure" at the time they took the oath. Men were uncertain as to how to respond to the Union's offer, given the elimination of Confederate authority and the absence of any legal precedent. In an effort to draw some historical comparison, Palmer cited the war between Philip IV of France and Flanders (Palmer called it the state of Holland) at the beginning of the fourteenth century. Although Philip resisted the attempt of Flanders to break away, he never forced an oath upon them, as was being done by Lincoln. Philip did not attempt to cancel the allegiance of the

Dutch people except through negotiations with the government to which they maintained their allegiance. Lincoln "grinds the citizens between conflicting jurisdictions, upper and lower millstones," Palmer claimed. Unable to conquer the South, the Union resorted to disgracing its citizens. Palmer specifically tied such conduct to Benjamin Butler and spent several pages chronicling Butler's oppressive acts. The dilemma was how to take the oath without surrendering one's loyalty to the Confederacy and at the same time maintaining some sense of personal integrity. Those willing to admit they swore "from the teeth out" strove to maintain their stake in the country they loved at the expense of truth, while those who would not renounce the oath despite their continued love of country preserved truth and honesty at the risk of "clouding with suspicion their civil fidelity."[5]

For Palmer, the use of the oath as a tool of war was damning. He explained to Perkins that an oath takes on the character of the religious nature of man. It is an affirmation in the eyes of God, a twofold covenant to both society and God. Thus, "to trifle with the sanctity of oath is to strike a fatal blow at law and religion . . . [doing so] destroys religion by weakening the sense of God's presence in the soul. In a legal sense it signals the loss of moral control for which no amount of civil penalties can compensate." Palmer argued that the oath was undermining the Confederacy in two ways: on the one hand, it was eroding citizen loyalty to the extent they honored the obligation to the United States; on the other hand, by swearing "from the teeth out," Confederate citizens were destroying the importance of oath in government. Swearing an oath that they had no intention of honoring undermined all oaths, including the ones taken from the inception of the nation, not the least of which was the U.S. Constitution. If jurors, for example, could swear only to the degree they wished, they were bound to no duty except their own. Thus, whether or not people intended to honor their professed allegiance to the United States, the Union's use of oaths undermined any sense of justice in the Confederacy via "a swearing that opens and shuts conveniently at the bidding of caprice." In the long run any real sense of authority in the Confederacy was destroyed.[6]

Palmer took exception to the Union oath process on conceptual grounds, and his criticism actually points to the genius, intended or not, of the oath of allegiance. Palmer argued that "it is one thing after submission, to swear allegiance, yielding in a sense to the rule of war. But another thing to allow a government of law to undermine citizenship before government of force has prevailed." What Palmer described was desertion. Confederate soldiers had been

DESERTION, IDEOLOGY, AND OATHS

deserting from Northern prisons and in the field under the authority of Union departmental commanders since mid-1862. The rule of war had yet to reduce the Confederacy to submission, but its soldiers were abandoning the army and the cause. What Palmer saw happening in Louisiana was civilian desertion. People unwilling to wait for the outcome, or looking at their situation and concluding that the rule of war in their little corner of the Confederacy had prevailed, took the final step to formalize the Confederacy's defeat. Once again the Confederate notion of nationalism, the protection of home and fireside, proved to be a double-edged sword, as soldiers and civilians looked not to the sustenance of the Confederacy's armies or the preservation of the capital as evidence that the Confederacy continued to live, but rather to the safety of home and family. Once *patriae* was subsumed, government of force had prevailed.[7]

For Palmer the choices were to take the oath or to refuse and suffer the consequences. There was no middle ground. If one took the oath, the damage was done. To honor the oath was to abandon the Confederacy. To refuse to honor it once it was taken was to abandon any sense of moral or social order. The Confederacy would either dissolve as its citizens abandoned it or would disintegrate from within. The only alternative was to refuse to take the oath, but that carried equally serious ramifications, and Palmer knew so. He understood that taking the oath offered some sense of protection for life and property, but he equated duty to country with duty to God, and it was on this crucial point that he lost touch with Southerners. Duty to country was not the equivalent of duty to God. Duty to country was based on something far more secular: contract.

Palmer believed that civilians should run the same risks as soldiers. "Can any good reason be assigned why they [civilians] should not run the hazard of confiscation, of imprisonment, of death, equally with those who encounter the risk of capture, of wounds, and death upon the field of slaughter? If those [civilians] may be justified in their apostasy because of the perils by which they were surrounded, why may not these [soldiers] be justified on precisely the same grounds for declining the gauge of battle in the presence of the foe?" What astounded Palmer was how the debate over the oath and loyalty had reduced "patriotism into an affair of simple contract. The inability of the Confederacy for the time being to protect them is viewed as dissolving the bond between them and it, like traders in the market, they bargain with another party, purchasing protection with loyalty." Patriotism had therefore become a word without meaning, and "allegiance" had become "the sport of accident and chance." Palmer concluded that he could not continue the debate on those grounds, and if the oath, once taken, cannot be withdrawn, then people should not try to defend having taken it but should allow it to stand as "a statement of human infirmity."[8]

Palmer's exasperation with Confederates' willingness to "switch loyalty" is understandable considering his religious background, but that background also clouded his perception of the foundation upon which Confederate nationalism was based. Southerners routinely claimed their struggle was the "Second American Revolution." A perusal of virtually every colonial constitution formed at or near the time of the Declaration of Independence recites in its preamble that the failure of the king of England and Parliament to protect the colonies and their willingness to make war upon them had dissolved the compact between ruler and people.[9] From the inception of the conflict, soldiers and civilians had been told that their duty was to protect home and fireside. Men had gone to war with the blessing of family at home, believing that they would best protect both by fighting in the Confederacy's main armies. From the beginning of the conflict the Confederate military had proved incapable of keeping the Union from invading and occupying the South, and government at the federal and state level had been unable to adequately provide for soldiers' families. Worse, the government could neither compel nor convince the elite class to contribute that "last dollar" for the benefit of the soldiers' families. The contract had been broken and the promise remained unfulfilled.

The Confederacy's leadership, at least at the state level, understood the contractual nature of loyalty and how crucial it was that soldiers know their families were safe. Addressing the Virginia legislature the first week of the new year, Governor Letcher continued to pound home the theme he had pressed the year before: "We have much at stake," he said, "and it becomes us to omit nothing calculated to insure success in the struggle. Dissension and division, strife and contention, crimination and recrimination, can have no other effect than embarrass and perhaps defeat plans and measures, upon the success of which the present and future of our cause and country in great measure depend." Letcher specifically pointed to extortion, endorsing Jefferson Davis's letter indicating that extortion hurt soldiers in the field as well as their families and others at home. Letcher did not see how it could be suppressed without some state action. He told the assembly that they should hear, as he had been compelled to, "the appeals of mothers and sisters, and children of soldiers, whose husbands, brothers and fathers are now and have been defending the freedom and

DESERTION, IDEOLOGY, AND OATHS

protecting the property of the extortioners." Letcher insisted that the soldiers' families had to be protected and that every solder should be able to say upon his return, "the government has protected those who were dearer to me than life, while I have been absent fighting its battles for freedom."[10] The key words were "its battles." These men were fighting at the behest of the government. Letcher understood that soldiers and citizens looked to the government for basic protection in return. Failure to provide it would be a breach of the contract between government and citizen. Letcher feared what might happen if the men fighting on the front came to understand what he and other leaders had already seen: that the Confederacy was beginning to implode.

At the far western end of the Confederacy, Governor Lubbock of Texas came to the same conclusion that Letcher had reached in Virginia. Addressing the legislature in February 1863, Lubbock stated that "there is an absolute necessity to provide for these [soldiers'] families." The county relief agencies had been working diligently, but the burden continued to mount and the state would have to step up to the task. The irony in Texas lay in the uneven distribution of wealth at the county level. The smallest counties gave the fewest troops but had the most wealth. If the state did not "ward off distress from the families of those who are nobly serving their country," Lubbock warned, "there will no doubt be destitution among the families," and the price of failure would be high. Although Texas experienced very little Union occupation during the war, even the limited incursion brought with it the dreaded oath. Lubbock reported that thus far most people remained loyal, but his observations pointed to the inherent flaw in a Fabian policy. The Union, "failing at arms and in battle has, whenever it has taken the country in the South, tried to induce citizens to swear allegiance and done so by all types of mean and despicable means."[11] Everywhere the Union occupied, the specter of the oath followed.

Confederate leaders feared that common citizens would renounce the Confederacy, but oath swearing also posed the threat that someone of prominence would break ranks. In 1862 that is exactly what happened in Texas, as former congressman and future governor Andrew Jackson Hamilton fled Texas by way of Mexico under the protection of the United States consulate. In March 1863 Governor Lubbock and Gen. John Magruder argued over how to treat Hamilton's family. In Magruder's opinion, Hamilton had departed the state, deserted the army and the cause, and thereafter "allied himself with the enemy." Hamilton's wife and children were trying to join him in the North, and Magruder clearly opposed allowing them to do so. Lubbock intervened in the matter and told Magruder that Hamilton's family had committed no crime that would preclude their leaving the country unless Magruder felt their departure would injure Texas or the Confederacy in some other way. Lubbock conceded that Hamilton might lead an invasion of Texas, at which time his family, if kept in the state, could be used as hostages. In the end Lubbock put the onus back on Magruder. Hamilton did lead an ill-fated invasion of southern Texas. Despite his actions in 1864, his family was allowed to join him in New Orleans.[12]

Hamilton represented an extreme example of the harm caused by desertion and oath swearing, but his experience would not be unusual. The dialogue between Lubbock and Magruder revealed yet another nuance of the oath process that created problems for Confederate leaders. An oath-swearing deserter left a family that could hardly continue to survive in his absence, much less support a government that had proved unable to provide for them. Letting families go might encourage desertion; forcibly preventing their departure placed the Confederacy in the position of having to coerce loyalty. Neither option was desirable. Union officials would try to capitalize on the deserter's need to have his family with him. As the war progressed the Union made it easier for the families of common soldiers to meet their husbands and fathers in the North by establishing a passport system that allowed families safe passage through Union lines. This in turn would put more pressure on Confederate authorities as women tried to go North to join their husbands. Letters like the one that Gov. Thomas Watts of Alabama received from Col. U. S. Murphy in January 1864 were not uncommon. Murphy wrote on behalf of his sister-in-law to request that Watts approve her passport. Her husband, and presumably Murphy's brother, had deserted to the North more than a year earlier, and she wanted to join him. Murphy could arrange passage through General Polk's lines if Watts approved her passport.[13]

In November 1863, as Lubbock prepared to leave office, his impressions of the situation in Texas and throughout the Confederacy mirrored those of most other Southern leaders and citizens. Whether or not Reverend Palmer wanted to accept it, Confederate loyalty was predicated on both a contract and a promise, and Lubbock, like so many others, saw the first breached and the second broken. The government was failing, and that failure was tied directly to the unwillingness of the wealthy to meet their obligations. Lubbock's observations revealed how this broken promise in turn tainted conscription and fueled desertion. Lubbock believed that both the Confederate Congress and the state legislatures had to do away with exemptions. He supported converting every man into a soldier and detailing men for short periods to perform essential tasks. The planter had been exempted in order to carry on his "legitimate business." In exempting farmers, stock raisers, mechanics, and professional men, "it was anticipated that they would supply the government and people with their produce, stock, fabrics, and services at a fair remunerative price. When they failed to do this, they violated their implied contract, and acted in bad faith." As a direct consequence, all exemptions should have been withdrawn. Lubbock saw a direct causal connection between conscription, exemption, extortion, breach, and damage. Conscription exemptions had not only created the perception of a "rich man's war but a poor man's fight" but had put the rich in a position to meet their obligation. Yet they had chosen to parlay their exemption into profit at the expense of those doing the fighting. Lubbock saw the actions of the wealthy as a breach of contract that made it impossible for the government to meet its obligations to its citizens.[14]

Lubbock was silent on desertion in his February 1863 address, but as he left office that November he admitted, "I am pained to say that occasionally there are desertions by Texans from the Confederate and also from the state service." Lubbock recommended harsher sentences but stopped short of suggesting death. He endorsed incarceration in the state penitentiary and forfeiture of citizenship for both deserters and those who encouraged or harbored them. While he suggested that desertion occurred only on "occasion," his need to address its prevalence and his plea to Texas women implied that it was worse than he was willing to publicly admit. He called specifically on women to "continue to frown upon the man who in this great emergency is wanting in patriotism. You must treat with scorn and contempt even though he be your relative or suitor, he who now in our day of peril shirks the service of his country." Lubbock concluded, "Should you hear any of our men complain that the range of their guns or the blades of their swords are too short to compete with the enemy, say to them in the language of the Spartan mother—shorten your distance." Having seen what was happening at home and warning his legislature of the potential effects of failing to provide for the home front, Lubbock nevertheless maintained the Confederate mantra: protect home by going to war. However, to shorten the distance between themselves and the enemy was to lengthen the gap between where they were and home. Many were coming to understand that killing or wounding Union soldiers was not putting food on their tables at home or clothing their families.[15]

Confederate defeat was only due in part to the pressures exerted by the enemy. Those pressures were not only causing the South to collapse from the outside but had begun to exploit internal weaknesses that were building to an explosion that would destroy the Confederacy from the inside out. Confederate leaders knew that at the heart of this internal explosion lay the failure of not only the government but the wealthy elite to provide, and in confirmation of their worst fears, by mid-1863 soldiers knew what was happening.

In August 1863, a lengthy letter appeared in Southern newspapers entitled simply "A Soldier's Reflections." Taking up a column and a half of the *Montgomery Weekly Advertiser*, the letter represented the fulfillment of Governor Letcher's prophecy just eight months earlier. It began by clearly stating that the failure of the Confederacy's elites was nationwide: "There is a state of circumstances existing in nearly every state, town, village and community in the Confederacy that if really known, would do more toward discouraging and demoralizing the men who are in the army than all of the abolition force that Lincoln could muster against them. . . . I write this to let the men fighting the war know what was happening at home."[16]

According to the author, who identified himself only as "R," men left home with their families depending on them for subsistence. Thus, everyone knew the mere act of leaving worked severe hardship. Once in the army, soldiers traded their constant labor at home for eleven dollars a month in Confederate scrip. With rations often short in the army, they had to use some of that money to survive, and the remainder was simply not enough to fill the hole their absence left at home. They had gone to war and "risked death for the altar of their country" while an entire class of men used their wealth to hire substitutes and remain at home. Those men possessed the South's wealth, and "it is their duty, beyond a shadow of a doubt to see that all of the soldiers' families, near or anywhere in their reach are supplied with the real necessaries of life." The elites owned the "plantations, Negroes, land and homes of southern luxury, for which so many of the poor men are daily and hourly battling in defense of." Rather than selling items like corn, wheat, flour, and meat at exorbitant prices, they should "bear in mind that the husbands, brothers and relations of these families are away on the arduous duty and hardship of a soldier's life, enduring privation, danger and disease and grim specter of death." The wealthy stood to benefit most from the struggle, and although some of them did their duty, "there are too many who demand from a sad, pale cheeked wife, widow or orphan of our brave soldiers, their last dollar for a scrap of meat, pound or two of flour, or a few ounces of sugar."[17]

Having described the conduct of the wealthy and laid blame at their feet, "R" then asked the same questions Letcher had asked the Virginia legislature, but in more graphic terms: "Can men who feel, hear and know such things to be true, can they fight with spirit, nerve and good faith? Fight and defend from ruin and degradation such a class of stay at home vampires?" The clear answer was no. The crucial term was "vampire." As the Southern soldier was fighting, the wealthy were sucking the very life out of the country. The South's self-consumption kept the elite temporarily alive, but it killed everything else. The wealthy should have been "gratuitously" bestowing their produce on the families of the men doing the fighting. The end result could only be to "demoralize and finally destroy our army."[18] Once soldiers were demoralized, the decision to desert became much easier. The Union's use of oath swearing gave men in this state of mind the opportunity to reject a government and elite that had breached a contract and broken a promise under circumstances that offered tangible benefits, namely the opportunity to safely return home and protect their families when both the wealthy and the government had failed. For civilians faced with starvation and the loss of the little property they had, swearing an oath to the Union seemed the prudent thing to do. And if civilians were abandoning the cause, soldiers had to question their own willingness to stay.

What Reverend Palmer saw in February 1863 as the "inability of the Confederacy for the time being to protect them" looked to many civilians and soldiers like a permanent situation that would only grow worse. And it did get worse. In late June 1863, B. Bradley, a man from Louisiana who was now living in Maine, wrote to an unidentified friend. "New Orleans is a wreck," he wrote. "The places of business for the most part closed, many dwellings abandoned, the levee a waste, thousands starving—thousands more in want . . . the plantations are many of them deserted. The Negroes are leaving their masters. The crops this year will be comparatively trifling. The military authorities seize the property of the loyal and disloyal. Widespread ruin is apparent to the eye." Bradley realized Lincoln's goal was one Union without slavery. From Maine he told his friend that civilians living in the North "know nothing of the desolation which follows the track of the army—of the poverty, starvation and misery of the destruction of property, as of a life which a military government carries with it." What Bradley described was happening in other places in the South as well. Writing from Port Hudson in June 1863, Captain Whitfield in the First Alabama told his wife, "What a struggle have I to encounter between my duty to my country and sincere regard for those tender relations that still engross my affections, nor less earnestly appeal to my manhood for defense."[19]

Civilians in Alabama were wrestling with some of the same conflicts. By the spring of 1863 a significant number of them had crossed the line. As of May 17 of that year, sources reported that seventy-four hundred people had sworn the oath since April 17, 1862, when Gen. Robert Mitchell issued an order allowing Alabamians to swear allegiance. In addition, another six hundred had sworn the lesser oath not to take up arms against the United States. Known as the noncombatant's oath, this lesser oath was less onerous on its face, at least regarding as its commitment to the Union. However, for the Confederacy the difference mattered little. Those who took the oath and were willing to stand behind it effectively removed themselves from the pool of potential soldiers.[20] Those who renounced it would enter the service in jeopardy of suffering a harsh punishment if captured by the Union and found to be in violation of the oath.

The debate over oath swearing played out not only among soldiers but also between soldiers and civilians—and even between a soldier and his family at home. Pvt. Jerome Yates of the Sixteenth Mississippi, assigned to the Army of Northern Virginia, had left his mother and sister. The situation that had begun to deteriorate in northern Mississippi in 1862 had by mid-1863 found its way to central and southwest Mississippi and the counties where the Sixteenth was formed, giving Yates a firsthand opportunity to evaluate the practice of oath swearing. In January 1863, Yates wrote his mother to tell her how pleased he was that folks had enough to eat and "that is more than any of the people up here has." The situation in Virginia was apparently as bad as Letcher and its citizens had perceived in 1862, yet parts of Mississippi seemed to be holding their own. That would change. In May 1863, Yates wrote his sister and specifically asked how she felt about the "Yankees getting in to that part of the country." Fabian tactics were at work, and the Union was pushing deeper into Mississippi.[21]

In August 1863 Yates wrote to his mother again. She must have written to him and specifically asked if he objected to her swearing the oath of allegiance to the United States. Yates's reply reveals much about the Confederacy and how such decisions had become a question of pragmatics and declining faith in the Confederate government. As far as he was concerned, the best person to make that call was his mother. She was there and he was not. He did not see taking the oath as wrong "in the least when people is in a destitute condition and that is the only way to save what they have or to get something to eat. Then I do not think there is anything which is wrong." He told her to do as she felt proper and not be influenced by anyone else. Despite his apparent understanding, however, he added that he was surprised his sister had sworn the oath. "I thought she was too good a secess for adversity to make her change so quickly." He feared she was not very strong in her faith in "Jeff." Although Jerome did not swear an oath, his faith was just as weak. In closing he told his mother to take the slaves to the center of the state, sell them, and buy gold.[22] If people were not giving up completely, they were beginning to hedge their bets. The difference between soldier and civilian lay in how they manifested their despondency. In distant Virginia, in the wake of Gettysburg, with the Army of Northern Virginia cracking down on desertion, Yates probably felt desertion was not an option, but his advice to his mother evidenced a clear loss of faith in the Confederacy, its sacred institution, and its currency.

The decision to swear the oath continued to weigh heavily on Jerome's mother. In mid-September Jerome responded to one of her letters and explained that he was not nearly as despondent as she was. He expressed a belief that if God was on their side, despite defeats, they would prevail. She had told her son that she was swearing the oath before everything was lost, and he cautioned her to be sure everything "would be lost before she does so." But he seemed to understand her plight. Since she was "a poor widow woman, a woman without protection, no one to provide for anything, I do not think it would be wrong." However, Yates's position on oath swearing was based on gender. "It is very different for a man, I look at a man who takes it [the oath] as good a Yankee as Abe has got." In the end he told his mother the same thing he had told her in August—to do what she thought was right and not listen to public opinion. By the end of October Yates learned that a family friend, Margaret, had left home and was in northern Mississippi "with the Yankees." His close friend Joe Murphy had tried to explain to him why she might have left, but Yates was not sympathetic. Murphy "gives a gloomy account of things in general in Mississippi," Yates wrote. "I cannot believe things are as bad as he represents."[23]

In the Confederacy, what men believed was often affected by what they learned secondhand. The South's newspapers tried to downplay the threat to family, implicitly realizing the importance of the home front on the morale of those at war. If the government and the wealthy could not protect those at home, perhaps the hardship could be marginalized. In late July 1863, an article entitled "Taking Care of Families" appeared in the *Montgomery Weekly Advertiser*. It began by acknowledging that nothing was more common than to hear men claim they were staying home to protect their family. The newspaper conceded that "normally" this is true, but "in war duty to family must take on a wider scope, if the nation fails and falls, what will be left?" The only way the Confederacy could hope to gain its independence was if the men did their duty. The writer believed that women were not "half as in need of protection as the men would have everyone believe" and suggested that women whose men were in the field fighting felt "as protected as if their protectors were at home."[24] Once again we find the recurring theme of protecting home by going to war. The rallying cry of 1861 had lost steam in 1862 and by 1863 had been shown to be empty, at least in some parts of the Confederacy. Clearly, not all men felt the need to return home, and some solders, like Jerome Yates, condoned conduct by those at home that he might not have supported in the army and that he found reprehensible for men. It is impossible to tell, but to some extent his attitude may have been shaped by his perceptions of the situation at home. He found it difficult to believe things were "that bad." Some men, like "R," did not have that problem, and for them going home became the only proper option, even if it meant swearing an oath to the United States. The reality was that Confederate soldiers had and would continue to swear the oath of allegiance.

In August 1863 the Union finally began keeping detailed records of Confederate deserters who entered Union lines and swore the oath of allegiance. Now oath takers had names, ranks, units, physical descriptions, and, perhaps most importantly, clearly defined homes, if only by state and county. The Register of Confederate Deserters to the Union Army, 1863–1865, provides some insight into just how widespread oath swearing was among Confederate soldiers.[25]

The Register provides us with the distribution of oath swearers by state. Without question, the leading state for oath-swearing deserters was Tennessee. Consistent with the fears of both Letcher and Lee, Virginia was second. Soldiers from North Carolina, the acknowledged leader of Confederate desertion, took another route home and finished fourth among the states (the distribution is shown in table 1).

Tennessee soldiers represent the largest number of deserters swearing the oath from any state. By the time the Union began keeping records, much of middle Tennessee from Clarksville to Chattanooga was in Union hands, and men who swore the oath could go home without fear of retribution or capture by Confederate military or civilian authority. Andrew Johnson had been working to return Tennessee's soldiers since March 1862. By September 1863 Union control was even more extensive, even if it did not have an absolute mastery

Table 1. Distribution of oath-swearing Confederate deserters by state

	Number in sample	Percent of total sample	Projected total number
Alabama	392	9.1	2,835
Arkansas	169	3.9	1,229
Florida	27	0.6	189
Illinois	4	—	—
Kentucky	126	2.9	913
Louisiana	75	1.8	567
Maryland	9	0.2	—
Mississippi	150	3.5	1,103
North Carolina	334	7.8	2,457
South Carolina	38	0.8	252
Tennessee	1,381	32.3	10,175
Texas	50	1.1	315
Virginia	638	14.9	4,693
West Virginia	107	2.5	788
Unidentified	781	18.2	5,733
Total	4,281		31,344*

* This projected total was determined by combining the 423 pages in book 1 and the 389 pages in book 2 of the Register of Confederate Deserters to the Union Army, 1863–1865 (812 pages total) and then multiplying that figure by the average 44 names appearing on each page. The half-filled pages of officers' names were omitted, as were the only partially filled pages at the end of each letter of the alphabet. If Georgians were added to this number, it would reach 34,712.

of the state. The county distribution of the Tennessee oath takers reveals three distinct patterns. The first pattern reflects the work that began with Johnson in early 1862 and the effects of two large armies living off the land. From Sumter, Jackson, and Overton counties on the Kentucky border running south-southwest to Wayne, Lawrence, Lincoln, and Franklin counties on the Alabama border, not only could virtually every county in middle Tennessee boast double-digit deserters, but many had more than twenty, and six counties had more than forty: Giles (92), Lincoln (75), Hickman (41), Wilson (42), Marshall (55), and Maury (58). The second pattern shows heavy desertion in the extreme eastern Tennessee counties of Knox (22), Granger (17), Jefferson (19), Hawkins (26), Greene (14), Sullivan (24), and Washington (24). A region opposed to secession in 1861 came under Union control in 1863. Longstreet's failed attempt to take Knoxville in December 1863 ended Confederate efforts to reoccupy the region, and Tennesseans in Longstreet's army would have found the Union policy useful. The third pattern resembles Georgia's experience in 1864 and reflects counties with heavy desertion toward the end of Bragg's retreat during the Tullohma campaign. Bradley (36), Polk (55), McMinn (30), Rhea (17), and Hamilton (50) counties reflect men deserting in the wake of the Confederate retreat from Tennessee. With so much historical focus on Virginia and the almost continuous occupation of that state by both armies, Tennessee gets lost. However, from 1862 onward it was the scene of a deliberate and successful Union effort to drive organized Confederate military resistance out of the state.

Desertion patterns in Alabama mirror those of Georgia. Alabama's northern counties, including the northeast mountain region, contributed 181 of the 392 in the sample, or almost half. A significant number (31) were from Mobile, Alabama's seaport counterpart to Savannah. A review of 1860 manuscript census data reveals the same "Irish"-heavy population in Mobile that was found in Savannah. [26]

North Carolina did not seem to need the benefits of the Union program. Its 334 oath-swearing deserters in this sample project out to 2,457, about 7 percent of the total number of deserters in the Register. While North Carolina had almost as many deserters to the enemy as Alabama, it makes up less than 10 percent of the more than 25,000 deserters attributed to the Tarheel state. North Carolina also did not show the same use of the oath-swearing process in its mountain regions that other southern Appalachian states displayed. While some mountain counties showed double-digit oath swearers, such as Ashe, Cherokee, Macon, and Wilkes, equally large numbers come from Randolph (22), Yadkin (16), and Northampton (10) counties. Letters, diaries, and other qualitative data indicate that desertion from the mountain counties was heavy, and these data do not refute that. They do, however, suggest that the benefits afforded by the oath-swearing process may not have appealed to western North Carolinians. The picture of the region during the war is one of chaos where neither the Union nor the Confederacy held sway. The deserter bands in the area seemed to have as much control as anyone. The region was supportive of deserters, and its harsh terrain made apprehension difficult, making safety less of an issue. [27]

Virginia, the state that contributed the second-largest number of soldiers to the cause, shows a county pattern of oath-swearing deserters that runs in an almost unbroken line from Rockingham County (19) in the middle part of the state, southwest through Autagua (22), Rockbridge (19), Botetour (12), Montgomery (14), Floyd (16), Carroll (10), and Washington (39) counties. The only other significant numbers are from counties on the state's southern border with North Carolina: Pittsylvania (11), Mecklenburg (12), and Norfolk (22) counties. The large number for Richmond County (118) is explained by desertion late in

1864 and early 1865. The trail moving southwestward runs into counties that had a significant amount of unrest during the war and those like Floyd County, which proved to be a haven for deserters.[28] Since the state of West Virginia did not exist when the war began, those who deserted and gave West Virginia as their home state when swearing the oath were Virginians when the war began. With "home" clearly breaking from the Confederacy in 1863 with the creation of the new state, those deserting and swearing the oath could not only safely go home but could return to a place that had already made a clear decision on where it stood in the conflict. If Virginia and West Virginia deserters are combined, the Old Dominion had 5,481 of its prized "Virginia Blues" not only desert but swear allegiance to the Union. Combining Virginians and North Carolinians, Lee's vaunted Army of Northern Virginia lost almost eight thousand soldiers to the oath-swearing process over the course of the war.

The rest of the West and the trans-Mississippi reflect the problem of distance and safety. The further south and west one goes, the fewer deserters to the enemy. Arkansas and Mississippi had 1,229 and 1,103, respectively, each more than 50 percent less than Alabama's 2,800, which itself was down about 600 from Georgia's 3,368. Tennessee's unique position as a border state, coupled with being the first state the Union was able to attack and occupy, reflects how the safety that came with the Union advance in the face of the Fabian retreat into the South made desertion to the enemy possible.[29]

The Register numbers indicate that oath swearing was utilized far more extensively by men in the Army of Tennessee than by those in the Army of Northern Virginia. What gives those numbers even greater weight is that unlike North Carolina and Virginia, the two states with the most soldiers committed to the war, Tennessee's contribution was not extraordinary. Isham Harris begged for recruits in 1862, and Louisiana's newspapers and governor suggested that the Volunteer state had not volunteered to the extent it could have, or perhaps should have. In a sense, its hesitancy to join the Confederacy and contribute to the fight played out in its soldiers' willingness to abandon the army as their home state fell quickly to the Union. But the common soldier's exodus from the army was not limited to the men from Tennessee. Consistent with the Georgia study, 84 percent of all Confederate deserters were privates. When noncommissioned officers are included, the total figure rises to well over 90 percent. Conscripts made up only a small percentage of the total. The Confederacy was losing men who volunteered to serve and then chose to leave.

By August 1863, the Union policy of allowing deserters to swear the oath and return home was having a clear effect. With the Confederacy slowly withdrawing, more of the South fell under Union control and more men could be assured of returning home safely and remaining there. In September, Union officials not only reported that "desertion from the rebel army is great" but indicated that some deserters were willing to fight for the Union. Gen. Henry Halleck authorized William Rosecrans to use his discretion regarding the enlistment of deserters. An exchange of telegrams on September 11, 1863, showed the Union moving with amazing speed to capitalize on the Confederate desertion situation. At 12:45 p.m. that afternoon, Rosecrans telegraphed Asst. Adj. Gen. E. D. Townsend to organize deserters and loyal Southerners into regiments instead of companies. It seemed the volume of men coming into Union lines wanting to take up arms now required units larger than the companies that had been previously authorized. At 2:00 p.m. on the same day, Rosecrans telegraphed Secretary of War Stanton directly for an "immediate decision" on his request to enlist deserters. These men apparently lived in areas still under Confederate control, and although they had deserted, they did not want to go North. As Rosecrans explained, "They cannot follow the avocations of peace, nor have the proper protections at home, and will soon be driven by causes founded in human nature to some course prejudicial to the public interests." Rosecrans had deserters who wanted to go home but could not. If he did not put them into organized units, they would disperse, end up in the mountains, and possibly begin to terrorize both the Union and other Confederate civilians. At 9:00 that evening, Halleck telegraphed Rosecrans indicating his wire to Townsend had been forwarded to him up the chain of command. Halleck gave Rosecrans the authority he requested, telling him to appoint competent men to serve as officers who would then be formally commissioned by the president. As for the new troops, Rosecrans was permitted to requisition all clothing, arms, and equipment that he might need. The numbers in the Register may actually understate the size of the Confederate desertion wave in August and September 1863. The speed with which the Union moved indicates that the rate of desertion was escalating to the point that it presented problems that Rosecrans moved to abate. In the process, Confederate soldiers were not only abandoning both the cause and its army but were willing to take the next step and join the army of its enemy.[30]

The Confederacy was a long way from admitting the harm caused by the Union policy, but tacit admission existed in its newspapers and among its citizens. In language that echoed that of "R," Mrs. Alliou Hundervant of Tallapoosa confirmed what the anonymous soldier had predicted: men were deserting. "The poor soldier has little at stake in this so far as property is concerned." While defending the property and firesides of those who stayed home, his wife and children suffer, "and the effect has already been seen and felt in Bragg's Army." Notices appeared rescinding furloughs in the trans-Mississippi. Georgia soldiers' furloughs were reduced to twenty days, Mississippi soldiers' to fifteen, and Alabama soldiers' to ten. Gen. John Pemberton ordered those Confederates captured at Vicksburg to report to their former organizations. Desertion and straggling were hurting, and Jefferson Davis pleaded for men to return to the front and equalize the odds. He openly told the states that the Confederacy was powerless to address the problem; if it was to be stopped, it had to be stopped at the state level. He conceded that appeals to honor, duty, and patriotism had failed. However, events in 1863 in some states would not only fail to stop desertion but actually encourage the practice. More importantly, it seemed that many stragglers were actually deserters and that many deserters were choosing the route home that ran through the Union and the oath. An article in the *Montgomery Weekly Advertiser* tried to dissuade men from deserting by painting a less-than-rosy picture of the fate of such men. As the Confederate army retreated from Tulloma to Chattanooga between January and August 1863, "a number of men deserted, or remained behind with the resolve to take the oath of allegiance and with the hope that they would by this simple process remain quietly at home." However, the writer indicated that based on a Nashville newspaper report, in every instance these men were arrested and detained in jail. Later they had the option of "joining the Yankee, Negro, Dutch army" or going North to be imprisoned until the end of the war.[31]

The article is significant for what it does not say. There was no mention of Confederate sanctions or legal consequences. The warning pertained to the Union practices. The gist of the article was, you will not get home, so do not desert. The official Union practice, or at least the process of recording oath-taking deserters, did not begin until July 1863. The practice had been in place, albeit confusing and internally inconsistent, since 1862. This article implies that enough men were taking advantage of the system to warrant some type of effort to discourage desertion and oath taking. In early August 1863 the adjutant general's office issued a blanket amnesty that allowed any man absent to return to his post without reprisal. The only exception was for men twice convicted of desertion, a lingering reminder of the price being paid for leniency. A week later an order from Bragg's headquarters to Confederate Cavalry commander Joe Wheeler instructed him to increase his pickets. Desertion was on the rise, and Bragg deemed it "highly important that some steps be taken to check this evil." The order also confirmed newspaper reports that furloughs had been terminated for men in the trans-Mississippi or those whose homes lay behind enemy lines.[32]

Lost in the debate over oath taking, at least on the home front, were those men taking the oath from prison. By 1862 the Union had come to understand the difference between prisoners and deserters. By 1863 taking the oath from prison would be more difficult. However, evidence suggests that as late as September 1863, Confederate POWs were taking the oath. J. S. Stockdale kept a diary of his time in Johnson's Island from 1863 to 1864, and it clearly refers to POWs swearing the oath in 1863. On September 9, 1863, Stockdale notes that thirty men were "taken out" of the prison who reportedly took the oath. The next day he makes reference to the same men and confirms that they took the oath. After taking the oath, they were sent back to Johnson's Island but told that they would not be exchanged as prisoners. Instead, they would be discharged upon posting bond in the amount of five thousand dollars. Stockdale made it clear that such men did not have good standing in the eyes of other prisoners and that "their lives here henceforth will not be pleasant."[33] Confederate soldiers clearly saw this as desertion. In a sense it was no better than deserting because camp life was becoming arduous. However, an argument can be made that by late 1863 POWs taking the oath did not really harm the Confederate war effort. These men were no longer going to be exchanged, and although their comrades deemed such conduct reprehensible, it did not hurt morale in the field. However, oath swearing from prison, itself a unique form of desertion, brought with it a similarly unique harmful aspect. Men leaving prison were allowed to join the Union army and go west.

Desertion's harm came in unusual ways, and one of them was in the service that some Confederate soldiers did for the Union fighting Indians. While the benefit may seem small, it must be measured against the same problem suffered by parts of the Confederacy as well as the complete inability of the government, state or federal, to bring any relief. In March 1863, Governor Lubbock wrote Davis to remind him of the acute Indian problem in Texas. Lubbock had been dealing with entreaties from the Texas frontier begging him for assistance. He had gotten all he could from his state legislature, about $300,000 to form units in twenty-five counties from the Red River to the Rio Grande. The governor hoped to prevail upon Gen. John Magruder for soldiers to patrol the Texas frontier, and he had begun to emphasize the need for counties to form local protection units. Lubbock reminded Davis of the December 21, 1861, Confederate act to provide for the defense of the frontier in Texas and expressed frustration at the Confederacy's failure to live up to the letter of the act. Texas had contributed both men and money to the cause, he reminded the president, and its contributions were limited only by its ability to contribute. "The very counties now being ravaged have supplied not only companies, but battalions to the CSA service." The Indian atrocities could have no other effect than to arouse the concerns of the men, many of whom were fighting in distant places. Six months later, Lubbock wrote Kirby Smith pleading for help. The inability to check Indian incursions served only to embolden them. Men, women, and children were dying regularly from Indian attacks, and some of the women and children belonged to families of soldiers fighting in the Confederate service. The money appropriated from the Texas legislature was sufficient to raise one regiment, and it patrolled the entire distance from the Red River to the Rio Grande. Lubbock flatly told Smith, "I fear this may be attended with bad effects upon our frontier men who are in the army." If Smith could release men to patrol the frontier, Lubbock concluded, it would give confidence not only to the people at home but also to the men in the service whose families were on the frontier. Lubbock went one step further and asked Smith to extend his proclamation of amnesty to deserters, allowing them to return to the command of their choice. He clearly wanted them to be allowed to serve at home, adding that a local force could not only patrol the frontier against Indian attack but could rid those areas of Confederate deserters.[34] In mid-September Lubbock repeated his request for local forces by asking the Confederate commissioner of conscripts, J. L. Ford, to exempt men from conscription to remain at home as local militia.[35]

While Lubbock was virtually begging for men to protect the Texas frontier, Confederates deserting from Northern prisons were beginning to fill the ranks of Federal units fighting Indians in Kansas and Minnesota. At the time these units began to organize, the situation in Kansas, Minnesota, and the Dakota territories had become critical. Union officials had considered using the deserters for this purpose as early as 1862 but were concerned that these men would simply leave the Union army once they were out of prison. There were also concerns that enlisting Confederates might adversely affect the prisoner exchange system. However, need overcame these concerns, and with the collapse of the prisoner exchange system in late 1863, enlisting prisoners no longer posed a problem of international law. The program limited those who could enlist to Confederate POWs of northern or foreign birth. By 1864 three regiments were formed to serve in Kansas.[36] Lubbock and his successor would have done virtually anything for three regiments to patrol the Texas borders. The fact that the Union sent Confederate POWs to Kansas made the entire oath-swearing business even more egregious to the South. At least eight hundred Alabama soldiers enlisted in six regiments, almost all of which formed prior to Lee's surrender in April 1865. These men served on America's frontier as early as 1864 and continued to do so after the end of the war. They protected the homes and firesides of men off at war to suppress the very rebellion in which they had once taken an active part. Another 150 Alabamians swore the oath out of prison and enlisted in the Union navy.[37]

The situation becomes more damaging when one considers that although the Union began to use Confederate deserters to fight in 1864, the Confederacy resisted allowing its own deserters to re-form into separate commands. Confederate Articles of War specifically prohibited such a practice, and for good reason—it allowed men to choose where they would serve by deserting. However, by 1864 some in the Confederacy believed it might be the only way to get deserters back into the Confederate military. That potential benefit notwithstanding, Confederate desertion policy consistently rejected this remedy.[38]

Whether from prison or the army in the field, desertion clearly drove the oath-swearing process at least until Lincoln's Proclamation of Amnesty in December 1863. Its use cost the South soldiers. Beyond the manpower drain, men like Reverend Palmer saw oaths as creating evils beyond simply inducing soldiers to desert. It ideologically undermined the Confederacy. A nation is to a great extent the ideas and concepts that it holds dear. Palmer saw oath taking as destroying the Confederacy's soul, but had he looked closer he would have seen desertion at work in yet another way that undermined the basis of the Confederacy by threatening its most sacred institution: slavery.

On January 22, 1863, three weeks before Palmer wrote his letter to Perkins, the Confederate House of Representatives ordered a bill to be printed, vaguely entitled "An Act to Increase and Strengthen the Army of the Confederate States." The bill had been read twice and then referred to the Committee on Military Affairs. House Bill no. 12 appeared on its face to be truly revolutionary. It authorized the president of the Confederacy to call out and place in service "such number of able bodied male slaves between the ages of 18 and 45 years as

DESERTION, IDEOLOGY, AND OATHS

may be necessary, from time to time to serve as teamsters, cooks, laborers and hospital nurses, for the armies of the Confederate States, so that the soldiers now engaged in such, may be relieved there from, and take their position in the army of the Confederate States." The bill placed the expense of feeding and caring for the slaves on the army and authorized a fee of ten dollars per month, paid quarterly, from any money in the Confederate treasury. All slaves within the target age group were to be immediately enrolled by Confederate marshals in every district of every Confederate state. Each marshal would in turn file a descriptive list of each slave. While in service, the slaves would be subject to such rules and regulations as prescribed by the president of the Confederate States.[39]

The depletion of the Confederate army in 1862 forced the Confederacy to turn to slaves, a class that by definition had no rights but would now be asked to serve in the military. Although slaves would not see actual combat, in some of their roles, particularly as teamsters and hospital nurses, they would be exposed to fire, disease, and death. Slaves had been requisitioned for most of the war to perform fatigue duty, particularly defense construction in places like Mobile, Petersburg, and other areas subject to Union attack. This bill took the next step by making them soldiers. They filled noncombat roles so white men could go into combat. The battlefield losses had now pushed the Confederacy to the point that it had to do something inconsistent with its own ideology. Slavery and slaves had been the mudsill of southern society. All white men were equal within a system that subordinated blacks.[40] Now the mudsill would serve because Confederate soldiers were deserting and Confederate civilians refused to serve, even when drafted. Thus Confederate losses were not just those killed and wounded. By 1863, desertion, straggling, and "absenteeism" were gutting both major armies and smaller commands throughout the Confederacy. If oath swearing served to undermine the Confederate legal system, desertion was now forcing the Confederacy to compromise its class structure. In 1864 Gen. Patrick Cleburne would destroy any chance he ever had for command above the division level by presenting a formal plan for making slaves soldiers. Yet in January 1863 Confederate authorities moved to enlist slaves, seemingly believing that so long as they did not fight, the social system would not be compromised. However, such a belief ignored the role of noncombat personnel in any army. Supply, transportation, medical services, and general noncombat fatigue duty were part of every Western army for more than four centuries prior to the Civil War. Every noncombat slave soldier freed a white soldier to fight. The numbers of Confederate killed and wounded alone might have prompted such a move, but desertion seemed to make it unavoidable. The "American practice" had threatened the core of Southern society. The antebellum social system, predicated on Herrenvolk democracy, had already proved to be an ineffective tool to maintain unity during war. To the degree anything remained of the prewar social system, it had completely disappeared by the second full year of the war. But desertion would not stop with the South's peculiar institution. While the cultural linchpin of the Confederate States of America was slavery, its political structure was predicated on the supremacy of the states. The willingness and ability of the states to undertake essentially "Confederate" obligations had become crucial. Davis and the Confederate Congress had all but conceded that without state intervention desertion could not be checked. At this crucial time, some of the states stepped away, and in North Carolina the recoil from responsibility would not only allow desertion to continue, it would exacerbate the problem.

By 1863 the Confederate government had all but conceded that the states would have to intervene if desertion were to be curtailed. If the state governments did not understand the urgency of the situation as communicated by Confederate officials, they should have seen it in the pleas of their own citizens. Correspondence continued to flood Governor Pettus's office in 1863, some of it demanding that Mississippi intervene to clean out deserters from the state. From Simpson County, Jackson, and Canton came requests for advice and reports on deserter activity. Sheriff Jason H. Thompson of Simpson County actually chronicled his successful efforts to round up deserters. His letter demonstrates the degree to which desertion had reached out of the army and into the very lowest levels of civilian life. To the extent that they could meet Davis's request for assistance in rounding up deserters, states relied upon both state and local authorities to capture, incarcerate, and transfer these men. The sketchy records for Mississippi contain a set of receipts kept by the sheriff of Chicasaw and Winston counties for the cost incurred in arresting and detaining Confederate deserters. With the exception of a few Tennessee and Texas units, most deserters in the state were from Mississippi regiments. In most cases they were held three days and the sheriff charged the state a flat fee of $5.00 per man and expenses that averaged $8.75. Of the seventy-five deserters captured and retained, all but thirteen were caught between July and December 1863. The remainder were apprehended in 1864.[41]

Governor Watts heard the same calls from Alabamians seeking state assistance to help round up deserters. Thirty-four citizens of St. Clair County signed a petition pleading with Watts for help. Some apparently had given up on Watts and simply asked for permission to raise and equip local units. One of the most vigilant state officials was Governor Brown of Georgia. Over the course of the war he raised three small armies; although they were dedicated to home defense, one of their principal tasks became the pursuit and apprehension of deserters.[42] In South Carolina the state adjutant general's office actively engaged the state troops in deserter control. In 1863, the Confederacy tried to use the Confederate Conscription Act to enlist the aid of state troops and local authorities to arrest deserters and seize conscripts who failed to report after being drafted. As interpreted by South Carolina officials, the Conscription Act allowed the governor to empower local sheriffs to arrest deserters without proof that they resisted or would resist. State troops worked in concert with Confederate forces, although their commanders were not legally required to report to General Lee. The focus of most efforts was the Greenville District, the portion of South Carolina that abutted the southernmost section of the North Carolina mountain region.[43]

Even North Carolina used its state troops to try to control the deserter problem, actions that led to violence in the mountains of western North Carolina in 1862. However, for all the efforts by the states, the perception remained that the obligation to find and bring back deserters from the Confederate army lay with the Confederate government. Governor Lubbock encouraged the Texas legislature to support the Confederate Congress and its national measures, but when asked about handling a deserter problem in Cook County he replied, "Over deserters and stragglers from the Confederate service I have no control— I will however bring the matter to the attention of the Confederate military authorities."[44] Lubbock's attitude appears to have been the exception, at least as a statement of formal policy. But North Carolina would make a statement that not only defined the extent to which it would use state military resources to hunt deserters but also defined the relationship between states and the central government in such a way that, in the crucial area of desertion, the Confederacy's goals of maintaining the army would prove incompatible with the state's conception of how the "Confederacy" worked. The pronouncement would come not from North Carolina's governor or its legislature but from its judicial branch.

In the Confederacy, state supreme courts occupied a unique position of power. Although the Confederate Constitution provided for a Confederate Supreme Court, one was never created. Therefore, in the Confederacy each state supreme court stood as the highest level of authority. The potential for each state to interpret acts of the central government loomed large, and in April 1863 the North Carolina Supreme Court did just that regarding the use of state troops and militia to arrest and return deserters from the Confederate army. At a point when desertion was escalating, the North Carolina court severely damaged efforts to return North Carolina troops to the Confederate service, and in the process it demonstrated how political ideology combined with this military crime to damage the South's war effort.

In the spring of 1863, Chief Justice Richmond Pearson of the North Carolina Supreme Court ruled that North Carolina state troops and militia could not legally be used to apprehend deserters from the Confederate army. For the most part the state judicial branches had refrained from interfering with acts of the Confederate government. Conscription had been challenged and upheld. However, the suspension of the writ of habeas corpus caused a more severe and less restrained reaction. The facts that gave rise to Pearson's ruling probably repeated themselves all over the South. A militia unit encountered a group of deserters in Yadkin County. After a brief but sharp encounter, two members of the militia were killed, and the deserters responsible for their deaths were apprehended. They sought out a writ of habeas corpus that was returned to Justice Pearson. Pearson ruled that the governor of North Carolina, absent some specific enactment from the Confederate Congress, had no right to arrest deserters who "pertained to the Confederate authorities alone." Therefore, the men had resisted an unlawful arrest and could not be detained for having committed no offense. The deaths of the two militiamen, while regrettable, did not constitute a crime.[45]

Pearson's decision made a bad situation worse. By May 1863 the desertion problem in North Carolina was getting out of hand. Secretary of War James Seddon wrote to Governor Vance on May 5, enclosing copies of a letter from Gen. Dorsey Pender that was endorsed by Lee. Pender was adamant that desertion among North Carolina troops was rampant, and Seddon agreed. He told Vance that unless North Carolina desertion was checked, it would destroy the discipline and morale of the army. Following on the heals of the victory at Chancellorsville that cost the Confederacy more than thirteen thousand casualties, including Stonewall Jackson, Seddon insisted that all able-bodied men needed to be with their commands. In less than two months Lee would invade Pennsylvania, and if desertion continued unabated he would face the same situation he had the year before when he went into Maryland. Unable to depend on state troops, Seddon directed that a regiment of Gen. D. H. Hill's division be detached for deserter duty in North Carolina.[46]

As the Confederacy scrambled to consolidate its army, Pearson's ruling exposed the danger desertion posed to the tenuous relationship between the central government and the states. With no Confederate Supreme Court, the possibility that a state supreme court would rule adversely to the Confederacy's interest and afford the central government no recourse had always loomed. Pearson's decision was in some ways the realization of one of the Confederacy's worst fears. He applied a judicial philosophy that treated desertion as "a dry question of law," ignoring the fact that the Confederacy was locked in a struggle for its very existence. In fairness, Pearson overruled an act of the Confederate Congress only once. But this limitation on the state's ability to assist the Confederacy severely restricted efforts to control desertion at a critical juncture in the war. William Graham's argument in 1861 regarding North Carolina's obligation to advance what he claimed were "Confederate objectives" had found judicial support. The political ideology of states' rights, which strictly defined obligations between states and the Confederacy, had joined with desertion to create a damaging combination.[47]

Governor Vance understood the urgency of the situation, and on May 11 he issued a proclamation condemning the numerous desertions. However, rather than just imploring that deserters return, he addressed his comments toward the civilian population, those who encouraged, incited, and then harbored such men. Pearson's ruling had not only emboldened soldiers to leave but strengthened the resolve of citizens, many badly in need of their men, to assist deserters. Vance insisted that "no crime can be greater, no cowardice more abject, no treason more base, than for a citizen of the state enjoying its privileges and protection without sharing its dangers, to persuade those who have the courage to go forth in defense of their country vilely to desert the colors." No plea could excuse such conduct, and Vance believed that the father or brother who encouraged his son or brother to desert should himself be shot. Vance addressed deserters by telling them that although he could not offer the pardon that many had already rejected, he could assure them that no man returning would be shot. Vance referred to the recent victory at Chancellorsville and the terrible cost in Confederate lives. Every man was needed at the front for the task that lay ahead. But the likelihood that deserters would return diminished in the face of a sentiment among those at home that condoned the practice.[48]

The governor's proclamation was well intended, but it was thunder and fury signifying very little, because as he explained to Davis two days later, Pearson had destroyed any authority he had to use his militia to apprehend deserters. He admitted to Davis that the information coming to him from North Carolina generals serving with Lee's army indicated that North Carolinians were deserting in droves. Those generals—Pender being one—had called on Vance for help. Vance had tried, but the problems were almost insurmountable. First, he had a hard time taking raw civilians and molding them into a militia force capable of policing North Carolina for deserters. Having assembled a force, it encountered the deserters in the Yadkin County incident that gave rise to Pearson's decision in April. He added that his efforts to persuade both the Confederate Congress and the North Carolina legislature to grant him authority to arrest deserters and use state troops for that purpose had failed. Vance could not move. If he sent his militia out under the current legal ruling, they could be shot with impunity by deserters. To make matters worse, Pearson's decision had increased desertion because of the way it was being reported. Vance explained that Pearson's decision was reported within the ranks as having declared conscription illegal. Soldiers were told that if they came home they would not only be safe from apprehension by state militia but would be entitled to the protection of the state authorities. "Desertion which had been temporarily checked," he told Davis, "broke out again worse than before."[49]

Vance was in an unenviable position. To a degree, desertion demonstrated the stark difference in leadership that existed between Vance or Davis and Abraham Lincoln, as well as the way public sentiment in the North differed from that in the South. While Pearson's ruling may have been legally sound, it represented practical national suicide. Just as Roger Taney's decision in *Ex Parte Merryman* had been legally sound, practically it meant that with Congress absent for at least five months, a sitting president was powerless under the Constitution to prevent an internal insurrection from succeeding by suspending the writ of habeas corpus in areas where local justice was at best questionable. Lincoln did the only sane thing; he ignored Taney's ruling and in the process preserved the Union in Maryland. Pearson's ruling was in some ways equally absurd. With the South in the midst of a struggle that would determine its very existence, a state judge rendered a decision which argued that the highest-ranking official in the state had no power to assist the central government in remedying an acute problem among troops from that very state who were hiding in North Carolina. Had Vance tried to send his militia to Virginia or South Carolina, Pearson's ruling may have made more sense, even if under the circumstances it would have been equally damaging to the war effort. The prudent thing for Vance to have done was to ignore the ruling. However, the public reaction to Pearson's ruling was decidedly favorable, and had Vance simply ignored the decision he may well have found his own constituents unwilling to support him. In light of Graham's speech on the sedition ordinances and his objections to North Carolina's being asked to perform an essentially "Confederate" function, Vance's hesitancy to ignore Pearson is understandable. But the ideological underpinnings of the Confederacy, the notion of states' rights, and the subordinate position of the central government allowed North Carolina to virtually turn its back on the desertion situation at a critical juncture.

Vance admitted to Davis that he did not know what steps other states had taken regarding deserters. He thought it fundamentally wrong for the Confederacy to draw on the North Carolina militia to arrest deserters, claiming that it suggested there were more deserters from North Carolina than from any other state, "which I hope and believe is not true." He did, however, concede a key element of desertion, one which implied that North Carolina could well be leading the Confederacy in desertion. "Our troops are nearer to their homes and therefore more tempted than those further south [to desert]." Vance touched on the centerpiece of oath swearing: the offering of safety to deserters. His own comments may explain not only why North Carolinians were so prone to desert but also why oath swearing among deserters was so prevalent in the Deep South. Thanks to Pearson's ruling, home was not only close, it had become safe, or at least safer. There was no need to seek out the assistance of the Union army. The North had yet to occupy the territory most North Carolinians called home. It controlled virtually none of Virginia so far as being able to create a safe haven for deserters. However, for Tennesseans, Mississippians, some Louisianans, and, by 1864, Georgians, safe passage home would be an important factor.[50]

In his long letter to Davis, Vance offered other insights into the problem that, although focused on North Carolina, was eating the Confederacy alive. First, he admitted ignorance regarding what other states were doing to solve the problem, raising an interesting point that citizens, soldiers, and leaders had already hit upon, namely, that the hardships and problems of the war were experienced differently depending on where one lived. However, different states also experienced many of the same hardships, and yet there was no coordinated effort to solve the problem. Desertion was certainly one of those problems. Extortion, deflation, food shortages, and scarcity of basic necessities were problems common to all states. Vance actually requested that Davis implement a coordinated plan to deal with desertion. More important for Vance, however, was dealing with the causes of desertion, and on that score he seems to have missed the point. "Homesickness, fatigue, hard fare, etc. have of course much to do with it," he wrote. He mentioned the lack of furloughs and placed particular emphasis on conscripted men's inability to join regiments with their neighbors.[51] All of these factors may have contributed, but the one cause Vance did not mention, perhaps because in his position he could not mention it, was that the government—North Carolina's, Davis's, and others'—had failed to protect the very thing it had sent these men off to fight for: home and family.

In late May 1863, Pearson's decision deepened a growing rift between North Carolina and the Confederacy. Now, however, the schism between Vance and Confederate officials had become personal. Vance understood the gravity of the desertion problem, but on May 25 he received a letter from Seddon that expressly blamed the Army of Northern Virginia's desertion problem on North Carolina troops. Seddon accused North Carolinians of allowing Pearson's decision to be construed as ruling conscription unconstitutional and providing a legal argument that the Confederate army could not keep North Carolinians in the service. Seddon told Vance that North Carolinians believed they had only to reach North Carolina's courts to receive all the legal protection necessary; furthermore, many believed that simply by reaching any of several western North Carolina counties they would "find no reprobation in public sentiment, but be secure of harbor and protection." Seddon's letter, whether accurate or not, explains several things about North Carolina desertion in May 1863. First, desertion gathered momentum from Pearson's ideological understanding of the relationship between the states and the Confederacy. Second, it appeared to be common knowledge that western North Carolina offered refuge and understanding, hence there was no need to swear allegiance to the Union for protection if one was either from one of those counties or willing to go "lay out" there. Although Seddon claimed it was not his place to tell Vance what to do, he demanded that the governor issue yet another proclamation condemning the actions of deserters and clarifying the judicial decision, using his "full official influence . . . to restrain the too ready interposition of the judicial authority in these questions of military obligation." In closing, Seddon cautioned Vance about "exposing by such proclamation the seriousness of the evil, which cannot fail to give hope and comfort to the enemy."[52]

Vance was clearly offended, and his response reflected his sentiments. He told Seddon that he had already issued a proclamation and enclosed his of May 11, 1863. Everything that he could do had been done, including ordering his militia to watch all fords, ferries, and public highways. As far as the problem of judicial intervention, Vance explained that he had written Davis and asked him to make an official requisition of the state militia, thereby curing any conflict between the North Carolina judiciary and the Confederate army. Then Vance expressed regret at Seddon's insistence on blaming North Carolina's desertion on Pearson's judicial intervention, claiming that such a belief "had its origin in political prejudice." Vance did not dispute that the decision had been misconstrued and that the misconstruction was indeed making its way through the army. But he did not know how the misrepresentation got started, and he placed blame at the feet of "our neighbors" and even among "our own citizens" for a willingness to "believe evil of the State." Clearly feeling defensive on the issue of desertion, Vance went on to point out that only North Carolina used its militia to arrest conscripts and deserters, "that she had better executed the conscript law; has fuller regiments in the field than any other, and that at the two last great battles on the Rappahannock, in December and May, she furnished over one-half the killed and wounded." Vance added that it "seems strange, passing strange, that desertion would receive official countenance and protection on her borders."[53]

Vance then set forth the problem that existed between coordinate branches at the state level and the comity that is often difficult to achieve between state and federal government. Pearson's opinions were published in the newspapers, and Vance claimed that any perversion of those opinions was by design, presumably by someone in another state. Vance agreed with Pearson that habeas corpus petitions carried heavy penalties for judges who wrongfully refused to grant them: "An upright Judge must deliver the law as he conceives it to be, whether it should happen to comport with the received notions of the military authorities or not." Vance then refused to use his influence to restrain or control "that co-ordinate branch of the government which intrudes upon nobody, usurps no authority, but is, on the contrary in great danger of being overlapped and destroyed by the tendency of the times." Despite Vance's claims that the North Carolina courts caused no harm and seized no authority, the desertion problem had become intertwined with the issue of states' rights and exposed a weakness in the relationship between state and federal government within the Confederacy. Vance intended to do everything he could to "sustain the common cause," but he would not undermine the authority or the decisions of his own judicial branch. The Confederate Congress had made the decision of any state supreme court the law of the land because no appeal from a decision rendered by such a court could be taken beyond the state level. As such those decisions were binding upon all parties. Vance then took offense that the letters of Seddon and Lee would create the impression that desertion was a bigger problem among North Carolina's troops than among those of other states, an assertion Vance refused to believe. Did the Confederate government call upon any other governor to issue proclamations? Did it employ the militia of any other state to arrest deserters? Has anyone threatened the "too ready disposition" of the South Carolina or Georgia judiciary "for almost similar decisions"? Vance did not think so, and although he begged Seddon's pardon for writing in such a tone, he felt that North Carolina's efforts were unappreciated.[54]

As North Carolina left the Union in 1861, the president of its secession convention had hoped that similarities of climate, pursuits, and institutions would bind together the various states. Two years later, that same state's governor made it abundantly clear that perceived similarities of culture and economics had failed to keep the diverse members of the new nation in step. Not even the notion of a shared commitment could override the political and ideological differences that desertion had begun to expose. Pearson's decision in April 1863 and Vance's steadfast willingness to support him would have been harmful under almost any circumstances, but when the events of 1863 combined with the willingness of the Confederacy's two great armies to cast a lenient eye upon the desertion that emerged in 1862, desertion had become a "justifiable crime" that had gained both legal and political support from the states. Desertion had worked with ideology to undermine the Confederacy, and in the process it was destroying many of the ideological foundations the fledgling nation held dear. But desertion would hurt more than the Confederacy's soul, as Reverend Palmer suggested; it was in the process of gutting its armies.

In January 1863, Robert E. Lee responded to a request from Gen. John Imboden to "keep" men who at one time had been a part of Lee's Army of Northern Virginia but were now within the ranks of Imboden's partisan corps in the Shenandoah Valley. Imboden wanted these men officially transferred to his corps. While Lee understood Imboden's reasoning and did not question his motives, he rejected the request. The men Imboden wanted to keep were from the area and offered the advantage of having local men fighting near home. But these men had "abandoned their colors," and Lee could not overlook the seriousness of their actions. He carved out a small exception for men who believed their term of service had expired and who had distinguished themselves after joining Imboden's corps. After making it clear that Imboden had to return all the other men, Lee cautioned against giving them any inducements for returning to their rightful commands, fearing that any "favors" might encourage others to desert. Lee had also become frustrated at the inability to bring conscripts into the ranks, and he told Imboden that he could keep as many of those as he could bring into the lines because "at present it is the only means of getting them into the service."[1]

Lee called the men hiding in Imboden's command absentees yet admitted they had abandoned the colors. Abandonment suggests the degree of permanence that rises to the level of desertion, yet still these soldiers remained "absentees." They were deserters. They had left their units and reenlisted in units that suited them. Lee's unwillingness to admit the extent of his problem would finally pass in 1863, but not before the situation reached a critical stage. His letter to Imboden revealed the existence of desertion on two levels. First, men were leaving their existing units and joining local forces. This was the equivalent of a North Carolinian leaving the Army of Northern Virginia to return to his home state and join the local militia. Second, conscripts were refusing to report. Continuing to characterize these men as absentees rather than deserters not only misidentified the true nature of the conduct but demonstrated a failure to see the symptoms. The Confederate military continued to look to the soldier's "intent" to determine if he really meant to stay away indefinitely. Unable to conclusively establish a soldier's state of mind, contemporary military leaders characterized the actions of deserters as something less onerous. The real problem continued to be that soldiers were gone when it mattered. Even without the intent to remain absent indefinitely, the problem was severe enough to deem the conduct desertion.

The Confederacy's approach to desertion is analogous to immigration studies that attempt to characterize the volume of immigrants by looking at growth rather than mobility. An increase in the size of a city like Boston from 175,000 to 350,000 over twenty years reflects significant immigration, since the increase exceeds that which could be expected from natural population growth. However, the phenomenon is shown to be even greater by records which demonstrate that during the same period of time 3.2 million immigrants moved through Boston, even if they did not remain indefinitely. Mobility shows the rush of immigrants in a way that growth does not. The same can be said for desertion. By playing down the number of desertions through a more lenient interpretation, Lee and others missed the point. The Army of Northern Virginia had become an army where only those who wanted to be disciplined accepted it. Men were leaving through every door possible, and 1863 would reveal just how many ways there were out of the army. What the year also revealed is that desertion was stripping the army of soldiers and making the Confederacy a very dangerous place to live.

Portents of things to come appeared early in 1863 and gave a stern warning to anyone watching and listening that the desertion epidemic about to strike the Confederacy in 1863 had already infected portions of the South. In January, Gideon Pillow, chief of the Volunteer and Conscription Bureau, wrote to Colonel Campbell, his principal assistant for middle Tennessee, telling him that Colonel Avery was to "sweep the County of Lincoln, arresting stragglers, absentees, deserters and all men liable to the conscript law." Pillow instructed Campbell to have Avery's command do the same in Franklin, Giles, and Lawrence counties and in that portion of northern Alabama lying along the Tennessee line contiguous with those counties. Pillow indicated that he would be going to Columbia, Tennessee, the next day, where he would "direct the operations of two other cavalry regiments." Not only was desertion spreading, but the Confederacy was allocating significant resources to combat the problem.[2]

Pillow's efforts show that by 1863 desertion had become something that had to be "fought." Samuel Cooper spent most of 1862 cloaking local officials, conscript enrolling officers, and government contractors with the authority to detain conscripts, absentees, and deserters. But giving civilians and military enrolling officers this authority was only the first step in the process. One can almost determine if "absentees" intended to return by looking at the measures required to bring them back into the army. In places like the North Carolina mountains, bringing soldiers back into the army required the zealous effort of other soldiers. As reflected in the tragic incident in Yadkin County in 1862, deserter duty was a nasty business.

With desertion on the rise, the Confederate government made the situation worse by confusing what seemed to be an otherwise clear directive from Lee. Lee had flatly told Imboden that men in his command who had left the Army of Northern Virginia had to be returned. In February 1863, Cooper's office issued General Order no. 19, which purported to clarify the "military state of certain persons in the army who have left their regular commands and joined others, under the impression they had the right to do so, but are claimed as deserters under existing laws." Lee had told Imboden that everyone other than conscripts had to be returned, although even he created an exception for men who had "distinguished themselves." Cooper's order now allowed men who had reenlisted, after their first term expired, to remain in their "present companies," provided the facts did not show "an intention to desert their former commands." Just how one was supposed to determine if men had intended to desert their former commands was not addressed in the order. To make matters more difficult, paroled prisoners whose terms had expired while they were on parole and had joined new companies would be allowed to stay in those companies per Cooper's General Order no. 44, of June 17, 1862. The most telling phrase of the order reflects the degree to which the Confederate military had become trapped within its own policies and definitions. The second paragraph of Cooper's order began, "All persons who have really deserted and have joined other companies will be returned to their original commands." Those who have "really deserted"? Hadn't they all? Given the lack of any clear definition and an obvious inclination to interpret desertion as mere absence, absence as straggling, and straggling as something else, the Confederate military and its officer corps were almost incapable of identifying a man who had "really deserted." Not only did officers have to figure out what "real" desertion was, but then, according to the order, real deserters would only be returned to their original commands in cases arising from a "mis-conception of the rights and duties under the re-enlistment and conscription law." By the time most officers had completed the interpretation process, it was unlikely anyone would be punished for desertion.[3]

Cooper's attempt to clarify the status of men moving from one command to another was but one of several orders he promulgated in the winter and spring of 1863. In February 1863, Cooper issued an order dropping officers from the ranks who were absent longer than thirty days, an action that had the effect of terminating their pay. In March he followed it up with an order that each officer absenting himself from his command for legal reasons was to be issued a certificate when paid. That certificate would in turn be deposited with the pay officer making the next payment in order that the army could keep track of officers on leave. Apparently Cooper's orders lacked sufficient force of law, because on April 16, 1863, the Confederate Congress passed "An Act to Prevent the Absence of Officers and Soldiers Without Leave," prohibiting any pay to officers or men AWOL.[4] The desertion signs were all there and had been for some time. Cooper's efforts to curb desertion reveal something important about the size of the problem. Robert Kean openly criticized Cooper for not knowing how large his army was in any theater. Based on the estimates historians routinely make as to the size of the army during the war, Kean's criticisms seem warranted. However, Cooper's efforts demonstrate that even without knowing the precise number of Confederate deserters, he knew the Confederacy had a problem.

By April the desertion situation forced the Confederate Congress to act, at least insofar as determining punishment for deserters. Cooper circulated a copy of "An Act to Prohibit the Punishment of Soldiers by Whipping," approved by Congress on April 13, 1863, throughout the Confederate army. Prohibiting "whipping or the inflicting of stripes," the act made death or confinement with hard labor the legally permissible punishment for desertion. A death sentence had to be approved by the commanding officer. Cooper had provided the legal and historical research that justified the law in a lengthy report he filed in January 1863 at the request of the House of Representatives. Punishment had become an issue after Private Seymour of the Fiftieth North Carolina was found guilty and sentenced to hard labor. having a letter "D" branded on his left hand, and thirty-nine lashes on his bare back every three months for the duration of the war. Cooper's report traced punishment for desertion from 1776 to 1861. Flogging had been discontinued in 1812 but was brought back in 1833. Branding, however, had been replaced with a tattoo of the letter "D." Apparently the tattoo was seen as a sufficient mark of disgrace without the inhumane practice

"THE NUMBER OF DESERTIONS IS SO GREAT"

of burning the letter into a person's flesh. Cooper observed that the Confederate Constitution copied the United States Constitution in many aspects and that in so doing it had outlawed cruel and unusual punishment. The act appears in no small part to have been a reaction to Seymour's sentence and Cooper's research into military law.[5]

The April 13, 1863, act did little more than repeat what was already in Article 20 of the Confederate Articles of War. The death sentence for desertion had always been on the books. Now, however, the Confederate Congress had placed its seal of approval on the use of death as a deterrent. However, making death the law was still only half the battle. The problem lay in persuading both the executive branch and the Confederate military to use the ultimate punishment.

As the summer of 1863 approached, the Confederacy continued to lose troops to desertion and struggled to bring conscripts into the army. The frustration with trying to maintain its armies began to show in the Confederate government's willingness to adopt harsher measures. Instructions in 1862 that directed government employers to return deserters hiding in their employment became military regulations prosecuting government contractors for allowing such conduct in 1863. The conscript office in Richmond finally made the failure to appear after being drafted the equivalent of desertion. A circular issued four days after the fall of Vicksburg and Lee's defeat at Gettysburg declared that "the evil of desertion from the army, with the determination to avoid and even resist future service, seems to be on the increase." Unable to spare troops from the regular army and uncertain of the extent to which it could rely on state units, the War Department had almost completely delegated the task of capturing deserters to the conscript agencies. District enrolling officers actually had authority to keep a sufficient number of conscripts out of the army for purposes of deserter duty and to pay civilians for the use of horses to mount these men. A law designed to bring men into the army, the Confederate draft now had conscripts trying to arrest other conscripts. The conscription circular authorized the use of state militia, but only if the governor of that state approved. As Vance demonstrated in North Carolina, governors would either resist such a use, insist on retaining authority over their militia, or look to the Confederate Congress for a law authorizing such a use. As of July 1863 such a law was not forthcoming. The circular had a sense of urgency underscored by the statement that "by the selection of suitable assistants and the exercise of the necessary vigilance and activity many men may be returned to service, and the evil of desertion effectually stopped."[6]

The ongoing pleas of military officers, conscription officials, and civilian governors in July 1863 reflected a problem that had gotten completely out of hand, although no one could ever provide precise numbers. Pillow estimated 8,000 to 10,000 deserters in northern Alabama and between 40,000 and 50,000 men of service age in Georgia who remained untapped or had deserted. The signs had been ignored, and by the summer of 1863 the disease had struck both major armies and almost every theater of war. Confederate commands in Tennessee, Georgia, Mississippi, and Louisiana were all overwhelmed by the sheer volume of deserters. Unable to arrest deserters in Harrison, Hancock, and Jackson counties in Mississippi, William Wren, the acting adjutant and inspector general for the state's sea-coast section, wanted authority to reorganize deserters into new companies just to get them back in the service. To make matters worse, deserters took their arms and accoutrements with them, often leaving them scattered across the countryside along their line of escape.[7]

On July 25, 1863, the entire general officer corps of the Army of Tennessee endorsed a letter to Cooper apprizing him of the urgency of the situation in the West. The message was clear: unless the ranks were filled immediately, the Confederate cause was doomed. There were sufficient men in the South to do the job, but they were not enlisting. By their estimate, 150,000 able-bodied men had hired substitutes, in many cases using fraudulent papers or providing diseased men who were of little use to the army. In addition to substitutes, "timid and effeminate young men" were constantly using political connections to have themselves transferred to safe locations. The war was at the front, and that was where they were needed. Bragg and his staff believed a quarter of a million men could be brought into the service at this crucial time. But it was more than just bringing men into the service, it was keeping them there once they arrived, and one of the main culprits was the Fabian policy. "With every inch of territory lost," they wrote, "there is a corresponding loss of men and resources of war. Conscripts cannot be got from the region held by the Yankees, and soldiers will desert back to their homes in possession of the enemy." The Union had only just begun to keep records of desertion into its ranks, yet the commanding officers of the Army of Tennessee already realized the damaging effects of the Union policy combined with the tactic of withdrawal. Some men deserted from "disaffection," others from war weariness, "and some to protect their families from a brutal foe." All of these causes combined with Union occupation to deplete the Confederacy of soldiers and diminish its ability to feed and clothe the army. The upper echelon of the Army of Tennessee finally admitted that "Fabian" was not the best policy. Far from weakening the Union, it strengthened it and allowed the Union's aggressive desertion policy to do its work. Jefferson Davis even acknowledged the severity of the problem by issuing a proclamation imploring men to return to the army.[8]

Just as the judiciary in North Carolina, South Carolina, and Georgia had undermined the army, politics was beginning to do the same thing in other parts of the South. Northern Alabama had been a hotbed of dissent since 1861, and on August 6, 1863, Maj. W. T. Walthall penned a letter to Col. G. W. Lay in the Office of the Commandant of Conscripts in Richmond. The situation in Alabama had gone from bad to worse, Walthall wrote. Recent state elections had brought what he called a "peace party" to power in the northern counties, and incumbents had been beaten by large majorities in some places. Virtual "unknowns" were now in office, and the elections signaled more than a popular resentment of the war. Walthall attributed the political swing to a secret sworn organization known to exist whose main purposes were to encourage desertion, protect deserters, and resist conscription. He had information that led him to believe that many of the votes necessary to elect these men came from Confederate soldiers paroled after the fall of Vicksburg. Desertion now had its own political party, and enforcing the conscription law was now virtually impossible.[9]

Despite all of this activity, there is a sense that nothing existed in the Confederacy if Robert E. Lee did not say it was so. In May 1863, Lee finally conceded he had a problem and took steps to prevent desertion among substitutes. Substitutes were never as good as the men they replaced, and some took the first opportunity to desert. Lee's order insisted that his officers carefully screen all substitutes. Almost in recognition of the wave that everyone else recognized, on July 26 Lee called upon all men "absent" from their commands to rejoin the army. His General Order no. 80 provided an amnesty and asked men to step up and strike a "decisive blow for the sanctity and safety of our homes." Finally, on August 17, he had to confront reality. He wrote Davis and admitted that "the desertions from this army is so great, and still continues to such an extent, that unless some cessation of them can be caused, I fear success in the field will be endangered." His amnesty proclamation of July 26 had backfired. Rather than come back, many left, mostly North Carolinians and, regrettably, "Virginians." The Virginians were leaving to join the partisan corps, and Imboden told Lee there were "great numbers of deserters secreting themselves" in the Shenandoah Valley. Some men took the route south, across the James River. Thirty left from one regiment and eighteen from another, and Lee finally conceded that "all has been done that forbearance and mercy called for." Nothing would remedy the problem except the "rigid enforcement" of the death penalty.[10]

Desertion was killing the Confederate army, and Lee's beloved Army of Northern Virginia was no exception. Even the common soldier was beginning to suspect the severity of the problem. William Smith wrote home to his girlfriend on July 27, 1863, that the situation seemed gloomy. Vicksburg had fallen, and Lee, who "had the finest army ever marshaled on a plain, met with defeat at Gettysburg, and has fallen back to Virginia." Smith claimed the army was worn out, but apparently the men were not too tired to run. On August 6, Smith wrote home again from his camp near Orange Courthouse. The men were grumbling about bad meat, poor clothing, and discipline. Desertions were becoming "fearfully numerous." Smith claimed fourteen men deserted from one regiment in his brigade. "I fear such work as this will ruin our army." On the other side of the Confederacy at virtually the same time, E. D. McDaniel saw the same thing happening in Arkansas. Union soldiers had actually crossed the picket lines to see if the Confederates were giving up in the wake of Vicksburg. McDaniel believed that there were sufficient men in the Confederacy to protect homes and families if "every man would only put their shoulders to the wheel." However, that was not happening, and McDaniel lamented that "some are deserters every week [and] the like of this may whip us."[11]

Lee finally came to the same solution that his military predecessors had arrived at in the eighteenth century: execution. Even men in Lee's command had come to realize that shooting deserters held the key to stopping the practice of desertion. Spencer Welch, a surgeon in the Thirteenth South Carolina, admitted on several occasions in letters home that as sickening as executions were, they were the only way to maintain discipline. Lee now told Davis the same thing. What seems strange is that despite the clear language of the Articles of War and the congressional act of April 16, 1863, Lee still felt compelled to ask permission to shoot deserters. Granted, men were shot in 1862 and 1863. William Smith described an execution in September 1863 in which ten men from the Third North Carolina were executed in front of the entire division. But even with such a spectacle, fighting the Confederate culture of leniency proved difficult. Col. Edward Porter Alexander, trained at West Point and hardened through battle, represented the best of the Confederate officer corps, and his actions in the wake of Gettysburg testified to the problem. British officers—men who shared little in common with those under their command—could apply the death penalty with cold effectiveness, but men like Alexander, products of a society that recognized a relative equality among white men of all classes, simply could not be as hard as they had to be. In the winter of 1863, Alexander's courts-martial had convicted two young men both who had deserted with impunity, and when they were captured Alexander felt they were his to shoot. Legality aside, Alexander's first inclination was to protect them. He immediately put one of them in irons to prevent him from being taken outside his jurisdiction. Alexander admitted he felt sorry for both, so much so that he was willing to allow one to escape. On the retreat from Gettysburg, he learned that the death sentences on both had been approved, and he felt trapped between two equally unpleasant choices. He wanted to go to Lee and plead for a commutation of both sentences. Yet he feared Lee's reaction to his unwillingness to make an example of deserters. The other alternative was equally unpleasant: shooting the men. Alexander expressed his sentiments to his subordinates; the next day, one man had miraculously escaped, and when he sent to Fort Thunder for the man he had placed in irons, no one could find him.[12]

Notwithstanding Alexander's hesitancy to execute the two men in his command, the sentences handed down by courts-martial boards in 1863 stood in stark contrast to those of 1862. Sentence after sentence carried the same solemn order, that the deserter be "shot to death with musketry at such point and time as the commanding general may direct." Death was being ordered, yet according to Lee it still was not universally carried out. Alexander provided an extreme example of the lengths to which commanders might go to prevent executing men, but he was not alone. Some soldiers continued to harbor the belief that executing a man for desertion made that officer a "vindictive and tyrannical man." Men were being executed in both major armies, and descriptions like the one provided by Smith stand in morbid testimony to the ritual.[13]

Despite an increased number of death sentences, by October 1863 the situation had apparently not changed and the debate continued. The problem stemmed from the civilian authorities, and Lee reluctantly deferred to their wishes. He wrote to Secretary of War Seddon acknowledging the receipt of a request to commute the death sentences of two deserters. Despite commuting both sentences, he cautioned Seddon that he had "serious apprehension of the consequences of a relapse into that lenient policy which our best experience has shown to be so ruinous to the army." Lee explained that he had shot some men in 1862 and then stopped, whereupon desertion immediately increased. Davis's July 31, 1863, proclamation implied that all men failing to report would be dealt with at the discretion of the military. Lee had apparently begun to shoot deserters, temporarily squelching the problem, but now he feared that leniency would not only return his army to its prior state but require even harsher means to stop desertion. Seddon told Lee that he approved of his policy regarding executing deserters, but he cautioned that men who voluntarily returned should receive some indulgence and that he had never known men returning on their own to be executed.[14] Seddon missed the point. Men returning voluntarily who could escape punishment would again leave when it suited them. Calling men who left at will "absentees" allowed for the same conduct that depleted Lee's army before each of his major invasions into the North. The ones who left and came back were gutting the army just as badly as those who left and had to be recovered. Both were gone when they were needed. But armies, particularly ones under the kind of pressure Lee's and Bragg's felt in the summer and fall of 1863, could not survive with men leaving at will. For Bragg it was especially hazardous because a soldier leaving to go home might find his home controlled by Confederates on one day and see it fall under Union control the next. The notion that desertion required an intent to remain gone had to give way to some kind of standard that questioned whether a soldier placed himself in danger of not being able to return, because once he got home and found it subsumed by the Union, he would be either unable to get back to his command or suddenly unwilling to do so.

What seemed to make desertion even more damaging was the inability to curb it by any other means. The Confederacy was exhausting itself on the federal, state, and local levels to find deserters and bring them back. In August 1863, J. E. Joyner, a Virginia civilian, wrote from Richmond to his friend Sidney Smith in Henry Courthouse, Virginia. His letter confirmed the extent of desertion and the patterns that had begun to develop. Joyner's health had been failing, and his doctors had sent him to the mountains to convalesce. Apparently recovered, he took advantage of the opportunity to travel around the state. To his surprise, he found "a most unfortunate state of things existing in many of these upper counties," specifically Botetourt, Roanoke, Montgomery, Giles, Floyd, Franklin, Patrick, Henry, and Pittsylvania. What Joyner called the "upper counties" were actually those in the southern and south-central part of the state. Botetourt, Montgomery, Floyd, and Pittsylvania were counties where significant numbers of their soldiers swore the oath of allegiance to the enemy. Roanoke, Giles, Franklin, Patrick, and Henry were contiguous to those counties. Joyner said the people in the region were greatly demoralized, and the situation in the North Carolina counties bordering Virginia was even worse. "A good many deserters are passing the various roads daily, and greatly increase the demoralization," he wrote. "These deserters almost invariably have their guns and accouterments, a problem other officials complained of, and when halted and asked to show furlough papers or leave authorization, they simply pat their guns and defiantly claim, This is my furlough." Joyner believed the demoralization of the civilian population was the product of misinformation. He suggested that speakers be sent to canvass the counties and explain that things were not as bad as they appeared. He also suggested that newspapers needed to be more vigilant in condemning desertion. Joyner believed there were thousands who ought to be in the service but that there "is not moral force enough in the country to bring them out." Unfortunately, he was right. Lee believed he was losing North Carolinians because of what appeared in the papers. Perhaps a reprint of Pearson's decision or just a general description of conditions at home was driving North Carolinians to desert. Consistent with Joyner's observations, Lee asked Seddon to post sentries at the ferries and bridges on the James, Staunton, and Dan rivers. He also wanted guards posted at the foot of the mountains in Halifax, Pittsylvania, Patrick, and Henry counties.[15]

Joyner's letter found its way to Col. J. C. Shields by way of the Conscription Bureau. Shields explained to the bureau that what Joyner had suggested was already being done. "All the agencies under my control have long since been directed to arrest desertions, all with good results," he wrote, "but the evil continues on the increase."[16] Not only did Shields state the obvious, but his statement that he was already using the newspapers indicated that the posted notices of desertion so common in virtually every Southern paper were doing nothing to stop the problem.

In the trans-Mississippi, Gen. Kirby Smith resorted to the same tactic that Lee had tried unsuccessfully in July. On August 26, 1863, Smith issued a general order providing for an amnesty consistent with Davis's July 31 proclamation. Smith gave all soldiers absent from commands east of the Mississippi until September 30 to report. His instructions for mustering men back into the service were significant because they reflected a belief that these men had left commands in Mississippi, Georgia, Tennessee, and perhaps Virginia and made their way home. Men in Arkansas were to report to the camp of instruction at Washington, Texans were ordered to Bonham and Houston, and Louisianans were ordered to Shreveport. Like Davis's proclamation and Lee's order of amnesty, Smith's order withheld amnesty from men who had deserted more than twice. The fact that such a category even existed was indicative of how serious the problem had become. Of equal importance was the demoralizing effect it had on those who had not deserted. J. B. Mitchell of Alabama wrote his father from Chattanooga in August 1863 with the sad news that he could not get a furlough. "It seems very unlike equity to pardon a deserter and allow him twenty days to remain at home," he lamented, "while every application of a good soldier who has done his duty is refused."[17] Thus mercy not only did not stop men from leaving, it undermined the strength of those who stayed and could not legally go home.

The disease had spread from one end of the Confederacy to the other. Everyone seemed to be trying something different to effect a cure or at least alleviate the symptoms. In the East, Lee saw no alternative but to execute deserters without hesitation. In the West, Kirby Smith tried what had already failed for Lee and Davis. At times the commands in the two theaters even worked against one another as officers in commands east of the Mississippi complained that trans-Mississippi commanders ignored their request to return deserters who crossed west over the Mississippi. Gen. William Hardee had actually written Gen. T. C. Holmes in April 1863 about a Capt. Thomas Newton who had either deserted or gone AWOL. Hardee replied, "His is but one of many instances I regret to say, when officers and men of this army have found refuge from justice in the Trans-Mississippi Department, the successive commanders of which I have learned have habitually refused to give up deserters and absentees without leave upon the application of proper officers." Hardee's frustration was understandable, but placing blame on the Trans-Mississippi Department for problems in his command ignored the situation much closer to home. By late July 1863 desertion had become so prevalent in Mississippi that Hardee instructed Brig. Gen. Jason R. Chalmers to "take energetic measures for the apprehension of deserters from this army with which the country is swarming." Hardee's order came less than a month after the fall of Vicksburg and coincided with the almost complete cessation of letters from Mississippi soldiers and officers to Governor Pettus for leave to go home. There was a reason why the letters had stopped: the men no longer needed Pettus's assistance. The soldiers captured at Vicksburg had been paroled and gone home. Whether they would return when exchanged remained unknown. Soldiers who had not been captured and paroled knew that Mississippi had fallen, and Hardee's order to Chalmers testifies as to what course those men took.[18]

The signs were everywhere. Col. Robert V. Richardson commanded the Twelfth Tennessee Cavalry, a partisan ranger group. In June 1863 he reported on the situation in western Tennessee and northern Mississippi, once again urging the suggestion made by Imboden back in January. Western Tennessee was full of deserters, many of whom were within Union lines. Richardson believed that many of these men would join his partisan group if given the opportunity, and that furthermore, only a fast-moving unit like his could even get within Union lines to reclaim them. Richardson wanted Seddon's permission to bring these men within his command, even though he knew they had deserted from other units. Seddon forwarded Richardson's report and his request on to Davis with a note stating that although the "example is pernicious and of dangerous precedent," it might be the only way to bring deserters within Union lines back into the Confederate army. Davis responded the same way Lee had answered Imboden: "No." The men had to return to their original commands, and once there, if they qualified for amnesty, they might be transferred.[19]

Desertion and retreat were proving a lethal combination for the Confederate army. No deserter beyond Confederate control would come back into the army under the conditions Davis set down. Thus deserters in western Tennessee were effectively lost, and Davis's only alternative would have been to backtrack on a policy of not allowing men to desert from one unit into another. The debate and conflicting policy directives from Lee and Cooper in the spring had already demonstrated how confusing the policy could be. By completely backing down, the Confederacy ran the risk of losing significant numbers of troops to a hodgepodge of partisan commands scattered throughout the South—in effect losing the ability to wage conventional warfare. This was exactly the scenario that Col. Robert Chilton, Lee's chief of staff, suggested to Imboden in November 1863. Chilton forwarded a list of deserters from the Army of Northern Virginia who were serving in Imboden's command. Imboden had ignored Lee's letter of January 1863, keeping not only whatever conscripts he could round up but also deserters from Lee's army. Chilton told Imboden that if men discovered they could desert into enemy lines and thereafter be taken back into partisan units serving close to home, "all anxious to serve in such vicinities have but to desert, thus destroying all military organization and discipline."[20]

Chilton and Lee were correct. Men did believe that desertion would actually allow units to be reorganized. The Ninth Texas Cavalry stood as a stark example of what could happen. In September 1863 one man wrote that Company H reported eleven men missing, Company B had ten men gone, and Company G "as many." The men believed that if enough of them deserted and went west of the Mississippi River, the regiment would be re-formed there and transferred. While what Imboden was doing and Richardson wanted to do may have seemed prudent in the short term as a way to bring deserters back into the army, if such a policy were extended throughout the army it would ultimately destroy it. Pillow believed that desertion from the infantry to the cavalry had already destroyed some units. He told Cooper in August 1863 that desertion from the infantry to the cavalry "is an evil of such magnitude as to demoralize the infantry and endanger its very existence" and claimed that two-thirds of the Mississippi cavalry regiments of Generals Roddey and Chalmers were deserters from the infantry. In September Pillow actually ordered Chalmers to stop the organization of any new cavalry units because the infantry in Mississippi had become so weak that it could not support the cavalry.[21]

August 1863 proved a pivotal month in the Confederate desertion story. Correspondence and official reports coming in from across the Confederacy spoke to the severity of the situation. Union efforts to deal with the influx of deserters during the same period, particularly in the West, confirmed what Confederate officials were seeing. But desertion had even infected places that it had previously touched only briefly. In late August, Gov. M. L. Bonham of South Carolina wrote Governor Vance of North Carolina to complain that armed deserters from North Carolina had begun to spill into South Carolina, threatening the border counties of Pickens, Greenville, and Spartanburg. Bonham pointed to the disloyalty and disaffection of the North Carolinians in the counties bordering South Carolina as the source of the problem. He ordered a unit of South Carolina's state troops to drive these men out, but at best all he could do was push them back into North Carolina. Without a concerted action by both Bonham and Vance the deserters simply relocated and waited for the opportunity to cross the border again. While Bonham had not underestimated the threat, he may have misallocated the blame. Many of these men were South Carolinians. Disaffection in the Greenville district and other upper South Carolina districts had reached extreme proportions, and deserters moved in groups of forty to fifty, plowed their fields, distilled liquor, and mended fences—activities undertaken by men who had returned "home." There were almost a thousand of them, and they controlled forty to sixty miles of the northern border areas. At Gowensville, northeast of Greenville, deserters had built a log fort for defense, and even Vance agreed that something had to be done to confront such an organized force. In response to Bonham's request for a coordinated effort, Vance ordered the state militias of Jackson and Transylvania counties to move to the South Carolina border and cooperate with the South Carolina state troops. The presence of a small deserter army along the border between the Carolinas did not occur overnight. It reflected a problem that began earlier and had never been completely squelched. In February 1863 Capt. E. Boykin was ordered to take a detachment to aid the sheriff of Marion County in arresting deserters and drafter evaders. Boykin was ordered to move quickly and with as much secrecy as possible because the deserters had concealed themselves a few miles from the North Carolina border and could flee beyond his reach if alerted. Events seven months later indicated that was exactly what happened. By September 1863 desertion had spread in some way into all eleven Confederate states.[22]

Not even Florida escaped the consequences of desertion. In the fall 1863 elections, Confederate deserters won positions as justice of the peace and seats on the county commissioner's court. Gov. John Milton of Florida was at a loss as to what to do and told Seddon that under Florida law he might be obligated to issue commissions to the new officials. Milton offered to withhold their commissions unless ordered to do so by the attorney general of Florida, but he added that electing deserters was only the surface of the problem in Florida. "There are deserters from the Confederate service who are citizens of this state and other states whose influence has produced much disloyalty," he wrote, "amounting to a disposition of what is termed 'reconstruction of the United States Government.'"[23]

There were many ways out of military service, and the longer the war dragged on, the more ways emerged to desert the Confederate army. Some simply ran off. R. H. Morris gave a clear description of men just leaving. Stationed at Fort Jackson in February 1863, Morris had come off picket duty and wrote home that "the boys have well nigh all skedadlled and some are leaving tonight." Disenchanted with the war and apparently their officers, Morris said that "within a few days we are all going to try and leave honorable as possible. If we do leave we do not wish to be very hasty there is some scouts sent out to the boys that have left." There were also guerrillas operating in the area, and Morris indicated they would leave armed so as to ensure their own safety and the ability to protect home and family once they returned.[24] Morris described basic desertion: leaving knowing you would be pursued and that the road home was dangerous. John Simmons of Smith County, Texas, described the same thing in August 1863. Stationed at Alexandria, Louisiana, the men in his unit were ill-clothed, half fed, and disgusted with the service. Simmons told his wife that twelve to fifteen men had just headed back to Texas. In September 1863, thirty men from his regiment left one night under cover of darkness, and countless others deserted from other regiments.[25] But there were other ways home, each avenue not only offering something different for the deserter but bringing with it its unique harm to the Confederate war effort.

From 1861 until the late fall of 1863 a prisoner exchange system had existed between the two sides. Captured soldiers were paroled, set free on their promise that they would not take up arms again until they were formally exchanged. Bragg had tried to prevent these men from going home by ordering all parolees to remain in camp. His reasoning was sound: once at home, soldiers who had been officially exchanged would have to be called back into service, and there was no guarantee they would return.

When Vicksburg fell on July 4, 1863, the Union army took more than thirty thousand POWs. The exchange system was still in effect, and these men were paroled. Contrary to Bragg's policy in the Army of Tennessee, the Vicksburg garrison serving under General Pemberton were allowed to go home. In one soldier's words, "the army scattered." Bringing it back again once it was formally exchanged would be crucial. On August 19, 1863, Secretary of War Seddon issued Special Order no. 197. A portion of that order called for the troops paroled at Vicksburg and Port Hudson who received furloughs to go home to report for duty to camps of instruction once their furloughs expired. The order specified four places of assembly: troops from Tennessee would assemble at Chattanooga under Bragg's command, men from Georgia at Atlanta under Gen. Alfred Cumming, Alabamians at Demopolis under Gen. W. M. Gardner, and those from both Mississippi and Louisiana at Morton, Mississippi, under General Hardee.[26] Less than a month earlier, Bragg and his senior officers had expressed the absolute need to replenish the ranks. An exchange of this size might not provide the quarter million men they believed were able to serve, but thirty thousand would surely help as Rosecrans moved toward Chattanooga.

Even before Seddon's special order was issued, word spread that furloughs were going to expire. A circular issued by Joseph Heigler on August 13 indicated that furloughs of men from the Fortieth Alabama paroled at Vicksburg would expire on August 23. Heigler requested help in "rounding these men up," and his notice indicated that transportation would be provided. The problem would be getting men interested in being transported back to the army. On August 27 Hardee began to press for the return of the Vicksburg and Port Hudson parolees. He gave notice that the Alabama camp of instruction had been moved from Demopolis to Enterprise, Mississippi, and called upon all men to report, saying that they should already be there. "Many are absent, you should repair at once." Governor Brown of Georgia confirmed Hardee's fears and the complete inability to get the Vicksburg parolees to return. Brown believed that many of the men had no confidence in Pemberton, their commander, and that only a small portion of the men would obey the call and return.[27] The prison exchange system clearly benefited the Confederacy more than the Union. With armies of unequal strength, a man-for-man exchange increased the proportionate size of the Confederate army. Now, however, the parole system actually facilitated desertion. Men had been given a free ride home and simply would not return. Some had homes behind enemy lines, others simply lived beyond the reach of the Confederate provost guard. It was more than a loss of faith in Pemberton. These men were home, and since many had lost faith in the Confederacy's ability to protect their homes, they were not voluntarily coming back.

Perhaps even more alarming is that once men actually got to the camp of instruction there was no way to ensure they would remain. J. J. Cowan wrote home to his wife from the camp at Enterprise in early December 1863. He had heard rumors that the exchange system was on the verge of collapse. By December there were only ninety men in camp, and Cowan told his wife that half of them were leaving after they got paid that day. As he was writing he got word that he had been exchanged, but he and others had their doubts. The newspapers indicated that the Union would no longer exchange prisoners unless the Confederacy agreed to treat blacks as POWs. Cowan claimed that no Confederate soldier would allow himself to be exchanged for a Negro, and that if the government agreed to such a thing it would lead to the disbanding of the army. On the other hand, knowing how strong the Union stance on black soldiers was, Cowan said many men did not believe they had been "officially exchanged." To take up arms would put them in violation of their parole and subject them to execution if found illegally in the Confederate army. Cowan claimed to believe his government, but it seemed clear from his letter that others did not.[28]

The demise of the exchange system may have driven desertion in yet another way. There is no correspondence or other records that indicate Confederate soldiers understood the distinction Union officials drew between deserters and POWs. By 1863, POWs found it much more difficult to swear an oath and secure their release from prison. The involuntary nature of their coming into Union custody tainted their oath. However, with no exchange system, parole would not be an option. But by deserting, a soldier on the verge of possible capture or who believed that the Confederacy's defeat had become a matter of time could desert and secure the same advantages previously enjoyed by paroled prisoners. The Union would even transport him as far as they maintained control.

Just as desertion undermined a system designed to strengthen the Confederate army, it would also severely hinder one of the few ways the Confederacy had to replenish its manpower: the healing and recovery of the wounded. The hospital records for the Army of Tennessee were kept in large, double-page ledger books. Inside the cover of one book appeared several handwritten notes. The last note stands as a testament to what Confederate hospitals became. Written in pencil is a two-line poem, an ode to desertion: "He who fights and runs away, lives to run another day." The ledger where this appears is the only undated book in the Samuel Hollingsworth Stout Papers. Although his efforts are the subject of one book, Stout has largely been forgotten in the vast abyss of Civil War memory. In a war renowned for its revolutionary aspects, Stout and his accomplishments certainly merit inclusion in the list of groundbreaking developments. Battlefield medicine benefited from the war as much as any other area of military science, in part because the huge number of casualties exposed the backward state of medicine in general and forced both the military and the medical profession to take a much closer look at the nature of disease, infection, and bacteria. Lost in this medical revolution is perhaps the most "military" of the innovations in battlefield medicine: Stout may well have invented the concept of mobile hospitals.[29]

Unlike its larger and more famous counterpart in Virginia, the Army of Tennessee fought over a much larger canvas. From 1862 to 1865 the it moved from middle Tennessee into the Carolinas. As it retreated southward, its hospital system retreated with it. In Virginia, Richmond became the medical center for the Confederate army, and eventually more than twenty hospitals would spring up in Richmond and remain there until the end of the war. Thus in the East medical facilities remained relatively stationary, much like the army they serviced. In the West, Stout developed a virtual archipelago of hospitals that eventually stretched deep into Alabama and Georgia. Linked together by rail, this vast network enabled Stout to send men deep into the South, away from the front, to places out of danger where they might convalesce.[30] However, in an effort to provide better care and a safer environment, Stout also created the means for soldiers in the Army of Tennessee to get home and desert.

At first glance, desertion from hospitals appears incidental to the larger problem of desertion in the field, avoidance of conscription, and failure to return when exchanged. While the numbers identify slightly less than eight thousand total deserters from hospitals in both major theaters, the observations of military commanders and civilian leaders point to a much larger problem. On May 1, 1863, the Confederate Congress approved a bill regulating the granting of furloughs and discharges from hospitals. The bill established procedures for furloughing men and required that all medical discharges be approved by the surgeon general. General Bragg had moved to more stringently regulate furloughs in January 1863, but in consideration of the benefit of allowing men to go home and leave the hospital environment to convalesce, the Confederate Congress allowed the practice to continue. Neither effort appeared to work, because by August 1863, with desertion out of control on all fronts, Sen. Benjamin Hill of Georgia remarked that not one man in three furloughed from a hospital ever returned to the army. That December the Senate took up a bill to repeal the furlough act. Senator Henry of Tennessee argued in favor of the bill, claiming that half of the army's absenteeism was attributable to hospital furloughs. Senator Orr of South Carolina saw no point in repealing a bill that he believed was a "dead letter." In his opinion the law had been totally disregarded anyway; why bother to repeal it? Senator Henry countered that the law was both regarded and respected. More importantly, when a man went into the hospital he passed from control of the commanding general to the surgeon in charge of the hospital, and some law was needed to prevent medical officers from allowing soldiers to leave. Henry's argument prevailed, and on December 29 the Congress passed a bill repealing the hospital furlough act.[31]

It is difficult to determine if the limitation or elimination of furloughs helped the problem. The Register of Confederate Soldiers for 1863 clearly showed men furloughed and thereafter listed as deserting. The number of furloughed men was staggering. The Department of Virginia reported 60,506 men furloughed between September 1862 and August 1864, an average of more than 2,600 a month. Stout's numbers do not exist for that period, but he claimed that during the month of June 1863, 1,882 of the 6,889 soldiers treated in the Tennessee hospital district received furloughs. If Senator Hill was right, the Confederate army lost more than 20,000 soldiers to hospital furloughs when men refused to return. The larger problem seems to be that hospital furloughs did not stop. The Army of Tennessee's records for 1864 show men receiving furloughs and using them to desert. The problem, however, was more complicated than just allowing men a healthy environment in which to convalesce. A man healthy enough to get out of bed, even if still too ill or injured to return to duty, needed to be moved to make room for incoming wounded. Furloughs served to ensure the continued availability of badly needed hospital beds. At the same time, medical passes allowed men to return home legally and gave them the means to get there, often by train. Already feeling he had paid a price for his country, and coming home to a family who must have been hurting, one man in three found it difficult to return to the war.[32]

The bigger concern should have been that men did not need furloughs to use their hospital stay to desert. Hospitals were loosely guarded, if at all. Men wandered from one ward to another, and those detailed to guard the other patients often used the opportunity to take whatever weapon they had been given and desert. With Stout's hospital chain reaching as far south in Georgia as Cuthbert, Fort Gaines, and Albany and to Eufala, Alabama, even men without furloughs were transported deep into the South, nearer to their homes. The Flewellen Hospital, established in Cleveland, Tennessee, on August 5, 1863, moved almost continuously for the next twenty-two months. It traveled as far south at Columbus, Georgia, then west to Mobile, Alabama. From Mobile it went north to Corinth, Mississippi, then south again to Meridian. From Meridian it went east to Selma, Montgomery, and Opelika before finally returning to Montgomery, where it remained for the duration of the war. Thus, whether on the move or at rest, Stout's hospital system provided soldiers with the opportunity to desert under circumstances where recapture was unlikely. Transportation from one hospital to another proved particularly advantageous. H. W. King, an acting assistant surgeon in Atlanta, provided a good account of how easy it was to desert. He left Atlanta with one hundred wounded and sick bound for West Point, Georgia, and then on to Montgomery, Alabama. At West Point the sick and wounded had to be transferred to another train. By 11 p.m. King had lost ten men. Two or three were seen leaving by their comrades, and the remainder took advantage of the throngs at the depot to easily disappear into the crowd. In January 1863 railroad hospital cars were created and special train surgeons were appointed. Frank M. Dennis was the first such man appointed, and he served for more than a year until he was killed on July 18, 1864, in a railroad accident. Dennis routinely complained of men deserting the trains, which were both unguarded and often stopped for long stretches of time en route to their destinations.[33]

Stout's ledgers for the Army of Tennessee suggest that there was less desertion from his hospitals than from the Virginia hospitals. The 2,851 men listed as deserters comes from a line-by-line review of all six ledgers from 1861 to the

"THE NUMBER OF DESERTIONS IS SO GREAT"

end of the war. Given the impressions by Seddon, the congressional concern over furloughs, and Bragg's and Lee's efforts to limit furloughs and the absences that resulted from them, that number seems low. Based on aggregate data in Richmond, it may well be that not all hospital ledgers survived the war. The only work to date on Stout and his hospital system does not attempt a numerical calculation of deserters. Incomplete data may well be the reason. However, even if the data are incomplete, the numbers and patterns of desertion revealed in the ledgers shed valuable light on who deserted and when.[34]

Several things are apparent from the 1863 data. First, most of the desertion from Army of Tennessee hospitals came in 1864, when Stout's mobile hospitals were forced deeper South and the war continued to go badly for the Confederacy. The hospital system stretched its tentacles into Georgia and Alabama, and most of the deserters were from those states. The desertion rate is fairly uniform, although there are more desertions in the summer months, perhaps because combat and casualties increase. These numbers also tell us something else. If the aggregate numbers are correct as set out in the secondary literature on the hospital systems in the East and the West, the ledgers in Stout's papers understate the problem. For example, the ledger that covers June 1863 supports eighteen hundred furloughs, but the desertion numbers in no way reflect that one in three, or six hundred men, did not return. Granted, the 1863 records are badly broken up, with one period covered only by morning reports, and June 1863 falls within that period. It is also not clear because the morning reports and the ledgers may duplicate information. The CSA morning reports in Stout's papers cover the period from April 1863 to July 1864, and it is conceivable that some of the information overlaps with surgeon morning reports. Nevertheless, it is clear that hospitals became easy avenues of escape for men who lived in the Deep South. Even if the numbers are low, they show that almost a regiment deserted from Army of Tennessee hospitals in 1863. By themselves the hospital desertion numbers are small, but when combined with other forms of desertion this path home contributed to the Confederate manpower shortage. Men the Confederacy counted on to return did not come back.

With parolees refusing to return, conscripts refusing to muster in, and hospital patients deserting, the path home through Union lines deserves a second look with an emphasis on 1863. One of the shortcomings of the Register lies in the general failure to record the time of desertion. Desertion has to be calculated based upon when these men took the oath. A detailed examination of Georgians determined that the lapse between date of desertion and date of oath swearing and release could be as little as a day and as much as three months. Thus when we look at the dates of release, it is appropriate to assume those dates reflect desertions that occurred thirty to forty-five days earlier.[35]

If we look at the data by state, only Virginians demonstrate any significant oath swearing in the months prior to December 1863. Most states have none or only a handful. Virginia has twenty-seven in October, twenty-four in November, and twenty in December. If the lag time is considered, these numbers reflect desertion beginning in late July or August. However, beginning in December 1863 one trend leaps from the page: Tennesseans were taking the oath-swearing path home. In December 1863, 156 Tennesseans from the sample group swore the oath and went home. With Bragg pushed out of the state by the fall and only Chattanooga under siege, the soldiers from the Volunteer state saw an opportunity to go home, unfettered by the Confederate army. If what Richardson said in June was true—that western Tennessee was substantially behind enemy lines— middle Tennessee was most assuredly in Union control by the late fall of 1863. In late November Grant broke the siege at Chattanooga and drove Bragg back into Georgia. The Tennessee numbers reflect the withdrawal of the Confederate army from the state and to some degree the willingness of the civilian population to abandon the cause. Jason I. Hall of the Ninth Tennessee told his parents in June 1863 that news of home no longer flowed as it once did now that the Union occupied the country. He was "afraid that a great many of our people in order to escape annoyance will take that most detestable of oaths . . . the oath of allegiance to the fed government. I cannot believe that any of my friends will take it."[36] Not only his friends but many of his fellow soldiers would take the oath. Whether because of Bragg's retreat, wavering civilian commitment, or both, the number of Tennessee soldiers swearing the oath remained high between December 1863 and March 1864. In the western theater only Georgia is close to Tennessee. In the East both North Carolina and Virginia show steady desertion to the Union (see table 2).

The North Carolina and Virginia numbers show some desertion to the enemy but nothing to rival that of the Army of Tennessee. While North Carolina's is significant, it is but a small percentage of its total desertion figure, reflecting the fact that North Carolinians did not see the benefits of the Union program. The mountains of western North Carolina had not fallen under Union control, and based on the correspondence from Lee, Imboden, and Joyner, that is where many of them went. With the Union presence in at least part of the state, the

Table 2. Number (from sample) of oath-swearing Confederate deserters to the Union Army, October 1863 to March 1864

	October	November	December	January	February	March
Alabama	0	1	9	23	19	9
Arkansas	0	0	8	22	12	1
N. Carolina	6	4	20	13	25	36
Tennessee	2	0	156	141	76	84
Virginia	27	24	20	63	54	24

Virginia numbers show the opportunity that it may have presented for some Virginians as 1863 came to a close. Joyner had commented on the disruption in the mountain counties, and the number of Virginians deserting to the Union in 1863 reflects a concentration of deserters in those counties.

The numbers are corroborated by the Union's reaction in the fall and winter of 1863. In September, Rosecrans spent all of one day obtaining authority to enlist Alabamians in the service. Whether they took the oath immediately or not, they were clearly deserting in numbers large enough to create an administrative burden and a potential crisis. From Chattanooga on December 12, Grant issued General Order no. 10, whose purpose was to bring some uniformity to the "disposition of deserters from the Confederate armies, within this military division." Grant directed that all such men be taken to the division or detached to the brigade commander, whoever was nearest to the place of surrender. If the commander was satisfied that the deserter desired to quit the Confederate service, he could go home after swearing the oath if his home lay within Union lines, but his arms and accoutrements were to be taken and stored. Passes and rations were allotted to each deserter, who received free passage on military trains and steamships. Grant even provided for employment in quartermaster and engineering departments. To prevent recapture, no Confederate deserter was to be enlisted in the Union army.[37] The lag time between desertion and oath swearing had in part been a product of Union disorganization, and Grant's order tried to alleviate the chaos caused by the wave of Confederate deserters coming into his lines.

Union occupation of the South facilitated its desertion program. As the year began, Private Gammage had assured his friend that the "Fabian" policy worked for the Confederacy. Events had proved just how wrong he had been, and by the end of the year there was no escaping the bitter reality: retreat drove desertion. On December 14, 1863, Brigadier General Chalmers filed a report on his withdrawal from Grenada, Mississippi. Feeling unfairly criticized for the condition of his command when the Union seized Grenada, Chalmers offered an explanation that in many ways described what had happened across the Confederacy that year and the damage desertion caused. His superiors, apparently as high up the chain of command as Lee, blamed him because his men deserted on the retreat from Grenada. Chalmers pointed out how desertion in the wake of retreat had become a recurring Confederate scenario. "General Bragg's Tennesseans always deserted him largely when he fell back from Tennessee," he noted, "General Price's Arkansasians nearly all left him when he retreated from Little Rock, and General Johnston's Mississippians when he fell back from Jackson." Chalmers pointed out that none of these commanders ever received censure because his men deserted. Chalmers lost almost a thousand men from his seventeen-hundred-man command. Desertion had figured prominently in the depletion of his command, but so too had capture at the hands of the enemy. His report implied that he stood accused of improperly deploying his troops. But he pointed out that Vicksburg had fallen and the entire country "was greatly depressed." All but forty men from the Second Arkansas had deserted. Two units totaling 479 men had been sent home by the commander of the state troops because their term of service was about to expire. Ninety-four men got cut off while guarding the bridge over the Tallahatchie River. Two regiments, Falkner's and McGuirk's, had been unavailable to Chalmers because they had been redeployed to arrest stragglers and deserters from Gen. Joseph Johnston's army. Chalmers forwarded Hardee's July 29, 1863, order and added that "the deserters were represented to be in considerable bodies, armed and threatening resistance." He believed that to have ignored Hardee's order under those circumstances would have been a dereliction of duty.[38]

Chalmers's observations of Confederate desertion patterns speak volumes as to what happened to the Confederacy in the West. Until 1864, Lee's army retreated only twice, both times back into Virginia and not out of that state. The Fabian policy never operated in the East. In the West the steady retreat from and through Confederate territory signaled that the Confederacy had abandoned those places to the Union. Men whose homes lay in these areas reacted accordingly no matter where they were from. Chalmers did not know it then, but Johnston followed up his Mississippi experience on a larger scale in Georgia. Georgians reacted just like other soldiers in the West. The desertion not only depleted the army but forced Confederate commanders to fight the Union and try to recover their own soldiers. Hunting deserters took two regiments away from Chalmers's command and left him unable to adequately engage the enemy when the time came.

Once again the common soldier saw the same thing his superiors reported, except he saw events as they unfolded. Alex McGowin, an Alabama boy, joined the Tenth Alabama and served in Bragg's Army of Tennessee. In July 1863 he wrote to his brother Thomas, who still lived in Alabama. The army was retreating toward Chattanooga, and Alex feared that before the year passed Alabama would be surrounded by the enemy. "Yes we all long to see home," he wrote, "but have almost despaired of ever seeing and enjoying sweet home again." He tried to look on the bright side, but it was hard. "If I should again pass home on the railroad as we did last summer it seems to me as if I could not keep from going home. It is hard to bear the name of deserter. Many have deserted from our regiment but not from our company." Men were tired, homesick, and ready to leave. McGowin would have needed transportation to desert, but as Bragg retreated, men from Tennessee did not, and if they did, the Union army stood ready to provide them with all they needed. McGowin saw what Chalmers, Rosecrans, and Grant all reported. As Bragg withdrew, soldiers deserted; some went straight home, but a significant number took advantage of the Union policy. McGowin's home may have been surrounded, but it was not occupied; if he planned to desert he would have to wait, at least until the train passed by home again. For Tennesseans desertion got easier once Bragg reached Chattanooga. McGowin told his sister in early November 1862 that only two hundred yards separated Union and Confederate pickets.[39]

Pvt. J. Searcy served with McGowin in Bragg's army. He did not report desertion, and the tone of his letters reflected a man who had not given up. He did, however, tell his mother that he remained in good spirits despite the fall of Vicksburg and Port Hudson and "the steady retreat being made back to Chattanooga." In fact, it pleased him to report that Bragg had not yet fallen back to Dalton, Georgia.[40] Bragg would indeed retreat to Dalton, and although he would not remain in command long enough to watch it happen, the retreat into Georgia would bring the same results that retreat brought throughout the Confederate West. Men close to home deserted. Southern newspapers confirmed what Chalmers, McGowin, and Searcy reported. The *Knoxville Daily Register* picked up a story in August 1863 from Mobile and Montgomery newspapers that originally ran the previous month. The story indicated that a "considerable number of Tennessee soldiers have deserted from Bragg's Army during the retreat."[41]

In Arkansas, soldiers reported the dreadful effects of retreat on Gen. Sterling Price's army and confirmed once again the "home" aspect of desertion. Lt. James Mitchell served in the Thirty-fourth Arkansas Infantry, and like McGowin and Searcy he witnessed the effects of Price's withdrawal from Little Rock in 1863. Writing to his wife, Lizzie, in September 1863, Mitchell believed the war would not last much longer west of the Mississippi. "Our men have deserted dreadfully since we left L. Rock . . . 11 in all, and some of the best soldiers we had—it is so in the whole army—they will not go South." Mitchell actually identified all eleven men from his company by name. He stayed, but one gathers from his letter that it was not out of devotion to duty. "I shall run no great risk in going home. There are too many Jayhawkers between here and home to make it safe for a few men."[42]

Johnston's command hung in the balance before he retreated. It was not just common soldiers who contemplated leaving, as some officers also entertained the notion of deserting. From Jackson, Mississippi, Horice Mortimer of Eufala, Alabama, wrote his wife, "It is a great struggle for me between duty and desire. At times I get up almost ready to start [for home], but with a kind of despairing sigh, fall back and say to myself, 'wait until after the next fight.'" He told his wife that he had never been as sick and tired of the service as he was then. If it were not for a law that required the commanding general to return deserting officers back to the ranks as privates, Mortimer would not have hesitated. However, as bad as his lot was, he did not want to trade it for that of a common soldier.[43] If officers had grown sick of the service, one could only imagine how disillusioned the enlisted ranks had become. Johnston's retreat provided all the opportunity the soldiers needed to desert.

Soldiers deserted on the march in Mississippi even after Johnston's withdrawal from Jackson in May 1863. The records for Company H of Lowry's Brigade describe what happened when that unit joined others in a march from Brandon to Camden, Mississippi, to meet a Union force of twelve thousand. Companies became mere skeletons of themselves, and after twenty-eight miles and twelve hours, Company H counted only twenty-eight men present for duty. Retreat had become a relative term. Even if moving to meet the enemy, if units left places soldiers called home, they were a good bet to desert.[44]

It is difficult to overestimate the significance of leaving "home." An example Chalmers did not cite, but one that clearly illustrates the effect of leaving home, is that of Gen. Nathan George Evans's Brigade of South Carolina. Stationed in the East, the unit fought at Kinston, North Carolina, in November 1862. Following

"THE NUMBER OF DESERTIONS IS SO GREAT"

a defeat there, the brigade was reassigned to Charleston, South Carolina. On May 11, 1863, it received orders deploying it to Jackson, Mississippi, to reinforce General Johnston. After two years of separation from their families and the attendant hardships of war, these yeoman farmer/soldiers had enough. The order to go west became a signal to desert. Over half of the unit deserted on the train ride to Jackson. But this was not an isolated incident. The Sixteenth South Carolina Volunteers, formed from men in the upper Greenville district of the state, also received orders to go to Jackson as part of the States Rights Gist Brigade. Rather than leave home, they deserted, and the unit arrived so depleted that it had to be replaced by the Fourteenth Mississippi.[45]

Alexander Campbell Hill described a similar situation in Louisiana among his Texas comrades in July 1863. Writing home to a friend, Hill described the demoralizing effect of the fall of Vicksburg and Port Hudson. His unit withdrew as a result of the twin defeats, and he admitted that the retreat disillusioned both citizens and soldiers: "What is to be the future of our little army here I cannot even conjecture. I hope it is done retreating . . . may heaven's mercy forbid that the federal army should ever desperage [disparage] the soil of Texas with their polluted footsteps."[46] It seemed the only solution was to stand and fight. Retreat from a soldier's state brought desertion. Withdrawing soldiers from their state to fight somewhere else likewise depleted the army. Hill hinted that the steady retreat which threatened Texas might also debilitate the army.

Resisting exchange, deserting from the hospital, entering Union lines, and just going home all provided ways out of the Confederate army. In Texas men could cross into Mexico. By 1863 Confederate desertion along the Rio Grande border had reached the same epidemic proportions that characterized other parts of the Confederacy. George W. Payne, a young Texan in the Confederate cavalry at Ringgold Barracks, Rio Grande City, reported that soldiers were deserting and that "fifteen out of our company crossed the river the other day." Like desertion in other parts of the Confederacy, going south into Mexico could be dangerous. In November 1863 Payne deserted with another young man and died at the hands of murderers twenty miles south of Camargo, Mexico.[47]

In addition to these other avenues, there remained at least one more major way to avoid military duty: refusing to comply with the conscription laws. The Conscription Bureau had offices and branches in every state in an effort to replenish the Confederate army. Gideon Pillow, the superintendent of the Volunteer and Conscription Bureau for the departments of Tennessee, Alabama, and Mississippi, had battled the problem since January 1863. By August he not only believed he understood the problems but offered what he deemed the only solution.

Pillow outlined his plan in a letter to Seddon in late August 1863. With Tennessee almost completely under Union control and Mississippi partly occupied and subject to Union incursions at every point along the river, Pillow did not see how either state could provide the conscripts to build the regiments Seddon wanted. Defeat and retreat not only drove desertion but put conscripts beyond Confederate reach. What exasperated Pillow further, however, was the growing practice among state governors to form state cavalry units, composed in large part of men liable to conscription. Disintegrating these commands and finding the conscripts posed a formidable task; Pillow wanted to simply take the units as they were and pull them into the Confederate service. Seddon wanted these units sent to Lee in Virginia, and Pillow agreed, but he could not do so without Seddon's authority. He also specifically asked Seddon to extend his jurisdiction into Georgia.[48]

The men Pillow described had "legally" avoided the draft by enlisting in state units, but Pillow had no better luck retrieving draft dodgers who were simply "laying out" at home. Unable to accomplish its primary purpose, the Conscription Bureau had also become the de facto deserter police for the Confederacy, a task that threatened to completely overwhelm the bureau. Pillow estimated that there were between eight and ten thousand Alabama deserters in the mountains, armed men who would resist efforts to bring them back. Assuming he could recover these deserters, Pillow wanted authority to send them to Lee in Virginia. They had deserted Bragg's army, many two or three times, and sending them back to Bragg made no sense. Pillow claimed that within ten days he would complete the reorganization of the state and that if his efforts could be duplicated in other departments, the Confederate army could double its present strength. The suggestion actually made sense because with Bragg in retreat, sending men back to his army under circumstances where they had already shown a propensity to desert, and would now be closer to their homes, seemed to invite desertion. Assistant Secretary of War John Archibald Campbell agreed. He endorsed Pillow's request and told Seddon flatly, "The rule that deserters shall be returned to their commands, under existing circumstances, is impracticable, and attempts to enforce it in all cases is injurious."[49] It was hard enough to round up conscripts without the added burden of repeatedly arresting deserters and sending them to Bragg, only to have to arrest the same men again, or worse, not be able to recapture them. Pillow's request reopened the debate that had been going on between Lee, Imboden, Seddon, and Richardson. With Pillow offering to send men to Lee rather than take them away, as Imboden had, the offer seemed more appealing. The danger lay in Chilton's warning that men would literally reorganize their own commands by deserting. One also had to keep in mind that Lee's gain would be Bragg's loss. But that is why Pillow wanted authority to draw upon Georgia. Estimates provided to him at the time indicated Georgia had more than forty-two thousand able-bodied men within conscription age who could fill the ranks of Bragg's beleaguered army. Pillow may have been correct, but by August 1863 desertion had literally created a type of "forum shopping" within the Confederate army as soldiers tried to get as close to home as possible and commanders began to place convenience and the hope of recovering soldiers above military discipline.[50]

Pillow's most important recommendation for dealing with the desertion epidemic in 1863 created the most controversy and revealed how the debate within the Confederate government hindered its ability to combat desertion. Pillow believed that the conscription law operated on the faulty assumption that men would come when ordered, "but this we know they will not do." Since voluntary compliance did not exist, the law had woefully failed to provide for an adequate force of officers and men to bring the "reluctant population" into the army. In Pillow's opinion, "No living man can take hold of the present conscript organization, and with its agencies, place the conscript population into the army." Pillow wanted to reorganize the Conscription Bureau and integrate the military officers into the various armies, giving them duties and authority to enforce the laws. In this way the bureau and army could work in concert and become a more efficient organization by making it a quasi-military body. Pillow argued that he had more experience in this area than anyone else and had enjoyed some success in his own department, earning the respect of the commanders in his three-state area. The system he proposed would extend into every Confederate state, "giving harmony to the service and embracing the labor necessary to keep up the armies in the field." By "thus combining the recruiting and conscript service and the labor of gathering up the stragglers, and directing the energies by the same head," Pillow argued, "our armies could be kept full and men would cease to desert or straggle, knowing that there was an organization covering all states with a net-work, making it impossible for them to stay home."[51]

Pillow's conclusions went to the heart of the problem. First, conscription and desertion were now tied together. Men unwilling to show up after being drafted were deserters, and there was no difference between hunting conscripts and hunting deserters. In fact, the bureau had become the Confederate arm responsible for doing both. The key to ending desertion and draft dodging lay in making "home" unsafe and inaccessible. The Confederacy could no longer do that in places the Union army occupied, but it had to be able to reclaim those areas it still controlled. The protection of home had been the Confederacy's rallying cry as it recruited these men. Now, unable to protect these men's homes and provide for their families, they were returning. The only way to stop the desertion was to make home unsafe for soldiers.

Pillow was not alone in his condemnation of the Conscription Bureau's organization. Five days before Pillow made his recommendation for overhauling the bureau, Gen. John Preston assumed control over the entire bureau and concluded that it had failed to work in any state. State recruiting efforts, military authority over conscription in four states, and the continued use of volunteering had destroyed conscription. Conscription had to bend to state and local law rather than being the supreme law of the land to which subordinate subdivisions yielded. Preston believed that if the Confederacy took half its armies and dedicated them to bringing in conscripts and rounding up deserters, it would bring but a tenth of its number. If, however, the bureau had authority to make both the state and the military comply with its orders, it could bring in five times the numbers at half the expense and within a short time. The bureau needed more men, and it had to have the authority to force army commanders to render temporary aid to arrest stragglers and deserters. Although Preston seemed to agree that the system did not work, his suggestions for fixing the system did not involve making the system a military organization. He wanted it brought back into the War Department and run by civilians with cooperation from the states and the military.[52]

Pillow argued that the cooperation Preston sought had not been forthcoming. States resisted efforts to turn their militias into deserter hunters, even though it had become clear that desertion was indeed a state problem. Pillow's recommendation sparked a renewed debate, and everyone concerned began to weigh in with an opinion. Seddon began by writing Johnston regarding Pillow's short-term suggestion of using military authority in Tennessee, Mississippi, and Alabama. Seddon granted Pillow temporary authority to use the military to effect the purposes of the conscription laws and to hunt deserters, but only in the three states where he currently held authority—he would not extend Pillow's authority into Georgia. Seddon explained to Johnston that although he

understood the military's need to recruit, an unbridled effort to round up conscripts and deserters as Pillow suggested had already caused problems. Pillow's
actions in hunting all men avoiding service "not unfrequently is compared to the
press gang, sweeping through the country with little deference either to the law
or the regulations designed to temper its unavoidable rigor, without detracting
from its legal force." Bitter and indignant criticism had come from all sectors in
1862, and the War Department had to be more careful in respecting the rights
and exemptions provided under the Conscription Act. Seddon believed that
Pillow's recommendations would cause more public dissatisfaction than good
in gathering up men.[53]

Preston also responded to Pillow's recommendations, having read Pillow's
August 7, 1863, letter to Cooper that outlined the same suggestions Pillow made
to Seddon two weeks later. Preston saw Pillow's efforts as an attempt to create a
nationwide military organization with Pillow in command. Generals Bragg and
Johnston and Governors Brown of Georgia, Shorter of Alabama, and Harris
of Tennessee had come out in support of Pillow's recommendations. Preston
admitted that when the conscription system began there was no official directive for gathering up conscripts, stragglers, deserters, and absentees. Gradually,
starting with General Order no. 7 in January 1863, deserter duty was made
part of the bureau's mission. The bureau as designed could have adequately
processed men into the army, but no one had contemplated that they would
not come voluntarily. The bureau lacked the resources to bring men back. So
while Pillow was correct that the bureau could not adequately handle the task
at hand, Preston concurred with Seddon that Pillow's methods would do more
harm than good: "Ten armed men in the mountain vastness, sustained as they
are by the sympathies of the people against the appearance of military force[,]
will require fifty of General Pillow's men." Preston believed the only solution
was "the due execution of the law, aided by the civil arm of the states, and that
arm properly sustained by the military force of the government." He insisted
that a plan based solely on military force would fail. Without state intervention,
the Confederacy had no hope of stopping desertion or bringing deserters back
to the army.[54]

Preston's beliefs were colored in part by a need to protect his own job. His
claim that Pillow's methods might cause dissatisfaction seemed to lose weight
given that three governors had endorsed Pillow's recommendations. Brown,
Shorter, and Harris knew full well how much dissension a rigorous military
effort to round up men would cause in their states. As the chief executives they

would face the brunt of the criticism, yet they all understood how serious the problem had become, both for the cause as a whole and in their respective states. They understood firsthand what the statistics, correspondence, and reports on desertion had been saying. Desertion had reached epidemic proportions, and nothing short of drastic measures could rectify the situation.[55] The end of 1863 validated Lee's prediction to Seddon that executing deserters might not be enough, that more drastic action would be required. Pillow now told Seddon that the number of deserters had become so great that they "could not shoot them all." But regardless of any personal motive, Pillow understood the key: home had to be made unsafe for deserters. Unfortunately, home had become unsafe, not for deserters, but for those who stood in their way. Pillow persisted throughout the fall of 1863 in implementing his program of a military-based, Confederacy-wide Conscription Bureau. Although his efforts to radically alter the bureau proved futile, he continued to work. Pillow claimed to have returned seventeen to eighteen thousand men to the Confederate army in September and October, but he believed in September that fully half of the armies of Tennessee and Mississippi had deserted. His report in November 1863 claimed that the number of deserters from the states of Alabama and Mississippi exceeded those for the states of Georgia, South Carolina, North Carolina, and Virginia. Given Tennessee's desertion figures and what we know of North Carolina and Georgia, Pillow's claim for the Mississippi and Alabama desertion numbers may have been high. However, he was in the thick of the hunt, and his firsthand observations at least served as a sense of how numerous deserters were in those regions.[56]

The Conscription Bureau continued to try to do what both Preston and Pillow knew it was incapable of doing with its present complement of officers and men. Efforts continued through the fall and early winter to rally the various branches of the bureau, and calls also went out from Cooper and the Conscription Bureau to commanding officers of regiments, battalions, and companies to prepare detailed lists of all deserters and absentees. Confederate leaders' general impression that desertion had become serious gave rise to a need for accurate data on the numbers of deserters. Robert Kean's appraisal of Cooper had been correct, and Cooper had no idea of the condition of any of his armies. However, he did know he had a severe desertion problem. Taking a cue from Pillow, in October 1863 Cooper issued an order forbidding recruiting officers from issuing any permits for conscripts or deserters to visit their homes for any purpose. The order seems almost absurd. By October 1863, to allow a conscript or a known deserter to return home would be to lose a potential soldier, and no Confederate officer should have needed an order to that effect.[57]

Pillow claimed to have kept records of deserters he collected, and in October he wrote Seddon again, reiterating a suggestion he made back in August, to send deserters from Bragg's army to Lee. He claimed to have six to eight thousand Alabama deserters, all from the disaffected mountain region. Seddon's reply showed just how little the Confederacy had learned in a year and the degree to which certain members of the government still believed that Lee's army was somehow immune to all of the desertion that plagued the Confederacy. Seddon acknowledged receiving Pillow's letter concerning conscripts and deserters from the disaffected regions of Alabama. In parentheses, after deserters, Seddon wrote, "who are, more correctly, only absent without leave or stragglers." After authorizing the transfer of these men to Virginia, he added, "but care must be taken not to make that gallant army a Botany Bay for ruffians or cowards." Seddon and Davis had abandoned their original position of forbidding men who deserted from being transferred to other units. In September, Seddon had authorized conscripts to be sent to Virginia but had refrained from allowing deserters to be sent, fearing the consequences of having Lee's army become a "receptacle for offenders."[58] Apparently Seddon had not read anything Lee had sent him. Desertion was running rampant in his army before and after Gettysburg. It was Lee who wanted to shoot these men and cautioned Seddon about being lenient. Lee actively tried to reclaim deserters from the Shenandoah Valley and the North Carolina mountains. Bragg's reclaimed deserters were no better than his own. Seddon's notion that these men were "absent or stragglers" was a blatant refusal to see reality. Pillow had to go out with armed troops and forcibly pry these men from the mountains of northern Alabama. They had deserted in every sense of the word, and unfortunately, uncoordinated military efforts to recover them were the best that could be hoped for. In other parts of the Confederacy, military units like the one Junius Bragg described in Arkansas met with some success. Bragg described the efforts of a Major Steele in November 1863 who took a cavalry detachment out for a week and caught thirty. He returned, rested two days, and went back out. But Steele's limited success could not obscure the fact that men were deserting and that the Confederacy continued to exhaust its resources in piecemeal efforts to bring them back.[59]

Lost in the desertion story are those soldiers who stayed to fight. As much as it hurt anyone, desertion hurt them and the cause to which they remained loyal. By mid-1863 some believed the Confederacy was finished. W. L. Barrett, a private in a South Carolina regiment in Longstreet's Corps, told his friend Jesse McMahan in July 1863 that the "Confederacy is on her way up the spout." Others, however, continued to believe. On Christmas Day 1863, Pvt. J. C. Conley of the Sixth North Carolina wrote home to his father and family. Camped near Rogersville, Tennessee, he reflected on the desertion that had become so prevalent. He assured his family he was "getting along fine" but admitted that he "was troubled by those men who have gone home, remain there and leave us to carry on the fight alone." Conley could never respect a man who would do such a thing. He felt that if everyone would do his part the war could easily be won without the distress so many people predicted. He closed by saying there was little chance he would be coming home until the war was over. Another letter, written from the Shenandoah Valley in June 1864, showed he was true to his convictions. He remained as resolute about the war and his service in it as he had ever been. What he probably did not know on that Christmas Day in 1863, but may have found out later, was that men going to their own homes and staying there may have left him and others to fight alone, but at least they did not wage war on their own. Perhaps one of the most egregious aspects of Confederate desertion lay in the actions of those who did not go home but who found places of sanctuary in the mountains and swamps of the South. From there they wrecked havoc on Southern civilians and provided one the most glaring example of how the South turned on itself.[60]

The heart of Gideon Pillow's argument for the prevention of desertion lay in making home unsafe for deserters. By 1863, however, the problem had become that home was unsafe for the people living there, and the danger could be traced directly to the Confederate army. Desertion had indeed taken on the qualities of a disease and spread out of the military into the civilian world. More than simply laying out, deserters staked out large areas of the Confederacy from Virginia to Texas and terrorized the civilian population. It is almost the supreme irony that the very conduct which Southerners feared and even attributed to the Union would ultimately be visited upon the South at the hands of its own soldiers.

Confederate politician William Miles had discussed the question of atrocity and retaliation with General Beauregard in October 1862. The Confederate Congress hesitated to adopt the "black flag," as Beauregard advocated, and Miles tried to explain to Beauregard that adopting such a policy would be unwise because the enemy would have too great an advantage while they held Southern cities and large portions of its territory. Occupation gave the Union the power "to arrest non-combatants, put them to death—insult women—burn houses and devastate the localities they occupy." If the Confederacy hung Union soldiers, the Union could not only do likewise "but would rob, murder and ravage in addition." Miles claimed the Union already robbed, murdered, and ravaged, although there is little historical evidence to support atrocity on that level.[1] But by 1863, the rhetoric of the "Union invader" ravaging civilians throughout the South paled in comparison with the reality of Confederate deserters, unable to reach home or with no home to return to, preying on Southern civilians.

Pillow erred in his assumption that making it impossible to return home would stop desertion. Deserters unable to reach home found refuge in the mountains and swamps of the South. As their numbers increased they organized into irregular units, and these bands put to rest one of the greatest fallacies of the Civil War: that the South shared some sense of collective unity and will. To understand the degree to which their were "many Souths," one need only look closely at what Southern men were willing and able to do to the wives, children, and families of other Southern men. This aspect of desertion may well have been the most harmful, but not only because it showed the extent to which the army had lost control of its soldiers. Once they began to operate, these bands crushed soldiers' morale by increasing the degree to which their families were already suffering. Shortages of food, salt, and necessities made life difficult enough. Now actual physical danger stalked Southern civilians.

It seems difficult to imagine Confederate deserters treating Southern civilians with brutality and indifference. However, one must consider that Southern soldiers were a product of the antebellum South, and a good portion of the South prior to the Civil War could best be characterized as frontier. Virginia, North Carolina, South Carolina, and portions of Tennessee had been developing since colonial times, but parts of Georgia, Alabama, Mississippi, Louisiana, Arkansas, and Texas were still isolated and growing when the war began. Historians have argued that the antebellum South maintained an air of violence, and frontiers are characteristically more violent and less orderly.[2] It is also clear that Southern loyalty tended to be local, even familial. A region that did not see itself as a nation had people who were not only accustomed to the harsh realities of rural, frontier life but whose sense of self-reliance led them to believe that all people had to fend for themselves. Their sense of loyalty may have extended to the immediate community, but generally they had no sense of community across state lines or even in places within their state beyond their local community. For example, people in the northwest corner of Georgia, northwest Alabama, and the area bordering Tennessee were more closely connected to one another than they were to other areas within their own states.

The Confederate army drew its soldiers from small localities all over the South. Those who deserted and could not get home found sanctuary in places inhabited by civilian populations to whom they felt no sense of allegiance or obligation. Warfare hardens men, and soldiers who survived the early shock of battle found that over time they became jaded to the death of comrades and the carnage that surrounded them.[3] This indifference to suffering did not stop when they deserted. The ability to abandon the military to some degree evidenced a willingness to put personal concerns above any collective need. When placed in a position where obtaining the essentials necessary for survival required taking them from others, the deserter bands that roamed the South showed no hesitancy to do so. Mark Neely argued that law and order hung in a precarious balance in the Confederacy throughout the war. Southern civilians showed a willingness to sacrifice certain civil rights and freedoms in order to be secure in their persons and property.[4] The looting and killing that became common practice among deserter bands undermined civilian morale and faith in the Confederacy because despite the sacrifices of those on the home front, they remained potential victims of their own soldiers. For those fighting on the front, seeing men desert created a sense of abandonment. When they learned that many of these men had not only abandoned their military duty but had turned on the families of those who continued to fight, disillusionment turned to anger, directed at both the deserters and the government. In a sense, Lizzie Neblett's dark prophecy may have come true. Lizzie had watched her husband, William, go off to war in 1862, and he apparently left with her pregnant. In April 1863 she wrote him of her distress over what the Confederacy had become: "Must I offer up this unborn warrior upon the altar of the country for that country's good—But on the contrary if the warrior turns out to be a maiden must I admonish her to multiply and replenish the earth with boys to fight this country's battles?" From her standpoint, Lizzie saw no end and wondered if the time was coming when "the Confederate states split and civil war is upon us again."[5]

In her groundbreaking 1928 study *Desertion during the Civil War*, Ella Lonn addressed what she called "deserter country." She even provided a useful map that showed concentrations of both Union and Confederate deserters. Using data from the *Official Records*, Lonn concluded that deserter pockets existed in every Confederate state. While her picture of Confederate deserter country is accurate, it is also incomplete. Deserter country encompassed even more of the South than her study suggested. In addition, Lonn argued that Mississippians found sanctuary in North Carolina, that North Carolinians hid in Florida, and that Louisianans lagged behind and hid in Tennessee. Clearly these men had no sense of loyalty to the indigenous population, and that helps to explain the brutality that followed.[6] But not everyone found sanctuary in places far removed from home. The evidence suggests that a significant portion of the terror created by deserters was inflicted on people within their own counties. To understand how this could be possible, one need only see the extent to which the South did not wholly support the war. Much of the terror and havoc inflicted by deserters came as a result of political differences over secession and the war. Deserters made it difficult for some of their neighbors to remain loyal Confederates, slowly sapping the life out of the Confederacy.

The possibility that deserters could become a threat to the Confederate home front surfaced in 1862. General Hindman saw evidence of it in Arkansas, as did Andrew Johnson in Tennessee. As Bragg moved out of Tennessee toward Kentucky in the late summer of 1862, Confederate soldiers saw signs of the bushwhacking tactics that would become commonplace later. Although these tactics were not attributed to deserters, those who observed the practice also took the time to evaluate the local population. Pvt. J. Searcy wrote home on August 31, 1862, from Dunlap, Tennessee. Bragg's army stood poised to invade Kentucky, and Searcy took time to evaluate the country and the people. He did not hold Tennesseans in high regard. Although the corn crop in eastern Tennessee seemed fine, "the people look fit only for the rocks." Searcy had not seen one house fit to live in and "only one or two honest looking people among the population." The women, he claimed, "are still worse, such people as you would suppose traitors to be made of." Searcy heard word of bushwhackers in the rocks and recounted an incident where one fired at his unit and got away.[7] Searcy came from Alabama, a state with its own mountain population that had already shown a propensity to resist the Confederacy. Yet he judged the honesty of the people he encountered by how they appeared. They were not his "people," and he had no qualms about labeling them as traitors or dishonest. His comment that the women "are still worse" leads one to believe that if faced was with the need to survive, he would have had little difficulty taking whatever he needed from them. There is no evidence that Searcy ever deserted, and certainly nothing to point to his taking up with a deserter band, but his observations raise the question of what he would have been willing to do had he been unable to get home to Alabama and had taken refuge in the mountains of eastern Tennessee.

Other soldiers had similar experiences. Just as citizens in northern Mississippi sold food for exorbitant prices and farmers removed their well buckets, Tennessee likewise mistreated soldiers. Pvt. Hugh McLaurin, from Mississippi, told his sister that Tennesseans charged triple for everything. Writing home from along the line of Bragg's retreat out of middle Tennessee, he claimed that everyone in Tennessee was a "Union man." McLaurin actually confronted an "old lady up here [and told her] that Mississippians didn't try to fool them when they sold them water, but the people up here did. I told her that when they wanted to sell water up here they mixed a little milk with it and sold it for milk. I tell you the old woman didn't talk about water to me anymore."

"WAR OF THE MOST WRETCHED AND SAVAGE CHARACTER"

These kinds of relationships between citizens and soldiers fostered an "every man for himself" mind-set that was already thriving in the South. Citizens extorted from one another to the injury of soldiers' families and each other. Soldiers routinely foraged for food or the Confederacy impressed it, and even when this was done legally under military auspices, citizens were deprived of food and supplies they could not spare. When citizens in turn extorted from soldiers, a belief that many had harbored from the beginning of the war was reinforced, that home and family was locality-specific and Southerners did not have enough in common to make them a cohesive unit capable of withstanding the rigors of war.[8]

William Nicholson, a Texan, had the opportunity to compare Tennesseans and Georgians. He did not share McLaurin's view of Tennesseans, but he found Georgians unpatriotic, particularly in the wake of Vicksburg. "There is a great difference between Georgians and Tennesseans," he wrote his sister in July 1863. "The former are not near as self sacrificing and patriotic as the latter, they love their pursuits. It may be that they have never felt the ravages of war as dealt by the enemy which causes the apparent difference." Nicholson did not understand what war had done to Georgia even without the ravages of the enemy. His comments, although not as scathing as those of other Southern soldiers, showed an inability to understand others' hardships—an absence of empathy that would make it possible for Southern soldiers to inflict harm on their own civilian population.[9]

Citizens also realized how tenuous the connections were among Southerners of different states. E. H. Rutherford of Mississippi, writing to the Cowans, friends who had fled the state into Alabama after the fall of Vicksburg, referred to them as "strangers in a strange land, homeless fugitives." Once in Alabama, the Cowans were hit by the same extortion that befell Southerners across the Confederacy. They had stopped in Eufala, Alabama, and when James Cowan realized that the local people were exacting the last dollar they could from his wife and other Mississippians, he claimed that "a people so lost to all principles of honesty are not worth defending and the sooner they feel the tyrant's heel and the dissolution of subjugation, the better. I have more respect for the yankees themselves." They felt like strangers in a strange land, yet they had only crossed the border into Alabama. This was hardly the type of cohesion that would foster tolerance when the "strangers" were deserters, with weapons and a willingness to use them to subsist while marooned in a strange land. By 1863 even the civilians in the South had lost any sense of empathy for their own.[10]

Most of the bushwhackers and guerrillas Southern citizens would come to fear lacked the notoriety of men like Bloody Bill Anderson and William Quantrill. These were not the irregular pro-Union or pro-Confederate forces associated with warfare in Kansas and Missouri. That is not to say that these bands and their leaders did not become infamous in their own localities. But unlike Anderson and Quantrill, this was not warfare in the strictest sense; these bands were at war with everyone and allied only to themselves. At least it started that way. One of the many harms caused by deserter bands in the South was to destroy any sense of order in Union-Confederate struggles at the partisan level.[11] In September 1863, when Rosecrans asked for the authority to enlist Alabama deserters as recruits, he told Halleck that the alternative was to deal with deserters as rogue groups of men.

By 1863 deserters had established themselves in all eleven Confederate states as quasi-military forces to be reckoned with. Their primary agenda was survival, which meant fending off Confederate efforts to bring them back to the army and finding sufficient food and clothing to survive in the country. Ironically, Lee's army, the one that Seddon told Pillow he did not want to turn into a "Botany Bay," provided one of the earliest examples of deserters living off civilians. James Kirkpatrick, a Mississippi planter, joined Company C of the Sixteenth Mississippi in 1861 and kept a diary for most of the war. His entry for November 2, 1862, stated, "Marched leisurely and camped in clearing near O.C.H. [Orange Courthouse]. On this march not half the army kept up. Straggling had become a practice that needs to be revisited by severe punishment. It has gone so long unpunished that it has become popular. The stragglers will range throughout the country in the wake of an army & sometimes ahead of it, living off citizens, plundering and pillaging."[12]

It is difficult to know which state's civilians suffered the most, but based on reputation alone it would seem that Tennessee and North Carolina had it the worst. Eastern Tennessee has been the subject of numerous studies, and North Carolina, the state with the "most soldiers and the most deserters," also had its share of deserter-driven violence. The problem with eastern Tennessee and other areas like it is that the debate has always been couched as a struggle between Unionists and Confederates. The fight went on between men from each side who stayed home and fought the war on a partisan level. Civilians who were brutalized came to misfortune because of their political beliefs. In 1863 deserter bands arose in the region and added their numbers to the mix. Deserters had only one concern, survival, and in an environment already rife with violence they had no problem plundering homes or fighting with either army, so they posed a serious danger to both soldiers and civilians. Their violence proved indistinguishable from the violence that preceded them in the first two years of the war. Nevertheless, desertion made the situation in eastern Tennessee worse in two ways. First, although the partisan warfare was "guerrilla," clearly defined sides existed and thus some clear legal parameters. Deserter bands blurred, and in some places destroyed, this legal fiction as men with no allegiance preyed on both sides for survival and in turn created the impression—depending on whom they victimized—that one of the two sides had perpetrated the atrocity. Second desertion made the situation worse by making it easier for well-armed partisans to move in and out of the regular Confederate army under the guise of hunting deserters, stragglers, and absentees. Because desertion reached such prolific levels, it became commonplace to detail small units for deserter duty. Some of these details served only to allow men to carry out personal vendettas against alleged Unionist civilians in the region; in effect, desertion allowed a type of furlough into the region to settle personal grudges.[13]

Middle Tennessee, the counties on the Alabama border, and the mountain counties experienced more clearly visible deserter violence. Because middle Tennessee had fewer mountains and swamps to hide out in, the violence most citizens encountered came from groups of deserters on the move, often on their way home. The effect was to force a rural population already devastated by the occupation of two great armies to virtually abandon their most fundamental community institutions, such as villages, towns, schools, churches, and court-houses. One woman from Montgomery County in 1864 claimed to not have seen Clarksville, a major town in that county, for two years. Jesse Cox ventured out to see a sick neighbor in 1863, and it was the first time in three months he had left his farm.[14] A more severe harm befell those unfortunate enough to cross paths with the deserter bands that roamed the mountains of northwest Georgia and northeast Alabama. The two regions had significant contact with Tennessee economically and culturally before the war, and that contact would continue during the war.

Since North Carolina bordered eastern Tennessee, it was inevitable that the partisan war waged in Tennessee would spill over into North Carolina's western mountain counties. However, North Carolina also experienced the effects of non-aligned deserter bands wrecking havoc throughout its mountain regions. In March 1863, General Edney of North Carolina applied to the War Department to have the conscript law suspended in the western counties, and Governor

Vance endorsed the request. Edney hoped to use some of the local conscripts to suppress the marauding bands of deserters and war refugees moving freely through the region. Seddon rejected Edney's application on the ground that it might create a form of civil war between citizens and deserters that would bring about the devastation of the entire region. Seddon offered to send Gen. Daniel Donelson to the area and to use nonconscripted local citizens to assist him in putting down the deserters, hoping that would be sufficient.[15]

It would not be. Desertion into North Carolina's mountains had evolved to the point that makeshift groups of civilians were unable to suppress deserters. Men began by "laying out," often alone, seeking help from friends and taking what they needed clandestinely if it were not offered. At best it meant a harsh existence, moving at night and taking on the habits of animals. But it did not remain that way. Deserters began to move in groups, some as large as a hundred men, forcing their way past bridge and ferry guards and finding refuge in the mountains. With all of their arms and accoutrements they became formidable groups, and by early 1863 they "owned" several mountain counties, at least by night. Friends helped them, and everyone else either helped out of fear or, as evidenced by Edney's application, complied because they were forced to do so. By June 1863 sizable deserter armies existed in Yadkin, Wilkes, and Caldwell counties. Wilkes County became home to a band of five hundred deserters that created a paramilitary unit, fortified their camp, and openly challenged the Confederate army to come and take them. A band of one hundred outliers roamed Cherokee County, disarming Confederate soldiers en route to their units and going on a shooting spree in broad daylight. In Henderson County deserters attacked the home of a prominent citizen where three deserters were being held, freeing them and terrorizing the owner. Even Piedmont counties to the east of Yadkin began to show sizable deserter contingents. It reached a point where people could no longer distinguish between armed deserters, Unionists guerrillas, and outlaws. At times deserters even allied with Unionists just to keep the Confederate authorities out of the mountains. The situation became so grave that Vance asked Seddon to send a unit from Lee's army, and the secretary of war reluctantly sent the Twenty-first and Fifty-sixth North Carolina under Gen. Robert Hoke. An area in Wilkes County known as Trap Hill became infamous because the contingent there grew so strong that it became a quasi-military force and roamed the countryside at will, harassing residents. Despite some limited success, Hoke's unit never found the Trap Hill gang. Once again, however, the efforts to control desertion bred yet another form of harm that further undermined the Confederacy. Soldiers in Hoke's unit succeeded in slowing down the deserter bands, but in the process they began to mistreat the families of deserters. People lost all of their property, and the families of many deserters were deprived of all means of subsistence and left to starve for the winter. Thus the efforts to control the problem ultimately undermined the civilian support that the operation had been designed to engender. By April 1864 Vance delivered to Seddon this sad appraisal of the situation in western North Carolina:

> I beg again to call to your earnest attention the importance of suspending the execution of the conscription laws in the mountain counties of North Carolina. They are filled with Tories and deserters, burning, robbing and murdering. They (the counties) have been robbed and eaten out by Longstreet's command, and have lost their crops by being in the field all day trying to drive back the enemy. Now that Longstreet's command is removed (and all of East Tennessee is in Union hands), the condition will be altogether wretched, and hundreds will go to the enemy for protection and bread.[16]

Not only had desertion in North Carolina depleted the army, terrorized the citizenry, and undermined civilian morale and faith in the government, but it had reached the point that, in combination with other aspects of war, it was driving people to the Union simply to survive.

The wrath of draft dodgers and deserters was also felt in Washington County, in the northeast corner of the state. More accurately, men passed in and out of the county as they raided civilians in Bertie County, which abutted its northwest border. In late 1863 draft dodgers and deserters living in and around Plymouth lurked just west of the United States military post. From there they could reach virtually every plantation in Bertie County by either the Roanoke or Chowan River. From this vantage point they preyed on plantation owners and yeomen alike, with some deserters actually remaining in Bertie County so as to be closer to their prey. John Pool, a local planter, described how four or five of these deserter bands robbed people traveling the local roads and even broke into a widow's home, confined her and a male companion in a room, and looted the main house and the meat house. Pool claimed that no military force could reach the bands because as soon as they become alarmed, they crossed the Chowan or signaled a passing boat on the Roanoke. In one case a planter had died and left his estate in Pool's care. Before Pool could find a suitable person to take charge of the property, the deserters and draft evaders came out of Plymouth, ran off eighty slaves, and robbed the estate of at least $15,000 in property.[17]

Washington and Bertie counties presented unique examples of deserter activity within wealthier plantation regions, but normally deserters took from those who had little to give. In the lower South, they most often found sanctuary and preyed upon the populations living in the mountains or in areas contiguous to swamplands. Hence they took from and terrorized the least-affluent people in those states. The black belts of Georgia, Alabama, and Mississippi did not face the brunt of the deserter problem, although northwest Alabama counties such as Marion had a significant planter population. Deserter violence would also spill into Mississippi's black belt later in the war, but it began in the north and south of the state. The mountain and piney wood regions of all three states would get the worst of the deserter activity.

The deserter problem in northeastern North Carolina added to an already-intense internal struggle among the area's residents. In this case it was the propertied class versus yeomen and laborers. Eventually the poorer Unionist faction utilized guerrilla tactics against its wealthier pro-Confederate adversaries, the plantation owners. Deserter bands confused the situation by preying on both sides with impunity, blurring any clear lines of demarcation and raising the level of anxiety.[18]

The Confederate government realized in the summer of 1863 that its efforts to subdue the deserter pockets in the Atlantic states had failed. In June 1863, Col. George W. Lay, then the acting chief of the Conscription Bureau, called Samuel Cooper's attention to the "evil of desertion from the army, with the determination to avoid and even resist future service [that] appears of late on the increase." Lay expressed a concern that deserters had become much more difficult to deal with because they carried their arms and accoutrements with them and banded together with other deserters and draft evaders. Enrolling officers, now charged with apprehending both draft evaders and deserters, found themselves being shot and the community kept in terror, a "state of things [that] exists more or less in each of our Atlantic states." Lay actually understated the problem when he told Cooper that "the various mischiefs resulting apart from the loss of soldiers to the Army are such as all good citizens are interested in putting down."[19]

The problem lay in the methods used to address the situation. The War Department looked to the conscription agencies to suppress desertion and its attendant ills, but the Conscription Bureau lacked the resources necessary to

"WAR OF THE MOST WRETCHED AND SAVAGE CHARACTER"

address what desertion and draft evasion had become. Trying to get help from the military usually proved futile. Army generals had their hands full dealing with the Union army; they expected state and local authorities to handle the problem. Despite having sent Hoke's two regiments in North Carolina, the military was reluctant to provide any force, even for a short time.[20] What had begun in the early stages of the war as a fifth column behind Confederate lines had literally turned into another front, drawing as much human and financial resources as the Confederacy could possibly feed into the effort with few tangible results. By mid-1863 desertion had not only exploded but had created military forces in the South that, although not as large as either army, proved every bit as formidable because they operated in geographic areas that made them difficult to find and enhanced the defensive capabilities of these forces. These were not just outlaws; they were bands of men with military training and in most cases combat experience. As the Confederacy groped to find a solution it threw citizens and militia against "regulars." The results were predictable. The Confederacy was devoting a significant portion of a nondisposable, male military pool to keep other Confederate soldiers from doing to its home front what it tried to convince Southerners the Union would do if they did not enlist in the Confederate army. The force it tried to use simply could not match its adversary, and it crushed the home front.

In North Carolina it had become clear that notwithstanding the beliefs of Pillow, Bragg, and others as to the untapped reservoir of men, Tarheel men were not coming in to meet the threat of the Union or to fight its own deserter problem. Six days after Pickett's charge ended the fighting at Gettysburg, Vance explained to Davis that he could not provide the seven thousand men Davis had called for. After receiving Seddon's request for troops, Vance issued a proclamation for statewide enrollment, and in his words, "the returns so far are gratifying to our state, but sad to contemplate." Vance said the North Carolina legislature had met in secret session and declined to draft men previously exempted. Vance raised eight hundred men in eastern North Carolina, and he wanted Davis to accept them toward his quota. There were five to six regiments along the Tennessee border that Davis authorized Vance to raise before the latest call, and Vance had to use them to fight the "tories, refugees and deserters who had congregated in the mountains and who carry pillage and murder in their path. It will be impossible to remove them without ruin to the loyal people." Deserter bands had grown so formidable that they had begun to offer their services to the state. Two weeks after telling Davis he could not meet his quota,

Vance wrote to Seddon telling him that there were twelve hundred deserters in the western mountains plundering and robbing the people. "Through their friends they have made me propositions to come out and enlist for defense of this state alone. Shall I accept it?" Despite conceding that the effect on Lee's army would be injurious, Vance saw no other way to get men into the local defense and stop them from devastating the people. Assistant Secretary of War Campbell endorsed the request, claiming that by extending the same offer across the Confederacy forty to fifty thousand men might be brought back into state service. Desertion had become so widespread and the deserter bands so strong that they were literally negotiating with the government. Lizzie Neblett in Texas had been right; it had become a civil war within a civil war. The disaffected soldiers had deserted, and now they negotiated with the Confederacy for terms to keep them from killing Southerners because the Confederacy could not put an adequate force in the field to stop them.[21]

Negotiating with deserters, even when they formed organized groups, proved tantamount to negotiating with terrorists in the twentieth and twenty-first centuries. But by September 1863, the point when all desertion to the enemy appears to really take off, the deserter bands had taken on a character no one had seen coming, one that lacked any American historical comparison. Colonel Lay's sense of desperation sheds light on why Pillow believed that only a military force could adequately deal with the situation.

Lay restated the obvious, that the forces at his disposal had always assumed that deserters would exist singly and unarmed and would receive no support from the local population. Even under that assumption the force had been inadequate, but now the "utter inadequacy now of any force that we command without potential aid from the armies will become apparent." Lay told his superior, John Preston, that desertion in some regions—particularly in central and western North Carolina—had "assumed a very different and more formidable shape and development than could have been anticipated." It was difficult to arrive at any exact numbers, but according to Lay the unquestionable facts were these: Men desert with arms and ammunition. They act as a unit to overrun the guards at bridges and ferries. When they arrive at their chosen localities they organize into bands of fifty to one hundred and sometimes more. Conscript authorities lucky enough to capture anyone admit they did so only by taking a few men by surprise. Deserters are often forced to retreat in the face of superior numbers and firepower, often using "circuitous routes" in order to keep from being intercepted at prearranged sites as they withdraw. Lay described the situ-

"WAR OF THE MOST WRETCHED AND SAVAGE CHARACTER"

ation in Cherokee County, where deserters seized a town, and in Wilkes County, where they continue to drill regularly, and he identified similar bands in Randolph, Catawba, and Yadkin counties. The civilians in the area were screaming for help and saw no end to the reign of terror. The Confederate government had been unable to help them, and now, Lay said, "letters are being sent by those at home to the army stimulating even more desertion." Originally concerned only with survival, the bands had become involved in what Lay described as political intrigue, fostered in part by the editorials coming out of "peace" newspapers like the *Raleigh Standard*. If the military evils that desertion had caused could not be squelched, Lay feared that a sort of civil war would develop within North Carolina. He asked that troops from the nearest local commanders and regular soldiers be detached from the units that had been depleted by desertion.

Lay's letter made its way all the way to Jefferson Davis with endorsements from Preston, Campbell, and Seddon. Campbell commented that the "condition of things in the mountain districts of Georgia and South Carolina menaced the Confederacy as [much as] either of the armies of the United States." Davis replied that his early detachment of Hoke's regiments had anticipated this need. But apparently there would be no other troops forthcoming. Hoke's absence depleted one of the corps in Lee's army, and eventually his effort went too far and his men alienated the civilian population by terrorizing the families of deserters. Although helpful, Hoke's force proved inadequate, and Lay contended that only a permanent detachment of two to three loyal regiments from the main army would suffice. In short, he needed regulars to fight regulars.[22]

Campbell's endorsement hinted at an additional problem already evident in Tennessee and North Carolina: the potential for deserter violence to spill over into contiguous states. Such was the case with South Carolina. John D. Ashmore, the chief enrolling officer for the Fifth Congressional District of South Carolina, had his hands full by early August 1863. His district bordered North Carolina, and he reported to Maj. C. D. Melton, the commandant of conscripts, that upon assuming his responsibilities on June 29, 1863, he found the enrolling offices in the Greenville, Anderson, Pickens, Spartanburg, and Union districts in a state of disarray. Books and records were kept haphazardly, and it was impossible to get an accurate count as to which men were liable for conscription and who had failed to appear. Ashmore determined that a sizable number of conscripts had not appeared and that they had been joined by deserters from the Confederate army. A force totaling more than five hundred deserters now roamed South Carolina's mountain areas abutting North Carolina. On July 13,

1863, Ashmore issued an order to these men to return to duty, but the only effect was to arouse ridicule from the deserters. They occupied 150 miles of the most mountainous terrain in the state, operating in bands of ten, twenty, and thirty, and Ashmore's attempts to seek an interview with their leadership proved futile. They were armed and well organized, and the local citizens claimed that only a military force of like strength had any chance of expelling them. Ashmore laid out in detail the rendezvous points for each deserter group by district. In South Carolina these bands not only harassed the local citizens but made it impossible for the state to send supplies to any Confederate army. Swearing they would die at home before being dragged back to the army, they made it impossible for anyone to obtain horses, food, or any other commodity. Speculation and extortion had risen to a new level as the deserter bands had locked down that part of South Carolina as a source of any type of supply for either the army or citizens in need. It had reached such proportions that Ashmore believed that "if the tramp of the enemy's cavalry were heard in every farm-yard throughout the land, in every tan yard, shoe shop, mill, cotton factory, wool carding machine, store yard, salt depot and slaughter pen, and they were to come with purses in their hand instead of drawn swords and loaded weapons, they could and would command whatever they wanted." To make matters worse, the deserters had begun to distill liquor in the mountains, taking badly needed grain crops by "traversing the country with traveling thrashing machines." No citizen could stand against them for fear of losing both life and property.[23]

The experiences of civilians in South Carolina had added a new element to desertion. Speculation and extortion would continue to drive men home as they received news that their families suffered from the lack of basic necessities, and now deserter bands actually added an economic aspect to desertion and became the source of speculation. More importantly, literally every state in the South had passed some law to control distilleries, and deserters in South Carolina's mountains openly disobeyed that law by stealing grain from farmers and distilling it. Within a few weeks matters got worse and pointed out a disturbing aspect unique to South Carolina. Ashmore identified some new deserters in the mountains as members of the Twenty-second South Carolina. The men had made the journey from Augusta, Georgia, meaning they were not a part of Lee's army. South Carolina's desertion problem now involved men from both armies in the late summer of 1863. Lay had sent out two officers to scout the situation, and they reported back on the building of a log fort at Gowensville, complete with firing loops.[24]

According to Melton, the harm went beyond what Ashmore described. Prior to the deserters' arrival, the areas they now infested had supplied some of the best companies in the service of the state. Their presence dried up that crucial recruiting pool. Poor and ill-informed, the people had identified very little with the struggle to begin with, and now "deserter" had ceased to be a term of disparagement. Worse, desertion from General Evans's brigade as it moved from Charleston to Jackson had bolstered the size of deserter bands in the region. The Sixteenth Regiment of Evans's brigade was made up of men from the mountains, and they quickly settled into the area, creating a strange situation where local Confederate soldiers actually preyed upon their own. Now, Melton conceded, letters coming out of South Carolina to soldiers in both armies told of the hardships and shortages in the region and the depredations committed by the deserters. Melton also observed that what plagued South Carolina likewise infested North Carolina as deserters from Clingman's brigade came into the region daily. Melton had solicited Governor Bonham's help, and he also suggested that Bonham approach Vance about coordinating their efforts to address the problem.[25]

Once again, Robert E. Lee would have the final word. On August 29, 1863, Preston wrote Seddon summarizing the events of the last several months in North and South Carolina. In his letter he asked that the governors of Virginia, North Carolina, South Carolina, and Georgia meet to discuss the problem and agree to cooperate with the Conscription Bureau. Seddon referred Preston's letter to Lee, adding that "some decisive measures are essential to arrest this fearful evil." In his brief response, Lee explained that Hoke had already been detailed for North Carolina and that Captain Boykin's cavalry had been sent by the governor of South Carolina. It was Lee's understanding that arrangements were being made to use men outside conscription age and to place them under the bureau's direction. "I do not know that anything more can be done at present," he wrote. Hoke had helped, but he had not remedied the situation, and Boykin's cavalry was already proving inadequate. The only other measure was to send boys and old men, the only two categories of men "not liable for conscription." Neither group had a chance against seasoned soldiers, hardened by war, fighting for their survival.[26]

The armies of both Lee and Bragg fed South Carolina with deserters, a dubious honor bestowed on the region because of its proximity to both armies. The state tried to respond to the urgency of the problem in December 1863 by passing a stringent deserter law that forced sheriffs to cooperate with state and

Confederate authorities and imposed a fine of one hundred dollars for each offense of noncooperation. It also imposed a fine of five hundred dollars on anyone harboring, aiding, or encouraging deserters. General Johnston actually sent troops to the South Carolina mountains in an effort to bring men from the Sixteenth South Carolina back to Mississippi in what proved to be a long journey for a dry run. For a short time in 1864 a Captain McGuire patrolled the mountain areas around Greenville. He enjoyed limited success and became known by local civilians as a terror to deserters, but his stay lasted only three months and he retired in November 1864. Small bodies of troops continued to be sent to the region until the end of the war, but with no real success. In the end, nothing worked in South Carolina. The *Charleston Courier* reported in March 1864 that deserter bands posing as Gen. John Morgan's cavalry stole livestock in the Pickens District town of Pendleton. Three months later the same paper reported deserters running wild in Greenville, stealing from everyone. The damage continued and even expanded beyond the mountains up to the very end of the war. That December the adjutant general ordered the commander of the state's Eighth Militia to Marion District to suppress a band of deserters killing people and terrorizing the local population. The deserters hid in the bays and swamps and came out only at night. "Our people at home shall not be disturbed by such characters," the adjutant general wrote, "their homes and firesides rendered insecure." Unfortunately, that is exactly what had happened. On January 9, 1865, a man wrote Governor Magrath asking permission to organize a company for local defense against deserters and skulkers. He actually wanted to use deserters as part of the unit. The next day a farmer wrote Magrath to tell him that deserters had broken into his barn and stolen three hundred bushels of rice. In February 1865, Magrath issued an order condemning deserters for taking private property under the guise of being part of General Wheeler's command. Three days after Lee surrendered, a letter to Magrath from the Headquarters District of Western North Carolina described the tremendous demoralization that deserters had caused among the local population in South Carolina. On April 17, 1865, Magrath received a petition from the citizens of Clarendon District requesting permission to raise a local cavalry unit to suppress the deserter bands in the area. The war was over, and deserters continued to prey upon people.[27]

Just north of Tennessee and North Carolina lay Virginia, and it fared little better against the deserter plague. On his travels throughout the state, J. E. Joyner had seen what deserters could do. They had accumulated a vast "number of muskets etc., and in all this country, and avow they shall be used against the Confederacy if there is any attempt to arrest them; and the depredations they commit are immense and outrageous. The papers are advising and urging the people to send them off and not feed nor lodge them, but these gentlemen editors know just nothing about it." Joyner added that the people in the southern Virginia counties and those bordering North Carolina had little home defense and were so cowed and dispirited that they did not even attempt to defend themselves.[28]

Virginia's most disaffected area, West Virginia, broke completely away in 1863 when it became part of the Union. Further south, most notably in the Shenandoah Valley, the presence of Mosby's and Imboden's commands posed problems for deserter bands throughout the war. Imboden's command was full of deserters from Lee's army, but as a rule they did not operate in the bands that characterized eastern Tennessee and North and South Carolina. However, after the war Jubal Early claimed that many deserters took refuge between Loudoun and Fauquier counties and professed to be part of Mosby's command whenever confronted by the Confederate authorities.[29]

Virginia had other mountains in the southwest portion of the state bordering eastern Tennessee, and there the same activities that plagued eastern Tennessee, North Carolina, and South Carolina took place. It is useful to look at the region where Tennessee, Virginia, and North Carolina border one another as being without boundaries, as an area defined in part by terrain and in part by internal strife exacerbated by desertion. Virginia's mountain southwest region experienced severe unrest not only because of internal political struggles but also because of the infusion of Confederate deserters. The most notable example was Floyd County.

Floyd County is considered part of southwestern Virginia. Directly north of Patrick and Carroll counties on the North Carolina border, it became a center for what one historian deemed both active and passive disloyalty during the war. Active disloyalty stemmed from the strong Unionist sentiment among some residents. As in eastern Tennessee and parts of western North Carolina, this division among citizens turned into partisan warfare. The influx of deserters—in this case men actually from the county—added fuel to an already volatile situation. Passive disloyalty took the form of citizen support for Floyd County deserters, and in the end it brought violence, intimidation, and murder to the county. When residents repeatedly sought Confederate assistance to rectify the situation and return the area to some sense of normalcy, the army units undertook a systematic campaign of terror against the families of deserters. In the end, the people remained as disaffected and disenchanted as they had been before. The remedy proved almost as harsh as the disease.[30]

Part of the problem in southwestern Virginia—particularly in Montgomery and Floyd counties—was a strong Unionist contingent. However, that was not the whole story. Judging from the correspondence that describes the energy exerted by the Confederacy, southwestern Virginia got out of control because it simply took the authorities too long to act. Joyner made his observations in the latter part of 1863, but based on official Confederate correspondence, serious efforts to rectify the problem did not get under way until almost a year later. In November 1864, Seddon tried to explain to Davis why yet another part of the Confederacy had become disaffected. The heart of the unrest lay, he said, with a secret association that had been uncovered through the efforts of detectives and spies sent into the area by Brig. Gen. John Echols, the department commander, and a Confederate commissioner, Maj. Henry J. Leory. The organization operated secretly with passwords, signs, and oaths, and its goal appeared to be the encouragement of desertion from the Confederate army. The organization also aided, abetted, harbored, and concealed all deserters coming into the area. Seddon claimed the organization may have been responsible for the death of General Morgan, and because of the service the organization rendered to the Northern war effort, the Union army left the group alone and protected its members' property. As a result of the group's efforts, numerous deserters and other violent men both from the Confederacy and outside its borders had collected in Floyd and Montgomery counties. They plundered and subsisted on the resources of the loyal Confederates and had so terrorized the residents that most would not take up an active defense or divulge the names of the participants. According to Seddon, this deserter organization had become powerful enough to enter the political arena and had elected a sheriff and several justices of the peace. The network had spread throughout southwestern Virginia and into the Shenandoah Valley to the north. Seddon feared their strength had grown to the point that they could do to southwestern Virginia what had been done in West Virginia: create a separate state. Seddon believed the organization had reached into the armies of Early and Lee, giving it a presence from within the military to help drive desertion. Confederate forces had been sent into the region to suppress this organization and reclaim the deserters, and like those in North Carolina, they had met with some success. However, the effort had come too late. The organization's information and communication network had become so strong that it knew the movements of desertion hunters as they were acting. Seddon recommended that the Confederate Congress consider suspending the writ of habeas corpus in the region so that ringleaders and other members could be arrested.[31]

Citizens had seen the effects of the organization even if they did not completely understand the source. In August 1864, two members of Montgomery County's Committee of Safety wrote to Major Leory, having learned of his plan to testify before the Confederate Congress regarding the state of affairs in southwestern Virginia. They wanted to be certain he included the information they had to offer. Montgomery, Giles, Floyd, and other counties adjacent to them had become infested with armed bands of deserters. The property of loyal Confederates was no longer secure, and some property had already been burned and citizens fired upon. The region's reserve forces, mostly militia, had tried to apprehend some of the deserter bands but had been overwhelmed. Those not captured had been dispersed. The presence of a secret society appeared to exist "in our midst," and the deserter bands had grown in strength to the point that they appeared capable of severing the Virginia-Tennessee railroad line.[32]

Leory did indeed make his way to Richmond with papers of introduction from General Echols that included a lengthy report on the situation in southwestern Virginia. Dated September 1, 1864, Echols's report stated that although they had suspected what was transpiring, not until "recently" had they been able to determine the existence and extent of the problem. Leory asked for Confederate assistance in the form of more detectives and the suspension of the writ of habeas corpus to fight the problem. He also feared that Virginia's governor, who had recently learned of the problem, was attempting a solution of his own that would conflict with Leory's, and Leory had appealed to Echols to stop state intervention. Leory's detective had clearly infiltrated the organization, and information continued to flow even after Leory went to Richmond. Through the efforts of Seddon and Echols, J. S. Bocock, the speaker of the Confederate House, returned with Leory to southwestern Virginia for a firsthand appraisal of the situation. Bocock confirmed what Leory had reported but concluded that the Confederate Congress could be of no assistance. "I have advised that the law as it now stands affords no adequate remedy for the evil," he wrote. "My opinion is clear that the only mode of successfully combating this alarming evil is by military authority, which can only be done upon legislation providing for its exercise and relieving it of interference by the civil authorities."[33]

Echols tried with the resources he had. In October 1864 he had requested men and officers to stop the deserter depredations. To its credit, the Confederacy sent men, much as they had in North Carolina, but in their zeal to stamp out the deserter problem they went too far. Although some order was temporarily restored, and deserters were both captured and some even executed, the authorities began deporting deserters' families and other civilians they suspected to be in complicity. This temporarily abated the problem, but the long-term effect was to alienate the civilian population. Echols feared that as soon as the soldiers left the deserter presence would return, and he was right. In early October reports from Montgomery County indicated that deserters from the East were passing through the county every week. They and their families were using three to four cattle a week, in addition to sheep and hogs. Some had tried to go over to the Union but learned they could not get their families through and returned to the county. A concerted military effort had been a good temporary solution, one that might have worked a year before, but in 1864 it served only to provide a hiatus from the problem. Desertion was too far out of control, and as Bocock stated, there was no "adequate remedy" for it as the "law now stands." There also did not appear to be any legislative help coming.[34]

The secret organization went by the name "Heroes of America," and the Confederacy was never able to suppress its activities. By November 1864, Lee and his army stood powerless around Richmond and Petersburg, unable to move. Sheridan had driven Early out of the Shenandoah Valley, and Sherman was days from starting his march to the sea. In southwestern Virginia the deserters had won. The situation had been allowed to grow unchecked, and in the Confederacy's defense, perhaps the organization was as secret and closely guarded as the reports indicated. Still, it is troubling that the real lesson in southwestern Virginia was that General Hindman had been right in Arkansas. Hindman lasted all of seventy days, largely because his methods had proved too harsh. However, they had worked, and what he tried to do in 1862 might well have been the key to victory; it was just that no one understood at the time.

There were other notable instances of desertion in the mountain counties of southwestern Virginia. It is interesting that the counties where the Heroes of America flourished also saw significant desertion to the Union by troops. A unit from Washington County found itself depleted almost entirely from desertion. When we take desertion in Virginia, North Carolina, and South Carolina as a whole, what we see makes Seddon's fear that Lee's army would become a "Botany Bay" sound almost ridiculous. No state and no army was immune.

Desertion actually brought out and defined the regional and local differences in the South in a way that clearly demonstrates the harm caused to country, cause, and citizen by an offense that traditionally had only military implications.[35]

As crippling as organized deserter bands were in the Atlantic states, it may be that the harshest experiences of the war were in the Deep South, particularly Alabama and Mississippi, where deserters ran freely through the mountain and swamp areas. Pillow claimed to know the true size of the deserter problem in Alabama. Data available in the Union's Register of Confederate Deserters provide us an excellent opportunity to look closely at the real numbers and see how large the problem was in the West, and in Alabama in particular.

The flash point came in 1863. The signs had been there, and Union military success in the West made the situation even more acute. There had been efforts to arrest deserters, and T. P. August, the Mississippi inspecting officer for the Conscription Bureau, told Colonel Lay in early August that some had been rounded up. However, August said that they were leaving faster than they could be captured. Based on information from a variety of sources, he estimated that there were at least five thousand deserters, stragglers, and absentees in the state at any one time. Mississippi had enacted a law similar to South Carolina's that obligated local sheriffs to vigilantly arrest Confederate deserters, but August conceded the law was a "dead letter." No one complied, and the courts could no longer compel compliance. August was certain that desertion could have been limited had these measures been undertaken, because "men would have been slow to desert with the certainty of speedy apprehension staring them in the face." Perhaps more telling than his estimations of the problem were August's revelations that even after he traveled to Brandon and Jackson, the records in the state were so poor that he could not ascertain what the troop strength was supposed to be, much less how badly it had been depleted. He feared the situation was about to get worse. Mississippi had significant numbers of men paroled at Vicksburg. By mid-August the call to return had gone out, but they were not returning. August heard rumors that they would resist coming back and were preparing to band together for that express purpose. He blamed the fact that General Pemberton remained in command, and there might have been truth to this, but the correspondence Governor Pettus had received over the preceding year indicates that blaming desertion on Pemberton's continued presence may have just been an excuse. Mississippi suffered in the absence of its soldiers, and many may not have been willing to return regardless of who was in command. In Mississippi, as in Alabama and many of the Atlantic states, public sentiment supported keeping these men home.[36]

The events of August 1863 had been preceded by subtle swings in the preceding months. In February an officer in northern Mississippi reported that just the presence of his unit had facilitated the capture and forwarding of deserters and conscripts to their proper places. In late March a citizen complained to the governor that two men had come to his northern Mississippi county and plundered the citizens under the guise of acting under proper authority to seek out and find goods brought in by the enemy.[37] In March and April a band of twenty-five deserters roamed Simpson County in southern Mississippi. The local sheriff captured and held several of them in jail, but their friends broke them out and soon no one in the county had the courage to stand up to the deserters. Letters from across Mississippi came into Governor Pettus's office between April and August 1863 imploring Pettus to help clear deserters out of Simpson, Scott, Leske, Lawrence, and Marion counties.[38]

According to Pillow, Alabama was in even worse shape than Mississippi. In August 1863 he told Seddon that he could send between eight and ten thousand deserters to Lee from the northern Alabama mountains alone. But as in other parts of the South, these deserters did more than simply hide. Pillow's estimates as of July 1863 reflected deserters in division strength who were robbing, burning, and murdering "the unarmed and defenseless population of the country with impunity." His reports mirrored what commanders in the Atlantic states saw: formidable forces, heavily armed and organized. Pillow blamed the increase on the withdrawal of the Conscription Bureau's cavalry from the region, but he conceded that the deserter force had reached proportions the bureau could not control. The deserters had spread to the whole of the eleven counties in northern and northeastern Alabama, and no one could safely travel the roads. The deserters, although non-aligned, had been joined by the Unionist population that had resisted the Confederacy, at least in spirit, since 1861. Although he had tried all year to return men to the army, Pillow felt that he had lost ground. The small force at his disposal had been driven out of the mountains. Bragg agreed completely with Pillow's assessment of the situation but could not provide men and resources. Pillow believed that central and southern Alabama offered little in the way of recruitment or troop recovery, so any addition to either the Army of Tennessee or the Army of Mississippi had to come from northern Alabama.[39]

Local citizens confirmed Pillow's observations. Not only did Alabama have severe problems with deserters, but the process of collecting them often bru-

"WAR OF THE MOST WRETCHED AND SAVAGE CHARACTER"

talized the civilian population as badly as the deserter bands themselves. An old man from Randolph County named "Mitchell" told the governor of being taken from his home and threatened with hanging and shooting because his son-in-law had deserted and come to the old man's home. The home guard responsible for collecting deserters abused all the citizens of the county, and the only defense citizens had was the law, which did not appear to mean very much. From Youngsville, three citizens wrote Governor Watts describing how deserter bands would come out of the mountain counties, raid, and go back. From St. Clair County came a petition in December 1863 with thirty-four signatories asking Watts to provide assistance in arresting deserters running free through the county. Requests like these created a real problem for Watts. They manifested legitimate civilian needs, but Alabama's state law conflicted with the Confederate law regarding arresting deserters and conscripts. Under Alabama law the Confederate government did not have jurisdiction to coordinate desertion-hunting activities. Watts wanted to know how he could both protect Alabama's citizens and strengthen the Confederate armies without a legal conflict. Pillow had obviously been pushing for national military authority, something Watts's predecessor in the governor's office, John Shorter, supported. Watts followed up his letter to Pillow with one to Seddon, claiming that Alabama's Class II militia could not be removed from the state but could be put to work arresting deserters. By January 1864 the conflict became clear. Watts's Class II militia was apparently subject to the draft, and Watts did not want to expose them to Confederate conscription when they were willing to volunteer at home. He may have had a valid point. Men willing to join the militia might actually join the ranks of the deserters if they were conscripted.[40]

To fill the army's ranks, the Confederacy risked alienating the population and turning deserter hunters into deserters. The choice was either to give up on Alabama as a source of soldiers or to risk replenishing the deserter population; either option would be crippling. Watts pressed for state control of conscription, claiming the Conscription Bureau had proved inefficient. His approach was the opposite of Shorter's, who had endorsed Pillow's plan, and at the end of 1864 the Confederate government rejected Watts's suggestions. Whether it would have made a difference is hard to tell. For Watts it would have ensured that Alabamians stayed at home to protect Alabama.[41]

Pillow was also responsible for Mississippi, and by September 1863 his observations of the Magnolia state confirmed what August had been telling Colonel Lay. Along the Mississippi coast a band of between three and five thousand men had sprung up, and Pillow's sources told him that about five hundred of them were Confederate deserters. What made this group even more damaging to the state and the Confederate cause was the trade they had developed with the Union. Pillow believed that if he could get fully staffed he would be able to drive a great many men back into the army in order to escape arrest.[42]

The year 1864 brought more of the same. Not only did Mississippi remain deserter country, but the deserters began to interfere with yet another aspect of the Confederate war effort: taxation. In late March, Maj. James Hamilton, the controlling quartermaster for taxation in Mississippi and eastern Louisiana, wrote Asst. Adj. Gen. T. M. Jack in Demopolis, Alabama. Hamilton explained that he was responsible for collecting the tax in kind in the Seventh District. "The deserters have overrun and taken possession of the country," he told Jack, and in many cases they had exiled anyone purporting to be loyal to the Confederacy, or sometimes just shot them in cold blood on their doorstep. They had ordered his agent in Jones County to leave, and Hamilton had not heard from him since. In Covington County, deserters had issued an ultimatum to Hamilton's agent to cease and desist from collecting the tax and to take what he had collected and redistribute it to their families. The agent lived in fear for his life. Deserters in Perry and Jones counties raided a tax depot in Augusta, Perry County, overran the small detachment there, and destroyed the public stores. Hamilton admitted that under these circumstances, he could not continue.[43]

Conditions in Mississippi actually improved by mid-1864, but only because the Confederate army dedicated its men and resources to hunting deserters. Lt. Gen. Leonidas Polk spent most of the spring working "energetically" to recover deserters. According to a release from his headquarters in Mississippi, Polk had rounded up almost a thousand men, and desertion and absenteeism had all but disappeared in Jones and Covington counties.[44] But Polk's success was temporary at best. Officials in Mississippi had reported at least five thousand deserters active at any one time; at best, Polk returned 20 percent of them. Although he did return some order to Jones and Covington counties, it disappeared when he did. By the time the order was filed with headquarters showing his returns, Polk was with Johnston in Georgia, retreating in the face of Sherman's advance. Polk himself had but a few weeks to live. His troops would eventually go with Gen. John Bell Hood into Tennessee, where what remained of the Army of Tennessee would disappear in the maelstrom of Franklin and Nashville.

Polk's success highlights a key point: to control desertion and deserter bands, the Confederacy had to militarily occupy its own country—something it proved both unable and unwilling to do. But one must question how effective Polk had been. By early May everyone knew that Sherman had designs on Georgia, and Johnston readied for the onslaught. Polk would have been moving his corps by then. In April 1864, reports came out of Perry and Jones counties that deserter bands still ran free. These bands molested travelers and caused considerable damage to farmers, suggesting that some of the deserters Polk claimed to have driven out may have simply relocated. The report indicated that Perry County deserters had gone down the Pearl River to Honey Island, where they existed in some force and held "the country in awe." Just as had occurred in Virginia, North Carolina, and South Carolina, the problem had begun to spill over into areas nearby. Reports from Marion County, Mississippi, told of deserter bands joining with deserters in Washington Parish, Louisiana, defying the Confederate government and claiming to have a government of their own. Once again, desertion had bred a civil war within another part of the Confederacy.[45]

Deserter resiliency cannot be underestimated. The deserter activity described in April 1864 occurred three weeks after an effort by Col. H. Maury with two hundred cavalry, a battalion of sharpshooters, and a battery of artillery to break up deserter bands in Jones County. Deserters there had threatened to interfere with the repairs being made to the Mobile and Ohio Railroad. In November 1863, correspondence to Johnston and Maury had indicated that deserters made it impossible to operate the line without an armed guard, and the railroad requested seventy-five men from the Confederate army. Maj. Gen. Dabney Maury claimed to have no official report, but he believed that Colonel Maury had performed his task and driven out the deserters. Colonel Maury supposedly executed some of the deserters and brought others back into the army, but Colonel Maury's dispatch confirmed that the deserters had merely relocated, some fleeing to Honey Island and the swamps. Colonel Maury also admitted that deserters had come from Perry and Covington counties to "whip" the cavalry. As he departed, he received a dispatch from "Garner," telling him, "Don't leave a company in Jones County." Maury did not understand the dispatch. As a postscript he told his commander the state of affairs that prevailed in Jones County, namely the want of protection of property provided by even a small body of troops in Perry, Covington, and Green counties. Maury explained that if the Confederacy was not as vigorous there as it had tried to be in Jones County, all of the southern counties in Mississippi would follow.[46]

Colonel Maury's experience brings several aspects of deserter fighting into focus. He brought a regiment, a battalion, and a battery of artillery to drive deserters from Jones County because militia and conscripts could not solve this problem. Having driven them out, he left, and although they appeared to vanish, they had merely relocated. Finally, the warning from "Garner" may have confused Maury, but it should have been clear: if a company was left in Jones County, it would not survive. One hundred men would be slaughtered or driven out. Deserters had literally become the third army in the American Civil War, turning the conflict into a two-front war for the Confederacy.

One soldier's experience demonstrated just how much harm deserters caused in Mississippi and how difficult it would be to remove them permanently. Capt. W. Wirt Thomson of the Twenty-fourth Mississippi returned to his camp in Dalton, Georgia, after a visit to his home in Greene County, Mississippi. Thomson had known before he left camp that Greene County had become home to a large number of deserters and conscripts avoiding service. What he did not realize was the degree to which they had organized and the extent of the violence and bloodshed they brought to his home. At the end of March 1864, Thomson told Seddon that the entire southern and southeastern section of the state had fallen prey to these renegade soldiers. These bands actively sought out loyal Confederates and killed or drove off anyone not willing to abandon the Confederacy. Officers or soldiers still serving in the army risked life and limb by even appearing in these counties. Thomson was impressed not only by their size but also by their ability to quickly form and surround anyone who appeared to threaten their control. He related the story of an officer in the Twenty-fourth Mississippi who went home in February 1864. His house was surrounded in daylight, and he escaped alive only by swearing never to serve in the Confederate army again. His fate was decided by a voice vote on the steps of his house. Thomson explained that every Confederate officer or soldier who was found in the county was given the following options: first, desert the army then and join them; second, take a parole not to molest them or give any information as to their whereabouts or rendezvous points; third, if unwilling to desert, leave the country immediately after taking parole. Citizens were petrified, government stores were in constant jeopardy, and Thomson observed that soldiers from almost every state in the Confederacy were among their numbers. They had a clear chain of command and the most up-to-date weaponry from the North and Europe. They had raised the Union flag over Jones County, and Thomson told Seddon that in his professional opinion, not less than a brigade of well-drilled infantry could exterminate these men. Cavalry alone could never do the job.[47] Thomson's observations revealed that even Confederate soldiers who were fortunate enough to obtain a furlough could not go home without risking death. In an ironic turn to what Pillow had advocated, home had become unsafe for everyone except deserters.

Within three months of Polk's departure the status quo had returned. In August 1864, Major General of Militia W. L. Brandon wrote General Maury from Enterprise, Mississippi. The Conscription Bureau had reported to Brandon that serious disaffection again existed in Jones and Jasper counties. In July and August 1864, Brandon had sent a company of cavalry to Jones County and a company of infantry to Jasper County, and it appeared that the deserters might be working in concert with the Union near Honey Island, with the goal of cutting the Mobile and Ohio Railroad at the same time the Union moved on Mobile. By July 1864 the Confederate provost in Mississippi reported that the deserters had returned in force to Jones and Jasper counties. They had seized 150 cattle originally destined for the Confederate army and turned them loose in the swamps where only the deserter bands could find them. They had also destroyed corn standing in the field. The local provost, H. C. Kelley, asked for a company of regular soldiers, since the unit he currently commanded had nothing but old men and boys and proved no match for the deserters. From September 1864 until January 1865, Pettus's successor as governor, Charles Clarke, continued to receive pleas from local citizens and soldiers regarding deserter bands in the state. One, a petition from citizens of Jones County, wanted Clarke to help clear deserters out in September 1864, four months after Polk left the state.[48]

Polk would not live to learn what happened after he left, since by late April 1864 he was on the move east. Writing from Demopolis, Alabama, he issued orders to duplicate his Mississippi success in Alabama and Tennessee, but time and the Union summer offensive were against him. Polk's success in Mississippi had taken more than a month and required the use of units within his army. His efforts in Alabama and Tennessee required that he move even more rapidly. Therefore, as part of his effort he resorted to using both the carrot and the stick. On April 16, prior to committing troops to hunting deserters, Polk issued a proclamation of amnesty, describing his experience in Mississippi and the return of Mississippians to the army. He then gave all absentees ten days to return to their units, but in no event would the amnesty apply to any man who returned after May 20. Polk hoped that deserters would take advantage of this merciful offering to wipe out "the disgrace which attaches to the[ir] characters." His proclamation stated that deserters had not only shown contempt for the claim their country had upon their services "but by banding themselves together had rendered the property and lives of peaceable citizens insecure and reduced society to the condition of lawlessness and violence."[49]

Ten days after Polk issued his proclamation, the operation began. Just as in Mississippi, it required speed and the use of a significant force of regulars. The plan required three separate forces: Gen. Philip Roddey was to picket the Alabama-Tennessee border, along the Tennessee River from Mississippi all the way across the state; Gen. Samuel Ferguson was to move north, driving these men toward Roddey; and Gen. Francis Cockrell was to proceed north along a line running from Tuscaloosa, sweeping men into the net toward Roddey. Polk added a brigade of Gen. Samuel French's infantry to the operation and then assigned Gen. Stephen Lee to take temporary command of the entire operation. A portion of Lee's cavalry no longer had mounts, and Polk ordered Lee to send the men to infantry units that corresponded to their state of residence, cautioning him to be careful that they did not desert in the process. Five days later, Maj. J. D. Bradford received instructions from Polk's headquarters to proceed from Tuscaloosa and help clear deserters from northern Alabama counties. Bradford was to coordinate his efforts with Roddey and Lee. He was also to be aware of a secret society in northern Alabama, similar to the Heroes of America in southwestern Virginia, made up of citizens and soldiers with the stated purpose of encouraging and facilitating desertion of Confederate soldiers to the enemy.[50] The deserter problems in northern Alabama had reached the level of civilian insurrection, and it is little wonder that Pillow's estimates for northern Alabama were so high. The citizens were helping to drive those numbers up by making it easier to desert to the Union army.

On April 28, 1864, Polk forwarded copies of the operations reports of Maury and Lowry in Mississippi and of Gen. Nathan Bedford Forrest in western Tennessee to Brig. Gen. George Hodge in Selma. Polk indicated that he had taken steps to ensure that the gains made in the deserter sweeps would last. Specifically, he had organized local commands and reopened the courts, both steps he hoped "would make it impossible for the deserters to return and remain away from the army hereafter." While his efforts were clearly well intentioned, they also required things to happen that were beyond his control. Whether the courts would remain open depended in great part on a continued Confederate presence in both Mississippi and western Tennessee. And his local commands had no realistic chance, because as his own operations had demonstrated, only coordinated efforts by regular infantry and cavalry could make even a temporary impression on the deserter problem.[51]

"WAR OF THE MOST WRETCHED AND SAVAGE CHARACTER"

The chaos that deserters caused in Alabama not only carried over from 1863 into 1864 and beyond but provided insight into the extent of the terror and the specifics of deserter conduct. On April 4, 1864, T. H. Baker wrote Maj. Gen. J. C. Denis, the provost marshal general. Baker, who served as chief provost marshal for the Second District of Alabama, enclosed a letter from local militia captain D. P. Watson and informed Denis of the recent activity in the area. Watson had a prisoner, one James Mayfield of Marion County, a deserter who had led an attack with fifteen other men on the home and family of one Mark Russell with the intent to rob, pillage, and possibly murder Russell and his family. Mayfield was wounded and captured, and both Baker and Watson wanted him to be moved to safer quarters before his cohorts tried to rescue him. The deserter activity in Marion, Walker, and north Fayette counties had reached appalling levels. The Confederate military had abandoned the area, and deserters roamed freely. Using Pikeville in Marion County as a base of operation, these bands, one of which Mayfield was a leader, made daily incursions into the adjacent counties to rob and pillage. Anyone suspected of being involved in deserter hunting or recruiting for the Confederate army was seized, hauled off, and usually murdered. Marion County had been completely demoralized by their presence, and Watson wanted Baker to give him a detail of sixty men to rid the county of deserters. Baker had forwarded Watson's request on to Denis with a report that his patrol had found five men tied to trees and shot through the head, all the work of deserters. One of them, McMinn, had been a lieutenant colonel in the army and a prominent citizen. People feared the worst, and Baker confirmed their fears.[52]

What became clear was that success, even temporary, came only with the use of Confederate regulars. In March 1864, the Thirty-fifth Alabama undertook operations in the Tennessee valley around Molton, Decatur, and Russelville. Its commanding officer, Col. S. S. Ives, reported that since arriving on March 14 he had recovered deserters from his own command and others. The job was difficult because the further north in Alabama they went, the more likely it became that they would encounter Union forces, and Ives reported a brief skirmish with the Union that his men won. The part of the country that he felt was most likely to yield deserters he described as a poor, hilly section. Ives had managed to get the loyal citizens in the area to sell him mounts, thus enabling him to turn his infantry into cavalry and to increase the range and effectiveness of his force. Of course, as people in Marion, Walker, and Fayette counties had discovered, that kind of assistance could prove fatal.[53] Desertion's evils had become so many and so widespread that the phenomenon literally redefined harm as time went on. In Alabama a new danger became clear, as citizens terrorized by deserters had to weigh the options of doing nothing and continuing to be preyed upon, or of helping the Confederate authorities and hoping they succeeded. If the Confederate authorities failed, it could mean death for anyone who assisted its efforts.

When large contingents of regulars appeared, deserters simply slid into the terrain and disappeared until the threat moved on. Fayette County, Alabama, served as a good example. When elements of First and Second Mississippi Cavalry moved through they expected to find between 250 and 300 deserters. They captured seven men, but after remaining four days and scouring all parts of the county, both units moved on. The people were described as basically loyal but unable to help. With poor soil and little resources in the area, its population barely subsisted, and the cavalry moved on because the county could not support it and its horses for more than a few days. One suspects that once the cavalry moved the deserters returned.[54]

Much as in South Carolina, nothing worked long-term in Alabama. In August 1864, with Polk dead, Johnston relieved of command, and the Army of Tennessee under siege in Atlanta, the white men of Covington County sought exemptions from the army to stay home and protect the county from deserters running free throughout the area. They began resisting even the militia call because they felt compelled to stay at home to protect their families. By the end of the year, conditions had changed little. On Christmas Day, Daniel S. Hood wrote his brother, John. Daniel had worked to get John out of the army and had secured a petition with 105 citizen signatures. The problem was tracking him down. He told John that deserters had recently raided the county, taking property and livestock, and had moved on through several other counties, killing men as they went. In January 1865 a Hillsboro County man told Alabama adjutant general Hugh Watson that "the woods are full of deserters and outlayers. The home reserves have done all they can to roust these men, but if they get one, it alerts the others and the terrain is so harsh that apprehending them proved impossible."[55]

Georgia's northwest mountains and southeast piney woods made ideal sanctuaries for deserters. In her history, Lonn picked up on the mountain problem but not the concentration in the southeast portion of the state.

Georgia's problems began as early as 1862. Its upcountry mountain region had voted Southern Democrat in the election of 1860 but had then reversed gears and voted strongly against secession, as did the southeastern piney woods. In the north some counties were so strongly Unionist that they sent companies to the Union army. In the winter of 1862–63, reports came from the upcountry indicating that the region had large numbers of tories and that deserters in increasing numbers had found sanctuary in the mountains. Whitfield and Gilmer counties were the first to appear as deserter havens. In June 1863 a Fannin County soldier wrote Governor Brown telling him that any country that could not protect soldiers' families from these bands was not worth fighting for. By October 1863, irregular bands filled with deserters, most likely from Joe Wheeler's Tennessee command, operated as far south as Pike County and north all the way to Dade County, where a place called Nick-a-jack served as a purgatory of sorts on the Alabama, Georgia, and Tennessee border for deserters to hide. Once a haven for runaway slaves, it became a source of safety for another type of runaway during the war. The governor took matters into his own hands as he had for most of the war. An advocate of Pillow's plan to centralize the conscription process under military authority, Brown formed state units that worked in concert with Confederate authorities and swept the Georgia mountains in 1863. He arrested fifty-three citizens and purportedly returned five hundred men of conscription age to the service. The Georgia upcountry, however, benefited from little Union incursion until 1864. In a reversal of the situation in Alabama and Mississippi, loyal Confederates routinely made life for deserters difficult. One hundred Confederate deserters who returned to Walker County in 1863 were hung, despite having formed a home guard to protect their own county.[56]

As far as uncontrolled deserter bands were concerned, Georgia may have benefited from Sherman's invasion in May 1864, since it drove Confederate authority from the area. On June 20, 1864, Sherman created the District of Etowah, which ran from northern Georgia into northern Alabama. Its purpose was to afford protection to the railroad line that served as his artery of supply. Sherman allocated significant men and resources to the area. Under the command of Gen. James B. Steedman, an average of 233 men per mile patrolled the railroad, manning blockhouses, pursuing Confederate raiders of all descriptions, and facilitating the exodus of Southern civilians who remained loyal to the Confederacy. Some were allowed to make their way South, while others found themselves shipped north of the Ohio River. Although Confederate deserters were not the intended beneficiaries of such a program, both they and their families realized a benefit of increased safety in the region. The Union military presence combined with the deportation of pro-Southerners changed the dynamic in the region. Those who stayed were already tired of the war and harbored Unionists sentiments, and hence the disruption and feuding that characterized the region before 1864—and other areas afterward—did not seem as intense in northern Georgia after 1863.[57]

Despite the steps Sherman took, however, pro-Confederate bands continued to roam the area. The irregular warfare took on a clear pro-Union versus pro-Confederate quality, and civilians suffered depending on where their sentiments lay. In December 1864, Robert Battey, a member of Samuel Stout's hospital corps, asked for a thirty day' leave from his post in Meridian, Mississippi, to return to his home in Rome, Georgia. Battey wanted remove his wife and seven children to a safer location because Confederate cavalry deserters were roaming northern Georgia and pillaging the civilian population.[58]

Northern Georgia did not have the corner on deserter activity. In the southern and southeastern part of the state, deserter bands operated with impunity by 1864. Lonn pointed to northern Georgia, specifically Henry, Dade, and Floyd counties, but recent scholarship reveals significant activity of deserter bands in southern Georgia that roamed across the state line into southern Alabama. Most of these men from Georgia appeared to have been eligible for the draft and simply refused to come in. However, the border between Georgia and Alabama was more fluid in the southern part of each state, and deserters from southeast Alabama flowed back and forth across the border.[59]

As was the case in Alabama, southern Georgia's deserter problem boasted a "secret society," in this case one that seemed to initiate the problem of organized bands in the wiregrass regions of both states. In December 1863 an entire command under Gen. James Clanton at Camp Pollard in south-central Alabama laid down their arms and refused to fight. The men, all of whom were from the wiregrass region and led by members of the Peace Society, refused to fight and took oaths to desert, to encourage desertion, and to protect deserters. Gen. Dabney Maury, then the commander of Mobile, arrested more than seventy men and sent them to Mobile for trial. For most of 1863 the swamps of the wiregrass regions of Georgia and Alabama provided sanctuary. Given the nature of the terrain and the ability to move back and forth across state lines, these men were hard to track. Some wiregrass civilians actually served as guides for deserters making their way to the Union lines. However, most deserters in the region chose to simply wait the war out in the swamps, at least initially. Local judges, unless accompanied by a military unit, refused to hold court for antiwar activities. Since citizens tended to be apathetic so long as they were left alone, the region offered relative safety.[60]

However, just as deserters had gotten out of control in other parts of the South, they became a hazard in southern Georgia and southern Alabama. Part of the change came with growth. As the deserter population grew the men began to band together into guerrilla units. Like deserters elsewhere, their primary goal was survival. Roaming through Dale and Clay counties in the southwest corner of Georgia's plantation belt, these bands raided plantations, attacked Confederate army depots, and drove off conscription officers and deserter hunters. One man in Dale County claimed he felt safer when he had fought with Stonewall Jackson in Virginia than he did now in his own home county. Loyal Confederate citizens began pleading with Governor Brown to send troops to drive these bands out.[61] Of course, the problem lay in jurisdiction. Bands driven out of Georgia were likely to slide into the safety of Alabama.

At least two groups achieved notoriety in the region. Ward's Raiders, led by "Speckled" John Ward, began when this former member of the Thirty-fourth Alabama, who had been mustered out of the army, received notification in September 1864 that he had been drafted. He went to the draft board and warned them against trying to bring him in, but his advice fell on deaf ears. When the conscription authorities came after him, Ward killed the conscription officers, formed a small band of deserters and draft dodgers, and set up shop in southeast Alabama. Perhaps the most famous—or infamous—deserter band in the region provides a good example of who these men were. The Confederacy's deserters came from the ranks of some of its best soldiers, and when they left they became some of its most formidable adversaries. John Sanders enlisted in 1861 with Company C of the Thirty-first Georgia. Made up mostly of men from the Alabama counties of Dale, Barbour, Henry, and Coffee, the regiment fought with Stonewall Jackson in Virginia, where Sanders gained a reputation as one of the bravest men in the unit. Initially elected as one of the company's sergeants, Sanders was elected captain by his comrades, but the regimental commander selected another instead. Encouraged by his men to return home and raise another company, Sanders went back to Alabama without an official furlough. Once at home he was considered AWOL by local authorities, so to avoid capture and possible execution he deserted and fled all the way to Florida. There he joined the First Florida Cavalry, a Union regiment, and served admirably until he was placed on "detached duty" in late 1864. He took command of an irregular unit and for the remainder of the war roamed through southeast Alabama, southwest Georgia, and northern Florida.[62]

Deserter activity led to atrocity on both sides, including instances where local Confederate authorities lynched men believed to be deserters. Some of the executed men had ridden with Ward or had been accused of rendering aid to his group. Others had no affiliation with any band and had come home only because their wives or families needed them. Putting aside for a moment the injustice of executing men based on rumor, these acts by and against deserters in southern Georgia and southern Alabama underscored the deep divisions among Southerners over the war, divisions that often changed deserter activity from mere survival into conscious resistance to the Confederacy and aid to the Union. Other bands roamed through the southern wiregrass from Mobile, Alabama, to Macon, Georgia, preying on plantations or poor farmers and lurking in towns for furloughed soldiers or refugees. Citizens in Worth County, Georgia, petitioned Governor Brown for help in October 1864, while others simply tried to protect themselves with vigilante committees. Deserters naturally tried to return home, but often the journey proved difficult and many found sanctuary between the Flint River and Okefenokee Swamp in Georgia. Some were fortunate enough to find sanctuaries specifically designed for them by local Unionists. The most famous sanctuary, Bone Pond, operated by Willis J. Bone in Irwin County, actually welcomed these men and made some pay for their stay by helping to clear land. By the winter of 1864–65 Bone Pond and other sanctuaries in southern Georgia actually called for reuniting with the North.[63]

Deserter encampments in southern Georgia varied from temporary sites in the swamps to established fortifications like those on Blackjack Island in the Okefenokee Swamp. The fortifications on Blackjack Island remained intact for fifteen years after the end of the war, and during the height of the conflict deserters not only survived off the wild game in the area but pillaged cattle herds in the region. Confederate attempts to eliminate these bands proved only moderately successful. Given the inhospitable terrain, the small population, and the area's relative poverty, conscription officers had to be pushed into actively hunting for deserters. The most active period of deserter hunting came in 1864, and the most prolific of these efforts came under the direction of George Washington Lee. Disliked by both his men and his superiors, Lee had few admirable qualities. Early in the war he enjoyed success hunting deserters in northern Georgia and led an expedition through the mountains that brought in five hundred men of conscription age. Unfortunately, he could not duplicate that success in the southern part of the state. Lee's Rangers, as his unit was called, spent four months in the southern Georgia counties of Wilcox, Coffee, Houston, and Clinch. Although Lee made some arrests, his efforts in the region generally failed. By the end of 1864 the Confederate government had all but given up trying to reclaim men from the region, leaving the job to local militia and home guard units. Efforts in Irwin, Berrien, Echols, and Coffee counties beginning in August 1864 produced such poor results that citizens in those areas questioned whether anything could be done to stop the deserter bands. The bands grew so strong by the winter of 1864 that units venturing into southern Georgia found themselves overmatched. Able to move from Georgia into Florida and back, sliding from swamp to swamp, deserters actually hunted the hunters and looted local stores and business establishments up to February 1865. They encouraged citizens in Blackshear, Thomas County, to withhold the tax in kind. As the deserter activity intensified, the local citizenry began to openly question the wisdom of carrying on a war that there was no hope of winning. By the end of the war deserter bands existed in Clay, Early, Decatur, Thomas, Irwin, Coffee, Worth, Berrien, Echols, Clinch, Ware, and Charlton counties. When Union general Benjamin Grierson passed through the lower Chattahoochee Valley in April 1865, he bore witness to what had transpired and the total inability of the Confederacy or local forces to abate the desertion problem. "The country was filled with armed marauders, composed mostly of deserters from the late rebel armies," Grierson wrote, "who have returned to find their families suffering from the neglect of the wealthy leaders, at whose instigation they joined the rebel ranks." It would be difficult to find a more concise summary of the Confederate desertion story.[64]

Florida gets lost in the entire desertion story in much the same way that the state played a backseat role during the war itself. Like most Confederate states, it was divided into regions. The northern portion resembled Georgia in both terrain and socioeconomics. Its plantation belt ran through the middle of the state from the Suwannee to the Apalachia River. Below that region was an area virtually uninhabited by white men. Consistent with what transpired throughout the South, Florida planters refused to change agricultural production from cotton to foodstuffs. By 1863 Florida soldiers knew this and threatened to abandon the fight if things did not change. Whether from the threats or from the Florida laws that created severe penalties for abusing the cotton quota, by 1864 the state's planters had begun to yield to the demand. Unfortunately, as the planters began to come around, shortages of iron hindered the ability to repair essential tools, and the plantations began to disintegrate. As the war progressed the Union army also made serious inroads, particularly in the St. Johns River Valley, and a state that began the war with a negligible Unionist presence quickly changed.

Unionism began in the eastern part of the state with the fall of Jacksonville in 1862, and although some Southern Confederates felt compelled to leave rather than swear an oath, most did not. Unionism alone did not make Florida a dangerous place, but when Confederate desertion combined with the growing Unionist sentiment in the state, both life and property became at risk. The Conscription Act forced men to evaluate their own sense of loyalty and to choose between home and country. Many of them feared for the health and safety of their families, and their concerns were justified. While the draft forced men to choose, the tax and government impressment made the plight of a poor people even worse as the inevitable shortage bred extortion and speculation. As early as May 1862, Union troops passing through Apalachicola found the citizens in "almost starving condition." For Florida men the choice was an easy one, and in 1862 the state's problems with desertion and conscription began. They would continue for the remainder of the war.[65]

In Florida the distinction between deserters (those who joined and left) and layouts (conscripts who refused to come in) completely disappeared. None of them wanted to be in the army, and they found refuge in many of the same places. They quickly banded together for their mutual survival and roamed freely in Lafeyette, Walton, Taylor, Levy, and Washington counties of western Florida and in the area of southwest Florida between Tampa and Ft. Meyers. On the Atlantic coast, deserter bands terrorized Volusia County and to a lesser degree Duval, Putnam, and St. Johns counties. While most deserter activity involved preying on civilians for survival, these last three counties involved conflict between Unionists and Confederates. Florida also provided another good example of how the Union used desertion as a tool to hasten the Confederacy's demise. Union forces provided the deserter groups with arms and supplies when possible, and as early as December 1861 the Union had a policy of accepting these men into the Union service. An ongoing Confederate presence early in the war limited the effectiveness of the recruiting effort, but nonetheless pressure was placed on the Confederacy to occupy and control the region, something it was not able to do for the entire war. In addition, most Confederates did not desert to join another army. However, since the Union was willing to allow Confederate deserters to use Northern weapons and operate on their own, the benefits often exceeded what could have been gained by having them in the

Union army. One group in Taylor County founded an organization called the Independent Union Rangers, wrote a constitution, and swore "true allegiance" to the United States. Despite their pledge of fidelity to the Union, however, they remained mercenaries, swearing to divide all spoils justly, to execute any spies, and to keep the organization and its whereabouts secret under the penalty of death.[66]

By late December 1862 stragglers and deserters skulked about the country freely. Unfortunately, the government's initial inclination was to treat the problem with a degree of leniency, and as happened everywhere else, that solution only made the problem worse. In 1863 and 1864 deserter bands became much more hostile, and Taylor County appeared to be the most dangerous place in Florida. One citizen wrote Governor Milton to say that something had to be done to "check the accumulation of deserters in Taylor County." Disloyalty ran rampant, and people did not feel the need to hide their sentiments. If something was not done quickly, the writer felt, the deserters would soon be difficult to deal with. The problem was that by the time people encouraged action to prevent the problem from getting out of hand, it had already escalated beyond control. Deserter bands that had been content in 1863 with making occasional raids on Confederate patrols, stealing from local plantations, and passing on information to Union blockaders turned to terrorizing entire areas of Florida in 1864. Slaves had to be moved to the interior to prevent them from being stolen. Even sparsely populated southwest Florida fell victim to deserters. By 1864 the region had become a significant supplier of Confederate beef, and deserters stole cattle and drove them south to the Ft. Meyers area, where they turned them over to the Union. The in-kind payment they received, in turn, allowed them to feed their families. Thus desertion harmed the Confederacy in yet another way by feeding its adversaries and taking food away from its own army.[67]

The theft of slaves emphasizes how Florida became a place where deserters preyed on the wealthy as well as the poor. In Lafayette and Levy counties deserters existed in large numbers. Men from as far away as Virginia found sanctuary in the swamps of those two counties and the counties contiguous to them. In Jefferson and Madison counties they raided plantations with impunity. Some of the bands grew so bold that they threatened urban areas like Tallahassee, Marianna, and Madison. West of the Apalachicola River the problem was even greater. Governor Shorter of Alabama complained that deserters used the swamps of the Chopola River as hideouts from which they terrorized both Florida and Alabama. As in southwestern Virginia, deserters managed to "contaminate elected officials" such as the sheriff of Washington County. Although there is no indication that they controlled the political process, they did managed to make the sheriff an ally, a significant advantage considering that states like Mississippi and South Carolina had laws compelling sheriffs to aid in hunting deserters. Governor Milton told Seddon that if deserters were not driven from western Florida, loyal citizens would forfeit their lives and property. It seemed no part of the state was immune. Even southern Florida with its sparse population had its own deserter band. The largest concentration existed in an area within the triangle formed by Tampa, Charlotte Harbor, and Lake Okeechobee.[68]

Deserters in Florida actually began working in concert with the Union, forming a true "fifth column" at times. In addition to providing valuable information, they stole supplies destined for the Confederacy, burned bridges, cut telegraph wires, and destroyed railroad trestles. As the war continued they even joined the Union army in significant numbers. As the Confederacy lost its grip on the state, more Floridian deserters took advantage of the opportunity to join the Union. At one point in the war, 1,290 Florida Confederate men had enlisted in the army, and a significant number had deserted from Confederate service. Late in the war the Union army formed a company in southern Florida composed entirely of Confederate deserters. Perhaps the height of arrogance came in February 1864 when one hundred deserters laid an ambush for Governor Milton just outside Tallahassee. Their objective was to capture Milton and turn him over to a Union blockading vessel. A loyal citizen in Calhoun County learned of the plot in time to warn the governor, who stayed home to avoid capture.[69]

In 1864, when the authorities in Richmond and Tallahassee made a concerted effort to stop the evils that desertion had visited upon the land. One method was to use the partisan ranger concept to form authorized Confederate guerrilla bands to act as counter-insurgency units—in essence to fight fire with fire. However, as militia, local defense leagues, and even Confederate cavalry and infantry discovered all across the South, these bands were organized and in many instances trained, and Florida's deserter-hunting units found the duty to be a nasty business. In their zeal to apprehend deserters, they employed a harshness that engendered sympathy for deserters among the local population. The atrocities committed against deserters' families not only did very little to reduce the numbers of deserters at large but actually increased the incidence of desertion. Men came home seeking retribution for the atrocities committed on their families as part of the government's sweep.[70]

The brunt of the Confederate effort focused on Taylor and Lafayette counties. Col. Henry D. Capers had the unenviable task seeking out and destroying the deserter bands. In March 1864 in Taylor County, home to the Florida Royals, formerly known as the Independent Union Rangers, Capers struck at the home of their leader, William Strickland. Finding no one home, Capers seized ammunition, weapons, supplies, and the organization's constitution. He arrested two deserters and sixteen women and children from the area. The fate of the two deserters remains unknown, but the women and children were taken to a camp and incarcerated in nine crude, double-penned log homes. Several other raids netted the same result: few deserters and lots of women and children. Capers created a wagon train he dubbed the "wagon brigade." Traveling through four counties, Capers and his men forced women and children out of their homes and into deserter camps in Leon County. Their homes were then put to the torch. The operation evokes images of Britain's creation of concentration camps for Boer women and children during the Boer War.[71]

Florida's experience with deserter bands demonstrated many consistencies with the problem throughout the South, while some aspects were unique to the state. The real tragedy for Florida and the Confederacy lay in the total failure to handle the problem. In addition to the harm caused by deserters to the cause and to the citizen population, the Confederacy utterly failed to bring back Florida deserters. Out of 2,219 deserters listed in the official records, only 220—10 percent—were returned to the army.[72]

The story of the deserter army that grew up within the Confederacy would not be complete without considering the trans-Mississippi. General Hindman saw desertion in Arkansas in 1862, and he tried to impose martial law because deserters roamed the state terrorizing the loyal citizenry. The letters and diaries of soldiers stationed in the state reveal that desertion occurred among units stationed there throughout the war. However, after 1862, guerrilla bands made up purely of deserters do not appear with nearly the regularity in Arkansas that they do in other parts of the Confederacy. A thousand Missourians refused to cross the Arkansas River with General Price in 1863, being joined by guerrillas in the northern part of the state. Correspondence of the time reveals at least an inclination toward deserting and bushwhacking. In May 1863, Gov. Thomas C. Reynolds of Missouri wrote to Col. W. P. Johnston that although the Missouri troops liked their commander, General Price, they liked their "own comfort & reputation" more. Price apparently told both Kirby Smith and Reynolds that if

Price were to leave the command, the Missourians would desert in large numbers and "behave badly." Reynolds believed Price was wrong, but he conceded that if anyone tried to take them to Kentucky or too far into Arkansas they would not stay. Reynolds then revealed something intriguing about the region: Missourians had "a horror of Arkansas and its bare mountains, and the old feud in 1861 between them and the Arkansasians can still be traced in their feelings." Since Price's departure, Reynolds added, the willingness of Missourians to continue to follow him had its basis in wanting to use the facilities of Arkansas to desert and return home or to take up bushwhacking. Apparently any love of Price had its physical limits at the Arkansas River, and once they deserted they roamed through an area in an armed band, preying on people they already held in contempt. Reynolds admitted that the Missouri troops were not well liked and that an invasion of Missouri would delight Arkansas's civilian population.[73]

Unfortunately for citizens of northern Arkansas, the Missourians did not leave, at least not all of them. However, while one cannot underestimate the harm that these men caused, Arkansas's home-front story was not dominated by desertion. As historian Robert Mackey put it, after 1862 Arkansas became a war of a thousand skirmishes between regulars and irregulars and between irregulars themselves. Guerrilla activity in Arkansas, even among Confederates, was actually "organized" by the Confederate army. While some deserters found their way into these units, they did not dominate them as they did in other states, nor did they organize into separate bands to the degree that prevailed throughout the Confederacy. However, the twin specters of defeat and retreat plagued Arkansas as it had the rest of the Confederacy. When General Price withdrew from his ill-fated Missouri expedition in the fall of 1864, isolated bands of deserters and stragglers joined the "official" Confederate bushwhackers. These deserters swelled the ranks of irregular bands and in general created problems for the Union and its sympathizers. However, loyal Confederate citizens suffered as well. In the last two years of the war, both major armies, jayhawkers, and bushwhackers of all varieties preyed upon the civilian population in order to sustain the war they all waged against one another. In essence they all competed to see who would burn the barns, steal the livestock, waste the corn, and drive off the slaves. In the end it mattered little to civilians which party perpetrated the act, since the suffering was the same. This complete breakdown of social order in Arkansas made it difficult to determine the extent to which deserters contributed to the chaos and civilian abuse.[74]

However, the desertion numbers in Arkansas would have been sufficient to cause this kind of harm. In September 1863, Col. William F. Cloud of the Second Kansas Cavalry reported on his activities in Arkansas and told his superiors that "the people come to me in the hundreds, and beg of me to stand by them and keep them from being taken by the conscript officers or from being taken back to the rebel army from which they have deserted." Many deserters brought their own guns and tried to join the Union army; others needed weapons, and Cloud recommended arming these men. Gen. William L. Cabell knew Arkansas had deserters running free within its borders, because many of them were his. In 1863 his unit, the First Arkansas Cavalry, attacked the Union post at Fayetteville and was beaten back. Afterward Cabell reported the steady decline of his unit strength from desertion, and by September 1863 only nine hundred men remained. During one skirmish he had to post a guard on eighty deserters to keep them from running off again. To add insult to injury, the force that defeated Cabell at Fayetteville, the First Arkansas, was a Union unit made up of Confederate deserters.[75]

Louisiana also seemed to lack the deserter dynamic that existed in the Atlantic and Deep South states. Although deserter bands found safety in the state, such as the one that crossed over from Mississippi and set up in Washington Parish declaring themselves separate from the Confederacy, the precise role that deserters played in the guerrilla warfare and bushwhacking that took place in Louisiana is difficult to surmise. Louisiana's slide into chaos and guerrilla war began with the Union occupation, in this case New Orleans in 1862. The most severe consequence of the sustained Union presence became the deterioration and demise of Confederate and local authority that maintained law and order. The other consequence was that the Confederate government virtually gave up on its efforts to reclaim the state, at least from the East. This in turn forced Governor Moore to fend off the Union on his own, and he took the only avenue available to him, the creation of partisan groups. In effect, Moore opened a Pandora's box in Louisiana, and while desertion played a role in what followed, one must ask how large a factor it was in the chaos that followed.[76]

West of Washington Parish in 1863, a band of three hundred skulkers and deserters plundered local neighborhoods, routing home guards and keeping the civilian population in a state of fear. Led by a Cajun man named Carrier, locals called the group the "clan," and because Southerners did not want to believe their own people could be responsible for such outrages, many thought the group was pro-Union. While probably not active supporters of the Union army or cause, the clan had formed a truce of sorts with the Union invaders. In exchange for information about and navigation through Louisiana's treacherous swamplands, the Union informally agreed to allow the group to plunder their own pro-Southern neighbors. With militia and home guards incapable of dealing with the irregulars, local authorities turned to Gen. Richard Taylor and his Confederate units. Taylor sent two companies of Texas cavalry into the area on the night of August 8, 1863, and the seventy-five mounted Confederates, under the command of Capt. A. A. West, moved against the clan. They took the area by surprise, surrounded homes where suspected deserters lived, broke in, and seized the men half asleep. With women wailing in the background, begging in French to spare their men, Taylor's troopers drove the deserters off in a group. The night's work netted about a dozen deserters, who were then turned over to home guards for escort to Opelousas for trial.[77]

The operation had almost been too easy. The next day would not go so smoothly. At breakfast that morning the guerrillas retaliated. Fifty men ambushed several Texans foraging for breakfast at the home of two free blacks. Appearing from the woods, the bushwhackers were upon the Confederates before they realized what was happening. Surprised and disorganized, the Confederate regulars were no match for the clan, and after suffering several casualties they fled back to the main party. Taylor immediately reinforced his cavalry with the Second Louisiana Cavalry and the remainder of the Fifth Texas Cavalry, and on August 10 the reinforced unit, now three hundred strong, swept back in to the clan camp. Several members of Taylor's unit were wounded, and one man died. Most of the clan fled, but four men were captured and shot on the scene, to the horror of their families who stood watching. The operation effectively destroyed the clan, and as a result of Taylor's efforts some deserters and conscripts actually turned themselves in to the authorities.[78]

To the extent that desertion played a role in the Louisiana home front, it resulted from a flaw in the Union's program to induce Confederate desertion. Until at least December 1863 many Louisiana deserters either refused to swear an oath to the United States or, once having sworn it, refused to honor their word. The problem was their military obligation to the Union once they took the oath. Like many freed blacks, Confederate oath swearers in parts of Louisiana occupied by the Union found themselves subject to the Union conscription law passed in 1863. Many of these men wanted to remain neutral, and when confronted with the choice of joining the Confederate army or being drafted by the Union they withdrew into deserter guerrilla camps and fought both sides in an effort to stay out of both armies. Grant cured the problem in December 1863 by exempting oath swearers from any form of Union service, but the damage had been done. When the two main armies moved out of southern Louisiana to other places, the conflict of pro-Confederate versus pro-Unionist returned and many of these guerrilla bands found themselves hunted by both Union and Confederate regulars who remained in the area to maintain order. However, both armies soon discovered how difficult it was to track down and subdue bands that could retreat into the swamps and disappear.[79]

The clan example does not appear to have been an isolated incident. Guerrilla bands remained prevalent in Louisiana up to the end of the war. In February 1865, Gov. Henry Allen authorized the issuance of firearms to members of the Louisiana legislature for distribution to their respective parishes. The goal was to allow citizens to protect themselves against predatory bands of jayhawkers. Allen identified the bands as pro-Union, but there is no evidence to clearly identify their allegiance. Given what was happening to Louisiana's soldiers in 1865, there can be little doubt that at least some of these bands contained Confederate deserters. The only condition for issuance of weapons was a certified statement by the parish legislator that his parish was "infested by such bands of predatory jayhawkers."[80]

The situation in Louisiana seemed to justify the order to issue weapons. Desertion in the northern part of the state reached epidemic proportions in 1865, with renegade bands roaming over the entire area from the Red River to the Mississippi. The groups varied in size from fifty to five hundred men, and a resident of Monroe claimed they maintained a "reign of terror" over the entire area. Allen's directive in February 1865 came after the Louisiana legislature authorized the distribution of ten pounds of powder and a thousand percussion caps to each legislator. It is a testament to the desperation of the times that a law providing the means for every man to defend himself represented the last act of the Confederate Louisiana legislature during the war. In essence it was one last act of defiance as the legal body that signified Confederate Louisiana drew its final breath, fighting chaos and disorder in conditions caused in no small part by Confederate desertion.[81]

At the far end of the Confederacy, Texas seemed to exist almost beyond the war itself. Texans fought in both major armies, serving in Arkansas, Louisiana, and at home. Yet Texas seemed to survive some of the more severe consequences of the war, specifically conquest. The eastern end of the trans-Mississippi saw Union occupation begin in 1862, dictating the course of the war for civilians in both Arkansas and Louisiana. Although Texas briefly relinquished Galveston, for most of the war the Union army could not gain a foothold in the state. However, like the rest of the Confederacy, Texas suffered. Shortages of food and necessities, inflation, extortion, speculation, and Indian raids all plagued the land. In fact, Texas suffered from desertion and the chaos that it brought to the home front to a greater degree than anywhere else in the trans-Mississippi. Long before Texans walked away from Kirby Smith's army in May 1865, deserters roamed across parts of the state, including the hill country of central Texas where its capital lay.

The presence of deserter bands in Texas resulted in part from the Confederate government's effort to crush the strong Unionist sentiment in northern Texas that surfaced before the war and continued after secession. Rumors of a Peace Party and secret societies abounded as the war began, and even Gov. Sam Houston opposed secession, a stance that resulted in his removal from office on March 16, 1861, for refusing to swear allegiance to the Confederacy. On January 15, 1861, two weeks before Texas seceded, residents of northern Texas circulated a document calling for that portion of the state to secede and remain in the Union. In 1862 Confederate conscription intensified the Unionist fervor because it forced people who remained loyal to the Union to fight for a country they did not support, and northern Texas was at the forefront of the opposition. Cooke County was not only the center of unrest there, but it would be the site of one of the most infamous incidents of the war, the Great Hanging of Gainesville.[82]

Although Texas was not technically a border state, its northern border ran along Indian Territory. From the beginning of the war, Texas citizens and officials feared a possible Union invasion using Indian Territory as an avenue of approach. With rumors of attack flying, clear evidence surfaced of a Peace Party or Union League in northern Texas. The group had passwords, handshakes, and signals and swore an oath to defend the United States Constitution. Their activities allegedly included hoarding ammunition and weapons to aid the Union invasion and communicating with Northern guerrillas. On October 1, 1862, local officials acting on these rumors swept into Cooke County and arrested more than seventy people. James Bourland, the local provost marshal charged with enforcing conscription and a slave owner, made it his personal goal to wipe out all dissent in his jurisdiction. Over the next ten days eight more men became prisoners as the local citizenry put the members of the Peace Party on trial. In the first week seven people were condemned and sentenced to hang, but when word got out that the seven condemned prisoners would be the only

"WAR OF THE MOST WRETCHED AND SAVAGE CHARACTER"

ones hung, the local mob that had watched the entire proceeding demanded that fourteen more people be lynched. The court capitulated and turned all the prisoners over to the mob, which quickly executed them. The bloodshed did not end there, however. On October 16, Col. William C. Young was murdered and the local citizenry blamed the Peace Party, claiming Young was killed in reprisal for the hangings. Within three days dozens more had been arrested, and on October 19 nineteen more people hung, two every hour. Aside from the tremendous animosity that developed between northern Texans and the rest of the state's residents, the events of October 1862 made its an ideal haven for Confederate deserters and conscripts unwilling to report.[83]

This entire area became the responsibility of Gen. Henry Eustace McCulloch. McCulloch possessed the kind of credentials one would expect to find in a man who hunted deserters, conscripts, and Unionists. Originally a sheriff in Tennessee, he commanded a company of Texas Rangers during the Mexican War. After that war he served as a United States marshal until the war broke out, when he accepted a commission as a colonel in the Confederate army. In 1861 he served as the district commander of San Antonio until promoted in March 1862 to the command of the Sub-Military District of the Rio Grande, where he began driving out Unionists among the German population that settled in the hill-country area around San Antonio, New Braunfels, and Fredericksburg. He eventually commanded troops in eastern Texas and Arkansas and led a brigade in Walker's Division during the Vicksburg campaign. In 1864 he returned to northern Texas, where he served as commander of the Northern Sub-District of Texas until the end of the war. McCulloch inherited a situation so violent and so rife with desertion that by January 1864 he called it a "sinking ship."[84]

The situation had not reached that point overnight. The atrocities around Gainesville merely made the area a haven for deserters; events that followed created the large numbers of deserters and thereafter the roaming bands, and once again the draft lit the fuse. Men who volunteered came to understand that after April 1862 they were committed for the war. With the situation on the Texas home front worsening, particularly on the frontier, men did not need much more of an excuse to desert, but military developments provided one anyway. In late 1863 Texas troops were ordered out of the state to fight. As the army moved into and through Louisiana, men deserted by the dozens and made their way back to Texas. They joined soldiers who had deserted from General Taylor's Louisiana units in early 1863. In July 1863, Taylor asked Gen. John Magruder to post sentries at all of the crossings along the Sabine

River because Taylor's men were leaving his command and heading for Texas. That same month, John S. Ford, the commandant of conscripts in Texas, saw desertion evolving into something else as deserters began to organize and arm themselves. Ford's enrolling officers needed the assistance of an armed force to subdue them, and Ford asked Gov. Francis Lubbock for permission to raise three companies made up of minors, old men, and those exempted from conscription for other reasons. He believed that such a force could arrest and disperse the renegade deserters, enforce the law, and preserve peace in the area. Lubbock agreed with Ford's appraisal of the situation and approved his suggestion.[85]

Ford's suggestion of sending boys, old men, and the infirm against Confederate deserters demonstrated the same ignorance shown by most Confederate and state officials in the summer of 1863. The motley crew he wanted to assemble would be no match for organized groups of former soldiers fighting for survival. But Ford at least understood the problem, even if he did not have a viable solution. What he described in the counties directly north of Austin in 1863 extended all the way north to the Oklahoma territory border. General McCulloch agreed with Ford's appraisal of the situation. In October 1863 he told Magruder that notwithstanding the possibility of a Union invasion from Indian Territory, "our domestic affairs are in a bad condition." There were at least a thousand deserters in the sagebrush country of his subdistrict. Within thirty miles of Bonham, between two and four hundred men organized themselves into three separate camps within ten miles of one another and could bring nearly the strength of a small regiment to bear against any adversary within two hours. They controlled every road and monitored ingress and egress to such an extent that not a man, woman, or child passed in their vicinity without their knowledge. McCulloch told Magruder that if they could not be induced to come out peacefully, "we will have trouble and bloodshed enough in this section to make our very hearts sick." McCulloch, who had been in the Mexican War, witnessed Indian fighting, and served during most of this conflict, promised Magruder that "a war of the most wretched and savage character will be inaugurated." Magruder estimated it would take him a month to get ready. He had counted on state militia and two regiments raised in the area, but he no longer felt confident of any of those troops.[86]

"War of the most wretched and savage character" was exactly what took place across the South. Just as had happened with Governor Vance in North Carolina, deserters in northern Texas took advantage of their position of strength to negotiate with the Confederate government. Henry Boren, the leader of the largest group in northern Texas, met in October 1863 with two Confederate officers and offered to serve on the frontier. The officers returned to McCulloch with Boren's offer, and McCulloch's answer became an ultimatum of war as he demanded to know how men "who had done so very wrong" could be allowed to choose where they would serve while others who stood by the colors and remained faithful should serve where they were ordered. Beyond deserting, Boren and his men "had banded together in defiance of the laws of the country, creating fear among the civil and quiet citizens of the country," exposing their homes to pillage and outrage. McCulloch offered a counterproposal that would allow Boren and his men to serve under his command and fight where and when they were ordered. He would expect them to fight Yankees and jayhawkers with the same zeal that they had shown in fighting Indians. In addition, they could not elect their own officers. McCulloch wanted them back peacefully, but he would not bend to Boren's terms, and he was committed to doing whatever was necessary to put an end to the lawless conduct in his command. He told Boren that he and his men need not fear for the safety of their families, for as long as McCulloch could protect them, he would.[87]

Boren agreed to McCulloch's terms, and in November 1863 more than six hundred deserters came out of the brush. McCulloch had to add a fifteen-day furlough to his offer, but he felt it was a wise concession considering the bloodshed he avoided. However, Boren's band had been only one of several, and when McCulloch prepared to move into northern Texas in January 1864 to arrest deserters and conscripts, the problem he faced seemed as formidable as the one he had just solved. His advanced guard informed him that deserters had stolen supplies of every description from the local citizenry and were seizing firearms ranging from shotguns to six-shooters. One old man, Mr. Craft, a loyal citizen with thirty slaves, had his horse and saddle stolen out from under him by a band of thirty deserters. As they parted, the deserters told Craft that he had "had his day and now they were going to have theirs." They claimed to be fifteen hundred strong, more than twice Boren's numbers, and said that in two months the Stars and Stripes would be flying over Texas. If they found Craft again they would kill him, they warned. Other sources from Denton and Dallas counties indicated deserter bands running freely through the area in groups as small as eight to ten men and as large as forty. One group, referred to as "Fox and his outlaw gang," were reputedly in league with the Indians. John Bourland, the infamous leader of the Gainesville hangings, served as a colonel with McCulloch and had 150 men with which to fight what seemed like a small army. Not only were the deserters numerous and active, but the local citizenry had all but capitulated to them. McCulloch had never seen a country "where the people were so perfectly worthless and so cowardly as here." Not only was there no hope of raising a home guard, but to add insult to injury, it appeared McCulloch had cut a poor deal with Boren in November. "There is not one bit of reliability in the deserters that have returned to service up here in mass; here and there a good man, generally bad, and steps must be taken to put the last one of them into his former command, the grave, or prison." McCulloch wanted out, but he refused to request a transfer from a sinking ship.[88]

In February 1864, McCulloch reported on his progress, and the news was not good. He needed more troops, and although he knew Magruder could not provide any from the coast, he hoped Kirby Smith could spare some men. Claiming that "there are deserters in nearly every county in it [his district]," McCulloch resorted to desperate measures and enlisted the aid of William Quantrill. By using the most infamous of Confederate irregulars, McCulloch had literally enlisted deserters to hunt deserters, because most of Quantrill's men had already deserted the Confederate army. At this point McCulloch did not care, and his only complaint was that Quantrill refused to follow orders. Once again the cure had become as dangerous as, and more damaging than, the evil it was supposed to fight. Most people in the district believed that Quantrill's men had committed much of the robbing and looting that had occurred recently, and even McCulloch admitted that they were but one step above highwaymen. They fought only when they had the clear advantage, and ran when they found things "too hot for them." McCulloch had tried, but the job was too difficult. Without "good" troops to suppress deserters, this section of the "country goes up." Faced with having to arrest Quantrill, McCulloch questioned whether arresting any deserters would make any difference. "Here it will do good for the present, but cannot tell if whether it will do good in the future if the war lasts long. Because they will desert, steal horses and come back for revenge if they are put in the army." McCulloch was tired, and it showed: "Well, it is now late at night and I must rest. I will not give up the ship nor 'shorten sail to get off a lee shore,' neither personal ease nor personal danger shall keep me from doing my duty as far as I have the capacity and means, but feeling I have but little of either compared to the great demand for both, I can but feel uneasy for my country. For myself I have no care. If I can only see my country free and peace restored I am content."[89] He had reason to feel uneasy: peace would come, but his country would be no more.

By March 1864 the deserter problem in northern Texas threatened to move beyond anyone's ability to bring them back, as deserters were gathering along the Concho River with the intention of taking themselves and their families to California. With some deserters threatening to leave, McCulloch's abortive solution to the deserter problem continued to haunt him as remnants of Quantrill's command were seen in the district wearing Union uniforms and pillaging the civilians. As if he did not have enough to do, McCulloch was ordered to apprehend these men and determine if they belonged to Quantrill.[90]

McCulloch and the Confederacy never solved the desertion problem in northern Texas. Unfortunately, southern Texas had problems of its own. Many of the state troops were stationed there, and in November 1864 one observer noted that in Goliad, Bee, Karnes, Refugio, San Patricio, Live Oak, McMullen, and Nueces counties, draft-age men walked about at will and at least two hundred deserters roamed the area. Anarchy was the result, as deserters banded together or with other outlaws and terrorized the civilian population.[91] Perhaps the most famous incident of desertion in southern Texas gets lost in the discussion of mutiny. In October 1863, Capt. A. I. Vidal, a Confederate deserter, took his company of Mexican nationals and rebelled. Deserting their post at the mouth of the Rio Grande River, they killed two soldiers and several civilians and threatened to march on Brownsville. The Mexican government intervened and routed Vidal's troops, bringing to a close a brief but violent chapter in Confederate desertion.[92]

By January 1865, desertion violence had not only reached epidemic proportions in northern and southern Texas but had spread into the heart of central Texas. In 1863, John Ford complained of problems in the counties north of Austin. In 1865, Col. T. C. Edwards received instructions from "Headquarters, Hardeman's Brigade" to move immediately through the counties of Bell, Williamson, Travis, Hays, and Comal, almost a direct line from south of Waco to just north of San Antonio. His orders were to arrest all deserters and outlaws marauding through that section of the state and return any absentees to their commands. The deserters were to be "swiftly arrested" and forwarded to the provost in Houston. Anyone without a pass was to be considered a deserter, and even men with passes should be closely scrutinized to ensure the pass had not been forged. Edwards also had authority to sweep deserters in any other county he might find them in. Four months later, as the war came to an end in the East, citizens reported bands of deserters in the hills fifteen to twenty miles above Austin.[93]

Unlike Arkansas and Louisiana, Texas fit the Confederate mold. Deserters ran rampant through the state and were clearly identified as undermining law and order. Attempts to stop their activities met with minimal success, and then only for a short time. In the end nothing stopped deserters and men fleeing conscription from terrorizing Confederate civilians. Early attempts to crush Unionism in the state merely created an environment that would later serve as a haven for deserters. People predisposed to resisting the Confederacy had paid a price for their belief and found harboring Confederate deserters to be an almost natural act. Once desertion infected the northern part of the state, there was little the overworked and undermanned authorities could do to keep it from spreading.

On November 26, 1863, Seddon admitted to Davis that "as the war has been realized in all its trials, repugnance and recusancy have, in some limited portions of the country, been manifest occasionally to the call of the conscription officers, and when desertion and straggling have added in those districts numbers of lawless and desperate men, there have been combinations and organizations for open resistance to the regular action of the law. It is always best," he continued, "to overcome such evils in their inception, and to prevent such lawless feelings from coming to the head of open violence and insurrection." In his letter, Seddon understated the extent and severity of the problem and demonstrated a failure to understand that violence and insurrection had already come to a head. Admittedly, it is always best to "overcome such evils in their inception"; however, the Confederacy never understood just how early the problem had begun. It had started back in 1862, and what everyone had deemed absenteeism, often tolerated because of what many called extenuating circumstances, was the beginning of what had overwhelmed both the army and the home front by the end of 1863. The truth was that every state had deserters running through it, and the violence had already reached epidemic proportions. Seddon suggested to Davis that it might be "expedient to use non-conscripts and the least available of the conscripts to form local or temporary organizations, which could be more constantly employed in arresting deserters and collecting conscripts." Everything Preston, Lay, Pillow, and others had told Seddon about desertion had run off him like water off a duck's back. Temporary organizations made up of men who had never fought before had no chance against well-organized, determined groups of former soldiers already hardened by war and fighting for their own survival. Seddon believed that a regiment would probably be sufficient in each state. Alabama's mountains had deserters in division strength, and that was just one state. W. Wirt Thomson told Seddon three months later that no less than a brigade of infantry would be needed to drive the deserters out of one county in Mississippi.[94]

The degree to which the Confederacy had allowed desertion to spread out of control became apparent in 1864. With deserter bands running freely through every Confederate state, officials at the federal, state, and local level tried to suppress what had essentially become an army. They discovered that only Confederate regulars had any chance against these bands of desperate men, and also that any success they achieved would be temporary. The harsh reality was that while deserters devastated the home front, the very fountainhead from which the notion of *patriae* flowed, the Union army threatened to destroy the Confederate army, and every available Confederate soldier was needed to meet the Union invasions of 1864. Every deserter represented a Confederate casualty, but after seeing what these men did to other Southerners and the Confederate army, it is impossible to ignore the fact that a deserter hurt the Confederacy much more than a dead hero. Had any of these men been killed in battle, their losses would have been mourned and their presence missed. As renegade deserters they were missed but not mourned, and they caused more harm and heartache than their deaths ever could have. Desertion had indeed become more damning than slaughter.

One of the most disturbing aspects of the deserter problem was the Confederacy's inability to get beyond the culture of leniency it created in the first eighteen months of the war. For all of Polk's zeal, his willingness to distinguish between "good" and "bad" deserters provides a vivid example of just how difficult it was for the Confederacy to be as harsh as it had to be. Martin Halls Burton, a soldier in Polk's corps, wrote home to describe the execution of a deserter. The man had deserted three times, and on the last occasion he had joined a band of "outlaws." He had apparently taken part in bushwhacking some of Polk's cavalry and paid the price. However, Burton described two other deserters whom Polk spared. The two men "only went home to make arrangements to keep their wives and children from suffering and I think the general done his duty when he spared them, the men all think the same way."[95] Two standards: good deserters and bad deserters. Going home to family was acceptable, bushwhacking was not. What Polk overlooked was that the two men he spared might desert again and, given the conditions of the country, find they had no alternative but to stay and band with others like themselves.

For all the harm roving bands of deserters caused to the Confederacy throughout the war, that growing army of renegades depended for its numbers on the continuing exodus of Confederate soldiers from the army. While the Conscription Bureau, state government, and local authorities struggled to deal with the chaos desertion caused at home, the Confederate army and government continued to try to close off the many ways out of the army. Yet the harder the Confederacy tried to close the gaps, the wider they seemed to become. At the same time, the Union stepped up its efforts to use Confederate desertion as a weapon of war.

It is difficult to overstate the Union's role in Confederate desertion in 1864. Two steps taken in December 1863—one by the military and the other by the United States government—enhanced the Union's ability to encourage Confederate desertion. An order by Grant while he was still in command in the West made it military policy that Confederate oath takers would not be put into the Union army by any means. This exemption from military service was repeated in Union orders and circulars throughout 1864. The previous year, the possibility of being drafted had led many Louisiana soldiers to either refuse to take the oath or to break it if they took it at all. In 1864 the Union launched a concerted offensive on four fronts designed not only to crush the Confederate armies but to open up larger portions of the South to Union occupation.

On December 8, 1863, Abraham Lincoln issued his Proclamation of Amnesty and Reconstruction, making the oath of allegiance for civilians the first step in a wartime reconstruction process. Although citizens throughout the South and soldiers in all of the Confederate armies had been allowed to swear an oath to the United States for almost two years, Lincoln's executive order made the oath of allegiance for civilians official. Every foot of Confederate territory occupied by the Union brought the possibility that both soldiers and citizens could desert the cause and begin to rebuild the Union within occupied Confederate states.

Lincoln's proclamation fit neatly into the context of desertion and the "broken promise," and its implementation effectively split the South by class. Those who had a hand in bringing about the war and promised to help the soldiers and their families were partially excluded from taking the oath. Confederate government officials, civil and diplomatic officials, all officers above the rank of colonel, and men who left seats in the United States Congress or resigned military commissions did not benefit from the amnesty proclamation. In effect, common citizens and soldiers were encouraged to act upon the breach of the contract between themselves and their government as well as the broken promise made by the elites.[1] With an official policy in place for both soldiers and civilians, Union invasion and Confederate retreat would drive desertion in 1864 just as it had in 1863. With home and family lying in the path of the Union advance, efforts by the Confederate army to advance or retreat, particularly across formidable physical boundaries such as rivers, would separate men from home and bring on desertion.

Stopping or at least slowing down the desertion epidemic would require preventative measures, because as the new year began Lee made it clear that he would no longer allow elements of his army to hunt deserters. Colonel Willis of the Thirty-first Georgia had been on deserter duty sweeping the Virginia counties of Rappahannock, Page, Madison, and Greene, arresting deserters and returning conscripts. He bagged approximately three hundred deserters and reported that in his opinion the conscript officers were incompetent and the exemption system created all kinds of abuses. "It is useless for me to arrest citizens for knowingly and voluntarily harboring deserters," he told Lee. "I made several such arrests, when the proof was indubitable, and the provost marshal was compelled to release them. Under these circumstances I have ceased to arrest them." Lee passed Willis's report on to Samuel Cooper and conceded, "I have no doubt that if I could send parties to sweep through every county of the state similar results and evidences of inefficiency and abuse would be obtained." He had sent Hoke to North Carolina on deserter duty, where he remained until early 1864, but Lee told Cooper that "these detachments weaken the army, and I have only resorted to them when in despair of otherwise mitigating the evil." Lee suggested that Cooper take steps to increase the efficiency of the Conscription Bureau's enrolling officers.[2]

Lee's letter testifies to just how severely desertion had hurt his own army. It also reflects the decision of a commander who had all but exhausted the resources at his disposal and would no longer continue to do so. Lee knew that it was only by using his army against the deserter "army" that he could hope to make any kind of meaningful headway, but that meant taking men and resources from the war against the Union in order to wage war against other Confederates. His willingness to do this came only during moments of despair, and like the temporary relief these units brought, it quickly passed as his focus returned to the Union threat. The Union offensive in the spring of 1864 took full advantage of Lee's unwillingness to use his army to combat the deserter problem. When Grant crossed the Rappahannock River into the Wilderness in May 1864, he tied up Lee and every soldier he could spare in an ongoing battle that would not end until both armies reached the gates of Petersburg and Richmond. At that point any chance Lee ever had to use his army to fight or collect deserters disappeared, and his suggestion of enhancing the efficiency of the enrolling officers would be useless. Deserters had become small armies, and enrolling officers alone had no chance.

On December 11, 1863, the Confederate Congress demanded to know what had been done to implement the last major piece of desertion legislation it had passed, the "Act to Prevent the Absence of Officers and Soldiers without Leave" of April 1863. The House passed a resolution and forwarded it to Secretary of War Seddon. Seddon attached copies of the orders issued by Cooper in February and March 1863 and forwarded the request on to Davis. In response to the request, Davis forwarded what material he had back to the Confederate House. To say the report was thin would have been an understatement. The only substance of any kind was Cooper's two general orders issued before the act had been passed, which, Davis claimed, had "anticipat[ed] it [the new law] as far as seemed practicable." Davis had asked Cooper if anything else had been done, and Cooper replied, "What additional measures may have been adopted by 'commanding officers' to secure the observance of this law, I regret to not have means of stating."[3]

Davis's response is perplexing, because he had far more knowledge of the situation than his feeble reply indicated. He had been briefed by Seddon in November 1863 and had corresponded with Lee following Gettysburg. Davis had even issued his own proclamation of amnesty, and to send the report he did clearly withheld what he knew. Perhaps even more troubling was Cooper's contribution to the report. Kean's evaluation of Cooper in the summer of 1863 rang true, Cooper did not have a clue as to the size of any army in the field, including Lee's Army of Northern Virginia, camped along the Rappahannock

River less than one hundred miles away. Why Cooper did not provide any of the numerous orders or correspondence he issued and received between April 1863 and January 1864 is also a mystery. Perhaps Cooper limited his disclosure out of a desire not to allow the true nature and extent of the evil to become public. It may not have mattered, since by January 1864 everyone knew the Confederacy had a problem, and the mere act of inquiring demonstrated how much the Confederate House already knew or at least suspected.

Whether in response to Davis's report or some other information, in January 1864 the Confederate government moved to outlaw activity that encouraged desertion and to prevent people from shirking their military obligation. On January 22 the Confederate Congress approved "An Act to Prevent the Procuring, Aiding, and Assisting of Persons to Desert from the Army of the Confederate States." Any person not subject to the rules and articles of war who procured or enticed a soldier to desert, aided or assisted any soldier to desert, enabled a person to enlist or join a command other than his own, interfered with the arrest of a known deserter, knowingly concealed or harbored a deserter, or purchased arms, equipment, clothing rations, or anything belonging to the Confederate state from a deserter would be subject to two years in prison and a thousand-dollar fine upon conviction before a district court of the Confederate States.[4]

Aiding and abetting a deserter had become a Confederate crime. The law made sense and appeared to have real substance, because almost any action taken by a civilian involving a Confederate deserter other than reporting his whereabouts or turning him in to the authorities became criminal. Feeding, housing, rendering medical aid, and an unlimited number of other unspecified acts now fell within one neat prohibition. But once again, the problem would be enforcing the law. Under Article 6, section 2 of the United States Constitution, the laws of the federal government were the "supreme law of the land," and all subordinate political subdivisions were obligated to honor and enforce them. Confederate laws occupied a different status in the minds of most citizens and state government officials. North Carolina openly disputed the obligation of a state to enforce the Confederate Conscription Law with state resources. Judge Graham had argued against North Carolina's enforcement of a state sedition act in 1861 because it arguably furthered a national purpose. In 1864, governors Brown of Georgia, Watts of Alabama, and Clarke of Mississippi contested the Confederate government's right to tax state property. States could not tax Confederate property, they argued, and therefore the Confederacy should not tax state property. A clear distinction had developed regarding which responsibilities were state and which were Confederate. To enforce this law, the Confederate army or the Confederate provost guard would have to be the arresting entity, and as Lee made clear, he was not inclined to commit Confederate troops to hunt deserters, much less to arrest civilians.[5]

The only other "national" force available to enforce the new law was the Confederate provost guard, an arm of the military that had literally disappeared from the discussion over desertion. The provost marshal's records indicate that despite its efforts, the provost guard had enjoyed little success in apprehending deserters. Polk's efforts in Mississippi and Alabama during March and April 1864 involved the use of his provost guard in coordinated efforts with regular troops. Given Lee's unwillingness to use regulars, enforcing the harboring statute became almost impossible. The provost guard operated ostensibly at or near the front, and its desertion duties and other peacekeeping functions were carried out in the immediate operational areas of the army to which it was attached. The reality of desertion, however, was that men did not stay at or near the front. They either crossed into the Union lines, went home, or disappeared into mountains and swamps. Therefore, if the state and local authorities refused to enforce the new law, the Confederacy would be unable to do so on its own.[6]

In April 1864, Seddon told Confederate attorney general Thomas Bragg that if the courts of North Carolina could efficiently and conveniently address the violations of the harboring statute, the Confederacy had no objection to proceeding in state courts. Again, however, Seddon glossed over the real problem. It was not a question of the power of the states to enforce the Confederate laws but of their willingness to do so. We find a good example of how difficult the law would be to enforce in Alabama in August 1864. The issue of desertion and state relief had come up, and Governor Watts had to decide to what extent desertion and the laws governing it affected state relief to soldiers' families. T. S. Pitman, a county judge charged with state distribution relief, posed the following problem: Both a woman's husband and her son were in the Confederate service. The son had deserted, but the father had not. However, the mother had apparently harbored the son, thereby violating the Confederate law. In the spirit of King Solomon, Watts "split the baby." While a deserter's family was not entitled to relief, and although harboring a deserter was a felony, harboring a deserter did not deprive the family of relief where its main breadwinner had not deserted. In this instance the family depended on the woman's husband for subsistence, not her son. Since the father was still in the service, the mother was guilty only of harboring and would still be entitled to relief. Therefore, although the woman was guilty of a federal felony, her state relief was unaffected, and there is no indication that she was ever prosecuted by the state authorities.[7]

The problem with enforcing desertion laws was not only convincing the states to act but getting them to act consistently. In Alabama families of deserters lost any right to state or county aid, but in Louisiana that would not be the case. A list dated July 10, 1864, from Calitoose and Concordia parishes in Louisiana identified fifty-six families entitled to receive state aid. Eleven women had the designation "deserter family" to the far right, and one woman's note indicated that her husband had not only deserted but had been shot. In Alabama none of these families would have received aid, but in Louisiana they had received and were continuing to benefit from state and county relief. Not only was the distribution of state relief inconsistent among the states, but the two different approaches underscored the dilemma state officials found themselves in because of desertion. To provide aid to deserter families, as Louisiana did, not only undermined the Confederate desertion laws but provided assistance to families whose male provider had deserted and might actually be home. To deny aid, as Alabama did, meant forcing families with as many as seven children to starve for the actions of the head of the household. If any of these women had brothers or sons, allowing the family to starve might drive other men to desert. A report filed six months later from De Soto Parish, Louisiana, had the same notations of "deserter family," but the roll did not show that those families received aid. One of two conclusions can be drawn: either the governor changed his policy, or within the state of Louisiana the treatment of deserter families was inconsistent.[8]

In an effort to combat desertion, the Confederate Congress suspended the writ of habeas corpus in February 1864 for all desertion cases and for cases involving the harboring and aiding of deserters. However, the suspension power was not absolute, providing judges with a level of discretion that was almost assured to undermine the law. Chief Justice Pearson heard writ of habeas corpus petitions in North Carolina in 1863 and would continue to do so in 1864. Pearson recognized that an enrolling officer could wrongfully accuse a man of desertion, and if access to the writ were denied, a citizen had no recourse. The problem was that it allowed every accused deserter to raise a defense and get his case before a judge. If the state and its judiciary proved resistant to enforcing Confederate law, it could simply find that the man had never legally owed military service and release him. The 1864 law suspending the writ of habeas corpus recognized the possibility of a wrongful accusation, and in cases of "palpable wrong and oppression by any subordinate officer, upon a person who does not legally owe military service," his superior officer could not only grant that person relief but could dismiss the subordinate officer.[9] The problem lay both in interpreting "palpable wrong and oppression" and in establishing the identity of subordinate officers. Often these men would be Conscription Bureau officers, and by 1864 many had so abused their positions that the local citizenry fought their authority with impunity. The likelihood of proving abuse at the subordinate level increased, and given the state judicial propensity to challenge Confederate law and the discretion built into the law, the exception could literally consume the general rule.

The week before the approval of the harboring statute, the Confederate Congress took an unprecedented step in trying to curb desertion and the avoidance of duty. On January 15, 1864, Senate bill 187 came out of the Judiciary Committee and was ordered to be printed. Entitled "An Act Declaring Persons Owing Military Service to the Confederate States, and Who Seek to Avoid Such Service by Removing beyond the Control and Jurisdiction of Said States, Alien Enemies, and Subjecting Their Property to Confiscation," the law applied the 1861 Alien Enemies Act and the 1861 Sequestration Act to draft evaders. The Alien Enemies Act declared citizens of the United States residing in the Confederacy to be alien enemies and ordered them out of the Confederacy. The Sequestration Act followed three weeks later and subjected the property of alien enemies to seizure and sale through the jurisdiction of the Confederate district courts. The new bill applied both laws by voiding any transfer of property belonging to a person who wrongfully left the country to avoid military duty if the transfer was made after that person left the Confederacy.[10]

This law divested of their citizenship persons who were unwilling to serve in the military and left the country to avoid service. Before the end of the year a debate would take place in the Confederate Congress over declaring deserters alien enemies. The measure would not pass, but the willingness to openly discuss desertion indicated that the problem had ceased to be a secret. The practice of leaving the Confederacy to avoid the draft had also become obvious. In his address to the Texas legislature in February 1863, Governor Lubbock asked what was to be thought of those who "left the country to avoid participation in the struggle expecting to return and join the successful party." His address suggested the situation was more than an isolated instance. The abandonment of military responsibility occupied a subheading of his address entitled "Citizens Voluntarily Absenting Themselves from the State during War." Was this desertion? Technically, no. The individual had not joined the service, nor had he been drafted, but the Confederacy now defined desertion as "the unwillingness to be liable to service." The severity of the penalty was greater than any sanction short of death. The loss of citizenship and the divestiture of property was almost the equivalent of a criminal's property escheating to the Crown under old English law. Harsh or not, the law finally evidenced a realization within the Confederacy that every able-bodied man counted. Just as the Confederacy had authorized the use of slaves as "soldiers" in a support role in 1863, in recognition that every noncombat role filled by a slave freed a white man to fight, many people now realized that even the sick and exempt could serve a role. "Every citizen is bound to serve and defend the state as far as he is capable," Lubbock contended. "None are naturally exempt from the performance of this duty by reason of age or infirmity, all are capable in some way, of being useful, the healthy and strong of bearing arms, and the infirm of doing hospital duty, and of aiding the families of those who are in the army, and of sympathizing with and giving aid and comfort to the cause in which we are engaged." Citizenship involved more than living up to the letter of the law, paying taxes, and hiring a substitute to go and fight. Not only were men staying behind, but at home they were "sow[ing] the seeds of discontent."[11] Lubbock called for a law that would divest such persons of citizenship and seize their property, and Senate bill 187 seemed to come in answer to his pleas.

Although Lubbock was the first to articulate the problem, the fact that the Confederate Senate acted upon it indicated that Texas was not the only state whose citizens eluded service by leaving. For some, however, the law did not go far enough. A Louisiana soldier in Lee's army actually suggested going one step further and applying the new law to civilian oath takers. Civilians who remained in the country but swore the oath had in effect abandoned the cause, and he felt they should have their property seized. The Confederate Congress would not go that far, but the 1864 Senate bill reflected a sense of desperation at the manpower shortage as the war moved into its third full year. Two months later, Governor Brown made a similar suggestion to the Georgia legislature, asking that the property of persons charged with disloyalty to the Confederacy on the Georgia border with eastern Tennessee be confiscated and sold with the proceeds divided among the loyal, along with laws that would forever "disenfranchise and decitizenize" such persons.[12]

The Georgia state bill never passed, but Brown's recommendation and the Senate bill demonstrated once again the Confederacy's delayed reaction to desertion. Lubbock's comments came in early 1863, so it is safe to assume the problem he articulated began sometime in 1862. The Confederacy finally took steps to address the manpower drain in 1864. By then it was too late.

The Confederacy had become a place where the unwillingness to agree with the cause could be deemed desertion. Certainly other than being shot it would be difficult to conceive of a penalty harsher than total divestiture of citizenship and forfeiture of property. However, the evil the government sought to address was real, as was the damage it caused. Year designations almost became meaningless because desertion in 1863 simply continued in 1864. On January 11, 1864, Kirby Smith issued an order to all commanders of the trans-Mississippi regarding the large numbers of deserters from east of the Mississippi who had crossed the river into his command. They were to be returned immediately. Smith not only had to take steps to send deserters from other commands back, but he had problems within his own jurisdiction. On January 12, 1864, W. A. Alston, assistant adjutant general for the District of Texas, New Mexico, and Arizona, issued an order to hunt down and arrest deserters from the Texas State Troops. Apparently with the coming of the new year these men walked out and headed home. They believed their terms of service had expired, although Alston pointed out that their service extended from August 6, 1863, to February 6, 1864, and that anyone leaving before that time was a deserter. In early February 1864, 157 men from Col. P. C. Woods's Texas Brigade walked away with all their arms and accoutrements. From the directions in the order to hunt these men down it appears Woods's unit was headed to Louisiana when his Texans walked away. The longer the war dragged on, the less willing men became to leave "home" to fight.[13]

Lee's reluctance to use his army to collect deserters seems almost suicidal considering what he stood to lose—and what he could have gained by actively hunting down these men. In mid-February 1864 Lee reported to Seddon the condition of Ewell's II Corps and provided a list of absentees. Early's division listed 3,227 absent, Rodes's 4,102, and Johnson's 4,045. Together with the 227 missing from II Corps Artillery, the total absent stood at 11,601. Lee reasoned that some of these men were prisoners, some deserters, some permanently at home disabled, and some properly detailed. His report was issued with "a view to adopt measures to bring back as many of the able bodied as possible before the opening of the spring campaign." Lee actually believed that the answer to his problems lay in the hospitals of Virginia, North Carolina, and South Carolina, and his solution was to send the surgeon generals of each of his three corps to the hospitals in those three states and Georgia to return as many men as possible. He asked Seddon to issue an order empowering his Commission of Surgeons to send men back to the army.[14]

It is little wonder that Cooper had no idea how many men he had in the field and where the rest had gone. Lee did not know. Out of more than eleven thousand absentees he could only speculate as to how many had deserted, how many were POWs, and how many were legally absent. While he looked to the hospitals for relief, he would find that those who were well enough to return and had not were probably no longer in the hospitals. If the numbers on hospital desertion are even close to accurate, Lee's hospitals served as the launching point for more than five thousand desertions, and if Lee was looking for men he could recover he needed to look to the mountains of southwestern Virginia and western North Carolina. He could also look north, to the Union lines, but those men were long gone. They were either prisoners who would never come back or deserter to the Union.

What made the desertion in early 1864 even worse was the Confederacy's return to the use of amnesty to bring men back. It was not so much that amnesty represented a continued policy of leniency but that an amnesty offer in the trans-Mississippi actually undermined the goal. The problem was the disjointed nature of dealing with the issue and a general breakdown in communication. On January 21, 1864, Gen. Richard Taylor penned a letter to Brig. Gen. William Richardson Boggs, chief of staff at the headquarters for the Confederate District of West Louisiana. Taylor enclosed a copy of letters sent previously to Gen. Henry Watkins Allen, who had been in the trans-Mississippi since August 1863 and would become Louisiana's governor in 1864. Sometime after Allen was appointed in 1863, headquarters gave him authority to offer amnesty to deserters. Allen's district had actually been within Taylor's at the time of his appointment, yet Taylor was never copied on any of the correspondence and knew nothing of the order. Taylor's complaint was twofold. First, deserters were being pardoned by an order from a general who did not command those men when they deserted. Thus Allen's deserter muster camps were turning into refugee centers for men Taylor had been pursuing who now obtained sanctuary. From Taylor's perspective this undermined the legitimate authority of commanders who did not acquiesce in the amnesty. Had they been informed and brought to agreement, at least the authority of those who had to lead these men could have been preserved. As it was, deserters could now play Confederate commanders off one another.[15]

Undermining military authority, however, was not the worst consequence of Allen's amnesty. Because Taylor had been unaware of its existence, deserters in his command continued to be subject to the harshest penalties. Taylor told Boggs that had he at least known of the amnesty he "might have avoided the spectacle of inconsistency recently presented of deserters caught, tried, and shot by my orders while in the adjoining or perhaps same parish General Allen was granting amnesties and pardons." In Taylor's opinion, "The very large number of desertions and absentees from every organization in the army may well inspire doubts whether the general amnesty lately granted by the President, as well as other lenient measures of more restrictive influence, have not increased the evil they were intended to remedy." Taylor was right. Leniency bred contempt for the law, but unfortunately for the Confederacy, the amnesty solution would continue to be utilized almost to the end of the war in all theaters. Beauregard issued an amnesty for deserters in Florida in March 1864, Polk did the same in Alabama in April 1864, and Price issued a proclamation of amnesty for Arkansas troops in May 1864. Despite grave concerns that amnesty would only encourage desertion, Lee followed these offers with one in August 1864 for the Army of Northern Virginia. While amnesty was clearly not the solution, desertion had become so widespread that it could no longer be solved by executing men. There were simply too many to shoot. Nevertheless, Taylor's experience shows the degree to which desertion had administratively overwhelmed the Confederacy as men in one command walked free while those captured in the next county got shot. The chance that one might get shot reaffirmed that desertion still posed certain dangers, and that possibility made the Union's oath-swearing program even more appealing. [16]

The year 1864 provides the first opportunity to examine Confederate desertion to the Union over a full year using the data from the Union Register. There is little doubt from the correspondence on both sides and at all levels that Confederate soldiers had deserted to the Union as early as 1862. The practice continued through 1863 and escalated in the summer of 1863 when the Union program developed concrete guidelines. Rosecrans reported to Halleck in late August 1863 that Confederate deserters from the Army of Tennessee were pouring into Union lines. Alabama newspapers confirmed large-scale desertion from both the Seventeenth and the Twenty-ninth Alabama, both regiments in the Army of Tennessee. The advertisements do not state how these men deserted, but the men from the Seventeenth came from counties in central and southern

Alabama. Getting home from around Chattanooga in July, August, or September 1863 would have required a considerable hike through Confederate-controlled territory. The men in the advertisement may well have been some of those whom Rosecrans reported as deserting into his lines. Union soldiers in Virginia saw the same thing at about the same time. Oliver Wilcox Norton, a surgeon stationed at Beverly Ford, Virginia, wrote home on September 7, 1863, that "deserters continue to come over from the rebels, and if one could believe the stories they tell, it would not take many troops to wipe out Lee's army." Norton did not believe Lee was that helpless, but his observation confirms that the Confederates took advantage of the Union policy.[17] However, while desertion to the Union clearly occurred in 1863, the Union did not begin keeping accurate records until July and August 1863. Although troops from several states availed themselves of the program in late 1863—Tennessee, Georgia, and Virginia being the most obvious—it was not until 1864 that Union records really help to show a picture of desertion to the Union across both main Confederate armies and in all states.

What Norton observed in September 1863 continued into the first month of the new year. Gen. A. A. Humphreys informed his cavalry commander, Gen. David Gregg, that all deserters from the Confederate army whom he picked up coming into Union lines were to be immediately forwarded to headquarters without allowing them to speak with anyone. Humphreys also identified three Confederate sergeants, two from the Fifteenth Louisiana Infantry and one from the Thirteenth Virginia Infantry, who had arrived within the last several days.[18]

The period from January to the end of April 1864 saw heavy desertion to the Union from the soldiers of four states: Tennessee and Georgia in the West and North Carolina and Virginia in the East. Alabama and Arkansas began the year with small but significant numbers of deserters to the enemy, but those numbers dropped off appreciably by May (see table 3).

Based on the date of oath swearing, Texas, Florida, Louisiana, Mississippi, and South Carolina had negligible desertion to the enemy in the winter and spring of 1864. However, for Mississippi and Louisiana it would not remain that way. The fighting that began in May on both major fronts apparently afforded the opportunity, and perhaps the motive, that men from these states needed to take advantage of the Union policy. On the other hand, not until the last two months of 1864 would Arkansas troops approach or surpass their volume of desertion to the enemy in the first two months of 1864. Texans did not use the

Table 3. Number of actual and projected Confederate soldiers deserting to the Union Army, January to April 1864

	January		February		March		April	
	Actual	Projected	Actual	Projected	Actual	Projected	Actual	Projected
Alabama	23	166	19	137	9	65	6	43
Arkansas	22	159	12	87	1	7	1	7
Georgia	40	269	61	405	55	349	40	246
North Carolina	13	95	25	183	36	264	13	95
Tennessee	141	1,049	76	573	84	610	24	173
Virginia	63	422	54	394	24	173	15	108*

* The numbers in the "actual" columns reflect each state's portion of the 4,281 deserters in the sample (see table 1). The figures are 15 percent of the total deserters in the Register of Confederate Deserters to the Union Army, 1863–1865. The actual data for each state each month represent 15 percent of the total. The numbers in the "projected" columns are the likely number of total deserters for that month. The actual numbers for Georgia also represent 15 percent of total deserters. (See Weitz, A Higher Duty, for the actual number of Georgia deserters.) Here, for example, the 61 Georgia February deserters represented in the sample are 15 percent of the projected total of 405 who swore an oath to the Union in February 1864.

Table 4. Number of actual and projected Confederate soldiers deserting to the Union Army, May to September 1864

	May		June		July		August		September	
	Actual	Projected	Actual	Projected	Actual	Projected	Actual	Projected	Actual	Projected
Alabama	12	86	12	86	37	267	47	339	31	224
Georgia	35	234	44	294	53	356	39	260	33	220
Louisiana	4	28	0	—	12	88	10	77	11	78
Mississippi	15	110	3	22	12	88	12	88	21	154
North Carolina	13	95	8	59	28	205	23	169	11	81
Tennessee	21	154	16	117	68	500	44	324	47	346
Virginia	28	206	21	154	69	507	26	191	15	110

Union program much at all during the war. Its 315 deserter oath swearers is the third-lowest total in the Confederacy. Texans did desert—as evidenced by the "official" figures, which claim that 4,600 Texans deserted during the war—but they found a way home other than through Union lines. At about the same time men from other states were taking advantage of the Union program in northern Georgia, Texans had used furloughs to get home and not return. In May 1864, William Nicholson wrote his father that Texans from his unit were rumored to have gone home. They had furloughs that forbade them from going through Union lines, and if they had returned to Texas that would be enough to have them deemed deserters. Nicholson wrote home a month later to tell his aunt that two other men had not returned and that the "furloughed men of the 8th and 11th Texas had acted very shamefully" and tarnished the reputation of his unit. As a result, furloughs would no longer be granted to anyone.[19]

In the West the two states with the most severe problems with deserter bands, Alabama and Mississippi, did not demonstrate high rates of desertion to the enemy in 1863 or in the first four months of 1864. The lack of a permanent Union presence within the interior portions of both states may account for that. When Vicksburg fell, men from both states were allowed to go home on parole, and they became deserters when they refused to return. Thus they took a different route out of the army. It might be significant that some Alabama civilians, particularly those in the Tennessee Valley running toward Dalton, Georgia, were actually leaving Alabama to cross into Union lines in Tennessee simply to keep from starving. One Alabama man actually warned Governor Watts that "if a soldier's family has to go across the lines to the Yankees to keep from starving he will desert and go to." Alabama soldiers deserted to the Union in sizable numbers in January and February, and then desertion picked up again during Sherman's invasion between May and September 1864. Three weeks before Sherman started his advance into Georgia, a Marshall County man wrote Governor Watts to tell him that the situation had grown worse. Women and children from De Kalb, Marshall, and St. Clair counties were crossing into the Union lines to get bread. If soldiers were to find out, the writer warned, they would desert. Some had come home, found their wives starving, and actually crossed with them into Tennessee. William Nugent, a Mississippi soldier, had seen the hardship that drove these people away. "I have witnessed scenes of distress since we became connected with the Army of Tennessee that would harrow the feelings of the most obdurate hearted person on earth," he wrote his wife. "Whole families ruined and thrown out upon the world homeless and without a particle of food. Our soldiers have become lawless to an alarming extent, steal and plunder to an alarming extent regardless of sex or age." Soldiers could not ignore what happened at home, and as the spring turned to summer, Alabama soldiers would take advantage of the opportunity to do something about the distress at home. In Mississippi in July 1864, civilians were swearing the oath just to be able to reoccupy their own homes. As news of a declining civilian will reached the front, some men's will to continue the struggle must have been undermined. Even when civilians swore the oath "from the teeth out," the message it sent to soldiers was that the Union now controlled areas where their homes lay and where surviving meant accepting Union control.[20]

Most men deserting and swearing the oath of allegiance welcomed the presence of the Union army, and it is difficult to overstate the importance of Union occupation to the "safety" component of its deserter program. The Confederacy continued to take the position that the Union oath had no legal effect, which meant that men could be being prosecuted for taking the oath if they returned to the Confederacy and were captured. However, Confederate oath takers could also be prosecuted by the Union if they took up arms with the Confederate army again and were captured by the Union. The key for men going home was to return to places where the Confederacy no longer had a presence. If anyone needed a reminder of the price one paid for being recaptured by the Confederacy after swearing an oath to the Union, Gen. George Pickett provided a lasting one in early 1864.[21]

In February 1864, Pickett hung twenty-two members of the First U.S. Volunteers, a unit made up of two regiments of North Carolina Unionists. They had never been in the Confederate army, although some admitted to having resisted conscription, which by 1864 made one a "deserter." Others had served in local units, and one had been a Confederate enrolling officer. They all swore an oath to support the Union when their regiments were formed. In early 1864 Pickett advanced on New Bern, North Carolina, and took the town and a number of prisoners before withdrawing to Kinston. After withdrawing he put members of the First U.S. Volunteers on trial for desertion, found them guilty, and hung them. Union officials were horrified. These men had never joined the service and were not subject to Confederate courts-martial. Their protests made little difference to Pickett, who had the dead bodies stripped and left to be picked up for experimental surgery.[22]

Tennessee's numbers reflect a state more firmly occupied by the Union army than any other Confederate state. Its numbers for December 1863 and January

1864 were higher than for any other state in any month of the war, and when the raw numbers are extrapolated out the magnitude of Tennessee desertion to the enemy is staggering. December 1863 saw 156 of the 1,381 Tennessee sample desert to the enemy. When the sample is extrapolated out, that means 1,149 Tennessee soldiers took the oath to the Union in December 1863, almost 12 percent of its 10,174 total. In January 1864, 141 Tennesseans in the sample took the oath, which projects out to 10 percent of the whole, or 1,037 men. It is difficult to overestimate the impact of the Union program on Tennessee troops. Running the projections of Tennessee soldiers through April 1864, 560 swore the oath in February, 610 in March, and 173 in April. From December 1863 through April 1864, 3,356 Tennesseans deserted and swore the oath of allegiance to the Union. That number is almost the same as the number of Georgia deserters to the Union for the entire war, but it was only slightly over one-third of Tennessee's total.

Union officers corroborated the figures in the Register. In April 1864, Gen. George Thomas wrote Gov. John Brough of Ohio to suggest that deserters coming into Union lines be sent North, and Thomas suggested Ohio. According to Thomas, his command received thirty deserters a day, men he could send as far as Nashville. Confederate deserters seemed like a viable labor pool for Ohio or any of the other western states that needed farm workers. Even though the Union had adopted a policy that trusted these men to return home and honor the oath, Thomas still had his doubts that deserters had "sufficient moral firmness to resist the natural depravity of their hearts." Thirty men a day into just his command would be more than nine hundred per month, numbers consistent with the volume seen in the Register and large enough to require a clear set of procedures. At the end of April 1864, James Wilson, the Union's provost marshal general for the Department of the Army of the Tennessee, issued instructions to all department provost marshals that specifically addressed Confederate desertion. Consistent with Thomas's concerns, deserters were immediately taken off the front lines and initially moved north. Reports were to be made biweekly indicating the disposition of each deserter. The Union efforts to deal with the volume supports the Register and shows that desertion to the Union in the West was on the rise by the spring of 1864.[23]

The East presented a different set of circumstances. The theater of war was confined to Virginia, and some portions of the state were almost always free of Confederate authorities, while others were never without Confederate occupation. Perhaps that is why the county distribution in Virginia runs southwest into the mountains, a continuous line to a place of sanctuary controlled by a strong pro-Union organization that facilitated desertion. Virginia had 4,693 total deserters to the Union, not counting the 913 who took the oath and claimed West Virginia as their home. Virginia lost 422 to the Union in January, 394 in February, 173 in March, and 108 in April. While this is not as many as for Tennessee, for a state with both armies fighting and living off the land, with a history of territory changing hands regularly, the numbers are significant. Virginians were willing to swear an oath under circumstances in which the Union might not be able to afford protection. Perhaps more significant is that of the states with large numbers of deserters to the enemy, only Virginia's total goes up in the month of May 1864 when the fighting resumes. A contributing factor to that increase was that for the first time in its history the Army of Northern Virginia retreated south in battle with the Union and by the end of the month was fighting in and around Richmond. Its raw number for May was 28, which projects out to 205 deserters. The only other state with comparable numbers of deserters to the enemy in May 1864 is Georgia, with 234 total deserters, or 6 percent of its desertion to the enemy in the month that Sherman began his move into the state's northern counties.[24]

North Carolina had slightly more than half as many deserters to the enemy as Virginia, yet its traditional total of almost twenty-four thousand led the Confederacy. Thus it seems that although only half as many Virginians deserted as did North Carolinians—slightly over twelve thousand—Virginians were almost twice as likely to take the route that led through the Union lines. During the last month of 1863 and the first four months of 1864, that trend held true. One hundred forty-seven men deserted to the enemy from North Carolina and swore the oath in December 1863. Over the next four months, 95 crossed into Union lines in January, 183 in February, 264 in March, and 95 in April, for a total of 637. By comparison, Virginia lost 1,097 during the same period.

If the damage is viewed from a theater perspective, the Army of Northern Virginia had more than seventeen hundred men deserting to the enemy in 1864 from North Carolina and Virginia alone before the fighting ever started. Lee's February 15, 1864, letter to Seddon that spoke of absentees from Ewell's II Corps may have included some of these men. In any event, while Lee went looking in the hospitals to replenish his army, his force continued to diminish in size as men accepted the Union offer and the protection that accompanied it. However, the real damage caused by this type of desertion fell upon Joe Johnston's hard-luck Army of Tennessee. In the first four months of the year, counting only Georgians (1,269) and Tennesseans (2,207), Johnston lost almost thirty-five hundred soldiers to desertion into Union lines. The total reached almost five thousand by the end of the year. While not every Georgian and Tennessean fought in the West, the vast majority did, and the study on Georgia shows that even though a large number of Georgians fought with Lee, the vast majority of Georgians taking the oath came out of Johnston's army. The Tennessee oath takers were almost exclusively Johnston's soldiers.[25]

In May 1864 the Union's summer offensive got under way with its two main armies engaging the two largest Confederate armies. The figures for desertion to the Union demonstrate some interesting trends from May through September 1864 (see table 4). In the East, desertion to the enemy in the Army of Northern Virginia continued to center around troops from Virginia and North Carolina. For both states the oath-swearing route spiked in July, the first full month after the armies went into what would become a siege around Petersburg. The Union also began circulating copies of its desertion policy to Confederate troops, which might have contributed to the spike. Virginia had 507 deserters, the most of any Confederate state in either theater. North Carolina's 205 is high but not near the numbers for Virginia or the other leaders in the West. It does, however, exceed the numbers for Mississippi and Louisiana combined. Lee suggested to Cooper in July that if his own men were deserting, Union soldiers were probably predisposed to doing so as well, and he suggested trying the same tactic.[26]

Reports from both sides support the desertion numbers in the Register. Life in the trenches had become harsh. Lee explained to Seddon in August that not only did men suffer from the heat and conditions in the trenches, but the Union circular had made the rounds among the men, promising immunity to deserters and exemption from military service. Seddon admitted to Lee that he had heard "with regret the increased tendency to desertion manifested by a portion of our army. I can well understand the discomfort and suffering which troops in this weather must suffer in the trenches, and I fear with you that the patriotism and self denial of our soldiers may not always be proof against the temptations offered by the Washington authorities." Desertion to the enemy had become a real problem. The Union pushed as hard as possible, and the Confederacy had begun to feel helpless to stop it. Desperation had literally pushed the South to utilizing the same tactic, and even if nominally successful, it would not save its own army.[27]

A key component of the Union's desertion plan was the exemption from service. Grant had addressed that point in December 1863, and in April 1864

Table 5. Number of actual and projected Confederate soldiers deserting to the Union Army in the East, October 1864 to February 1865

	October		November		December		January		February	
	Actual	Projected	Actual	Projected	Actual	Projected	Actual	Projected	Actual	Projected
North Carolina	41	301	10	73	37	272	10	74	5	37
Virginia	45	331	44	323	76	559	33	242	7	51

Table 6. Number of actual and projected Confederate soldiers deserting to the Union Army in the West, October 1864 to February 1865

	October		November		December		January		February	
	Actual	Projected	Actual	Projected	Actual	Projected	Actual	Projected	Actual	Projected
Alabama	45	325	15	108	11	80	10	72	15	108
Arkansas	14	101	38	276	20	145	3	28	4	29
Louisiana	4	—	2	—	7	—	3	—	1	—
Mississippi	22	161	23	169	2	—	4	—	1	—
Tennessee	76	559	31	228	41	302	280	2,062	89	655

the United States provost marshal for the Department of the South issued a circular out of Jacksonville, Florida, that repeated Grant's December statement and attached a copy of General Order no. 64, issued by the United States War Department on February 18, 1864. "All refugees from the rebel lines and deserters from the rebel armies, and all persons desiring to become such," it read, "are hereby informed that they will not under any circumstances be compelled to serve in the U.S. army against the rebels." In August 1864, Grant repeated the offer of transportation to all deserters whose homes lay within Union lines and added the inducement of employment in a Union military office. Whether it was the inducements or the terrible conditions in the trenches, Lee's army was leaving, and a good number were taking the route into Union lines.[28]

From August to the end of September, desertion declined from its July high but stayed relatively heavy, a trend that continued through most of 1864 and into 1865 (see table 5). Troops from the two major states of the Army of Northern Virginia reflect the steady drain of desertion, as the war in the East became a daily grind of trench warfare with the outcome all but decided by the winter of 1864. North Carolina's desertion to the enemy spikes again in October 1864, giving that state its highest month of the war. Virginia's desertion rate was likewise up, but while North Carolina's goes down in November and then back up in December, Virginia's stayed steady and then spiked again in December 1864, with its 559 deserters exceeding even its July total. Lincoln's election results would have come in late November, and in addition to the other hardships, both in the trenches and at home, that news certainly crushed what little morale remained. While numbers were down in the first month of 1865, they remained high before tapering off until the end of the war. In the last three months of the war Lee's army would lose almost nineteen hundred Virginians and North Carolinians from an army already badly depleted and being stretched further and thinner by Grant's steady attempts to flank it.

Correspondence and reports during this period support the numbers. In one day in November 1864 Pickett reported one hundred men in his guardhouse, all charged with desertion. The letter went up the chain of command, and Lee's endorsement indicated that "desertion is increasing in the army notwithstanding all my efforts to stop it," and only "rigid execution of the law" would abate the problem. Davis added that once a deserter is captured, tried, convicted, and sentenced, the civil authorities cannot criticize the commander's decision. Lee did not say these men should be executed, but his endorsement certainly suggested such a measure. Davis all but said that civilian authorities would no longer review sentences and grant reprieves. As November 1864 came to an end, Confederate authorities, at least in the East, appear to have swung back toward harsh treatment of deserters. That December, Union commanders continued to report the influx of deserters to the Union lines. The Confederates seemed so predisposed at that point it was suggested that Grant's desertion offer be printed up on "very thin paper" and be let off from signal stations in high winds because disseminating information to the Confederate soldiers was proving difficult by any other means. Even Confederate commanders were reporting the daily desertion of their troops, sometimes two to three a night. The Confederacy was slowly bleeding to death, punctuated on occasion by large losses. On December 1, 1864, Maj. Gen. A. P. Hill provided a long list of deserters from his corps and claimed that all went over to the Union. Desertion through the lines had increased to such a point that Confederate officers began offering a thirty-dollar reward to any soldier who apprehended a deserter going through the picket line. What is interesting is the Confederacy's continued inability to deal harshly with desertion. The Union also had a desertion problem in and around Petersburg; their pickets were offered a twenty-day furlough for shooting a soldier trying to go through Union pickets. Harsh but effective; it is much easier to shoot a man than to capture him. [29]

In the West the numbers reflect several trends. First, Georgians left as the army retreated through their state. Georgia desertion numbers for May and June exceed even Tennessee's desertion numbers. But beginning in July, the month Sherman reached Atlanta and the advance turned into a siege similar to the one in Virginia, Tennessee's numbers skyrocket again. Tennessee had 500 men desert to the Union in July, almost 150 more than Georgia. As in the East, July is the spike month for every state except Mississippi. Alabama begins slowly, but its July numbers are third overall, its August numbers exceed those of every state in the Confederacy (including Tennessee and Georgia), and its September numbers exceed those of every state but Tennessee. It seems clear that in the West the encirclement of Atlanta began the exodus for soldiers other than Georgians. When the city fell the desertion continued through September, then dropped off again for most states except Alabama, Mississippi, and Tennessee. It is significant that in September the Army of Tennessee moved out of Georgia, camped briefly in Alabama, and then moved north for the campaign that would all but destroy it as an effective fighting force.

In early July 1864 deserters poured back into Tennessee. The main center for deserter relocation prior to their release was Nashville. However, they were being released in other parts of Tennessee, and certain places presented a hazard. Knoxville lay across the border from Virginia and close to North Carolina. Apparently, so many deserters were being released that the provost marshal general for eastern Tennessee, S. P. Carter, feared that if they were let go in Knoxville the city would soon be filled with spies pretending to be deserters. Carter suggested they be sent to the rear and released in either Nashville or Chattanooga. The fact that he thought a spy could hide within the deserter population speaks to the large numbers of Confederates coming into Union lines. July proved to be the peak month for the soldiers of every Confederate state, and Carter's concerns therefore seem justified.[30]

Soldiers from the Army of Tennessee continued to desert after the fall of Atlanta by going into Union lines (see table 6). Aside from the general level of morale and the condition of the home front across the Confederacy, the winter of 1864–65 in the West reflects both military developments and opportunity.

Georgia's desertion to the enemy does not appear on the chart. It declined appreciably after September 1864. Ninety-three men left in October, 86 in November, and 106 in December. Of the December deserters, most were Irish Confederates from Chatham County, where Savannah is located. From January 1865 until 1866, when the last men appear in the Register, only 354 men deserted and swore the oath to the Union. Georgia's exodus effectively ended in September 1864.[31] However, Alabama's remained strong through October with 325, and then steadily declined with a slight jump in February with 108 and March with 101. April saw 80 men desert and swear the oath. The big month of October may be attributable to the return of the army to Alabama in September and its subsequent move north. Gen. John Bell Hood camped in northern Alabama, a region teeming with deserters, and Alabamians may have taken advantage of the location. It is more likely, however, that the oath swearing in October has some lag in it and that these men actually left earlier, before the army departed. When Hood took the Army of Tennessee out of Georgia, very little prevented Alabamians from leaving Georgia and going home.

Leaving a soldier's home state or retreating in defeat clearly had a direct effect on desertion, whether he went to the enemy or straight home. Junius Bragg, the surgeon serving in an Arkansas regiment, told his wife in February 1864 that "the men are beginning to desert again, they are getting so far from home." His unit was only moving south from Arkansas into Louisiana, yet the men were unwilling to stay if it meant being too far away from home. In October 1864, Richard Taylor complained to Braxton Bragg that Kirby Smith had "pardoned all the men who deserted from his army when ordered across the river." Taylor did not identify the river. He wrote from Selma that he had captured all or most of the men who deserted, but in light of Smith's amnesty he now believed it was useless to send further orders to move troops across.[32] By late 1864 men refused to cross formidable physical barriers. Missourians had deserted when Price tried to take them across the Arkansas River. Texans had deserted when confronted with having to leave the state, and had they continued east their likely destination would required them to cross the Mississippi. Bridges and ferries across major rivers were sparse and always guarded. Deserters leaving Virginia going into North Carolina actually banded together to storm guarded bridges or mountain passes. Crossing a river put that barrier between a soldier and his home and forced a decision. The time to leave was before he was forced to cross, and as Taylor and Price discovered, many did just that. The choice got easier as it appeared that the Confederacy had begun to lean toward not shooting men who voluntarily returned. Thus, if they deserted and then had to return, the chances of being shot appeared less, at least in Mississippi.

The Confederate leadership could never overcome the desire to be lenient, a subject that put Richard Taylor at odds with Governor Clarke of Mississippi. Clarke clearly advocated forgiveness, and while Taylor was not in a position to challenge the governor's authority, particularly in Mississippi, he argued that some punishment should accompany desertion even if men came back voluntarily. Taylor deferred to Clarke since the deserters in question were Mississippians, but he added that although Clarke could use his influence to apply the "best correction to the evil," in his opinion, the prevalence of desertion alone had prolonged the war.[33] The fact that Taylor, Lee, or any other military officer had to defer to the civilian authorities regarding punishing deserters revealed a serious problem in and of itself. That aside, based on Smith's pardoning of the men who refused to cross the river and Clarke's predisposition to pardon men who voluntarily returned, the Confederacy seemed to have so little control over its armies that it felt that only by being lenient could they hope to replenish their ranks. Rather than clamp down hard on desertion in the face of the Union amnesty program, the Confederate army and government chose to fight the Union amnesty with one of their own. The effect seemed to run contrary to what was desired. The inclination toward amnesty prevailed across the West and at all military levels. In December 1864, the Georgia Reserve and Militia District Headquarters issued an order that offered amnesty or "the most favorable consideration of their respective generals" for any absentees who voluntarily returned. Governor Brown endorsed the amnesty for all men returning within twenty days of the order.[34]

In the winter of 1864 the Union continued to push its deserter program, stepping up its efforts in areas outside the main theaters of operation. From New Orleans in October, Maj. Gen. Stephen Hurlbut issued General Order no. 151, which recited General Order no. 82 from Grant in August. All deserters if they so desired would be given employment in the Quartermaster's Department and paid the same as a civilian working in that department. In addition, there would be no attempt to force any deserter into the service or into any duty that would subject him to capture by the Confederate service. In December came a letter from Union Headquarters, District of Little Rock, which indicated that a concerted effort was being made to influence Confederate soldiers in Arkansas to desert. It repeated the standard offer of employment and the complete exemption from military service. It also offered to take any deserter as far north as Cairo.[35]

Did the Union's increased efforts in Louisiana and Arkansas have any effect on the desertion of Confederate troops from those states? In Louisiana it seems unlikely. The highest levels of desertion for its troops came in July, August, and September 1864. Even then the levels were low, and over the course of the war only 535 men deserted to the enemy. States like Virginia and Tennessee had that many desert to the Union and swear the oath in one month. Perhaps Louisiana soldiers never overcame the experience in 1863 of being drafted once they deserted into Union lines. Based on the *Official Records*, Louisiana had the third-lowest total of deserters for the war, behind only Florida and South Carolina.

Arkansas also did not show significant desertion to the Union, although the *Official Records* indicate that more than ten thousand of its soldiers deserted. Arkansas's most prolific months of desertion to the enemy were October, November, and December 1864. In November, 22 percent (276 men) of its total desertion to the Union occurred. December saw a decline, yet 145 soldier still sought refuge in Union lines. Arkansas and Louisiana seemed to have a different desertion experience from most of the rest of the Confederacy. Although guerrilla activity hurt both states, the desertion aspect of it came early in Arkansas, and later activity did not seem driven by deserters. The key to Arkansas may lie in the fact that for some of its soldiers willing to desert, protection afforded by the Union was unnecessary, and in areas of the trans-Mississippi where the Confederacy continued to hold sway, the Union's ability to offer protection was diminished and the program therefore lacked appeal. Nevertheless, Arkansas soldiers deserted, and in 1864 they did so when Sterling Price retreated back into the state after his failed invasion of Missouri. Just as Georgians disappeared in the wake of Johnston's retreat, Arkansas soldiers deserted as Price withdrew from Missouri on October 30, 1864. His expedition had been a disaster, and it not only emboldened the Union but demoralized his army. Men fell sick on the retreat, and desertion escalated. Some men simply left, while others got furloughs to go home and never came back. To the extent his soldiers felt any sense of loyalty to Price, that loyalty disappeared in the wake of disaster. Likewise, civilians in Arkansas saw the Missouri debacle as the last straw. By the end of 1864 in Arkansas, both soldiers and civilians were beaten.[36]

Mississippi desertion to the enemy remained heavy through November 1864, when it dropped to almost nothing. Like Arkansas and Louisiana, Mississippi did not have a high rate of desertion to the enemy, but to the extent it took place, Hood's movement out of Georgia up into Tennessee seems to have provided an opportunity. Mississippi's countryside, like Alabama's, was inundated with deserters—they just took another route home that seldom led into Union lines. The *Official Records* attributed more than eleven thousand deserters to Mississippi troops, and most did not see the benefits of the Union program.

A variation of "The Yellow Rose of Texas" tells the story of Hood's 1864 Franklin and Nashville campaign: "You can talk about your Beauregard and sing of Robert E. Lee, but John Bell Hood of Texas played hell in Tennessee." The most dramatic desertion to the Union came from Tennessee troops, and Hood's return to the state and subsequent disaster appears clearly tied to Tennessee's use of the Union desertion program. From 346 in September 1864, Tennessee's desertion increased to 559 in October before declining again in November (228) and December (302) while Hood was actively campaigning in the state. However, in January 1865, following the army's retreat out of the state, 2,062 Tennesseans deserted and swore the oath, a figure that represents 20 percent of its total desertion to the enemy over the course of the war. Six hundred and fifty-five men followed in February. Although comparatively it would decline in March (383) and April (302), both months were almost as high or higher than all of Georgia's desertion in 1865. By the end of 1864 Tennessee soldiers had had enough, and with Joseph Johnston once again in command and in pursuit of Sherman in the Carolinas, the Union program offered Tennessee soldiers the opportunity to end the war and go home. They took that opportunity in overwhelming numbers.

The office of the provost marshal general for the Department of the Cumberland issued a report in February 1865 for Confederate deserters received at Nashville and those received outside Nashville for the period from September 7, 1864, to January 31, 1865. The aggregate number of Confederates swearing the oath in the Department of the Cumberland alone was 2,207. While the number is small compared to the total numbers presented in the Register, Nashville was only one place designated for release of deserters. Deserters swore the oath in at least eleven cities in the South. The most frequent place of release was Chattanooga, with Nashville second, Knoxville third, and Fort Monroe, Virginia, fourth. The February report therefore provides only a fraction of the oath swearers, but it supports the existence of a number large enough that established procedures and record keeping were required. The Union had created a web of receiving cities and spread itself out across the Confederacy to welcome deserters into its lines. Over the course of the war almost thirty-five thousand took this route out of the Confederate army. These men not only abandoned the military but rejected the Confederate cause. The numbers alone reflect real harm, but as with Johnston's army in Georgia and Tennessee, the desertion to the enemy reflected an abandonment of hope at crucial times. It was a sign that these soldiers had been as close to war as possible and determined that either the cause was hopeless or that those they left at home had been abandoned. In either case it signaled a weakening of the Confederate effort, both in terms of military resources and citizen will.[37]

Perhaps a more important question is how many deserted to the enemy before the Union began keeping records. In Tennessee, Andrew Johnson made sure the Union program received top priority beginning in March 1862. The fact that the Union army had to develop a procedure indicated that desertion occurred in significant numbers. The thirty-five thousand in the Register represents only eighteen months of desertion. How many left in the first half of the war? Accurate numbers are difficult to establish because they represent men leaving under circumstances in which not only the Confederacy had no idea how many men it had at any one time, but most states could not determine with any accuracy how many had enlisted. In October 1864, Alabama's adjutant general, H. P. Watson, responded to Governor Watts's inquiry as to how many troops from Alabama enlisted prior to the 1862 Conscription Act. Watson told Watts he could not give an exact number and could only estimate. The Confederacy's recorded keeping was at least consistent—consistently poor.[38]

The years creep slowly by, Lorena;
The snow is on the grass again;
The sun's low down in the sky, Lorena
The frost gleams where the flowers have been.
But the heart throbs on as warmly now
as when the summer days were nigh;
Oh! The sun can never dip so low
adown affection's cloudless sky

A hundred months have passed, Lorena
Since last I held thy hand in mine,
And felt the pulse beat fast, Lorena
Though mine beat faster than thine.
A hundred months—'twas flowery May,
When up the hilly slope we climbed,
To watch the dying of the day
And hear the distant church bells chime. [39]

By 1864, "Lorena" had the distinction of being banned in both Union and Confederate camps because officers discovered that hearing the song made men long for home and desert. Reading the lyrics, it is easy to see how the words would lead men to think of happier days, far from war. That feeling would have been even more intense for men lying in hospitals, and for those able to move about it would have been easy to take advantage of the loose security of hospitals and desert. For those fortunate enough to get a medical furlough, the hospital might well be their last contact with the military. Once safely home, they would not return.

Desertion from hospitals had been going on since 1862 in the East. Notwithstanding his suggestion that hospitals could be a good a source from which to replenish his army, Lee also must have understood that soldiers healthy enough to fight were healthy enough to run, and if left in the hospital too long they would desert. Not only were men susceptible of leaving and heading home, but Lee had learned that Gen. John Morgan had visited several hospitals in Richmond promising men clothes and two months' furlough if they joined his command. Morgan pulled thirty-five out of one hospital in Richmond, and his "recruiting officers" seduced another 200 to 250. Lee demanded that Davis intercede and return all of the men to their proper commands. [40]

What should have troubled Lee more than Morgan's taking troops was the ease with which men left hospitals on their own. Lee was right—hospitals had lots of able-bodied men—but he was wrong to believe that hospitals were a reliable source for troop replenishment. The Army of Northern Virginia lost 5,895 men to desertion from its hospitals between September 1862 and August 1864, an average of 256 a month. While desertion from Army of Tennessee hospitals does not appear to have been as prolific, with 2,851 leaving from roughly late 1862 until April 1865, the records for Samuel Stout's mobile facilities provide a more detailed picture of hospital desertion.[41]

The underlying data for the analysis of the Army of Tennessee hospitals come from the Samuel Stout Papers, specifically ten hospital registers from December 1862 until the end of the war in 1865.[42] Stout's hospital system began in Tennessee, but it eventually extended well into Georgia and Alabama. The same Union offensive that drove Johnston into retreat likewise drove the army hospitals south, and as Johnston retreated, Stout withdrew his medical facilities. Just as retreat drove desertion from the army in the field, the same withdrawal would facilitate desertion from its hospitals.

In 1864, 1,839 Confederate soldiers took advantage of the opportunity to convalesce and deserted from Stout's hospitals, the most of any year of the war. However, it was more than simply a matter or being in a place where military discipline did not exist. Stout's system was built around several receiving hospitals, usually close to where the actual fighting occurred, that funneled the wounded directly out of the field and into these short-term facilities. From there they were dispersed to smaller hospitals in the area, and then eventually men were sent to hospitals much further south. A wounded soldier could find himself in Atlanta one month and the next month be in a hospital deep in southwest Georgia or southeast Alabama. Under normal circumstances a soldier could never have hoped to get transportation that far, and for men who lived in Alabama and southern Georgia, the hospital system provided the means to desert and return home.

The desertion from Stout's hospitals was fairly well spread out in 1864, peaking when one might expect, from the start of Sherman's Atlanta campaign until the fall of Atlanta in September 1864 (see table 7). The majority of the deserters came from three states—Georgia (460), Alabama (372), and Mississippi (204)—with Tennessee (83) a distant fourth. Most of the Alabama and Georgia troop desertion took place between March and December 1864. The web of hospitals plunged progressively further south as the year wore on, and by the time Atlanta

Table 7. Number of Confederate soldiers deserting from Army of Tennessee hospitals in 1864 and early 1865

1864			1865
January to May	June to September	September to December	January to April
738	774	327	178

Note: These data were gathered by tallying every deserter during the period covered by a particular hospital register. With the exception of records designated as "morning reports," which list deserters only by hospital, the registers identify each patient by name, state, and unit.

had fallen and Hood took the army out of the state, Stout's hospital network could have taken a Georgian as far south as Fort Gaines and Albany, east to the South Carolina border at Augusta, or into the Georgia wiregrass/pine barrens at Fort Valley and Americus. One of the difficulties of deserting was getting home or to a place of safety, but for soldiers well enough to walk, Stout's network of hospitals provided the long-distance transportation necessary to make desertion possible.

Sherman's invasion had serious consequences for hospitals and desertion because as the casualties poured in, the facilities became overcrowded, forcing Stout to find additional space. As he moved his hospitals south, particularly into Alabama, he was forced to use churches, grocery stores, and literally any building that would accommodate men. The facilities were poor and often improperly supplied, and for men able to desert, the conditions in these places made desertion an even more desirable option.[43] Mississippi's hospital deserters came later but followed the same pattern. More than half (124) deserted between September 1864 and April 1865, and part of the reason lies in the network of hospitals extending down into Alabama by that time. One of the more mobile facilities of the war, the Flewellen Hospital, was in either Mississippi or southern Alabama from October 1864 until the end of the war.[44]

There appeared to be no single regiment more susceptible to desertion. Since all these men shared the same plight, having become ill or been wounded, the commonality among them was their condition. What is interesting, however, are the notations in the registers. They give some idea as to the circumstances of each deserter, and in many cases they support the observations of Confederate civilian and military leaders.

Some men apparently were admitted and incapable of doing anything for some time. There are examples of "admitted May 5th deserted July 24." Other entries, however, vindicate Lee's belief that hospitals were full of men capable

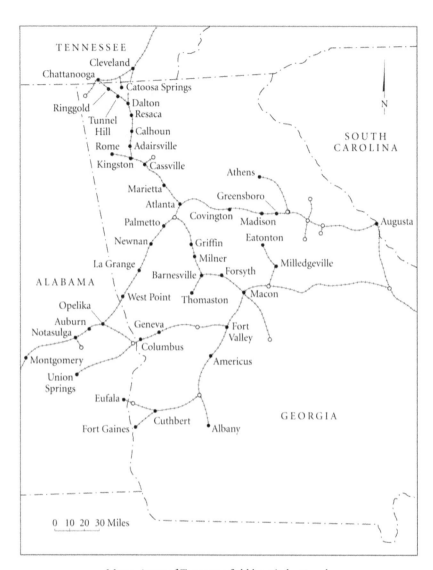

Map 1. Army of Tennessee field hospital network

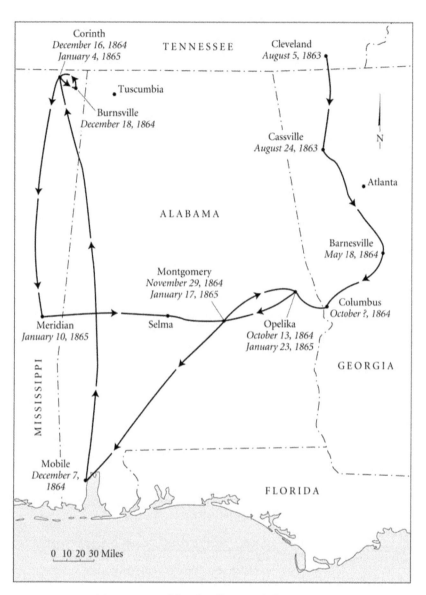

Map 2. Route of the Flewellen Hospital, 1863–1865

of returning to duty. The most conspicuous example comes in the notation "Admitted August 1, deserted same day." A man capable of deserting the same day he was admitted had either not been as badly hurt as was first believed or had been moved from a hospital where he was initially admitted to a place further from the front. Lee would have argued that he should have been sent back to the army, not furloughed or transferred south for more convalescing.

The most obvious example of an abuse unique to hospitals was the medical furlough. Bragg had seen the potential and actual harm in his army in late 1862, but the Confederate Congress had nevertheless continued the practice until as late as April 1863, in great part based on the research to that point that demonstrated how important convalescing at home was to a soldier's recovery. However, by late 1863 even the Confederate Congress realized what the hospital furlough system had done to army strength. The repeal of the law, however, did not seem to affect the granting of furloughs. The case of Cpl. W. R. Holder from Company F of the Thirty-ninth Alabama is typical: "Admitted to Milner July 15, Furloughed, deserted August 24, 1864." Milner lay immediately south of Atlanta on the railroad, and Holder's wounds had taken him out of the immediate theater of operation around Atlanta. His furlough enabled him to travel legally from Milner to wherever his home lay, and thereafter he chose not to return. Holder's furlough came not from any real need to heal at home but from the realization that with the campaign raging around Atlanta, the Confederacy needed the hospital beds. What is significant about the soldiers deserting in the July 22, 1864, hospital register is that by that point in the war Stout's hospitals were well south of Atlanta. Milner, Griffin, Columbus, and Forsyth (see Map 1) were all south of the siege in Atlanta. Vineville, another hospital that shows up frequently among the deserters, was located near Macon. Alabama hospitals also figure prominently in the desertion of Alabama troops, particularly hospitals located in Montgomery and Eufala.[45]

In one sense it is amazing that more men did not desert from Stout's facilities. With security virtually nonexistent both in the hospital and while in transit, opportunities to desert abounded, and thanks to the Confederate military, the transportation problem had been solved. Perhaps the answer is that most men in hospitals were too sick or injured to desert. The death rate for wounded during the war was almost twice that of any other American war. The more salient question is, Of those capable of deserting, how many did so? The bigger question is, Did the desertion from hospitals hurt? The answer is clearly yes. Alone, eighteen hundred men might not have mattered. But given the desertion that occurred everywhere else, from going to the Union, refusing to answer conscription, ignoring the call to return once exchanged, and just leaving the army and going home, hospital desertion compounded the problem. It represented yet another aspect of the Confederacy that desertion infected. Kirby Smith's 1865 experience notwithstanding, there are very few instances of mass desertion. Even five hundred men in a month like July 1864 comes down to sixteen a day. It was not always dramatic, but desertion never let up. Its killing effect lay in its persistence. Hospital desertion also hurt from another perspective. The Confederacy lost soldiers trying in effect to save them. It sent men to the rear, to safety, in the hopes that some could recover and return to aid the cause. The danger that one might not recover in a hospital was real. Edward L. Wells from South Carolina received a bullet wound, and for several weeks there was no problem. But then the fever set in, and with what he called "the impure air of the hospital," contracting typhoid fever became a possibility. Wells got his furlough and apparently healed and returned to duty. However, men in Stout's hospital system used the transportation provided and the furloughs to escape service. To stop hospital desertion the Confederate army would have had to either commit combat soldiers to guard duty or keep men closer to the front and not allow them to convalesce, in effect running the risk that fewer would die from illness and wounds than would desert. Clearly, this was one more dilemma that desertion posed for the Confederacy.[46]

Desertion to the enemy and hospital desertion clearly drew significant numbers out of the Confederate army. But while the Union kept records, as did Stout, the state of Confederate record keeping continued to decline or failed to improve. H. C. Lockhart, the commandant of conscripts in Alabama, admitted in late November 1864 that there were 7,994 deserters from Alabama alone on his books and that every one of them had been recorded since April 1, 1864. His records indicated that 4,323 had been returned to the army, but that still left 3,671 deserters at large. The fall of Atlanta not only crippled the Confederacy militarily but stopped any reporting of troop strength. Lockhart claimed there had been no updating of deserter numbers since September 2, 1864. He believed Alabama had no less than six thousand deserters at large, giving each county an average of three hundred. As if deserter bands had not caused enough havoc, Lockhart explained that the presence of such groups in Florida, Georgia, and Mississippi made it impossible to get an accurate count for counties bordering those states. As 1864 came to an end, the Confederacy had no statistical idea how bad desertion had become.[47]

Although scattered, evidence of desertion in 1864 existed beyond the Union Register and Stout's hospital registers. Junius Bragg referred to desertion as "the order of the day" in February 1864. He commented on how just it was to shoot two deserters, claiming that if they did not do so then everyone "should quit and go home." On February 5, 1864, the *Selma Morning Reporter* listed twenty-nine men who failed to report to parole camp when exchanged. In April a reward poster founds its way onto walls and fenceposts in southern Texas, offering thirty dollars for the apprehension and delivery of any one of nine deserters from the Thirty-third Texas Cavalry. The men came from Atascosa, Bexar, Goliad, and Refugio counties of southern Texas and Williamson County in central Texas, just north of Austin. In Alabama on August 17, 1864, Governor Watts advised Maj. David Compton to "send for every man who is liable for service and bring them back by force if necessary." Watts wanted advertisements posted for all deserters and rewards offered. In early September 1864, correspondence came to Watts indicating that Autauga County had large numbers of deserters running through it. On September 30 he issued a notice addressed to "All Soldiers Absent from their Commands" that covered several forms of desertion. Some soldiers may have stayed at home after their furloughs expired "not intending to desert" and now were afraid to go back for fear of the penalty. Many had left their commands without leave under the "mistaken notion that the highest duty required you to provide sustenance and protection to your families." Every man's motive differed, claimed Watts, but he did not believe any of the men now absent intended to abandon the South's cause and gave them forty days to return without the threat of the death penalty.[48]

The day before Atlanta fell, Governor Clarke received a petition from Jones County asking him to station the company of one M. H. Barkley within the county for the protection of the local citizenry because "deserters" had returned and the people were helpless. The next day a request came from Erata to leave the local state troops within the county for protection from deserters. Every month until the end of the year Clarke received some kind of correspondence from a Confederate official, local magistrate, or citizen asking his assistance in dealing with desertion.[49]

The notices, letters, newspapers, and proclamations demonstrate the severity of the desertion problem even if they do not provide precise numbers. Col. William Fowler's records of Alabama troops in the Army of Tennessee was destroyed in the final months of the war, but his records of Alabama troops in Lee's Army of Northern Virginia remain partially intact. Fowler had given explicit instructions for how each commander was to complete the data on his troops, but people seldom followed directions. Some companies have desertion dates, others simply say "deserted" or "deserted to the enemy." Without dates it is impossible to establish any kind of pattern, but where company and regimental commanders did date their information, those records reinforce the correspondence and the newspapers of the day as well as Union records. What remains today are the raw data from Fowler's work, and it is significant because it represents one of the few sources on desertion from the Confederate side at the unit level, prepared during or immediately following the war. They allow for a glimpse into desertion at the regimental and company level within the ranks of Lee's army and demonstrate just how severe the problem had become in 1864.[50]

Records for the Fourth Alabama survived and provided both names and dates of desertion. Every company except Company A had deserters. The 1864 desertion occurred almost exclusively between May and September, the period from the start of the overland campaign until the end of the summer. Judging by the county affiliations of the soldiers, Companies F, H, and K appeared to be full of northern Alabama boys and showed the most desertion, with some notations indicating desertion to the Union. James H. Davis of Macon, Alabama, deserted to the enemy on August 4, 1864. Calvin Cassidy, F. L. Chapman of Jackson County, James M. Frayser of Florence, Alabama, and Epheraim Hawkins of Bristol, Tennessee, all left on the same day as Davis.[51]

Records for the Eighth Alabama demonstrate not only the amount of desertion but the problem with Confederate record keeping. The individual company rolls list 107 deserters up to December 31, 1864, but there is a regimental summary at the front that purports to total the company data, and it indicates there were 141 deserters. Some of the companies in the Eighth listed dates of desertion while others did not. Even within the company data there are dates for some men and none for others. However, once again Fowler's records show that soldiers were deserting from Lee's army from as early as May 1864 to the end of the year, and many were going into the Union lines. The regimental records for the Eighth Alabama indicate that 14 men deserted and went to the enemy, and the detailed company data actually lists more, but it raises the following question: if 14 out of 107 deserters in one unit took the route through Union lines, and over the course of the war 35,000 deserted to the Union, what does that say about the total numbers for Confederate desertion?[52]

The purpose in looking at units like the Fourth and the Eighth is to show not only that desertion occurred but also that it involved large numbers. The impact gets lost because many times men trickled out a few at a time. But when two or three men from every company left every day across the entire Confederate army, the overall impact was lethal. It did not happen every day of every month of every year, but once it began to pick up in 1863 it never stopped.

Union records in Mississippi also support the other indicators of heavy oath swearing among Confederate deserters in 1864. A Union prison record from Natchez lists twenty-nine Confederate deserters from Louisiana, Missouri, Mississippi, and Texas units who swore the oath to the Union between August 12 and September 21, 1864. The notes in the record indicate that the men were sent north to one of the release points and then set free. At about the same time, the *Daily Mississippian* published a list of eighty deserters from eight different units, all but one of whom was from Mississippi.[53] Again, this does not suggest that men deserted in June and ended up in the Natchez prison by August; it simply shows the many different contemporary records that testify to the extent of the desertion epidemic in the Confederacy.

One of the most interesting records is the isolated field returns for a division in Polk's corps commanded first by Jones Mitchell Withers and then by Thomas Hindman. The returns are incomplete and hard to read, but they show the weekly numbers in one division over a period of several years. It is difficult to tell whether the desertions listed each week reflect the total deserters still gone or if each week reflected new men who had deserted. Based on the numbers, it would seem to be the former. If not, then this division lost between a half and a full company of soldiers almost every ten days. If the records are cumulative, they reflect some interesting things about desertion and record keeping. One of the problems the Confederate army faced was knowing what its strength was throughout the war. Kean blamed Cooper, yet even Lee had to speculate about the whereabouts of his absentees. These divisional reports have desertion numbers that shift every week. What this may indicate is that men were listed as deserters one week if they could not otherwise be accounted for, and then, if they returned from a furlough or a detail or were located in a hospital, their names were removed from the desertion category. In 1862 the weekly division returns listed no fewer than 11 deserters and as many as 156 in one week in June. The returns, however, are incomplete, and a large gap exists between January and April 1863. Hindman took command of the division in August 1863, about the time the Union desertion program became finalized. His returns run from the end of August 1863 to April 28, 1864. For September, October, and November 1863 his division never had fewer than 53 deserters listed, and for the week ending September 30 it listed 145. The numbers drop in December and then pick up again in January 1864. The report for March 1864 lists 122 deserters. On average, Hindman's division had 60 men listed each week as deserters.[54]

Despite the condition of the company, regimental, and divisional records, three important aspects of desertion emerge. First, desertion begins in 1862, regardless of what people chose to call the problem. Absenteeism had a connotation of temporary absence, and these records show that men left on a permanent basis. Second, no one really had a grasp of just how many men deserted. Like Lee's army, Polk's corps and most likely the rest of Bragg's and later Johnston's army was a revolving door. Some men left and returned while others simply left. Third, once desertion began in earnest it never let up. Hindman's returns show a jump at the same time the Union began to push its desertion program. Whether these men deserted to the Union is impossible to tell, but the returns reflect a clear increase in desertion. Hindman's division averaged eighty-eight deserters for every weekly return from August 30 to November 20, 1863. Something had to account for the higher rate.

Causation in 1864 followed the previous years with an added element, as unfulfilled hope and unrealized expectation appeared to drive desertion. An Alabama soldier writing from Mobile spoke confidently of the cause as late as August 1864. Mobile Bay had already fallen to Farragut, but Pvt. J. Little Smith still believed the South could survive. He thought that enough would happen between then and the November election for the North to come apart, and he expressed "big hope" for Sterling Price's upcoming invasion into Missouri out of Arkansas.[55] For those who had not given up, defeat on the field or at the ballot box could prove twice as damaging. For soldiers pinning their hopes on a turn of events, the fall of 1864 must have been devastating. Atlanta fell three days after Smith wrote home. Price's invasion proved to be a disaster. If Smith was demoralized, what must Price's soldiers have felt? Arkansas desertion, both among men going to the enemy and those going straight home, went way up in the wake of his defeat. Likewise, the numbers on desertion to the enemy show the effects of Lincoln's November victory, particularly in the East among men mired in trench warfare. But Southerners everywhere were hoping Lincoln would lose.

A Texas man admitted that if Lincoln won there was no "telling when it will end."[56]

Expectation or simply hope of Lincoln's defeat existed across the South and was dealt a fatal blow in November 1864. Just as Lincoln's election took the steam out of people across the South, one did not have to go to Arkansas to find troops demoralized in the wake of defeat and retreat. Lewis E. Parsons wrote home from outside Atlanta on September 11, 1864, "I have the blues dreadfully & all of the men have the blues as so many of the boys have been killed." So many dead and apparently for nothing. The Confederacy had lost Atlanta, and Parsons was despondent that Hood had withdrawn. Alabama desertion to the Union escalated in the wake of Atlanta's fall, and that Hood left the state in Union hands made matters worse. It is little wonder that as the army withdrew out of Georgia and into Alabama that Alabama soldiers left the army and headed home. Despite his disappointment, there is no evidence that Parsons ever deserted, but defeat apparently weighed more heavily on other men. A notice posted in the *Selma Morning Reporter* on September 14, 1864, called for the return of all men from the Forty-fourth Alabama who had disappeared. Four months earlier the men of this unit had pledged themselves as "Soldiers for the War."[57]

By October 1864, some men had experienced so much defeat on the battle-field that Lincoln's election no longer seemed to matter. An unnamed soldier wrote home in late October from a camp near Cross Plains, Alabama. He had recently come out of Georgia with the army, and as far as he was concerned the election no longer mattered. "For my part," he wrote his wife, "I would not hesitate to accept of a restoration with the Union as much as I hate the Yanks—because our government has become a despotism, which is intolerable and will continue to be despotic if our independence is acknowledged, hence I believe a larger share of liberty will be enjoyed in the old Union." This man claimed he would continue to fight as long as the Union regarded Southerners as slaves, but his message was clear, and Governor Watts had warned Seddon this might happen. In January 1864 Watts complained about the Confederate government's practice of seizing private property. It was bad enough that the government had proved unable to provide for and protect soldiers' families, but Watts warned that "if our independence is lost it will be due to a breaking down of the spirits of the people." Governor Allen of Louisiana found himself mired in the same debate with Davis three months later. Allen wanted a commission appointed to look into deprivations of property and rights by Confederate authorities. While Davis agreed that the key to the success of the cause was "a perfect understanding between the state and Confederate authorities," he all but ignored Allen's requests and told him to consult Kirby Smith. By 1864 the "perfect understanding" most people had was that the Confederate government had failed its citizens, both at home and in the army. John Sandidge, Louisiana's chief of ordnance, said it best: "The government can no longer protect the citizenry and they should be at least left in the best possible condition to take care of themselves." It was not that people had failed to develop some attachment to a larger cause, even if the cause was sold as a defense of home. The government had simply failed to deliver on its promise. The anonymous soldier had camped near Tuscaloosa four months earlier and been astonished by the poverty and suffering in the area. By October defeat and suffering at home seemed to convince him that Confederacy was not the way to go.[58]

The unnamed soldier chose to remain in the army, or at least that is what he said in late October. Many soldiers, however, did not. While camped near Petersburg, Timothy Morgan wrote home on December 30, 1864, and described the desertion reflected in the Register and documented by both Union and Confederate officials. "Our men are deserting and going over to the Yankee's lines nearly every night and some officers is going," he wrote his wife. Again, it is difficult to discount the effect of unrealized expectation. In April 1864, Pvt. R. S. Jones wrote from his camp in Dalton, Georgia, to tell his aunt how happy he was that the deserters in Covington County had been captured. He hoped they would "be dealt with as they richly deserve." Johnston had been shooting deserters, and Jones believed such men deserved what they got, but by October the situation had changed. David L. Jones, R. S.'s brother, had returned to Alabama, and his letter reflected the disappointment that came with unfulfilled hope. Men in his unit received letters from home daily describing how both the Yankees and Confederate deserters threatened the country. The corn in the fields rotted from the lack of anyone to harvest the crop, and blacks and whites alike had fled into Yankee lines. One of Jones's friends was going home and hoped to stay, as it appeared men were badly needed there. For David Jones and his comrades, the election would matter. If Lincoln won it would mean four more years of war, and they would not fight for four more years.[59]

Despite the efforts of Polk and Pillow, deserters continued to terrorize civilians, further demoralizing men already reeling from defeat on the battlefield. Catherine Powell of Greene County, Mississippi, wrote Governor Watts of Alabama complaining that deserters had pretended to leave the county but stayed in the area looting women and children, taking food, clothing, and other necessities. She claimed it was wrong for her and others to have their husbands and sons off fighting for men who were at home stealing from their families and that Southern soldiers would not allow this to go on. Those at home could barely get bread, much less feed these deserters.[60] The government could not protect them, and all the help these women had in the world was in the army. No longer willing to have their men leave the county, citizens of Chambers County, Alabama, petitioned the state legislature to have their men brought back from state duty to patrol their own county against deserter bands. This was exactly the kind of situation the Union desertion policy counted on.

People in need got no relief or protection from those they had depended on before the war, and not only did the government prove unable to effectively protect people, but its officials exploited the system. A fifty-nine-year-old man from Desoto, Alabama, told Governor Watts that he had four sons in the army, three of whom "now sleep the sleep of death." He did not understand why Alabama men would hide behind the protection of government employee "exemptions" provided to bailiffs, justices of the peace, and conscription officers. Let the old men fill those positions, the man insisted; the young needed to fight. As far as the writer was concerned, it was Watts's responsibility and he did not want to hear Watts claim not to be the legislature. Watts had been elected, and everyone expected him to protect the state. In 1864, Confederate enrolling officers had become a real problem. A man from Tallapoosa County claimed the state commandant and his minions were "dashing about in buggies seeking some poor devil to devour." It is little wonder the Conscription Bureau officers could not handle the deserter problem. Many had lost the respect of the local population by abusing their station. As the Tallapoosa man put it, "Old men are forced into the army and widows and children left homeless."[61]

Letters like these make it easy to understand why men began to abandon their duty. With little help from the government and life at home in turmoil, maintaining a fight for a cause that seemed to be dying in some places and was already dead in others no longer made sense. A soldier in the Twentieth Alabama watched as two men were shot for desertion in Tennessee in May 1864. He told his parents that both men died because they tried to desert after they got letters from home, and he cautioned his own family to "think of this ye mothers and wives, when you write letters to your sons and husbands, thus causing them to desert—oh, dreadful is the consequence."[62] The nation they supposedly fought for was being choked by its political subdivisions that refused to enforce national laws, help maintain the national army, or even aid the nation when it need it most. Thomas Watts told Governor Brown of Georgia that he could send no troops to protect Georgia without violating Alabama law. Yet he also claimed that "When Georgia suffers, Alabama suffers." Brown wanted troops to stop Sherman, but Watts said his state militia laws forbade such a transfer. Two days before that, Watts had told John Bell Hood essentially the same thing. Hood would invade Tennessee within two months and needed more soldiers, but Alabama's state militia law did not allow men to leave their own counties.[63] It seemed almost insane for the Confederacy to ask men to keep fighting for a cause when the political subdivisions within it were willing to commit national suicide to maintain the letter of the law.

The South's governors knew there was a problem. In October 1864 the governors of Virginia, North Carolina, South Carolina, Georgia, Alabama, and Mississippi met in Augusta, Georgia. The meeting served as an appraisal of where the Confederacy stood in late 1864 and what the states should do to further the cause. One of the resolutions passed dealt with the use of state troops outside state lines. The governors agreed that the interest of each state is identical and that "wisdom and true patriotism dictate the military force of each should aid the others against subjugation and invasion." The governors resolved to appeal to their legislatures to lift any prohibition against sending troops outside state lines. They also resolved to recommend to their respective legislatures that stringent laws be passed for the arrest and return of all deserters to the Confederate army and that it be made the specific duty of all state and local officials, under appropriate penalties, to enforce these desertion laws. But the governors had one request of the Confederate government: eliminate passport agents on all trains except those near the immediate theater of operations.[64]

It is significant that not every state governor attended the conference. However, even among those who attended, the resolutions reflect several key points about the Confederacy that undermined not only its ability to wage war but ultimately the willingness of its soldiers to continue the fight. First, to the extent that Confederate desertion resembled that of other eighteenth-century American and colonial armies, the Confederate executives also resembled the revolutionary governors. Both were effectively hamstrung by strong state legislatures that handicapped them in both war and peace. All of the resolutions at the Augusta meeting state that the governors will "recommend" certain measures to their legislatures. Watts actually tried before the conference ever met, but to no avail. The Alabama legislature met in September and adjourned in early October, and it did not address the manpower situation or the desertion question. The state

THE ORDER OF THE DAY

legislatures had refused to allow the state forces to become arms of the Confederate military. Just as Vance had refused to challenge North Carolina's judiciary when Pearson ruled that state troops could not arrest Confederate deserters, Watts refused to challenge the Alabama legislature's authority to restrict the movement of its state troops. Second, some of the measures proposed already existed as laws in Mississippi and South Carolina, and officials in Mississippi admitted that the laws were all but dead. Finally, the suggestion that the passport agents be taken off trains outside the areas near the front reflected a clear failure to understand just how severe the desertion problem had become. Confederate officials would never eliminate passports, and by 1864 the main reason was the desertion problem.[65]

Perceptions are crucial to the entire desertion story. Retreat clearly drove desertion, but while some retreats were clear, such as Price's from Missouri and Johnston's through Georgia, others were not. Soldiers could often designate redeployment as retreat, and if they felt that something was being abandoned, they used the move as a basis for desertion. James J. Cowan of Mississippi, whose family became refugees in Alabama, was part of Polk's corps. When Polk moved out of Mississippi into Alabama on his way to join Johnston in Georgia, some men, including Cowan, characterized Polk's movement as a retreat from Mississippi. To Mississippi troops leaving their state, it may well have seemed like a retreat. Cowan boasted that "fewer desertions occurred than ever before on a retreat." Polk refused to give battle, and Cowan claimed that no one deserted until they reached Morton, Mississippi. Cowan claimed he lost only 20 out of 350 men, and some of those returned by the time he reached Demopolis.[66] Cowan's experience confirmed that retreat could be deadly to an army's discipline. Mississippians reacted to leaving their home state by characterizing what was essentially the redeployment of a corps as a retreat, and retreat translated into defeat. Cowan's observations suggest that some Mississippians went into Georgia "defeated" insofar as they had failed to hold their own state, and Johnston's subsequent retreat to Atlanta could not have strengthened their conviction to serve.

Despite all the indications that desertion had been driven by hardship, retreat, the desire to protect home, and the inability of the Confederate or state governments to protect their citizens, there remained those who believed desertion was the product of disloyalty. On February 28, 1864, John Paris, chaplain of the Fifty-fourth North Carolina, gave a funeral sermon for the twenty-two men hung as deserters by Pickett. In Paris's opinion, the dead were unfortunate "yet wicked and deluded." Deserters had but one biblical analogue, Judas Iscariot, and Paris proceeded to detail Judas's road to desertion. Paris segued from his biblical example to a theme so prevalent in the war on both sides, the American Revolution. He spoke of Benedict Arnold, a man whose name towered "high on the scroll of infamy." Using these two infamous deserters, Paris argued that any man who takes up arms in defense of his country and then basely deserts belongs in both principle and practice with Judas and Arnold. Paris claimed that the twenty-two men had joined the Confederate service, accepted the bounty, sworn the oath, and then rejected everything they had held dear—honor, reputation, land, and state—to enter into an agreement with the enemy and swear an oath to the United States. All but two of these men had claimed that they were influenced to desert by other men. "The great amount of desertion from our army are produced by, and are the fault of a bad, mischievous, restless and dissatisfied, not to say disloyal influence that is at work in the country at home," Paris claimed. He argued that the letters coming from home to soldiers from supposed friends claiming the state was going to secede and other falsehoods amounted to spreading treason.[67]

Paris made a compelling case for the stain that desertion cast upon a man, and he argued vehemently for the loyalty men owed to North Carolina. But the reality was that opinions differed as to how committed the twenty-two deserters had ever been to the Confederacy and whether any or all had ever joined the service. More importantly, Paris ignored completely the state of affairs throughout the Confederacy. Letters indeed came from home, and some may have spoken of the dissolution of the Confederacy, but many more spoke of the dissolution of community, the absence of law and order, and the destruction of the family. Desertion was much more complex than simply a renunciation of a clear obligation. Confederate soldiers fought an enemy that considered all of them disloyal rebels. They went to war for a nation that had existed for only two months before the conflict began. Most soldiers benefited little from the institution that defined the South and went to war based on what they deemed was a contractual obligation between themselves and the Confederacy. They relied upon the promise of the rich that home would be well cared for, and both the contract and the promise had been breached. Many felt no obligation at all and felt a much deeper connection with those they left when they went to war. Desertion was much more than an evil driven by the disloyal. It was the reaction of men who had been loyal and felt betrayed.

Thirty years after the Civil War ended, Edward Porter Alexander, reflecting on the situation in 1865 as Lee's army and the Confederacy headed toward the war's end, wrote that "the situation of the country at large was one of almost as great deprivation & suffering as that of the army itself; and many localities even of much greater." Georgia and the Carolinas had been overrun by Sherman and were economically devastated, and although "the other Southern states had not been so generally over run, . . . in all there had been many districts more or less ravaged by raids and marches. Naturally, the wives and mothers left at home wrote longingly for the return of their husbands and sons in the ranks in Virginia. And naturally, many of them could not resist their appeals, & deserted in order to return and care for their families." The situation had reached absurd levels as whole commands started to desert. Captain Poor of the Twenty-fifth North Carolina had gone to the western mountains of North Carolina. He had fifty men in his command when he left the Army of Northern Virginia and claimed to be hunting deserters when in reality he and all his men were deserters themselves. The Sixty-second and Sixty-fourth North Carolina did likewise, and once these men got into the mountains they never returned.[1]

Alexander's description of Lee's army in Virginia applied across the Confederacy. Reports flowed into the Headquarters of the Military Division of the West Mississippi that certain areas of Louisiana could not be reached because of the condition of the Confederate forces. Citizens and refugees described the army as in "a state of great discontent and insubordination." Poor pay, insufficient rations, and the destitution of their families had turned it into a rabble. Desertions occurred daily, and military authorities had once again moved to the other extreme, forsaking amnesty and leniency for harsher treatment. Punishment took on almost a retributive quality. Executions in Louisiana took place on Fridays, with one regiment shooting fifteen men at one time. In Alexandria one brigade mutinied and tried to desert, and thirty-five men were shot as a result. Troops in Louisiana and Arkansas were seen headed into Texas with civilian refugees accompanying them.[2]

The war ended four months into 1865. Entire books have been written about the last month of the war, the end of the Confederacy, and the military aspects of the last days. That is not the case with the Confederate desertion story. For years, Civil War scholarship pointed to 1865 as the great wave of Confederate desertion. The reality is that desertion was a disease that infected the Confederacy long before the end of the rebellion. Ella Lonn concluded her story of Confederate desertion with the comment that "the miracle is not that the Confederacy fell, but that it did not collapse in 1863."[3] The nation remained standing because those in the army continued to fight, but those who stayed could not do it alone. The disease that ultimately killed the Confederacy began in 1862, took hold in 1863, and never let go. Shortages of food and necessities, extortion, conscription, and the inability of a society strongly based on a semi-subsistence agriculture to continue in the absence of its male workforce all weakened the Confederate cause, and these same elements contributed to desertion. Although desertion began in the military, it spread out into the home front and eventually became something far bigger and more lethal than the simple unwillingness of men to fight. By the end of 1863 desertion depleted the army, taxed the ability of government at all levels to bring men back, spawned a military force in the South that eventually became a small army, and in the process allowed Southerners to prey upon the very people whom soldiers had gone to war to protect. The year 1865 is an appropriate conclusion because the last four months of the war represented a recapitulation of the things that had been happening for almost three years. The desertion continued, the Confederacy tried many of the same remedies that had failed it for most of the war, and the Confederate Congress passed new laws that came too late to make any difference.

In January 1865 the Confederacy stepped up efforts to preserve what remained of its army in the West. From Richmond came orders to send a portion of the provisional Confederate army to northern Georgia to rid the area of deserters and stragglers and break up whatever illegal organizations were found to exist. The partisan war in northern Georgia had continued, and the Unionists appeared to be winning. The massive desertion of Tennessee troops in the aftermath of the Franklin and Nashville disaster had apparently struck, and both the Union and Confederate armies were put on notice to be aware of deserters. George Thomas's superiors cautioned him to be wary of Confederate deserters from a forced retreat, claiming the trustworthiness of such men was suspect.

Meanwhile, John Bell Hood, desperately trying to salvage what he could of an army already decimated by slaughter, discovered that what the Union had not killed or wounded, desertion threatened to take away as large numbers of his soldiers crossed the Union lines in Tennessee.[4]

In an effort to more effectively punish desertion and prevent its occurrence, the Confederate House passed House bill 319 on January 3, 1865. The bill required that any officer absent for more than a month be dropped from the rolls. Any regimental officer who in the opinion of his commanding officer willfully or carelessly neglected the care and comfort of his men or exhibited undue laxity of discipline would be suspended for three months. The most important aspect of the bill called for any officer to be dropped from the rolls who kept a man in his command whom he knew or had been told was a deserter. Finally, any man deserting would have his name forwarded by the adjutant general's office to all the governors of the respective states and the generals in command of the departments.[5] Like so many other measures in 1865, this law was too little, too late. It implied that desertion flowed from a lack of discipline and care, but officers could not provide food and clothing they did not have. The discipline needed should have come in 1862 when men began deserting. Dropping officers from the rolls or suspending them would do nothing. The Confederacy should have executed men in 1862 when the evil first began. Instead, leniency dominated all aspects of the military justice system.

On January 10, 1865, with Sherman poised to drive into the Carolinas and Grant slowly wearing Lee down around Petersburg, the Confederate House passed a law designed to bring deserters back into the army. Entitled "An Act to Provide for the More Efficient Execution of Conscription and the Arrest of Deserters and Absentees from the Army," it reorganized the Conscription Bureau and created the post of superintendent, which was to be filled by a brigadier general who had the authority to call upon the Confederate reserves in any state to assist in hunting and apprehending deserters. The law further made it more difficult to secure medical exemptions from the draft and gave the superintendent the same power to order a general court-martial as that accorded to generals commanding armies.[6] In reality, however, the law changed nothing. The job of collecting deserters was still not a purely military function, and the act only allowed the bureau to borrow reserve troops. It created no independent force. Despite the experiences of the last two years, the Confederate leadership appeared to have learned nothing.

On February 2, 1865, the Confederate Senate passed a bill designed to strengthen its January 22, 1864, act that prevented the harboring of deserters. To the extent that the act could be enforced at all, people accused of harboring deserters hid behind the claim that they did not know a man had deserted when they fed, clothed, or housed him. The amendment stated that in prosecuting someone for harboring a deserter, the "general representation that such a soldier or officer is a deserter, shall be taken as prima facie evidence of the fact of desertion."[7]

Not every suggestion for bringing the Confederate army back to full strength had been tried before. There were actually some novel ideas, and one in particular, although impractical, revealed that the elites knew the war had become a poor man's fight. J. W. Ellis suggested to Jefferson Davis that to "successfully manage" the war, every soldier should be given a stake in slavery. Ellis reasoned that 3.5 million slaves existed in the South and that there were one million men in arms, half of them owning slaves. He suggested that each non-slaveholder be given one slave and fifty acres of land, since by doing so "every man became a slaveholder" and every family would have a stake in the war. Then Ellis suggested that the Confederacy adopt the Union plan of inducing desertion by offering a slave and fifty acres to Union soldiers who deserted and swore the oath to the Confederacy.[8]

Ellis's plan has the distinction of never having been tried, but with desertion continuing to escalate the Confederacy needed a more practical solution. In February 1865, John Preston, superintendent of the Conscription Bureau, took another shot at convincing Lee to create independent local forces working in conjunction with the bureau to bring deserters back into the army. Preston claimed that Pillow's plan had been tried and had failed "almost ridiculously," but it is hard to say Pillow's idea failed when the Confederacy never devoted the permanent military forces necessary to make it work. Efforts by Confederate army units had succeeded, but their success had been brief; moreover, when they left an area the deserters returned, and as desertion continued the deserter bands got larger. Putting aside his rivalry with Pillow, Preston nevertheless had some sound ideas. He suggested to Lee that in addition to establishing a permanent deserter force, the states needed to pass desertion laws similar to or identical with the Confederate laws. The laws needed to at least imply that civil authorities could be used to hunt and return Confederate deserters. Furthermore, state courts had to be empowered to prosecute offenders under Confederate law. Although Preston's plan had merit, Lee was not the man to implement it. He did not believe an independent force was needed, and he had no power to persuade state legislatures to do anything. Once again the reality of Confederate desertion was that a federal problem had became a state problem, and it would only be solved by a proactive participation by the states. That level of participation never came.[9]

Lee's solution to the problem was to offer yet another amnesty, approved and endorsed by Davis. Upon assuming the position of general in chief of the Confederate armies on February 9, 1865, Lee resorted to leniency in the hope that men would respond and that those at home would force deserters back to the army. Lee's latest amnesty pardoned all deserters and absentees who returned to the army within twenty days. The pardon did not apply to those who deserted to the Union, those who deserted after taking advantage of a previous pardon, or those who deserted after receiving a pardon under the present amnesty offer. Lee's order stated that "this was the last such pardon that would ever be offered."[10] He was right: the war would be over in less than two months, and this latest offer would do nothing. The offer of amnesty had proved a conspicuous failure, and over the course of the war the Confederate military had wavered back and forth between full pardons and executions. In January 1865 officers in Louisiana were shooting men every Friday, and the following month Lee wanted to pardon deserters throughout the Confederacy. Without a consistent approach, the military had lost all legitimacy with the men it purported to lead.

In March 1865, Confederate leaders continued to debate the best way to curb desertion. Lee steadfastly maintained that a new independent force was unnecessary and that reserves could be used to fight deserters on the home front. Preston disagreed, as he had for most of the war. After getting no satisfaction from Lee, Preston approached the new secretary of war, John C. Breckenridge, and told him that there were one hundred thousand deserters running free in the Confederacy. Sixteen-year-old boys and old men could not hope to bring these deserters back, and desertion had become so common that it had lost its stigma. Will Crutcher had been right in 1861: desertion had become a "justifiable crime."[11] Preston's arguments, while sound, no longer mattered. The time to act was two years past, and the same argument Preston made then had been rejected. Whether it would have worked or whether Pillow's concept of militarizing the job of collecting deserters was the answer no longer made any difference. A week before the end of the war, the Confederacy continued to resist efforts throughout the South to enroll deserters in new organizations. Samuel Cooper repeated the mantra that had been stated and restated for two years: deserters had to be returned to their original commands.[12]

On the front lines in the East, the slow and steady trickle of Confederate deserters into Union lines continued. Notwithstanding the Union policy that no deserter would be forced into the Union ranks, Confederate authorities told their men that Confederate deserters were being impressed into the Union army. To avoid any confusion on the issue, Confederate pickets began to conference with their Union counterparts to determine if there was any truth to what the Confederate military was saying before they deserted into Union lines. It must have been painful for Lee to report deserters from some of the proudest units in his army. Between February 15 and February 25, 1865, Longstreet's corps had 148 men desert, Early's corps reported 143 deserters, and A. P. Hill's corps lost 586 men. Anderson's corps had only one division, Bushrod Johnson's, and during the same ten-day period he lost 217 men deserting into Union lines. One thousand ninety-four men in ten days, and it all started within a week of Lee's amnesty offer. Even when Lee tried to shoot a deserter, the civilian authorities intervened to commute the sentence.[13]

As March rolled around, men got bolder. Georgians began to leave under the belief that they could go home and join local units. Soldiers began to induce one another to desert, and the practice became so common that Lee issued an order reminding men of the penalty for encouraging desertion. All of this fell on deaf ears. The war in the East had been over for some time as men ran out the last days of the struggle in miserable, cold, wet trenches. By March 1865 even those afraid of the consequences had reached their limit. North Carolinians continued to lead the way, and despite his best efforts, Governor Vance could not stop the steady exodus out of Virginia. Lee took steps to guard river crossings, but because men generally took their weapons with them when they deserted, such efforts were to no avail.[14]

What Lee experienced in Virginia, Kirby Smith felt in the trans-Mississippi. Men from the Third, Sixth, Ninth, and Twenty-seventh Texas had deserted. Apparently, Texans at home encouraged these men and others to desert and come to the Lone Star state, where apprehending deserters had become very difficult. Soldiers east of the Mississippi were deserting, and Smith could not stop men on either side of the river. In early January 1865 he republished copies of the law prohibiting aiding and harboring deserters, but by then the law meant little to the citizens of the Confederacy.[15]

"WE CONQUERED OURSELVES"

Lee's amnesty proclamation did not reach parts of the West until March, and when it was published in the newspapers, confusion arose as to when the twenty-day period for returning would commence. Governor Clarke of Mississippi ordered Richard Taylor to republish the notice and clearly set out the time period for returning. Amnesty by this point in the war meant little to soldiers. When 1865 began, conservative estimates by Confederate authorities in Mississippi put the number of deserters in the state at seven thousand. There is no evidence that any of them responded to Lee's offer. In Alabama, soldiers of the Sixteenth, Twenty-seventh, Thirty-fifth, and Forty-ninth Alabama regiments were all at home in the mountains, and they would not return without coercion. The Union continued to press its amnesty policy and to correct any flaws that developed in its implementation. Some commanders had failed to abide by the regulations concerning Confederate deserters and had actually treated them like prisoners. George Thomas intervened to ensure the continued exodus of Confederate soldiers by emphasizing that deserters were taken back to Nashville only to record their names. Once properly recorded, those from the Army of Tennessee would then be free to return to any portion of Tennessee, northern Alabama, or northern Georgia. In the first four months of the new year, Confederate soldiers in the West continued to take advantage of the Union program led by the Tennesseans. Union reports from Nashville claimed that 4,045 men had sworn the oath, with another 2,506 swearing allegiance in Chattanooga.[16]

This flurry of desertion activity provides a vivid picture of a phenomenon that had no remedy. Lee's army was exhausted, as was Johnston's. While men deserted from Petersburg every day, Tennesseans left Johnston's army in record numbers. It was more than a shortage of food, clothing, and shelter and defeat on the battlefield. The story had come full circle, and it is now easy to see how Kirby Smith's army virtually dissolved in April and May 1865. Shooting men only drove them away. Amnesty offered no enticement. The war had outlasted the Confederacy's ability to maintain its limited cohesion, and exhaustion set in long before 1865. Davis as much as admitted the Confederacy had reached a point of exhaustion in early 1864. In an address to the Confederate Congress in February 1864 he stated:

> It has been our cherished hope that when the great struggle in which we are engaged was passed we might exhibit to the world the proud spectacle of a people unanimous in the assertions and defense of their rights and achieving their liberty and independence after the bloodiest war of modern times without the necessity of a single sacrifice of a civil right to military

necessity. But it can no longer be doubted that the zeal with which the people sprung to arms at the beginning of the contest has, in some parts of the Confederacy, been impaired by the long continuance and magnitude of the struggle. [17]

Davis's comments came as he lobbied the Congress to suspend the writ of habeas corpus. His comments on desertion revealed a problem that had spiraled out of control and displayed a frankness that had been absent from his report to Congress the previous month. But Davis implied that the suspension of the writ would be the "first" instance of sacrificing a civil right to military necessity. Impressment of property, tax-in-kind, conscription, and myriad unspecified acts by the Confederate army had pushed the civilian population to the limit of its tolerance for most of the war. Contrary to E. P. Alexander's observations, wives and mothers had been writing "longingly" for years. Despite what Chaplain Paris believed, these letters were not from "treasonous friends." The Confederacy had taken all its people had to give and had been unable to give back. The length and magnitude of the struggle had demonstrated that loyalty ran both ways and that the government and the wealthy had been unable, and in some cases unwilling, to reciprocate.

The Confederacy became inflicted with many diseases, and although desertion was but one of these maladies, it fed off all the others. In many cases men left for war knowing their families were unprepared for what lay ahead. Every hardship that struck the home front pulled at them to return. Government intervention and the support of the wealthy were the only things short of their returning home that could have alleviated the suffering at home and the apprehensions of those at the front. While the failure of the government must have been troubling, the unwillingness of the wealthy to provide the support they promised proved much more destructive to a soldier's will. These men had no prior experience with government-based intervention and aid. This was a time when "good government" stayed out of everyone's lives. But the poor and the rich in the South had developed a relationship of mutual support and aid that spanned decades. Before the war it had been enough that the poor and yeomen acquiesced to the leadership of the wealthy and demonstrated a work ethic that merited assistance. Going to war and fighting a battle that J. W. Ellis admitted the poor had never had a real stake in seemed to the common man like a greater sacrifice than had ever been asked for or made. To hear that the elites not only withheld assistance but actually took advantage of the hardships and shortages of the war undermined and ultimately severed any sense of loyalty to the Confederacy, its cause, and its army.

It seems almost redundant to harp on causation. So many reasons existed to justify desertion that one could literally pick and choose, and therein lay the problem with controlling what happened. The Confederacy, its army, and its citizens redefined desertion based on motive. There was "good," or justifiable, desertion and unjustifiable desertion. In 1862, a military culture developed that showed, if not outright approval, at least an understanding for men who deserted to return home to their families. The culture remained so strong throughout the war that as the Confederate army completed the process of disintegration in 1865, soldiers continued to diminish the severity of the crime based on why men left. Maj. William Marion Walton, known affectionately by his men and peers as Major Buck, described Texans leaving in the winter of 1865. Many had been within almost a "stone's throw of home" but were never allowed to leave. "The men commenced to deserting—and a great many went off without leave or license. It was not exactly desertion—they were going home to see their folks." Walton told his superior, Gen. William Steele, that he would not desert if the enemy threatened, but since it did not, "I cannot and will not stay idly here while the life of my wife goes out."[18] Going home in response to need was justifiable desertion, and the army never overcame this mind-set. By the end of the war most poor and yeomen soldiers could claim their families needed them. A culture that excused desertion under such circumstances made it impossible to condemn and punish the practice.

The Confederate military and government simply did not see the signs, or if they did they did not recognize their significance. Desertion was indeed a process that grew worse by degrees. The potential had existed from the beginning, and the signs began to appear in 1862. Contrary to Davis's claim in 1864, not everyone joined with zeal in 1861. The need for conscription attests to the unwillingness of many to join the fight. When soldiers began to desert in 1862 the military leadership insisted on referring to them as absentees, and court-martial charges of desertion were routinely reduced to absence without leave. All of this reflected a belief that no one really intended to leave and not return. What the Confederacy never understood was that determining what qualified as desertion was up to the army, not the soldier. If a soldier disappeared for two months, returned only after being captured, and missed the entire summer campaigning season, the army did not have to ask if he "intended" to never return. He was gone when he was most needed. He had deserted. The Confederate

Articles of War contained all the authority the military needed to deal harshly with desertion, including imposing the death penalty. Yet when it came time to execute these men, an officer corps tied to its soldiers in peacetime community relationships simply could not do what was necessary. British officers crushed men of a different social class with impunity. Confederate officers could not do likewise. The willingness to excuse "justified" desertion and to demonstrate leniency made it impossible for the Confederacy to establish the kind of discipline it would need when matters became really hard a year later.

Leniency had another downfall: fairness. Justice was not always blind, and sometimes whether one was convicted or acquitted, whether one received lenient or harsh treatment, depended on wealth and status. In late 1864, James Phelan, a close friend of Davis's, wrote the president with a plan for returning deserters to the army. Sending good soldiers after bad ones, wrote Phelan, not only failed to bring anyone back but reduced good soldiers to a state of uselessness. Phelan suggested a pardon for all deserters, which is exactly what Lee offered in 1865. However, Phelan included several conditions of his own. The pardon had to be issued to everyone. He had seen commanding generals abuse their power to commute sentences of the military courts and knew that such abuse would destroy the power of a pardon. Phelan provided an example from early in the war in which a group of men stood accused of desertion. Two of the deserters came from "family and fortune." Able to afford able counsel, they escaped conviction on the desertion charge and were found guilty of absence without leave. Almost immediately their families took steps to have them pardoned of the lesser conviction, and shortly thereafter both men "were parading the streets with their friends." In contrast, several "poor, plain men who could not pay counsel nor provide petitions and affidavits" were charged with desertion and suffered the full punishment of the court. Thus leniency had not only undermined military discipline but had separated the army by class, creating an atmosphere in which not all soldiers were the same in the eyes of the law.[19]

Phelan described Mississippi as overrun by deserters, and his suggestion of a pardon, even if applied equally to all soldiers, had been tried on numerous occasions and found as wanting as the coercive polices he denounced. The numbers that exist attest to the Confederacy's inability to deal with desertion as it should have. Over the course of the war, 4,236 men faced court-martial for desertion, and of that number 255 were acquitted. The court-martial records indicate that a large number of those accused of desertion were convicted of the lesser offense of absence without leave. The records also reveal something else: desertion to the enemy did carry a certain degree of safety. Of the nearly four thousand men convicted of desertion, only thirty-seven were convicted of desertion to the enemy. Pickett executed twenty-two at one time in 1864, which means that only fifteen men were convicted of desertion to the enemy outside of the unfortunate members of the First U.S. Volunteers. But even if one chose another route home, the court records indicate that apprehending deserters of any kind was difficult. If deserters could get beyond the immediate area of operations into the Confederate rear, avoiding the trains and other areas where the passport system operated, they stood a good chance of escaping. Even if home proved too far away, they might still find sanctuary in the countryside. Assuming that the 103,400 figure for Confederate desertion is accurate, the Confederacy captured less than 5 percent of its deserters. However, even if apprehended, few men convicted of desertion were executed. During the war, Confederate military courts handed down about thirteen hundred death sentences. Records indicate that Davis pardoned approximately six hundred of those, and that number does not include those sentences commuted by blanket amnesties. From December 1861 until the end of the war the Confederacy executed only 229 men—204 by firing squad and 25 by hanging—a punishment generally reserved for those caught deserting to the enemy. North Carolinians accounted for more than half the executions, more than twice Virginia's 48, which came in a distant second. The small number of executions confirms the leniency that prevailed in the Confederate army, but given the state of Confederate record keeping the numbers could be low, and the numbers for Tennessee deserters certainly support that possibility. Union records and correspondence from both sides point to widespread desertion among Tennessee troops, but according to the court-martial records only 18 Tennessee soldiers stood trial for desertion. The Union Register lists more than ten thousand Tennessee deserters to the enemy, and the *Official Records* give Tennessee the distinction of the second most deserters in the Confederacy, barely edging out Virginia for the title of runner-up to North Carolina. With all of this desertion it seems hard to believe that only eighteen Tennessee soldiers stood trial for desertion.[20]

Confederate records clearly lack the accuracy the army needed during the war, and although Union records help fill this void, even the United States government did not record all of the desertion it caused from the Confederate army. New Orleans was the westernmost place of release for Confederate deserters to the Union. Texas had no official place for swearing, recording, and releasing deserters to the Union. Yet correspondence from 1862 shows that the U.S. consulate in Mexico, working in conjunction with the Mexican government, induced soldiers to desert and cross the Rio Grande. Correspondence from 1865 indicates that Confederate soldiers continued to desert from Texas outposts across the border into Mexico, but no one kept records of how many.[21] Based on the total body of desertion reporting and record keeping for Confederate desertion, it seems that the overall numbers are low. In March 1865, Preston told Breckenridge that more than 100,000 deserters ran free in the Confederacy. Is that the same number that appears in the *Official Records*? To say that 100,000 deserters were at large in the spring of 1865 is not the same as saying that 103,400 men deserted over the course of the war.

If court-martial records and execution numbers are understated, it would seem logical to assume that the total desertion figures are likewise low. The only place where the statistics may actually overstate numbers is in the area of Confederate deserters returned to the army. The *Official Records* indicate that 21,056 deserters were returned to the army, but from the face of the list it is clear that the numbers were added incorrectly. The total is slightly over 33,000. If we look more closely, the data show that the numbers for three states were as of February or August 1864, one state's data were as of August 1863, and another's stopped in September 1862.[22] The omission of several years for almost half the Confederate states lends credence to the idea that more men may have been returned than the numbers indicate. However, efforts to actively hunt and return deserters did not get under way until 1863. The records do not show how the men were returned, whether voluntarily, through coercion, or because of an amnesty. It is also possible that men deserted several times and returned and were therefore counted more than once. Almost every amnesty offered by the Confederate army in any military department stated that it did not apply to men who had deserted before. Multiple desertions by one man occurred with enough frequency to exclude that class of men from the pardons. This is one more item of proof as to the failure of leniency. But regardless of the actual numbers and the statistical inadequacies, desertion became an epidemic that never received the stern treatment that might have stopped it or at least slowed it down. When men were executed the process served as a macabre spectacle, but despite the profound impression it made on those who witnessed the event, it occurred far too infrequently to serve as an enduring deterrent.

The inability to successfully deal with the desertion problem caused other harm, not the least of which was the resort to methods that not only could not

"WE CONQUERED OURSELVES"

stop desertion but also served to further alienate a people whose identification with the nation and its cause had always been tenuous. Davis's February 1864 speech in which he described the exhaustion caused by war came in the context of a plea that the legislature suspend the writ of habeas corpus. Admitting that desertion had become "the order of the day," Davis argued that the Confederacy's only hope in addressing the problem was to suspend the writ. He also claimed that the history of the Union offered no parallel to the Confederacy's plight, and he pointed out that over the last one hundred years England had resorted to such a remedy when threatened by invasion.[23]

George Washington and Nathanael Greene might have disagreed with Davis's view of history, since the armies of both men had been plagued by desertion during the Revolutionary War. However, Davis was correct that since the creation of the Union in 1789 desertion had never posed such a problem to any American army. Nevertheless, suspending the writ of habeas corpus struck a nerve with most Americans, both Union and Confederate. Davis eventually got his wish, but given how the Confederacy dealt with deserters one must ask if suspending the writ accomplished anything positive. First, state courts continued to grant writ applications under the belief that Confederate law did not bind them. Second, suspending the writ enabled a government to hold citizens without bail. Its main purpose was to prevent captured deserters from seeking civil court relief. However, if the military and the government refused to deal harshly with deserters, what was the purpose of holding them without bail? In either case the deserter escaped execution. Even if he was held and then sent back to the army, he lived to "run another day." In the end, a government already despised by many of its citizens took away their most sacred right under circumstances where it would do little good.

Shortly after the war, W. D. Herrington of the Third North Carolina Cavalry published a novelette entitled "The Deserter's Daughter." The story centers around Captain Forrester, a Confederate cavalry officer in charge of a unit that is hunting deserters in North Carolina. Forrester uncovers the existence of a "secret league" whose avowed purpose is to defeat the cause by inducing soldiers to desert. Forrester locates the organization's camp and lays an ambush for the deserters. Before he can spring the trap, however, a little girl appears along the road, and Forrester brings her into camp. Her name is Lula. She claims to have no mother and no home, and she will not respond to questions about her father. Believing she is withholding information, Forrester has Lula held under guard. Eventually he captures a column of deserters moving toward the house where the league is suspected to be operating. In the house the Confederates discover a girl named Julia, Lula's older sister. Julia tells Forrester that she had been held hostage by her father, her two brothers, and their cohorts. Ultimately the reader discovers that Julia and her mother are being used by her father as lookouts for the secret league. In the course of performing her vigil, Julia's mother is shot and killed. Seeking revenge against the Confederate cavalry, the father had sent Lula into their camp with enough arsenic to poison their water supply. The story ends with Julia doing the "right" thing by turning her father and his band over to the Confederate cavalry. Because she remains true to her country and its cause, she wins the heart of young Captain Forrester.[24]

Herrington's story reflects several aspects of "real" Confederate desertion. Men used the familiarity of home and the support of family to desert and remain free. They drew strength in numbers, actively opposed the Confederacy, and showed a willingness to kill Confederate soldiers if necessary. Desertion became more than just a depletion of the army that needed more troops than it could possibly muster given its significantly smaller population. It loosed a terrible plague upon the land as large bands of these men, either aligned with some partisan cause or merely trying to survive, preyed unmercifully upon a civilian population already suffering from deprivation of basic necessities like food and clothing. In addition to its other shortcomings, the government proved unable to provide one of the basic needs of its people: safety. Confederate deserters undermined morale more severely than any Union occupation force. To combat this army of deserters the Confederacy sent old men and young boys and watched as they were ground to dust by men already tested in combat and fighting for their own survival. The only alternative was to dedicate seasoned troops to the effort, and although such efforts were temporarily successful, they could never be sustained because those men were needed at the front. Deserter bands began as fifth columns and evolved into the third army of the war; desertion sucked men from the Confederate army and then took from it again by forcing the army to redeploy troops. Sometimes soldiers did not return from such service, dying at the hands of men they might have fought alongside a year before. Deserters contributed to the economic turmoil in some areas as they took an active hand in speculation and extortion. In the end the very families that Confederate soldiers had gone to war to protect found themselves at the mercy of their own people.

Desertion hurt because it exploited some of the very programs designed to replenish the Confederate ranks. Prisoner-of-war paroles and exchanges benefited the Confederate army more than its adversary, since each man traded on a one-for-one basis increased the Confederate army by a greater percentage than the Union army. But desertion severely tainted this program because eventually by paroling prisoners, the Union took the first step in effecting their desertion. Once men returned home on parole they often did not return. To his credit, Bragg understood this problem early in the war and began keeping parolees in camp. He also saw the exploitation of another aspect of the war that in theory should have returned men to the front. Battlefield medicine entered the war almost as a nonexistent field. Although it left much to be desired when the war ended, it had come a long way in four years. Once again, however, removing men from the front to hospitals in the rear and then furloughing them home to recuperate cost the Confederacy soldiers. Bragg stepped in to stop this abuse before any other military or civilian official. By the end of 1863 even the Confederate Congress understood the harm of medical furloughs, but the realities of war would not allow for the elimination of the practice. With the heavy fighting in 1863 and 1864 the wounded filled hospital beds faster than the hospitals could care for them. Men able to travel were only too happy to accept transportation deep into the South, where getting home was easy. Once these men returned home, getting them back proved difficult.

Desertion hurt in other ways. As Reverend Palmer argued in 1863, the use of oaths, a prominent feature in Confederate desertion, threatened the underlying foundation of law and order in the Confederacy. When the Union combined deserter oath swearing with a civilian amnesty program it placed both the soldiers and those at home in a situation where the decision of one could affect the other. When civilians swore the oath it hurt soldiers' resolve. When soldiers swore the oath and returned home it encouraged civilians to swear the oath also. Palmer expressed disbelief that loyalty had been reduced to a mere "contractual obligation." While his shock may have been sincere, many people throughout the South understood the contractual nature of military service and how important it became that the wealthy share what they had with the poor. Government officials like Joe Brown, John Letcher, Zebulon Vance, Francis Lubbock, Thomas Moore, and Charles Clarke understood the contractual nature of citizen loyalty. Southern newspapers implored planters to forego growing cotton and plant food crops instead, and then they lamented when the wealthy refused. More importantly, soldiers and civilians understood the nature of service and loyalty, and they expressed their displeasure. When it appeared that their words fell on deaf ears, soldiers deserted in a variety of different ways. Oath swearing served as a unique way for both citizens and soldiers to renounce the Confederacy and the military obligation it imposed.

Aside from contributing to the depletion of the army and the demoralization and terrorization of the civilian population, desertion hurt in yet another way: it became the focal point for all other debates. Extortion hurt. Why? Because it struck the families of poor and yeomen soldiers who might then desert. Shortages of food hurt. Why? Because it led to hunger and starvation among soldiers' families, thus driving soldiers to desert. Conscription hurt. Why? It forced the poor to fight while the rich were exempted. Conscription made the war a poor man's fight, and when the other ills struck the Confederacy and hurt those at home, the draft became one more topic that drove desertion. Desertion put the Confederate government at odds with the states. It justified the creation of local and state forces to protect the home front, thereby not only depriving the Confederacy of soldiers but also never adequately protecting the home front. Later, when the Confederate government and military debated on how to most effectively control the problem, desertion demonstrated the inability of the military and civilian administration to reach a consensus.

Not even Robert E. Lee escaped the ill effects of the disease, and despite his brilliance on the battlefield he never demonstrated a solid grasp of the problem except to understand that it became serious. In 1862 he saw the problem as "temporary absence," almost refusing to concede that men left and stayed gone. By 1863 he admitted that desertion threatened to gut his army, yet he never believed that bringing deserters back was the army's job. Although he did detach small units like Hoke's brigade in North Carolina, he steadfastly maintained that desertion was a state problem and that Confederate soldiers could not be spared. Like Washington and Greene, Lee argued for executing deserters, but by the time he pressed the issue in earnest it was too late. Thus, while Lee outmatched his contemporaries on the battlefield, Bragg demonstrated a better grasp of the ramifications of desertion and how to address the problem. Perhaps it was the difference in military fortunes. Large Confederate forces surrendered at Forts Donelson and Henry in 1862, creating large numbers of prisoners. Bragg saw early in the war how paroles and straggling were connected with and led to desertion. While Lee fought almost exclusively in Virginia and kept the Union in the northern part of Virginia for most of the war, the Confederate army lost parts of Tennessee, Mississippi, Louisiana, and Arkansas early in the war. Retreat brought desertion and forced Bragg to deal with the problem.

In May 1865, J. W. Yale wrote his daughter to confirm that Kirby Smith had surrendered. "We are a subjugated people," he admitted. He could not believe his own words and would never have believed it was possible. "But how did it befall us—that is the worst part, we conquered ourselves," he continued. "Committed suicide—such [a] people does not deserve independence. Corruption yes, in high places and there is any wonder that privates should get demoralized, none."[25] The South had imploded. The anonymous soldier whose letter appeared in the papers in 1863 had actually used the term "vampire." It was an accurate description of what happened. The Confederacy served as a glaring example of a people and a region that literally began to feed on its own as the war lasted beyond the people's limited ability to endure. Desertion had indeed proved to be more damning than slaughter and became but one way the South committed national suicide. Dead men martyred on the battlefield did not terrorize the home front. Fallen heroes did not deplete government resources pursuing deserters throughout the South and fighting them as they formed bands to resist efforts to return them.

Desertion also served as proof of something else. Confederate nationalism did not fail; in fact, it succeeded beyond all aspirations. What failed was the government and the rich. The Confederacy convinced its diverse and essentially "local" population that the government could best protect their homes and firesides. To succeed in war, men had to be willing to leave home and fight in the Confederate army. By seizing on the notion of home, something that everyone could identify with, the Confederacy found a concept that in effect represented a national will. Despite Herculean efforts in the field, Confederate soldiers could not keep the Union out of Tennessee, Mississippi, Louisiana, and Georgia. It seemed to many that the government gave up on the trans-Mississippi without a fight. Soldiers deserted because they bought into the Confederacy's notion of *patriae*. Protection of home and family was the most important goal, and Confederate soldiers simply reached a point when they no longer believed that the government could live up to its own promises.

The irony of desertion is that the story was not told by deserters but by those who remained in the field or suffered at home. Men like Lee, Bragg, Davis, and Seddon are well known even today. Samuel Cooper, John Preston, and Gideon Pillow, while minor figures in many mainstream histories of the war, come to the forefront in the struggle with desertion. We know that these men survived the war. However, others told the story and saw it unfold from the ground level, yet we know so little about what happened to most of them. William Crutcher, the

Mississippi officer that told his wife that desertion would become a "justifiable crime," survived the war but lost what he had in Vicksburg. He relocated his family to Texas before the war ended. Jerome Yates, the Mississippian who patiently advised his mother on the issue of taking the Union oath, remained true to his convictions. While it was permissible for an old woman to do what was necessary to survive, he could not. After being captured he spent time in Fort Delaware, but his obituary indicated he surrendered at Appomattox and was murdered while traveling from Edwards, Mississippi, to his home at the end of the war.[26] Lizzie Neblett, the Texas woman who predicted that civil war would split the Confederacy, survived the birth of a daughter. Although initially happy, she came to hate the child's very existence. The depression that dominated her correspondence continued, although she seemed relatively affluent and her husband never left Galveston. William Nicholson, the boy from Bastrop, Texas, who found Georgians so disloyal, never left the state. He died there in October 1864.[27]

There were others whose lives after the war remain unknown—no less important, just undocumented. What all of these people, rich and poor, North and South, soldier and civilian, attested to was the unique place that Confederate desertion occupied in one of the most celebrated civil wars in human history. In the hands of the Union, desertion became a weapon that worked in a unique way as it spread like a disease out of the army into the entire Confederacy. In Jefferson Davis's words, it had no parallel in history. Working in concert with the Confederacy's many other problems, desertion truly crippled the Confederate war effort and in the end hurt much more than slaughter.

Among Louisiana soldiers, oath swearing was overwhelmingly found in Orleans Parish. Thirty-three of the seventy-five deserters identified in the sample were from Orleans Parish. Occupied continuously beginning in April 1862 and readily accessible from the sea, Orleans Parish and New Orleans offered soldiers deserting and swearing the oath of allegiance in 1863 both safe passage and a safe haven. Given the conditions that prevailed in New Orleans at the time, these numbers are hardly surprising. They may also cast some light on why Rev. Benjamin Morgan Palmer (see chapter 6) felt compelled to address the issue of oaths. The Register only identifies men who took the oath from July 1863 onward, but clearly men were taking the oath prior to the start of accurate record keeping. Palmer therefore seems to have witnessed not only civilian unrest and declining resolve but an influx of Confederate soldiers back into the parish who had taken advantage of the opportunity. Louisiana's remaining oath takers are scattered throughout the state, illustrating no significant pattern.

Mississippi also lacks a distinct pattern, although northern Mississippi clearly has the larger numbers. The smaller total number of Mississippians taking the oath and the scattered pattern also seem to indicate the possible absence of any real need for the benefits of the Union program. Letters to Governor Pettus from soldiers and officers in 1863 showed a determined effort to secure details, furloughs, and in some cases unconditional releases to return home to care for destitute families. The letters came from men in both the Confederate service and the state guard and begin in January and run through the end of June. A January 1863 letter from forty-seven members of the Mississippi Scouts begs Pettus to return them to the state from service outside Mississippi. They were unaware when they left that Mississippi was in such danger. In February, seventeen men from Company L of the Mississippi Minute Men asked to be detailed for protection of Marshall County in northern Mississippi, claiming the county was in a "destitute condition." One hundred fifty members of Lafayette County asked to be released from military service to return home in view of the "distressed and unprotected condition of the county." In March the officers of the Fourth Regiment of Mississippi state troops asked Pettus to release their troops so they could return home and plant crops. A petition from members of the Fifth Regiment of state troops asked Pettus to disband the unit so they could return home to "see to their destitute families." These are only a few examples of the many letters that flooded Pettus's office, a flood that suddenly ceased with the fall of Vicksburg. The POWS at Vicksburg were some of the last men to reap the advantages of the parole and exchange system on a large scale. Once paroled, they were allowed to return home, and as the desertion story unfolds they do not return. In short, they got home by legal means; their desertion would come later when they refused to report after being exchanged. See Petition of 47 members of Mississippi Scouts to Pettus, January 1863, Petition of 17 Members of Co. L., Miss. Minutemen to Pettus, February 14, 1863, One Hundred fifty members of Lafayette County to Pettus, February 20, 1863, Mississippi Governors' Records, CAH, Ramsdell Collection, Microfilm Reel no. 786.255, series E, vol. 59; Officers of the Fourth Regiment of State Troops to Pettus, March 9, 1863, Colonel A. L. Grumby, Panola County, Miss., to Pettus, March 11, 1863, Petition of Members of Fifth Regiment Mississippi State Troops to Pettus, March 23, 1863, Mississippi Governors' Records, CAH, Ramsdell Collection, Microfilm Reel no. 786.255, series E, vol. 60. Letters like these run up to the end of June 1863 and spill over into series E, vol. 61. They cease with the fall of Vicksburg.

Arkansas and Texas reflect the problems of distance. As in North Carolina, this does not imply that men from these states did not desert; to the contrary, desertion would plague both states, just not oath-swearing deserters. Arkansas soldiers benefited from the Ozark Mountains in the northwest. Oath-swearing deserters in the state, strangely enough, are concentrated in the middle part of the state in Pulaski (21), Prairie (13), and White counties (16). Texas has only 50 in this sample and a projected total of only 315. For Texans in the Army of Northern Virginia or the Army of Tennessee, the Union policy held little advantage unless these men were willing to remain in the North. Texas is a long way from Virginia and Georgia, and the journey home would have had to be made across country still controlled at least in part by the Confederate authorities. Furthermore, Texas remained "Confederate" for most of the war, so even if they made it home, safety was not assured. Those serving in Kirby Smith's forces might find it worth taking a chance to go directly home. At least the journey was shorter. Only Dallas and Galveston counties have as many as five deserters; the remaining counties have between three and one. The pattern, to the extent one exists, shows deserters concentrated in the counties of northern Texas, particularly those bordering the Oklahoma Territory and Arkansas. It was in this area that significant Unionist sentiment seemed to exist, both before the war and after it began.

Abbreviations

ADAH   Alabama Department of Archives and History, Montgomery

AJP   *The Papers of Andrew Johnson*. Ed. Leroy P. Graf and Ralph W. Haskins. 16 vols. Knoxville: University of Tennessee Press, 1967–2000.

CAH   Center for American History, University of Texas–Austin

GWP/CS   *The Papers of George Washington: Colonial Series*. Ed. W. W. Abbot et al. 10 vols. Charlottesville: University Press of Virginia, 1983–95.

GWP/RS   *The Papers of George Washington: Revolutionary War Series*. Ed. Philander D. Chase et al. 13 vols. Charlottesville: University Press of Virginia, 1985–.

LDAH   Louisiana Department of Archives and History, Baton Rouge

MDAH   Mississippi Department of Archives and History, Jackson

NARA   National Archives and Records Administration, Washington DC

NGP   *The Papers of General Nathanael Greene*. Ed. Richard K. Showman et al. 12 vols. Chapel Hill: University of North Carolina Press, 1976–.

OR   *The War of the Rebellion: The Official Records of the Union and Confederate Armies*. 128 vols. Washington DC: U.S. Government Printing Office, 1880–1900.

RG   Record Group

SCDAH   South Carolina Department of Archives and History, Columbia

SHSP   *Southern Historical Society Papers*. 52 vols. Millswood NY: Krause Reprint, 1977.

TSA   Texas State Archives, Austin

Introduction

1. Kirby Smith, Soldiers of the Trans-Mississippi Army, April 21, 1865, in Booth, *Records of Louisiana Confederate Soldiers*, 1:3.

2. Edmund Kirby Smith, Proclamation, May 30, 1865, Edmund Kirby Smith Papers, Ramsdell Collection, CAH, microfilm reel no. 786.210: 210A.

3. Vegitius, "In re Militari," 75–76; Frederick the Great, "The Instructions of Frederick the Great to His Generals," 311–13; Bonaparte, "Military Maxims of Napoleon," 425–26; Jomini, "Jomini and His Summary of the Art of War," 458–59.

4. McKiven, review of *A Higher Duty*, 874; Bohannan, review of *A Higher Duty*, 270–71; Gallagher, *A Confederate War*.

5. War Department Collection of Confederate Records, NARA, RG 109, microfilm, 1,500 reels.

6. William H. Fowler, To the Officers and Soldiers of the State of Alabama, January 25, 1864, Alabama Adjutant and Inspector General's Records, ADAH, SG 24872, no. 15, microfilm, folder 6; Owen, *History of Alabama Dictionary of Alabama Biography*, 3:607–8; Owen, "Work of Fowler."

7. Owen, "Work of Fowler," 178.

8. Samuel P. Moore, Surgeon General, Order, April 25, 1863, Civil War Papers, ADAH, PB/Range H/Sec 7, Shelf C.

9. Kean, *Inside the Confederate Government*, xiv–xv.

10. Kean, *Inside the Confederate Government*, 89 (July 28, 1863).

11. Register of Confederate Soldiers Deserting to the Union Army, 1863–65, NARA, microfilm, RG 598, reel 8. A comparison of Georgia soldiers found in the register with muster rolls of their units, compiled during or shortly after the war, revealed men who were listed as missing or AWOL who appeared in the register as deserters. In other instances, the muster roll correctly identified these men as deserters to the enemy. See Weitz, *A Higher Duty*.

12. Beamer, "Galvanized Yankees in Kansas," 18; Brown, *Galvanized Yankees*. See also Current, *Lincoln's Loyalists*.

13. Weitz, "Preparing for the Prodigal Sons."

14. Weitz, "Preparing for the Prodigal Sons."

15. Cunningham, *Doctors in Gray*, 90. Records from the Department of Virginia show that 5,895 soldiers deserted between September 1862 and August 1864, an average of 256 per month. Schroeder-Lein, *Confederate Hospitals on the Move*, 120, 128. Secondary works on Stout and his mobile hospitals speak of desertion but record no hard numbers. The extent of the desertion from Stout's hospitals does lie within his papers, however, and will be extracted later in this study.

16. Receipts for Deserters of the Army Arrested by the Sheriff of Chickasaw County, MDAH, RG 9, series 404, box 8372, vols. 35 and 143; A Descriptive List of Soldiers Who Have Deserted from the Confederate States Army, Louisiana State Records in the War Department, Collection of Confederate Records: Letters Received by the Executive, 1860–1863, LDAH, microfilm reel no. CR.004; United States Military Prison Record, CAH, box 3B59, 62–64, 150.

17. Manarin, *North Carolina Troops*; Bearman, "Desertion as Localism."

18. Booth, *Records of Louisiana Confederate Soldiers*, 3–5.

19. Booth, *Records of Louisiana Confederate Soldiers*, 6.

20. Salley, *South Carolina Troops in Confederate Service*.

21. Lonn, *Desertion during the Civil War*; Martin, *Desertion of Alabama Troops*; Weitz, *A Higher Duty*. In addition to these three books, there have been several recent theses/dissertations that address desertion either exclusively or as a major part of the study: Dotson, "'Sisson's Kingdom'"; Carlson, "Wiregrass Runners"; and Maars, "Dissatisfaction and Desertion."

22. Borgwald, "Desertions from the Confederate Army"; E. Taylor, "Discontent in Confederate Louisiana"; Bardolph, "Inconstant Rebels"; Reiger, "Deprivation, Disaffection, and Desertion"; Otten, "Disloyalty in the Upper Districts"; R. Reid, "A Test Case for 'Crying Evil'"; G. D. Davis, "An Uncertain Confederate Trumpet"; B. H. Reid and White, "A Mob of Stragglers and Cowards"; Bardolph, "Confederate Dilemma"; Sterling, "Discouragement, Weariness, and War Politics"; Hallock, "The Role of Community in the Civil War"; Bearman, "Desertion as Localism"; Emerson, "Leadership and Civil War Desertion"; Giuffre, "First in Flight"; Damico, "Confederate Soldiers Take Matters into Their Own Hands"; Weitz, "Preparing for the Prodigal Sons"; Weitz, "I Will Never Forget the Name of You"; Maars, "Dissatisfaction and Desertion" (*Proceedings*).

1. The American Practice

1. Bauer, *Zachary Taylor*, 53; Vargas, "The Military Justice System"; *Army and Navy Chronicle*, May 30, 1839, 345.

2. McDermott, "Were They Really Rogues," 165; Miller, *Shamrock and Sword*, 151–66, 172–76, 180.
3. From all indications, units made up of African Americans enjoyed a low rate of desertion that was attributed to strong morale. W. Leckie, *Buffalo Soldiers*, 98–99. Buffalo soldiers served on the outer fringes of the frontier, and while strong morale certainly contributed to low desertion, one must also suspect that isolation also contributed. Men simply had nowhere to go in territory that was extremely hostile. For statistics on desertion between 1865 and 1891 and an excellent list of the late-nineteenth-century desertion periodical literature, see McDermott, "Were They Really Rogues"; and McAnaney, "Desertion in the United States Army." The same year General Order no. 130 was issued, the adjutant general's office published a compilation of laws, rulings, and other legal decisions on desertion as well as how desertion affected claims filed against the U.S. government. Drum, *Laws, Rules, and Decisions Governing the Military Crime of Desertion*.
4. Woodbury, *A Study of Desertion*. Woodbury's Civil War numbers are undocumented and appear at page 5.
5. For a discussion of America's penchant for well-trained and effective citizen armies see Hanson, *The Soul of Battle*; and Weitz, "Drill, Training, and Combat Performance."
6. Middlekauf, *The Glorious Cause*, 363; R. Leckie, *George Washington's War*, 171, 232, 316; Lancaster, *The American Revolution*, 155, 260. The exodus had actually been going on for most of 1776, but it seemed to pick up in earnest in late 1776. Robert Hanson Harrison to John Hancock, November 3, 1776, GWP/RS, 7:80. Colonial authorities began to take steps to ensure that no one whose enlistment had not expired was allowed to leave. Washington to William Livingston, and Washington to Hancock, November 30, 1776, GWP/RS, 7:232–33, 236–37.
7. John Martin to Washington, August 30, 1755, GWP/CS, 2:103; Washington to Robert Dinwiddie, October 11, 1755, GWP/CS, 2:11–12; Adam Stephen to Washington, November 11, 1755, GWP/CS, 2:190; Washington to Stephen, December 3, 1755, GWP/CS, 2:195–97; Robert Stewart to Washington, December 5, 1755, GWP/CS, 2:205.
8. George Mercer's Orders, December 25, 1755, GWP/CS, 2:229–30; Washington to Adam Stephen, February 1, 1756, GWP/CS, 2:310; Memorandum respecting the Militia, May 7, May 17, May 18, 1756, GWP/CS, 3:97, 145, 151.
9. Washington to Robert Dinwiddie, May 23, 1756, GWP/CS, 3:171–72; Dinwiddie to Washington, May 27, 1756, GWP/CS, 3:178–79; Dinwiddie to Washington, September 30, 1756, GWP/CS, 3:424–25. Leniency plagued provincial armies. Fred Anderson's analysis of Massachusetts troops provides a good example of discipline problems and laxity of punishment in colonial units during the Seven Years' War. See *A People's Army*, 127–31.
10. Orderly Book, September 15, 1758, GWP/CS, 6:37; Robert Stewart to Washington, December 20, December 31, 1758, GWP/CS, 6:171, 174. Inadequate supplies, poor compensation, and overextended enlistments contributed to at least nineteen instances of mass desertion or mutiny among the Massachusetts provincial army alone. Anderson, *A People's Army*, 187.
11. Morris, *America's Armed Forces*, 30. Philip Schuyler to Washington, May 26, 1776, GWP/RS, 4:388–89; Schuyler to Washington, July 12, 1776, GWP/RS, 5:286–88; Washington to Schuyler, July 17, 1776, GWP/RS, 5:365; Horatio Gates to Washington, July 29, 1776, GWP/RS, 5:499; Hugh Mercer to Washington, August 9, 1776, GWP/RS, 5:651; William Heath to Washington, September 19, 1776, GWP/RS, 6:342–43.
12. From the Essex County Committee of Safety, May 14, 1776, GWP/RS, 4:297; General Orders, April 27, May 2, May 3, May 12, May 14, May 16, May 27, May 31, June 2, June 5, June 9, June 11, 1776, GWP/RS, 4:141, 183–84, 189, 228, 282, 295, 310, 392–93, 407–8, 425–26, 438, 445–46, 468–69, 497. The list could go on. Whipping continued to be the general means of punishment, and execution

appeared later in the war. William Livingston to Washington, August 12, 1776, *GWP/RS*, 5:683–84; Hugh Mercer to Washington, August 11, 1776, *GWP/RS*, 5:666–67; Philip Schuyler to Washington, June 17, 1776, *GWP/RS*, 5:27; General Orders, July 20, 1776, *GWP/RS*, 5:396. Reprieves often involved an elaborate staging process whereby it appeared a man would be punished, only to be spared at the last minute. Chadwick, *George Washington's War*, 160–61.

13. Schuyler to Washington, July 12, 1776, *GWP/RS*, 5:286; Washington to Schuyler, July 17, 1776, *GWP/RS*, 5:363; Gates to Washington, *GWP/RS*, 5:597.

14. Schuyler to Washington, August 16, 1776, *GWP/RS*, 6:42. Some of those deserting even went so far as to swear an oath of allegiance to the British Crown. Oath swearing became a prominent feature of Confederate desertion during the Civil War. Henry Beekman Livingston to Washington, September 11, 1776, *GWP/RS*, 6:282; General Orders, October 31, 1776, *GWP/RS*, 7:58–59; George Washington to John Augustine Washington, September 22, 1776, *GWP/RS*, 6:374; Washington to Jonathan Trumbull Sr., October 8, 1776, *GWP/RS*, 6:512.

15. Washington to Hancock, September 25, 1776, *GWP/RS*, 6:394–96.

16. Washington to Hancock, September 25, 1776, *GWP/RS*, 6:396–99; Hancock to Washington, November 9, 1776, *GWP/RS*, 7:122. Women lay at the heart of this obligation, as Washington understood. He had allowed women to follow the army in the hope that it would keep their men in the service. In 1778 women visited the camps at Valley Forge and convinced their men to desert. Raphael, *A People's History*, 151, 163.

17. James Thompson to Greene, October 5, 1779, *NGP*, 4:438; Greene to Robert L. Hooper, September 17, 1779, *NGP*, 4:385; Green to Henry Hollingsworth, August 2, 1779, *NGP*, 4:291; Greene to Jonathan Trumbull, July 20, 1779, *NGP*, 4:248–49; Greene to Washington, August 26, 1780, *NGP*, 6:233; James Livingston to Greene, October 11, 1780, Greene to Livingston, October 11, 1780, *NGP*, 6:368–69; General Greene's Orders, October 13, 1780, *NGP*, 6:372–73.

18. Greene to Washington, November 19, 1780, *NGP*, 6:485–87. Part of the problem was the lack of a quartermaster to facilitate the rapid gathering and distribution of clothing and equipment. Greene to Edward Carrington, December 29, 1780, *NGP*, 7:15; Greene to William Preston, February 24, 1871, *NGP*, 7:143, Daniel Morgan to Greene, February 20, 1781, Andrew Pickens to Green, February 20, 1781, Greene to Pickens, March 5, 1781, *NGP*, 7:324–25, 399; Marquis De Malmedy to Greene, March 11, 1781, *NGP*, 7:428.

19. Honeycut to Greene, December 26, 1780, *NGP*, 7:3.

20. Inscoe and McKinney, *Heart of Confederate Appalachia*, 117, 124–25.

21. Middlekauf, *The Glorious Cause*, 556–57; Raphael, *A People's History*, 385; Greene to Joseph Reed, President of the Pennsylvania Council, May 4, 1781, *NGP*, 8:199; Marquis de Lafayette to Greene, July 4, 1781, *NGP*, 8:497; Thompson and Thompson, *The Seventeenth Alabama Infantry*, 74, 134.

22. F. Anderson, *A People's Army*, 187–94.

23. Southern antebellum rhetoric embraced the notion that the South was a place that clung to simpler values, and social historians have explored the idea that the South continued to be a throwback to an earlier time. See J. W. Harris, *Plain Folk and Gentry*, 33–34. James McPherson explores the idea of the South as a throwback to an earlier era in "The Distinctiveness of the Old South." He cites David Potter's thesis that what made the South distinctive was a "folk culture" with an emphasis on traditional rural life, close kinship ties, and a hierarchical social structure.

24. Wiley, *The Life of Johnny Reb*, 330. Wiley's study takes 107 companies from Alabama, Arkansas, Georgia, Louisiana, Mississippi, North Carolina, and Virginia. McPherson, *For Cause and Comrades*, 181. McPherson's study looks to the motivations of the Civil War soldier. By definition the study requires men who left written record of their motives. However, his data show that over

half of enlisted men were farmers, as does Wiley's study. Desertion will be shown to have been a phenomenon of the enlisted ranks, and thus the occupation of officers becomes less important.

25. Weitz, *A Higher Duty*, 77, 172.

26. Bodnar, *Worker's World*.

27. Woodbury suggests this push-pull characteristic of desertion in his conclusion. He argues that desertion occurs when the pull outward, or away from service, exceeds the pull inward. He then admits that some desertion occurs when an individual experiences a push outward. Woodbury, *A Study of Desertion*, 46.

28. Miller, *Shamrock and Sword*, 174. World War II at 5.3 percent was the highest; Vietnam at 4.1 percent was second. No other war saw desertion rates exceed 2 percent. Woodbury, *A Study of Desertion*, 6.

29. As stated in the introduction, total Confederate enlistment numbers vary from 800,000 to 1.2 million. At 800,000, 104,000 deserters yields a rate of 13 percent. At 1.2 million the rate is over 8 percent. Given the disparity of white population and the fact that the Confederate army was generally always outnumbered, that number is significant.

30. Woodbury, *A Study of Desertion*, 1, 4.

2. My Country . . . My Home

1. E. N. Edwards to Jefferson Davis, May, 1861, *Confederate Imprints*, RG 3517, reel 48, no. 1697 [hereinafter cited by record group: reel: document no.: page if applicable; e.g., 3517: 48: 1697].

2. William Moore Diary, January 1, 1861, William E. Moore Papers, 1807–1944, CAH, file 2F5; Diary of Henrietta Embree, April 23, 1861, Henrietta Embree Papers, CAH, file 2Q505.

3. Carp, "Nations of American Rebels," quote on 5–6.

4. Murphy, *Trial of William Smith*; Warburton, *Trial of the Officers and Crew of the Privateer Savannah*; and Woodruff, *Sequestration Cases*. These three trial transcripts came from court cases in 1861. The sequestration cases involved the Confederacy's nationwide efforts to drive out alien enemies and to seize their property. The piracy cases saw lawyers on each side debate the issue of the Confederacy's de facto existence and point to the Confederacy's ability to impose national control as evidence of its legal existence.

5. W. C. Davis, *"A Government of Our Own"*; W. C. Davis, *Look Away, Look Away*; Thomas, *The Confederate Nation*. An older work, Frank E. Vandiver's *Their Tattered Flags*, also sees a form of nationalism in the Confederacy's structure and government.

6. Beringer et al., *Why the South Lost the Civil War*, 66.

7. *American Heritage Collegiate Dictionary*, ed. Robert B. Costello, 3d ed. (Boston: Houghton Mifflin, 1997), 908; *Merriam-Webster Online* http://www.m-w.com/cgi-bin/dictionary.

8. Carp, "Nations of American Rebels," 6; B. Anderson, *Imagined Communities*, 5–7; Kohn quoted in Beringer, "Confederate Identity," 78; Potter, *The South and the Sectional Conflict*, 51–57, 68–78.

9. George Fredrickson is one of the leading proponents of the idea that Herrenvolk democracy was the source of Southern antebellum unity. See his *The Black Image in the White Mind* and "White Supremacy and the American Sectional Conflict." See also Ford *The Origins of Southern Radicalism*. For a perspective on how tenuous such unity was, even in regions of high slave populations, see J. W. Harris, *Plain Folk and Gentry*, 64–93.

10. Gallagher, *A Confederate War*, 63, 64, 72–83, 77; Bonner, *Colors and Blood*; Faust, *The Creation of Confederate Nationalism*, 6–7. This list is far from exhaustive. For a good discussion of these and other theories of Confederate nationalism see Carp, "Nations of American Rebels."

11. Thomas, *The Confederate Nation*, xv, 297; Beringer, "Confederate Identity," 79–81.
12. McPherson, *For Cause and Comrades*, 104–16; Higginbothom, *War and Society in Revolutionary America*.
13. Gallagher, *A Confederate War*, 61, 63.
14. Freehling, "The Divided South."
15. Ash, *Middle Tennessee Society Transformed*, 1–10. Ash even refers to middle Tennessee as a "third South between East and West Tennessee." Weitz, *A Higher Duty*, 12–13; Rogers et al., *Alabama*, 135.
16. Inscoe and McKinney, *Heart of Confederate Appalachia*, 211–13.
17. Neely, *Southern Rights*, 103–17.
18. Bennett, *Days of Uncertainty and Dread*, 1–3.
19. Williams, *The Georgia Gold Rush*, 117–23; Moneyhon, "The Die Is Cast," 1–8; Woods, *Rebellion and Realignment*, 1–2, 5; Dougan, *Confederate Arkansas*, 2–11.
20. J. W. Harris, *Plain Folk and Gentry*, 90–91, 143–53.
21. Rogers et al., *Alabama*, 55, 58–60, 67.
22. For general discussion of wartime resistance in Georgia's wiregrass see Williams, *Rich Man's War*; Williams, Williams, and Carlson, *Plain Folk in a Rich Man's War*; and Carlson, "Wiregrass Runners." For an excellent study of Jones County and its history of resistance see Bynum, *The Free State of Jones*.
23. Rogers et al., *Alabama*, 62.
24. Frazier, "'Out of Striking Distance,'" 151–52.
25. Griffith, *Alabama*, 422; Dougan, *Confederate Arkansas*, 63; Beringer, "Confederate Identity," 83.
26. Heitman, *Historical Register*, 2:285. These numbers are slightly less than the aggregate numbers Heitman provided, and they reflect the aggregate reduced to a three-year standard. Heitman's numbers reflect no soldiers from Georgia, which is incorrect. Gilmer County in northern Georgia supplied several units directly into the Union army at the start of the war. However, even without Georgia numbers the figures reflect a significant number of men unwilling to embrace the Confederacy and willing to risk their lives at some level for the Union. Beringer, "Confederate Identity," 83. Current (*Lincoln's Loyalists*, 213) sees the number at 86,007.
27. McPherson, *For Cause and Comrades*, 94–95.
28. Gallagher, *A Confederate War*, 72.
29. "Government or No Government, or the Question of State Allegiance: A Tract for Churchmen" (Mobile: Farrow, Dennett, Book and Job Printers, 1861), 2–3, in *Confederate Imprints*, 3517: 91: 2757.
30. "Government or No Government," 6.
31. Nolan, *Lee Considered*, 30–58; McPherson, *For Cause and Comrades*, 96–98.
32. "Our Cause," *Mobile Daily Tribune*, April 28, 1861.
33. Reply of Jos. J. Nicholson, Rector St. Mary's Church Mobile to Bishop Potter, May 22, 1861, in "Government or No Government," 12–15.
34. Beringer, "Confederate Identity," 90–91.
35. Weitz, "'Shoot Them All,'" 330, 335–36.
36. Flanagin to Davis, January 5, 1863, in Beringer, "Confederate Identity," 94.
37. "To the People of Tennessee," *Union and American Extra*, May 1861, Ramsdell Collection, CAH, microfilm reel no. 786.51.
38. McPherson, *For Cause and Comrades*, 98–99.
39. Weitz, *A Higher Duty*, 142.

40. Ash, *Middle Tennessee Society Transformed*, 80; Weitz, *A Higher Duty*, 165.
41. G. Wood, *The Creation of the American Republic*, 601–2.
42. Rhett, *A Fire Eater Remembers*, 6–9, 13–16.
43. W. C. Davis, *"A Government of Our Own,"* 120, 127.
44. Weitz, *A Higher Duty*, 33.
45. J. C. Harris, *On the Plantation*, 138–39.
46. "Provisional and Permanent Constitutions of the Confederate States," in *Documenting the American South*. For two older but nevertheless good studies of shortage in the Confederacy see Massey, *Ersatz in the Confederacy*; and Lonn, *Salt as a Factor in the Confederacy*.
47. F. Anderson, *Crucible of War*, 219–21.

3. Into the Breach

1. Gallagher, *A Confederate War*, 143–44; OR, 4th ser., 1:106, 114, 117, 127–31.
2. "British Articles of War 1765," in Bunch, *Military Justice in the Confederate Army*, 164–65.
3. *Militia Laws of Tennessee*.
4. Weitz, *"'Shoot Them All,'"* 326.
5. Radley, *Rebel Watchdog*, 1–3.
6. Radley, *Rebel Watchdog*, 3.
7. "Irishmen to the Front," *Richmond Dispatch*, July 5, 1861; *Selma Morning Reporter*, June 1, 1861.
8. Jones, *Rebel War Clerk's Diary*, 1:8; W. D. Wynne to Sister, September 16, 1861, Civil War Miscellany, CAH, 2C477, W. D. Wynne file.
9. C. C. Taylor to Father, July 14, 1861, C.S.A. Records, 1856–1915, CAH, 2C484, folder 1: Soldiers' Correspondence.
10. C. C. Taylor to Father, October 10, 1861, C.S.A. Records, 1856–1915, CAH, 2C484, folder 1: Soldiers' Correspondence.
11. Mrs. Charles Besser to Husband, June 29, 1861, Civil War Miscellany, CAH, 2C447, Charles Besser file; R. B. Hardman to Brother, August 28, 1861, Civil War Soldiers' Letters, ADAH, LPR 78, box 1, folder 25; D. E. Twiggs to Governor Pettus, September 21, 1861, C. J. Dahlgren to J. J. Pettus, September 27, 1861, Mississippi Governors' Papers, Military Telegrams, 1861–63, Ramsdell Collection, CAH, microfilm reel no. 786.254B, series E, vol. 63; James Thrower to Steven, n.d., 1861, Civil War Soldiers' Letters, ADAH, LPR 78, box 1, folder 1; Jesse Ogden to Pettus, May 16, 1861, John Dickerson to Pettus, May 18, 1861, Mississippi Governors' Collection, Ramsdell Collection, CAH, microfilm reel no. 786.254B, series E, vol. 52.
12. The secondary literature likewise emphasizes the zeal of early enlistment without addressing the fact that not everyone answered the call. McPherson, *Battle Cry of Freedom*, 317–18. In his classic work *The Coming Fury*, 401–2, Bruce Catton refers to thirty-five thousand to forty thousand men already in Richmond by May 1861. His tenor, like McPherson's, is of the rush to join. It is interesting that even in A. B. Moore's 1924 study of conscription, *Conscription and Conflict in the Confederacy*, 12–14, he states that conscription was necessary because of defeats in the West. He quotes Davis as advocating conscription to correct the mistake of short-term enlistments, to create uniformity and regularity in the military, and to equalize the burdens of military service. There is not even a suggestion that men were slow to enlist. J. W. Harris echoes these sentiments in his discussion of enlistment in the Augusta, Georgia, area. However, he does hint at problems to come even if he does not indicate that filling the ranks in 1861 was a problem. See *Plain Folk and Gentry*, 140–44. The situation in 1861 is perhaps best told in the words of the citizens and government officials who grappled with the problem.

13. L. P. Walker to T. Moore, June 19, 1861, Walker to Moore, June 30, July 17, August 7, 1861, La. State Records in the War Department Collection of Confederate Records: Letters Received by the Executive, 1860–63, LDAH, microfilm reel no. CR.004.

14. James Chestnut Jr., Report of the Chief of the Department of the Military of South Carolina to His Excellency, Governor Pickens, 1862, Ramsdell Collection, CAH, microfilm reel no. 786.47.

15. Mrs. W. H. C. Lane to Governor Pettus, June 15, 1861, G. W. Smith to Pettus, June 16, 1861, John Johnson to Pettus, July 17, 1861, Mississippi Governors' Collection, Ramsdell Collection, CAH, microfilm reel no. 786.254B, series E, vol. 52; I. L. Walton to Pettus, August 12, 1861, Petition of 58 Members of Pontotoc Dragoons, August 30, 1861, Mississippi Governors' Collection, Ramsdell Collection, CAH, microfilm reel no. 786.254B, series E, vol. 53.

16. Weitz, *A Higher Duty*, 91.

17. Emily Moxley to William Moxley, September 1, 1861, William M. Moxley Papers, 1854–1901, CAH, 3B28, folder 1; D. N. Moxley to William Moxley, November 27, 1861, Emily to William, December 10, 1861, William to Emily, December 17, 1861, Emily to William, December 25, 1861, Moxley Papers, CAH, 3B28, folder 2. Another Alabamian, Joseph McGowin, described the same situation in eastern Tennessee. As Deep South men moved into northern Tennessee and Virginia, sickness followed with the change in climate. Joseph McGowin to People, October 9, 1861, Civil War Soldiers' Letters, ADAH, LPR 78, container 2, folder 5.

18. C. B. and M. F. D. Mason to W. H. Mason, November 3, 1861, Civil War Soldiers' Letters, ADAH, LPR 78, box 1, container 2, folder 9.

19. James Thrower to Starling Thrower, November 25, 1861, Civil War Soldiers' Letters, ADAH, LPR 78, box 1, container 1, folder 1.

20. Alabama Muster Rolls, 4th Alabama Infantry, ADAH, SG 25011. Samuel Downing, born in Maryland and living in Huntsville, deserted on May 31, 1861. William Warren, born and raised in Chambers County, deserted on August 31, 1861. David Samples of Scottsboro deserted on July 25, 1861. George M. Mosley to Pettus, December 24, 1861, Mississippi Governors' Collection, Ramsdell Collection, CAH, microfilm reel no. 786.254B, series E, vol. 54; *Richmond Dispatch*, July 2, 1861.

21. Earnest Forestall, Aide de Camp for the Adjutant and Inspector General to Thomas Moore, September 12, 1861, Letters Received by the Executive, 1860–63, LDAH, microfilm reel no. CR.004; Diary of George L. Griscom, December 10, 1861, CAH, 2R6; "$30.00 Reward—Deserted," *Charleston Mercury*, August 17, 1861, August 19, 1861; John Pemberton, Circular Order, HQ 4th District South Carolina, December 29, 1861, Records of the Confederate States Army, Fourth Military District, South Caroliniana Library, University of South Carolina, Columbia; *Richmond Dispatch* July 5, 1861. "War, War, War" appeared as part of an advertisement for Davis, Davis & Bro. for uniforms and other provisions. *Richmond Dispatch*, July 9, 1861.

22. William Crutcher to Wife, Emily, December 1, 1861, Crutcher-Shannon Family Papers, 1822–1905, CAH, 2E511.

23. Will Crutcher to Emily, December 12, 1861, Emily to Will, December 13, 1861, Will to Emily, December 25, 1861, Crutcher-Shannon Family Papers, CAH, 2E511.

24. "Patriotic Move in West Baton Rouge," *Richmond Dispatch*, July 6, 1861.

25. "Weather and Crops in Alabama," "Crops & Corn in Georgia," *Richmond Dispatch*, July 11, 1861.

26. *Augusta Daily Chronicle and Sentinel*, December 27, 1861.

27. "An Act for the Protection of the Frontier of Texas," December 21, 1861, C.S.A. Congress, in F. R. Lubbock, Address to Members of the State House of Representatives, February 5, 1863, Executive

Record Books, Francis R. Lubbock 1/25/63–11/4/63 through A. J. Hamilton 7/25/65–8/13/65, TSA, microfilm reel 6.

28. Governor Joseph Brown, "Special Message to the General Assembly relative to the transfer of the State Troops to the Confederate Service, December 5, 1861," *Confederate Imprints*, 3517: 39: 1572.

29. Brown, "Special Message, December 5, 1861."

30. Brown, "Special Message, December 5, 1861."

31. For an explanation of Alabama's militia system see T. H. Watts, Proclamation, July 22, 1864, in Governor Thomas H. Watts Administrative Files, ADAH, SG 24872, microfilm, Reel 19.

32. McCarthy, *Detailed Minutiae of Soldier Life*, 2–3.

4. Desertion in the Heartland

1. James Thrower to Starling Thrower, January 6, 1862, George Athey to Father, January 18, 1862, Civil War Soldiers' Letters, ADAH, LPR 78, box 1, container 1, folder 1.

2. See Weitz, "Preparing for the Prodigal Sons."

3. See Weitz, "Preparing for the Prodigal Sons."

4. Weitz, "I Will Never Forget the Name of You," 45–46, 49.

5. Ash, *Middle Tennessee Society Transformed*, 85–88; E. K. Smith to Wife, June 27, 1862, Kirby Smith Papers, Ramsdell Collection, CAH, microfilm reel no. 786.209.

6. G. D. Davis, "An Uncertain Confederate Trumpet," 35–36, 41.

7. Isham G. Harris, Proclamation, February 19, 1862, Ramsdell Collection, CAH, microfilm reel no. 786.51.

8. Connelly, *Civil War Tennessee*, 30; G. D. Davis, "An Uncertain Confederate Trumpet," 32–33.

9. G. D. Davis, "An Uncertain Confederate Trumpet," 34; Hattaway and Beringer, *Jefferson Davis*, 193. There is an argument that Davis had begun to abandon the trans-Mississippi by late 1862, which might lend credence to Alcorn's belief that the trans-Mississippi had always been a "second rate" front in Davis's mind. For an analysis of this argument see Woodworth, *No Band of Brothers*, 51–69.

10. R. B. Hardman to Mother, November 2, 1862, in Hardman Family Correspondence, ADAH, LPR 78, box 1, folder 25.

11. Ash, *Middle Tennessee Society Transformed*, 49–51, 81.

12. Weitz, "I Will Never Forget the Name of You," 45–46.

13. Nathan T. Allman to Johnson, March 8, 1862, AJP, 5:190; Robert G. Bails to Johnson, March 18, 1862, AJP, 5:249–50; Johnson to Edwin Stanton, March 13, 1862, AJP, 5:201.

14. C. C. Taylor to Father, September 28, 1862, C.S.A. Records, 1856–1915, CAH, RG 2C484, folder 1.

15. James Haggard to Johnson, June 2, 1862, AJP, 5:434.

16. Petition From Work House Prisoners, September 2, 1862, JAP, 6:6–7; Robert S. Northcutt to Johnson, AJP, 5:161, see also 6:9; William Hoffman to Johnson, September 25, 1862, AJP, 6:14, see also 5:634, 6:3; Peter Zinn to Johnson, November 18, 1862, AJP, 6:63; William Campbell to Johnson, November 2, 1862, AJP, 6:46.

17. Jas. I. Hall to Parents, June 29, 1862, in Fleming, *Band of Brothers*, 98–99.

18. G. D. Davis, "An Uncertain Confederate Trumpet," 50.

19. Report of Maj. Gen. Thomas Hindman, OR, 1st ser., 13:29–30.

20. *Random House Unabridged Dictionary*, 2d ed. (New York: Random House, 1993), 715.

21. Gen. Thomas Hindman, General Order no. 5, June 5, 1862, Letters Received by the Executive, 1860–63, LDAH, microfilm reel no. CR.004.

22. Junius Bragg to Josephine, January 24, 1862, in J. N. Bragg, *Letters of a Confederate Surgeon*, 24.

23. Report of Thomas Hindman, 1862 [no month or day], in Evans, *Confederate Military History*, 14:115–16. The report seems to have come after Hindman was relieved of command. His stint was short, but he did effectively curb the ills that plagued Arkansas. In *Southern Rights*, Mark Neely describes Hindman as "either a fanatic or an unprincipled despot or both" (17). He was also "energetic, explosive and unpredictable" (27). Despite Hindman's being relieved after only a seventy-day tenure as commander of the Trans-Mississippi Department, Neely concluded that he had mobilized a "prostrate state" and created a "minor economic miracle." His ruthless use of martial law had put Arkansas in a position to wage war (11).

24. Bunch, *Roster of the Court-Martial*. The roster is alphabetical and identifies men by name, rank, unit, date of trial, charges, and sentence. The numbers in this text reflect a simple count by date of trial and sentence.

25. Evans, *Confederate Military History*, 14:116–17.

26. Miss Howard W. Wilkinson to Governor Pettus, January 1, 1862, W. J. Reeves to Pettus, January 5, 1862, William L. Duncan to Pettus, January 7, 1862, in Mississippi Governors' Collection, Ramsdell Collection, CAH, microfilm reel no. 786.254, series E, vol. 53.

27. G. W. Humpherys to Governor Pettus, January 13, 1862 (request for return of his neighbor who has dozens of slaves to look after), M. H. Carr to Pettus, January 17, 1862 (wants an honorable discharge to care for his destitute and penniless family), Mr. Phelen to Pettus, February 10, 1862 (from Aberdeen, a former senator, he writes about general issues of recruiting and drafting men), Report of Columbus Meeting and Citizen Resolutions, February 10, 1862 (general issues of volunteering, the draft and citizen cooperation), James Burnitt to Pettus, February 18, 1862 (from West Pt., Mississippi, writes of efforts to avoid the draft and the governor's call for a thousand men), Lewis Pipes to Pettus, March 5, 1862 (Franklin County draft bleak, no police board), L. A. Webster to Pettus, March 24, 1862 (writes from Holmes County, wants his overseer exempted), W. J. Fryday to Pettus, March 25, 1862 (reports on "Union men" and asks that they be deported form Calhoun County), A True Southern Girl to Pettus, April 17, 1862 (reports on anti-Confederates in Greensboro and affirms her loyalty to the cause), R. W. Roberts, Benjamin King, and W. F. Green to Pettus, April 21, 1862 (reports suspicious persons in the Gallatin area, might be spies, wants steps taken to ensure everyone's safety), A. Six to Pettus, April 24, 1862 (from Vicksburg, wants his minor son Jesse Six exempted from the draft, says he has already sent his older son Phillip), H. T. S. Dabney to Pettus, April 28, 1862 (wants martial law declared in Raymond, asks that the provost marshal arrest Union spies), Petition of Citizens of Countryside to Pettus, April 28, 1862 (Rankin citizens want their physician exempted), Petition of Soldiers of Winston County to Pettus, April 30, 1862 (want two men exempted from service so they can protect their destitute families), in Mississippi Governors' Collection, Ramsdell Collection, CAH, microfilm reel no. 786.254, series E, vol. 56; A Planters Wife to Pettus, May 1, 1862 (from Warren County, wants able-bodied men left on every plantation), E. Mathis to Pettus, May 2, 1862 (seeks an exemption to protect home folks in Quitman; endorsed by two other men), Benj. W. Bedford to Pettus, May 2, 1862 (requests overseer exemption), David Harrison to Pettus, May 2, 1862 (suggests men on plantation not be conscripted) in Mississippi Governors' Collection, Ramsdell Collection, CAH, microfilm reel no. 786.254, series E, vol. 57.

28. The volume of correspondence escalated from May 1862 to the end of the year. The letters are too numerous to set forth individually. A true sense of what was happening in Mississippi comes from looking at them as a group. See Mississippi Governors' Collection, Ramsdell Collection,

CAH, microfilm reel no. 786.254, series E, vols. 57 and 58. *Natchez Daily Courier*, October 3, 1862; Special Field Order no. 21, Oxford, Mississippi, December 12, 1862, OR, 1st ser., 27, pt. 2:405.

29. J. W. Ward to Father and Mother, March 1, 1862, J. W. Ward Family Correspondence, 1861–1864, in C.S.A. Records, 1856–1915, CAH, RG 2C484, folder 12.

30. Anonymous to Governor Pettus, October 28, 1862, from De Soto County, Anonymous to Pettus, October 28, 1862, from Hancock County, Mississippi Governors' Collection, Ramsdell Collection, CAH, microfilm reel no. 786.262, series E, vol. 58, Sept.–Dec. 1862.

31. P. G. T. Beauregard to John Pettus, June 9, 1862, Mississippi Governors' Papers, Military Telegrams for 1861–63, Ramsdell Collection, CAH, microfilm reel no. 786.262, series E, vol. 63.

32. Hugh McLaurin to Father, September 17, November 18, 1862, H. McLaurin to Sister, December 7, December 27, 1862, in Hugh A. McLaurin Papers, 1862–1864, Ramsdell Collection, CAH, microfilm reel no. 786.391. The soldier he saw shot may have been Pvt. Asa Lewis of the First Kentucky Brigade. Lewis had tried several times to leave and go home to see his mother. Braxton Bragg finally decided to make an example of him. See W. C. Davis, *The Orphan Brigade*, 143, 147–50.

33. *Daily Advocate*, Saturday evening edition, March 22, 1862.

34. Thomas Peebles to Father and Mother, May 26, July 15, 1862, Civil War Soldiers' Letters, ADAH, LPR 78, box 1, container 3, folder 5.

35. E. W. Halsey to Governor Moore, March 1, 1862, Letters Received by the Executive, 1860–63, LDAH, microfilm reel no. CR.004.

36. Moore to Davis, June 3, 1862, Letters Received by the Executive, 1860–63, LDAH, microfilm reel no. CR.004.

37. Moore to Davis, June 3, 1862, Letters Received by the Executive, 1860–63, LDAH, microfilm reel no. CR.004.

38. Citizens of New Orleans to Thomas Moore, July 28, 1862, Mansfield Lovell to G. W. Randolph, June 14, 1862, Moore to Thomas Hindman, June 14, 1862, Letters Received by the Executive, 1860–63, LDAH, microfilm reel no. CR.004.

39. Trial Record of Flugence Gregoine and Jacques Gregoine Jr., 1862, Letters Received by the Executive, 1860–63, LDAH, microfilm reel no. CR.004.

40. Descriptive List of Soldiers Who Have Deserted from the Confederate States Army, December 9, 1862, Letters Received by the Executive, 1860–63, LDAH, microfilm reel no. CR.004; Bergerion, *Reminiscences of Uncle Silas*. It is not clear whether planter meant wealthy farmer or just farmer. All the men were privates, and most were young, and hence planter may therefore have actually meant farmer. In any event, the signs from home, the increasing length of service, the reverses on the battlefield, or a combination of all three seemed to be taking their toll.

41. William H. Hinson and Mary Hinson to Father, February 28, 1862, Anonymous to Mother, March 9, 1862, Civil War Miscellany, CAH, 2C477, Thomas O. Moore file; Serena to L. S. Neblett, March 27, 1862, Neblett (Lizzie Scott) Papers, CAH, 2F81, folder 3.

42. Lizzie Scott Neblett to Cousin, March 23, 1862, Neblett Papers, CAH, 2F81, folder 3; Cornelia M. Noble, March 3, 1862, March 10, 1862, March 25, 1862, Cornelia M. Noble Diary, CAH, 2Rl28.

43. William Morris to Governor Lubbock, February 24, 1862, Correspondence Concerning Conscription, 1862–1864, TSA, RG 401, box 401, folder 829-1c.c.c. 1862; Petition to Governor Lubbock from Citizens of Colorado County, Texas, 1862, Correspondence Concerning Conscription, TSA, RG 401, box 401, folder 829-3. Both folders are full of exemption requests ranging from shoemakers to court officers and tax collectors to artisans.

44. Chief Justice of Bee County to Adjutant General of Texas, March 13, 1862, Correspondence Concerning Conscription, TSA, RG 401, box 401-829, folder 829-1.

45. To Lubbock from 21 Citizens from Bandera County, March 11, 1862, Correspondence Concerning Conscription, TSA, RG 401, box 401-829, folder 829-1; Petition to Governor Lubbock from Citizens of Medina County, Texas, April 5, 1862, Correspondence Concerning Conscription, TSA, RG 401, box 401-829, folder 829-2.

46. Sallie Lauderdale to Adj. Gen. J. Y. Dasheil, July 1862, Correspondence Concerning Conscription, TSA, RG 401, box 401-829, folder 829-2.

47. Sallie Lauderdale to Adj. Gen. J. Y. Dasheil, July 5, 1862, Correspondence Concerning Conscription, TSA, RG 401, box 401-829, folder 829-2.

48. Weitz, *A Higher Duty*, 91–92; Thomas Moore, Decree, February 11, 1862, Judah Benjamin to Moore, February 2, 1862, Letters Received by the Executive, 1860–63, LDAH, microfilm reel no. CR.004.

49. L. B. Fielder to Sister, February 1, 1862, Hardman Family Correspondence, ADAH, LRP 78, box 1, folder 25.

50. Junius Bragg to Josephine, April 17, 1862, in J. N. Bragg, *Letters of a Confederate Surgeon*, 50.

51. Thomas Moore to P. G. T. Beauregard, June 3, 1862, Letters Received by the Executive, 1860–63, LDAH, microfilm reel no. CR.004.

52. General Hospital Franklin & El Paso, Texas, June & July 1862, C.S.A. Records, 1856–1915, CAH, RG 2C490.

53. H. E. McCullough to Don Santiago Vidaurri, April 17, 1862, in *U.S. Department of State Papers*, 1:752.

54. Weitz, *A Higher Duty*, 46.

55. General Order no. 7, Headquarters, Exchanged Prisoners, October 27, 1862, *Daily Mississippian*, November 9, 1862.

56. "Report of the Select Committee, Appointed by the Senate of the Confederate States to Examine the Condition of Hospitals and Report by Bill or Otherwise, 1862," *Confederate Imprints*, 3517: 5: 247-1: 8–9.

57. Braxton Bragg, General Order no. 4, January 19, 1863, C.S.A. Records, 1861–1865, CAH, RG 2C485, folder 7.

58. Report of W. P. Price, Superintendent of Georgia, in *Second Annual Report of the Central Association for the Relief of South Carolina Soldiers for 1864* (Columbia: Evans & Cogswell, 1864), Ramsdell Collection, CAH, microfilm reel 786.47.

59. Senate Resolution from 1st Confederate Congress, 2d sess., Senate, Wednesday, August 20, 1862, SHSP 45 (1925): 184.

60. Davis to State Governors, n.d., in E. W. Halsey to P. D. Hardy, Secretary of State, November 7, 1862, Letters Received by the Executive, 1860–63, LDAH, microflim reel no. CR.004.

61. "A Traitor to the Confederacy," *Montgomery Weekly Advertiser*, October 1, 1862, November 19, 1862. For First Alabama affiliation in the Army of Tennessee see McMorris, *History of the First Alabama Regiment*.

62. *Montgomery Weekly Advertiser*, October 1, 1862.

63. Executive Council Chamber, Resolution Adopted by Governor and Council, July 21, 1862, Adjutant General, Scrapbook of Published Orders, 1862–1865, SCDAH.

64. "Desertion from Our Army," *Montgomery Weekly Advertiser*, December 10, 1862.

65. *Montgomery Weekly Advertiser*, December 13, 1862.

66. "The Excitement in Northern Texas," *Selma Morning Reporter*, November 21, 1862. The article was reprinted from the *Houston Telegraph* and claimed the organization had been "nipped in the bud."

67. Military Volunteer Family Assistance Records, 1861–66, ADAH, microfilm, SG 16064; *Charleston Courier*, April 9, 1862.

68. "Public Resolution," *Augusta Daily Chronicle and Sentinel*, March 18, 1862.

5. Desertion in the East

1. Ms. N. L. Beckley to Lizzie, April 2, 1862, Women's Writings, Neblett Papers, CAH, RG 2F81, folder 3. For the slave exodus see also Sutherland, *Seasons of War*, 176.

2. For stories of wartime hardships see Faust, *Southern Stories*, 176–92; Gallagher, *A Confederate War*, 63; Powers, *Lee's Miserables*, 435, 442.

3. Lee, *Wartime Papers*. Desertion first appears on page 587, the section covering Lee's correspondence and reports from August to September 1863. OR reflects a similar void. Although Union documentation, particularly regarding oath taking and desertion, is active in 1862, the Confederate perspective does not start to appear until 1863.

4. "Samuel Cooper, Adjt. & Inspector General's Office, General Order no. 16, March 21, 1862," *Staunton (VA) Spectator*, April 1, 1862.

5. "Soldiers on Furlough," *Staunton Spectator*, April 1, 1682.

6. Special Order no. 107, May 9, 1862, OR, 4th ser., 2:1120.

7. Weitz, *A Higher Duty*, 72–73; Lee to Randolph, July 12, 1862, in Lee, *Wartime Papers*, 231.

8. Sutherland, *Seasons of War*, 194–95.

9. For language of the oath not to bear arms see Weitz, *A Higher Duty*, 38; Lee to McClellan, July 21, 1862, in Lee, *Wartime Papers*, 234.

10. The order of battle for the Army of Northern Virginia during the Manassas campaign lists regiments from every state except Arkansas. Virginia boasted 50 infantry regiments, 10 cavalry regiments, 1 infantry battalion, 1 cavalry battalion, and 31 artillery batteries. Georgia boasted the second-most regiments, with 27 infantry, 1 cavalry regiment, and 1 artillery battery. North Carolina had 13 infantry regiments, 1 infantry battalion, and 1 artillery battery. South Carolina had 15 infantry regiments, 1 infantry battalion, an undefined unit of sharpshooters, and 4 batteries of artillery. Alabama contributed 10 infantry regiments, 1 battalion, and no artillery. The army is primarily a Virginia army and secondarily an eastern army, with troop numbers from other states diminishing as one moves further west. OR, 1st ser., 12, pt. 2:546–51.

11. Lee to Clark, August 8, 1862, in Lee, *Wartime Papers*, 248–49.

12. Address of John Letcher, Wednesday, May 7, 1862, Journal of the Senate of Virginia, Ramsdell Collection, CAH, microfilm reel no. 786.88.

13. Address of John Letcher, Monday, September 15, 1862, Journal of the Senate of Virginia, Ramsdell Collection, CAH, microfilm reel no. 786.88.

14. Address of John Letcher, Monday, September 15, 1862.

15. Address of John Letcher, Monday, September 15, 1862.

16. Robertson, *Civil War Virginia*, 108; Sutherland, *Seasons of War*, 128–31, 160–61, 177, 194–95.

17. Blair, *Virginia's Private War*, 62–64.

18. Blair, *Virginia's Private War*, 61. Blair's study of Virginia encompasses more than desertion, but his study of ten regiments represents the best study of Virginia desertion to date. He took one regiment from the Tidewater region, three from the Piedmont, three from the valley, two from southwestern Virginia, and one from western Virginia. The Twenty-second Virginia, from western Virginia, had more in 1861, as did the Sixty-third Virginia, from the southwestern portion of the state. The Twenty-fourth Virginia, a Piedmont unit, had more deserters in 1863

and 1864 than in 1862. The Thirtieth Virginia, also a Piedmont unit, had more deserters in 1863, as did the Fifty-first Virginia, a southwest Virginia regiment.

19. Radley, *Rebel Watchdog*, 103.

20. *OR*, 1st ser., 11, pt. 3:614–15.

21. Harry Heth, To Whom it May Concern, June 9, 1862, *OR*, 1st ser., 51, pt. 2:584; General Order no. 43, June 13, 1862, *OR*, 4th ser., 1:1151; Robert Chilton to S. Cooper, September 23, 1862, Abstract for Field Return, Army of Northern Virginia, September 30, 1862, *OR*, 1st ser., 19, pt. 2:621, 639. It is difficult to identify exact times of departure, but on September 22, 1862, Longstreet and Jackson's Corps combined totaled 36,407. By October 1, 1862, that number had grown to 48,689. Twelve thousand men represented a significant force on a day that Lee scrambled to keep from being driven into the Potomac.

22. Lee to Davis, September 21, 1863, *OR*, 1st ser., 19, pt. 1:143; General Order no. 102, Lee to Davis, September 7, 1862, *OR*, 1st ser., 19, pt. 2:592, 597; Davis, "Message of the President with attached Findings of a General Court Martial in the Case of Persons charged with Desertion and Absence Without Leave for 1862, February 11, 1863," *Confederate Imprints*, 3517: 20: 1272: 5–6. The attached findings contain dates for every court-martial proceeding after September, but the first entry is not dated beyond providing September as the date of the general order reporting the findings. The August starting date was arrived at by matching men found in the list with Bunch, *Roster of the Court-Martial*, 53. William Callum appears in the list of findings and in the roster. The date of his trial in the roster is August 15, 1862.

23. "Findings of a General Court Martial in the Case of Persons Charged with Desertion and Absence Without Leave for 1862 under General Orders no. 93," *Confederate Imprints*, 3517: 20: 1272: 6–7.

24. "Findings of a General Court Martial," *Confederate Imprints*, 3517: 20: 1272: 1–18.

25. "Findings of a General Court Martial," *Confederate Imprints*, 3517: 20: 1272: 19–29.

26. "Findings of a General Court Martial," *Confederate Imprints*, 3517: 20: 1272: 32–36.

27. "Communication from W. S. Barton, Assistant Adjutant General, February 26, 1863," *Confederate Imprints*, 3517: 20: 1272. For Lee's order of ritual executions see Blair, *Virginia's Private War*, 65. Blair's source is a letter from a North Carolina soldier dated February 26, 1863. With Lee's army on the move in 1862 and the virtual absence of court-martial death sentences, the scene he describes is unlikely in 1862. It is more likely that the ritual executions occurred in August 1863, when Lee becomes overwhelmed by the desertion numbers. See Lee to Davis, August 17, 1863, in Lee, *Wartime Papers*, 591.

28. "Findings of a General Court Martial in the Case of Persons charged with Desertion and Absence Without Leave for 1862 under General Orders no. 7 and 35," *Confederate Imprints*, 3517: 20: 1272: 38–61. Bunch, *Roster of the Court-Martial*, 39, 194.

29. Radley, *Rebel Watchdog*, 124–25, 150; Adjutant and Inspector General's Office, General Order no. 49, July 14, 1862, General Order no. 52, July 23, 1862, General Order no. 64, September 8, 1862, General Order no. 96, November 27, 1862, *OR*, 4th ser., 2:5, 14, 78, 214–15; William H. Richardson, Attorney General, to George W. Randolph, Secretary of War, September 17, 1862, *Doc No. IV Communication Transmitting Correspondence between State and Confederate Officers Relative to Conscription, October 1, 1862*, Ramsdell Collection, CAH, microfilm reel no. 786.88.

30. "List of Deserters," *Montgomery Weekly Advertiser*, October 28, 1862.

31. "Deserters," *Selma Morning Reporter*, August 25, 1862.

32. "Notice," *Selma Morning Reporter*, August 12, 1862. It offers a thirty-dollar reward for Isaac Littleton, a private in the Twenty-fifth Alabama, with a notice that all men from the Twenty-

fifth then absent should return. "Deserters," *Selma Morning Reporter*, October 10, 1862, listed four deserters from the Fourth Alabama.

33. "An Act to Better Provide for the Sick and Wounded of the Army Hospitals, September 27, 1862," in Cunningham, *Doctors in Gray*, 38.

34. Cunningham, *Doctors in Gray*, 39–40, 90.

35. William A. Graham, "Speech in the Convention of North Carolina, December 7, 1861, on the Ordinance concerning Test Oaths and Sedition," *Confederate Imprints*, 3517: 91: 2758: 29–30. The ordinance appears in the appendix to Graham's speech.

36. Graham, "Speech in the Convention of North Carolina, December 7, 1861," *Confederate Imprints*, 3517: 91: 2758: 18–19, 26–27.

37. Inscoe and McKinney, *Heart of Confederate Appalachia*, 3, 103–4.

38. Inscoe and McKinney, *Heart of Confederate Appalachia*, 106–7.

39. Inscoe and McKinney, *Heart of Confederate Appalachia*, 106–9.

40. D. W. Siler to Governor Vance, November 3, 1862, in Inscoe and McKinney, *Heart of Confederate Appalachia*, 112–13.

41. G. J. Huntley to Tincy Huntley, March 19, 1862, in Taylor, *The Cry Is War*, 67–68.

42. Inscoe and McKinney, *Heart of Confederate Appalachia*, 113; Norm Harrold to Jefferson Davis, January 11, 1863, in Moore, *Conscription and Conflict*, 19–21.

43. Inscoe and McKinney, *Heart of Confederate Appalachia*, 113–20.

44. Neely, *Retaliation*.

45. Weigley, *A Great Civil War*, 143.

46. McPherson, *Antietam*. McPherson argues that in September 1862 the survival of the Union was in doubt. Second Manassas had struck a hard blow to the North, and England seemed ready to act if the South could but finish the job it started in northern Virginia in August. For accounts of the straggling see Alexander, *Fighting for the Confederacy*, 155.

47. George Randolph, Confidential Circular to the Governors of the State, July 17, 1862, OR, 4th ser., 2:7.

48. John Gill Shorter to James Seddon, December 23, 1862, Joseph Brown to George W. Randolph, July 30, 1862, OR, 4th ser., 2:22, 259.

49. Zebulon Vance, Address to the General Assembly of North Carolina, November 17, 1862, OR, 4th ser., 2:186.

50. "For the Spectator," *Staunton Spectator*, December 30, 1862.

51. "General Order 96," *Montgomery Weekly Advertiser*, December 13, 1862; "Breadstuffs in the South," *Montgomery Weekly Advertiser*, December 17, 1862.

52. *Selma Morning Reporter*, October 4, 1862; James Chestnut Jr., Report of the Department of the Military of South Carolina to His Excellency Governor Pickens, Ramsdell Collection, CAH, microfilm reel no. 786.47.

53. "Our Resources," *Selma Morning Reporter*, November 20, 1862.

54. General E. Kirby Smith, "Headquarters Army of Kentucky," September 4, 1862, *Confederate Imprints*, 3517: 11: 651.

6. Desertion, Ideology, and Oaths

1. W. L. Gammage to William Bonner, January 1863, Civil War Miscellany, CAH, RG 2C447, M. H. Bonner file.

2. Joint Resolution of Confederate Congress, January 13, 1863.

3. General Order no. 286, August 26, 1863, OR, 2d ser., 6:212. This order established the policy for releasing deserters and required a descriptive list to identify men who violated the oath. The

Union was keeping records. By late 1862 the Union army was issuing forms to Confederate deserters to prove they had sworn the oath to the United States. The goal was to prevent them from being harassed by Union provost guards on their way home. The problem, however, was that in the South that same piece of paper was proof of desertion to the enemy. See William Hoffman to Maj. J. G. Fonda, September 1, 1862, and Hoffman to Col. Jesse Hildebrand, September 3, 1862, OR, 2d ser., 4:479, 485.

4. Rev. B. M. Palmer to John Perkins, February 10, 1863, published as B. M. Palmer, *The Oath of Allegiance to the United States Discussed in Its Moral and Political Bearings* (Richmond: McFarlane & Ferguson, 1863), MDAH, call no. 973.751/P180.

5. Palmer, *Oath of Allegiance*. Palmer's analogy to Philip and the Netherlands ignored the fact that the Union did not recognize the Confederacy as a nation. Therefore the Latin doctrine of *nemo poteste exure patriam* ("no one can cast off his own country") did not apply.

6. Palmer, *Oath of Allegiance*.

7. Mark Grimsley suggests that the Union policy was always designed to coerce behavior from Southern civilians. The goal was to encourage loyal behavior, and although few commanders believed they could do so en masse, they never stopped trying to do so on an individual scale. The oath process was clearly part of that effort. Even when the Union moved to a more "hard war" approach, evidenced by Sherman's march and Sheridan's Shenandoah Valley campaign, those actions were designed not so much to crush Southerners as to show them that they could be hurt and that their government could not protect them. See Grimsley's *Hard Hand of War*, 208–15. In theory, the same lessons the Union sought to teach Southern civilians about their own helplessness could drive the desertion of soldiers who believed their loved ones were in danger. Palmer, *Oath of Allegiance*; Weitz, "Preparing for the Prodigal Sons."

8. Palmer, *Oath of Allegiance*.

9. The constitutions of New Jersey, New York, and Pennsylvania provide excellent examples of the colonial contractual understanding of government and the breach of that contract as the justification for rebellion. See Thorpe, *The Federal and State Constitutions*, 5:2594, 2623, 3081.

10. John Letcher, Address to the Virginia Assembly, January 7, 1863, Journal of the Senate of Virginia, Ramsdell Collection, CAH, microfilm reel no. 786.88.

11. F. R. Lubbock, "Address to the Members of the State House of Representatives, February 5, 1863," Executive Record Books, TSA, microfilm reel 6.

12. F. R. Lubbock to John Magruder, March 30, 1863, Executive Record Books, TSA, microfilm reel 6.

13. Col. U. S. Murphy to Thomas Watts, January 17, 1864, Thomas H. Watts Correspondence, 1863–1865, ADAH, SG 21977, microfilm reel 20. For a discussion of the passport system see Halleck to Maj. Gen. George Foster, September 23, 1864, OR, 2d ser., 7:865–66.

14. F. R. Lubbock, "Address to the 10th Legislature, November 4, 1863," Executive Record Books, TSA, microfilm reel 6.

15. F. R. Lubbock, "Address to the 10th Legislature, November 4, 1863, Valediction, November 5, 1863," Executive Record Books, TSA, microfilm reel 6.

16. "A Soldier's Reflections," *Montgomery Weekly Advertiser*, August 5, 1863.

17. "A Soldier's Reflections."

18. "A Soldier's Reflections."

19. B. Bradley to Dear Sir, June 21, 1863, Civil War Miscellany, CAH, RG 2C447, B. Bradley file; Captain Whitfield (1st Ala. from Port Hudson) to Wife, *Selma Morning Reporter*, June 10, 1863.

20. *Montgomery Weekly Advertiser*, May 27, 1863. The item is actually dated May 17.

21. Jerome Yates to Ma, January 1863, Yates to sister Marie, May 11, 1863, C.S.A. Records, 1856–1915, CAH, RG 2C484, folder 8: Jerome Yates Letters. The Sixteenth Mississippi formed from eight counties in central, southern, and southwest Mississippi: Pike, Smith, Simpson, Copiah, Adams, Jasper, Claiborne, and Wilkinson.

22. Yates to Ma, August 21, 1863, C.S.A. Records, 1856–1915, CAH, RG 2C484, folder 8: Jerome Yates Letters.

23. Yates to Ma, September 13, October 28, 1863, C.S.A. Records, CAH, RG 2C848.

24. "Taking Care of Families," *Montgomery Weekly Advertiser*, July 29, 1863.

25. Register of Confederate Soldiers Deserting to the Union Army, 1863–65, NARA, microfilm, RG 598, reel M8. For this study, data on 4,267 Confederate deserters were taken from the record. The record contains almost 35,000; men were selected by taking every man with a last name beginning with A–F. My numbers exclude Georgians (the subject of *A Higher Duty*). Georgians accounted for 3,500 identifiable deserters, of which 132 were duplicates. Taking those 3,500 from the estimated 35,000 leaves 31,500 deserters from states other than Georgia.

26. Bessie Martin counted 2,800 Alabamians who swore the oath in the Register and an additional 800 to 1,400 who swore the oath as POWs before the Union put severe restrictions prisoner oath swearing. The 392 in this sample represent 14 percent of Martin's total number of 2,800 and 9.2 percent of the 4,267-man sample in this study. She concluded that between 3,600 and 4,000 Alabamians deserted to the enemy. However, that number includes not only those found in the Register but also those she could find from prison rolls indicating POWs who took the oath in 1862. Her county analysis showed the same distribution as that demonstrated by this data run. The most deserters came from the northern counties, with the exception of Mobile County in the extreme southwest corner of the state. Martin determined that "at least 2800 took the oath" and were entered into the Register. Her estimation is not explained, but based on how data are kept, the 2,800 figure probably reflects those who were absolutely identified as from Alabama. She may not have counted men who served in Alabama units but did not have a state or county designation. Martin, *A Rich Man's War*, 234–39; United States Manuscript Census, Mobile County, 1860, ADAH.

27. North Carolinian's choice of desertion options becomes more revealing when compared to the "official numbers" of those states whose soldiers did make heavy use of the Union desertion program. According to Ella Lonn, Alabama had only 1,583 deserters, of which all but 5 were enlisted men. The 2,800 listed in the Register are twice that number. Lonn indicates Georgia had 6,876, of which only 79 were officers. The state's 3,368 men in the Register are half that number if we assume it is a portion of her total, and 33 percent of the total if we assume that it is not included in Lonn's number. Tennessee had almost as many men desert to the Union as Lonn attributes deserted in total from Tennessee (12,155). Lonn, *Desertion during the Civil War*, 231.

28. Dotson, " 'Sisson's Kingdom.' " Dotson clearly argues for a Confederate home-front collapse in Floyd County. The war created clear divisions of loyalty within Floyd County and made it a favorite destination for Confederate deserters. As will be pointed out later herein, not only did the county's sons return, but those who found the area's terrain and hospitality appealing also came, and their presence created desertion problems of a different nature.

29. See the appendix.

30. Rosecrans to Townsend, September 11, 1863 (12:45 p.m.), Rosecrans to Stanton, September 11, 1863 (2:00 p.m.), Halleck to Rosecrans, September 11, 1863 (9:00 p.m.), OR, 1st ser., 30, pt. 3:529–30.

31. Mrs. Alliou Hundervant to Thomas Watts, December 24, 1863, Watts Correspondence, ADAH, SG21977, microfilm reel 20; *Montgomery Weekly Advertiser*, August 12, August 26, 1863.

32. Samuel Cooper, General Order no. 109, August 11, 1863, George Wm. Brent to Joseph Wheeler, August 17, 1863, OR, 1st ser., 30, pt. 4:489, 502.

33. Diary of J. S. Stockdale 1863–1864, September 10, 11, 1863, Prisoner of War Records, ADAH, SPR 352, folder 2.

34. F. R. Lubbock, Address to Members of the State House of Representatives, February 5, 1863, F. R. Lubbock to County Court of Lampasas County, February 21, 1863, F. R. Lubbock to Col. James Bourland, March 11, 1863, F. R. Lubbock to Jefferson Davis, March 27, 1863, F. R. Lubbock to Kirby Smith, August 31, 1863, Executive Record Books, TSA, microfilm reel 6. Lubbock's February 5, 1863, address claimed Texas sent 33 cavalry and 19 infantry regiments to the Confederate service, 30 of which were organized after February 1862, evidence of the effect of conscription on volunteering. He estimated that a total of 63,000–68,000 men were gone by mid-1862.

35. F. R. Lubbock to J. L. Ford, Commissioner of Conscripts, September 18, 1863, Executive Record Books, TSA, microfilm reel 6.

36. Beamer, "Galvanized Yankees in Kansas."

37. Martin, *A Rich Man's War*, 236; Brown, *Galvanized Yankees*.

38. Samuel Cooper, General Order no. 40, March 29, 1864, James Seddon to L. Polk, April 13, 1864, Jesse Glenn to Davis, October 7, 1864, with endorsement of Seddon, October 19, 1864, OR, 4th ser., 3:255, 295, 714–15.

39. Confederate House of Representatives, "An Act to Increase and Strengthen the Army of the Confederate States, January 22, 1863," *Confederate Imprints*, 3517: 6: 288.

40. For slavery as a unifying force in the antebellum South see J. W. Harris, *Plain Folk and Gentry*.

41. J. Z. George to Pettus, March 24, 1863, P. T. Norman, Canton, to Pettus, March 27, 1863, Lucretia Curtis to Pettus, March 31, 1863, Jason H. Thompson to Pettus, March 31, 1863, William T. May to Pettus, April 2, 1863, Officers of Co. D. 1st Batt. Miss. State Troops to Gen. T. C. Tupper, April 4, 1863, Mississippi Governors' Collection, Ramsdell Collection, CAH, microfilm reel no. 786.254, series E, vol. 60; Receipts for Deserters of the Army Arrested by the Sheriff of Winston and Chicasaw Counties, MDAH, box 8372, series 404, RG 9, vols. 35 and 143.

42. O. G. Dark, C. V. Gamble and T. C. Shauston, Youngsville, Alabama, to Watts, October 31, 1863, Undersigned Citizens of St. Clair County to Watts, December 19, 1863, Watts Correspondence, ADAH, SG 21977, reel 20. For a study of Brown's state troops see W. H. Bragg, *Joe Brown's Army*.

43. A. G. to "Captain," February 17, 1863, A. G. to Maj. C. D. Melton, August 20, 1863, A. G. to Capt. E. M. Boykin, August 22, 1863, A. G. to Col. J. C. Witherspoon, n.d., Special Order no. 226, November 1, 1863, Adjutant General's Order Books, 1861–1865, 3 vols., SCDAH, vol. 2.

44. F. R. Lubbock, Address to Members of the State House of Representatives, February 5, 1863, Lubbock to Col. James Bourland, June 23, 1863, Executive Record Books, TSA, microfilm reel 6.

45. Neely, *Southern Rights*, 69; Vance to Davis, May 13, 1863, OR, 1st ser., 51, pt. 2:709.

46. Seddon to Vance, May 5, 1863, OR, 1st ser., 51, pt. 2:702.

47. Neely, *Southern Rights*, 68.

48. Zebulon Vance, A Proclamation of the Governor of North Carolina, May 11, 1863, OR, 1st ser., 51, pt. 2:706–8.

49. Vance to Davis, May 13, 1863, OR, 1st ser., 51, pt. 2:709.

50. Vance to Davis, May 13, 1863, OR, 1st ser., 51, pt. 2:709–10.

51. Vance to Davis, May 13, 1863, OR, 1st ser., 51, pt. 2:710.

52. Seddon to Vance, May 23, 1863, OR, 1st ser., 51, pt. 2:714.

53. Vance to Seddon, May 25, 1863, *OR*, 1st ser., 51, pt. 2:715.

54. Vance to Seddon, May 25, 1863, *OR*, 1st ser., 51, pt. 2:715–16. Actually the Confederacy had asked all state governors to help per Randolph's July 14, 1862, circular. Brown had actually issued a proclamation similar to Vance's in January 1863. See Proclamation by Joseph Brown, Governor of Georgia, January 17, 1863, *OR*, 4th ser., 2:360–61.

7. "The Number of Desertions Is So Great"

1. Lee to Imboden, January 12, 1863, *OR*, 1st ser., 51, pt. 2:669–70.

2. Pillow to Campbell, January 26, 1863, *OR*, 4th ser., 2:374.

3. Samuel Cooper, General Order no. 19, February 17, 1863, *OR*, 4th ser., 2:401.

4. Samuel Cooper, General Order no. 15, February 6, 1863, General Order no. 28, March 12, 1863, and the Congress of the Confederate States of America, "An Act to Prevent the Absence of Officers and Soldiers without Leave, April 16, 1863," *Confederate Imprints*, 3517: 20: 1289.

5. Samuel Cooper, General Order no. 44, April 16, 1863, *OR*, 4th ser., 2:496; Samuel Cooper, Report of the Adjutant and Inspector General, January 31, 1863, *Confederate Imprints*, 3517: 29: 1423.

6. Samuel Cooper, General Order no. 94, July 4, 1863, J. H. Binford, circular, July 7, 1863, *OR*, 4th ser., 2:618.

7. Gideon Pillow, General Order no. 1, July 27, 1863, Jno C. Burch, General Order no. 2, July 27, 1863, G. W. Lay, Acting Chief of Conscription Bureau, Circular July 27, 1863, Daniel Ruggles to Col. B. S. Ewell, July 27, 1863, Pillow to Col. Benjamin S. Ewell, July 28, 1863, William Wren to Jefferson Davis, August 12, 1863, P. N. Page, circular, August 20, 1863, *OR*, 4th ser., 2:676–79, 708, 736.

8. H. D. Clayton, Wm. B. Bate, P. R. Cleburne, M. P. Lowrey, Alex P. Stewart, L. E. Polk, St. John R. Liddell, J. M. Withers, T. J. Churchill, D. H. Hill, L. Polk, Z. C. Deas, O. F. Strahl, John C. Carter, Preston Smith, A. M. Manigault, Braxton Bragg to Samuel Cooper, July 25, 1863, Davis, Proclamation, July 31, 1863, *OR*, 4th ser., 2:670–71, 687–88.

9. W. T. Walthall to G. W. Lay, August 6, 1863, *OR*, 4th ser., 2:726–27.

10. Lee, General Order no. 60, May 8, 1863, General Order no. 80, *Confederate Imprints*, 3517: 11: 657–58; Lee to Davis, August 17, 1863, Lee to Imboden, August 17, 1863, *OR*, 1st ser., 29, pt. 2:649–50.

11. William Smith to Sunshine, July 27, August 6, 1863, William Adolphus Smith Papers, 1862–1877, CAH, RG 2.325/B15, AR 91–251; E. D. McDaniel to Wife Lizzie, August 23, 1863, C.S.A. Records, 1861–1865, CAH, RG 2C485, folder 6.

12. Spencer Glasgow Welch to Wife, March 5, September 16, September 27, 1863, in Welch, *A Confederate Surgeon's Letters*, 44–45, 77–79; William Smith to Sunshine, September 6, 1863, William Adolphus Smith Papers, CAH, RG 2.325/B15, AR 91-251. For another description of an executed deserter in Lee's army see W. Wood, *Reminiscences of Big I*, 41–42. For a description of deserters executed in the trans-Mississippi see John Simmons to Wife, March 17, 1863, in Harrison, "The Confederate Letters of John Simmons," 32. For report of deserters shot in 1862 in Texas see Simpson, *The Bugle Softly Blows*, 18–19; Alexander, *Fighting for the Confederacy*, 191–93.

13. Bearss, *Confederate Diary of Felix Pierre Poche*, 14; General Order no. 62, Courts Martial Proceedings, Army of Northern Virginia, May 12, 1863, Circular, Courts Martial Proceedings, Army of Northern Virginia, August 14, 1863, *Confederate Imprints*, 3517: 11: 655, 659.

14. Lee to Seddon, October 30, 1863, Seddon to Lee, November 4, 1863, *OR*, 1st ser., 29, pt. 2:806–7, 820.

15. Joyner to Smith, *OR*, 4th ser., 2:721–22; Lee to Seddon, July 30, 1863, *OR*, 1st ser., 27, pt. 3:1052.

16. Jno Withers to Col. J. S. Preston, August 18, 1863, C. B. Duffield to Col. J. C. Shields, August 19, 1863, Shields to Duffield, August 23, 1863, OR, 4th ser., 2:722–23.

17. Kirby Smith, General Order no. 38, August 26, 1863, OR, 1st ser., 27, pt. 2:580; J. B. Mitchell to Father, August 8, 1863, Civil War Soldiers' Letters: Mitchell Collection, ADAH, LPR 78, box 1, container 3, folder 2.

18. Hardee to Holmes, April 27, 1863, William Hardee Letterbook, December 20, 1862–April 30, 1863, in Civil War Papers, ADAH, PB/Range H/Sec 7, shelf C, folder 37; Hardee to Chalmers, July 29, 1863, OR, 1st ser., 51, pt. 3:829.

19. Report of Col. Robert V. Richardson, August 10, 1863, Seddon to Davis, August 17, 1863, Davis to Seddon, August 19, 1863, OR, 1st ser., 52, pt. 1:72–74.

20. Chilton to Imboden, November 24, 1863, OR, 1st ser., 29, pt. 2:844–45.

21. George L. Griscom, Adjutant, 9th Texas Cavalry, September 4, 1863, Diary of George L. Griscom, CAH, RG 2R6; Pillow to Cooper, August 28, 1863, Pillow to Chalmers, September 7, 1863, OR, 4th ser., 2:775, 795.

22. Bonham to Vance, August 22, 1863, Vance to Bonham, August 26, 1863, OR, 4th ser., 2:741, 765; Order to Captain, February 17, 1863, Adjutant General's Order Books, SCDAH, vol. 2; Otten, "Disloyalty in the Upper Districts," 102.

23. Milton to Seddon, October 22, 1863, OR, 4th ser., 2:879–80.

24. Morris to Margaret Ann Roe Morris, February 22, 1863, Civil War Miscellany, CAH, RG 2C447, Robert Morris file.

25. Simmons to Wife, August 30, September 13, 1863, "Letters of John Simmons," 35–36.

26. J. E. James to Parents, July 21, 1863, in Elkins, *Letters from a Civil War Soldier*, 25–26; Jno Withers, Special Order no. 197, August 19, 1863, OR, 1st ser., 52, pt. 2:516.

27. Jno Heigler, 40th Alabama, Circular, August 13, 1863, William Hardee, Order to Paroled Prisoners of Vicksburg, August 27, 1863, Civil War Papers, ADAH, PB/Range H/Sec 7, section C, folder 15, 37; Joseph Brown to James Seddon, August 10, 1863, OR, 4th ser., 2:753.

28. J. J. Cowan to Wife, December 9, 1863, James J. Cowan Family Papers, CAH, RG 2E555.

29. Register of Confederate Soldiers, n.d., Stout Papers, CAH, RG 4L252. This undated volume appears to be for the year 1863. Months and days are provided, but this volume, unlike the other five in the Stout Papers, has no year identification. Several factors lead one to the conclusion that it is 1863. First, the general receiving hospital is in Chattanooga. That would not have been the case for either 1864 or 1865 as the Confederacy lost Chattanooga for good in December 1863. There is also a hospital in Ringgold, which would not have been the case in 1864. It is unlikely it was for 1862, because the Army of Tennessee was not formed as an entity until late that year, and earlier combat in Tennessee focused on the western part of the state and Corinth, in northern Mississippi. In addition, casualties—or at least patient records—for April are simply not high enough to reflect the fighting at Shiloh. The Chattanooga hospital was established on November 17, 1862, so its first records would logically be 1863. Schroeder-Lien, *Confederate Hospitals on the Move*, 197.

30. Schroeder-Lien, *Confederate Hospitals on the Move*, 120–21; Cunningham, *Doctors in Gray*, 47, 52–54. There were hospitals in Charlottesville and Danville, and North Carolina actually had eight way hospitals. There were also several smaller hospitals in South Carolina and Florida.

31. Cunningham, *Doctors in Gray*, 40–41; A Bill to Repeal "An Act Regulating the Granting of Furloughs and Discharges in Hospitals," Senate, First Congress–Fourth Session, December 29, 1863, SHSP 50 (1953): 138–39. Hill's statement about losing one in three men to hospitals furloughs apparently came from Seddon.

32. Cunningham, *Doctors in Gray*, 41.

33. H. W. King, Receiving and District Hospital, Atlanta, Georgia, May 30, 1864, in Daily Remarks and Reports 1863–1864, Stout Papers, CAH, RG 2G386; Cunningham, *Doctors in Gray*, 98, 142; Schroeder-Lien, *Confederate Hospitals on the Move*, 128.

34. Register of Confederate Soldiers, n.d., Stout Papers, CAH, RGS 4L250, 4L251, 4L252, 4L259; C.S.A. Army of Tennessee Morning Reports, April 1, 1863–July 17, 1864, Stout Papers, CAH, RG 4L248. The earliest ledger runs from November 2, 1861, through March 17, 1863. It has 177 total pages with 82 lines to a page. Only about half the pages are full. For 1861 and 1862 the ledger lists only six deserters, all from a hospital in Cairo. One is Michael Welch, the first such man to desert, or at least the first to be recorded. He left on Christmas Day 1861. The ledger lists fifty-four men who deserted between January 1 and March 17, 1863. The dates are those the men were admitted. Some deserted as late as April 28, 1863. The data are then picked up on two separate types of records. One is the Army of Tennessee morning reports for April 19, 1863, through July 19, 1864. This report provides no names, only locations, but lists 728 men deserting from hospitals, mostly in Georgia during 1863. Thereafter, a series of general ledgers records men admitted and deserting. A general ledger for the period starting in July 1863 lists twenty deserters, all between August and October 1863. The ledger that begins in November 1863 runs into 1864. From 1863 it lists twenty-one deserters for November and December 1863. Finally, the undated record that appears to be for 1863 fills the gap between the ledger that ended in April 1863 and the one that picked up in July 1863. It lists fifty-nine deserters for the period from May to mid-July 1863. According to the existing ledgers and hospital morning reports, in 1863 the Army of Tennessee lost 882 soldiers to desertion from hospitals. To the extent that the records identify individual soldiers, most of the deserters came from Alabama, Georgia, and Arkansas.

35. Weitz, *A Higher Duty*, 62–66.

36. Jason I. Hall to Parents, June 25, 1863, in Fleming, *Band of Brothers*, 100.

37. Ulysses S. Grant, General Order no. 10, December 12, 1863, OR, 1st ser., 51, pt. 3:396.

38. Jas. R. Chalmers to Maj. G. W. Holt, December 14, 1863, OR, 1st ser., 51, pt. 3:828–29.

39. Alex McGowin to Thomas McGowin, July 13, 1863, Alex McGowin to Sister, November 2, 1863, Civil War Soldiers' Letters, ADAH, LPR 78, box 1, container 2, folder 5.

40. J. Searcy to Mother, July 21, 1863, Civil War Soldiers' Letters, ADAH, LPR 78, box 1, container 1, folder 15.

41. *Knoxville Daily Register*, August 6, 1863.

42. James Mitchell to Lizzie, September 17, 1863, in Mitchell, "Civil War Letters of James Mitchell," 314.

43. Horice Mortimer to My Own Darling, May 24, 1863, Civil War Soldiers' Letters, ADAH, LPR 78, box 1, container 1, folder 9.

44. Howell, *Going to Meet the Yankees*, 202–3.

45. Otten, "Disloyalty in the Upper Districts," 100–101.

46. Alexander C. Hill, Second Texas Brigade, to Judge Rector, July 28, 1863, Civil War Miscellany, CAH, 2C447, A. C. Hill file.

47. Ellsworth, "San Antonio during the Civil War," 54; Irby, "Line of the Rio Grande," 163–67.

48. Pillow to Seddon, August 23, 1863, OR, 4th ser., 2:741–42.

49. Pillow to Seddon, August 23, 1863, with J. A. Campbell Endorsement, OR, 4th ser., 2:742–43. There are no records to verify Pillow's numbers, but newspapers show an increase in deserter postings. A notice for Canty's brigade appeared in the *Independent Gainesville*, September 5, 1863, and listed 103 deserters from the Seventeenth and Twenty-ninth Alabama regiments.

50. Richardson to Seddon, August 22, 1863, OR, 4th ser., 2:739–41. Richardson was a professor of mathematics at Georgia Military Institute, and using two methods he came up with 42,689 and 41,944 able-bodied men available for service in Georgia.
51. Pillow to Seddon, August 23, 1863, OR, 4th ser., 2:743.
52. Preston to Seddon, August 17, 1863, OR, 4th ser., 2:723–26.
53. Seddon to Johnston, August 25, 1863, OR, 4th ser., 2:749.
54. Preston to Seddon, August 25, 1863, with enclosure of Pillow to Cooper, August 7, 1863, OR, 4th ser., 2:749–51.
55. Harris to Seddon, August 8, 1863, Brown to Seddon, August 10, 1863, Seddon to Shorter, August 13, 1863, OR, 4th ser., 2:752–54.
56. Pillow to Cooper, September 13, 1863, Pillow to Seddon, September 21, 1863, Pillow to Cooper, November 2, 1863, OR, 4th ser., 2:805–6, 819–21, 963–65.
57. Circular, Bureau of Conscription, September 10, 1863, Samuel Cooper, General Order no. 122, September 11, 1863, General Order no. 125, September 1863, General Order no. 135, October 15, 1863, Circular no. 59, Bureau of Conscription, December 4, 1863, OR, 4th ser., 2:798–99, 801, 827–28, 874, 1022–23.
58. Seddon to Pillow, September 28, 1863, Pillow to Seddon, October 5, 1863, Seddon to Pillow, October 12, 1863, OR, 4th ser., 2:830, 853–54, 869.
59. Junius Bragg to Wife, November 19, 1863, in J. N. Bragg, *Letters of a Confederate Surgeon*, 183–84.
60. W. L. Barrett to Jesse McMahan, July 18, 1863, in Heller and Heller, *The Confederacy Is on Her Way Up the Spout*, 102–3; J. C. Conley to Father and Family, December 25, 1863, J. C. Conley to Family, June 3, 1864, Civil War Soldiers' Letters, ADAH, LPR 78, box 1, container 1, folder 16.

8. "War of the Most Wretched and Savage Character"

1. Miles to Beauregard, October 15, 1862, Civil War Miscellany, CAH, 2C447, William Miles file. For the absence of Union atrocity during the Civil War see Neely, *Retaliation*.
2. Franklin, *The Militant South*.
3. Lindermann, *Embattled Courage*, 243–44.
4. Neely, *Southern Rights*, 29–42.
5. Lizzie to William Neblett, April 13, 1863, from Grimes Co., Texas, Women's Writings: Neblett Papers, CAH, 2F81.
6. Lonn, *Desertion during the Civil War*, 1–2, 65. Lonn's map was excellent for its day. She must have identified every reference in the *Official Records* and then charted those counties or areas on her map. More recent scholarship has shown deserter bands in areas beyond what she depicted. Much of the information that identifies these bands comes from primary archival sources that had not yet been assembled. Lonn's primary sources are restricted to the material that had been published in the years after the war, most of which were from high-ranking officers and officials, See Lonn, *Desertion during the Civil War*, 239–41.
7. J. Searcy to Mother, August 31, 1862, Civil War Soldiers' Letters, ADAH, box 1, container 3, folder 12.
8. Hugh McLaurin to Sister, June 10, 1863, McLaurin Papers, Ramsdell Collection, CAH, microfilm reel no. 786.391; Watts to Seddon, April 12, 1864, Governor Thomas A. Watts Administrative Files, 1863–1865, ADAH, SG 24872, microfilm reel 19. Watts enclosed a letter from a Perry County resident and told Seddon he was at a loss. Watts learned that in Alabama alone 10 million pounds of bacon had been impressed. Divided among all the states east of the Mississippi, this would give every Confederate soldier in the field half a pound of bacon each month for twelve months.

"The people are willing to submit to almost anything when a necessity exists," Watts wrote, "but it is well of the government to consider the disastrous policy of harassing the producers."

9. William Nicholson to Sister, July 28, 1863, from Rome, Georgia, in Women's Writings, Nicholas-McDowell Family Papers, CAH, 3J306; Weitz, *A Higher Duty*.

10. E. H. Rutherford to Mr. and Mrs. Cowan, October 7, 1863, Cowan Family Papers, CAH, 2E555. The Cowans had also just suffered the loss of two children in eleven days, making the flight from Mississippi all the more painful. James J. Cowan to Wife, December 3, 1863, Cowan Family Papers, CAH, 2E555.

11. For Civil War guerrilla warfare see Fellman, "At the Nihilist Edge," 519–40.

12. Diary of James Kirkpatrick, 1861–1864, CAH, 2E293.

13. Fisher, *War at Every Door*, 62–81; Cooling, "A People's War," 123–25. For an older work on the subject see Seymour, *Divided Loyalties*, 26–38.

14. Ash, *Middle Tennessee Society Transformed*, 95.

15. Seddon to Vance, March 26, 1863, OR, 4th ser., 2:460–61.

16. Trotter, *Bushwhackers*, 139–47, Vance quote on 146; Inscoe and McKinney, *Heart of Confederate Appalachia*, 124–29.

17. Durrill, *War of Another Kind*, 180–81.

18. Durrill, *War of Another Kind*, 166–86.

19. Lay to Cooper, June 24, 1863, OR, 4th ser., 2:607.

20. Lay to Cooper, June 24, 1863, OR, 4th ser., 2:607.

21. Vance to Davis, July 9, 1863, OR, 4th ser., 2:619; Vance to Seddon, July 25, 1863, with J. A. Campbell Endorsement, OR, 4th ser., 2:674.

22. Lay to Preston, September 2, 1863, endorsed by Preston, Campbell and Seddon, and Davis to Seddon, 4th endorsement, OR, 4th ser., 2:783–86; for Davis order to Hoke see Vance to Seddon, OR, 1st ser., 29, pt. 2:676. For evidence that Hoke's efforts met with some success see "Gathering Them In," *Jackson Mississippian*, October 10, 1863, which picks up a story from Raleigh, North Carolina, telling of deserters coming back from North Carolina and other states.

23. Ashmore to Melton, August 7, 1863, OR, 4th ser., 2:771–73.

24. For a survey of every state's distillery laws see Tanner, *Encouragement of Food Crops in the Confederacy*, 30, CAH, 2R 204; Ashmore to Melton, August 16, 1863, OR, 4th ser., 2:773.

25. Melton to Preston, August 25, 1863, OR, 4th ser., 2:769–70.

26. Preston to Seddon, August 29, 1863, with Seddon endorsement to Lee, Lee to Seddon, September 15, 1863, OR, 4th ser., 2:768–69.

27. Otten, "Disloyalty in the Upper Districts," 103–4; Maars, "Dissatisfaction and Desertion" (*Proceedings*), 44–45; A. G. to Brig. Gen. A. Godbold, December 8, 1864, Adjutant General's Order Books, SCDAH, vol. 2; J. A. Dill to A. G., January 9, 1865, Adjutant General: Abstracts of Letters Received, 1864–1865, SCDAH; A. Duffie to McGrath, January 10, 1865, HQ Dist. Western N.C. to McGrath, April 12, 1865, Petition of citizens of Clarendon District to McGrath, April 17, 1865, Governor McGrath, Letters Received and Sent, 1864–1865, box 1, folder 14, box 1, folder 40, box 1, folder 50; McGrath Circular, February 22, 1865, Adjutant General, Scrapbook of Published Orders, SCDAH.

28. Joyner to Sidney Smith, August 15, 1863, OR, 4th ser., 2:721–22.

29. Jubal Early, "The Advance on Washington in 1864, letter to the editor of *The Republican*, SHSP 9 (1881): 302.

30. Dotson, " 'Sisson's Kingdom,' " 2.

31. Seddon to Davis, November 7, 1864, OR, 4th ser., 3:802–4.

32. Robert L. Custin and James P. Hammet, Members of Committee of Safety, Montgomery County, to Maj. Henry Leory, August 28, 1864, OR, 4th ser., 3:804–5.

33. John Echols to James Seddon, September 1, 1864, Henry Leory to Seddon, September 20, 1864, with enclosure of September 12, 1864, detective's report, R. G. H. Kean to War Office, November 9, 1864, with endorsement of detectives report dated October 10, 1864, Leory to Seddon, November 4, 1864, Echols to Seddon, November 9, 1864, N. F. Bocock to Seddon, November 8, 1864, OR, 4th ser., 3:805–15.

34. Echols to Maj. J. Stoddard Johnston, October 10, October 27, 1864, OR, 1st ser., 43, pt. 2:889–90, 907–8; J. H. Otey to Major Cloyd, October 8, 1864, OR, 1st ser., 43, pt. 2:890.

35. For Washington County desertion see Mann, "Ezekiel Count's Sand Lick Company."

36. August to Lay, August 10, August 15, 1863, OR, 4th ser., 2:717, 761–63.

37. Capt. W. D. Windle to General George, February 10, 1863, Affidavit of H. F. Miles, March 28, 1863, Adjutant General's Correspondence: Letters to Various Commanders, MDAH, RG 9, box 394, vol. 116, folder 3.

38. Bettersworth, *Confederate Mississippi*, 240–41; William T. May to Pettus, April 2, 1863, Officers of Company D, First Battalion Mississippi State Troops to T. C. Tupper, April 4, 1863, Samuel Houston to Pettus, May 13, 1863, John S. Neal to Pettus, May 31, 1863, James Drane to Pettus, August 21, 1863, Mississippi Governors' Collection, Ramsdell Collection, CAH, microfilm reel no. 786.254B, series E, vols. 61 and 62.

39. Pillow to Seddon, August 23, 1863, Pillow to Brigadier General Mackall, July 14, 1863, Pillow to Benjamin S. Ewell, July 28, 1863, OR, 4th ser., 2:638–39, 680–81, 741–43.

40. Robert W. Fortes to George Parsons, November 7, 1863, Civil War Soldiers' Letters, ADAH, LPR 78, box 1, container 3, folder 4; O. F. Dark, C. V. Gamble, and T. C. Shauston, from Youngsville, Alabama, October 31, 1863, Undersigned Petition of Citizens of St. Clair County to Thomas Watts, December 19, 1863, Watts to Pillow, December 12, 1863, Watts to Seddon, December 14, 1863, Watts to Seddon, January 1, 1864, Watts Correspondence, ADAH, microfilm, SG 21977, reel 20.

41. McMillan, *Disintegration of a Confederate State*, 59, 108–9.

42. Pillow to Benjamin S. Ewell, September 1, 1863, OR, 4th ser., 2:782.

43. Hamilton to Jack, March 31, 1864, OR, 1st ser., 32, pt. 3:727–28.

44. P. J. Ellis Jr., Return of Leonidas Polk, June 3, 1864, OR, 1st ser., 32, pt. 3:729.

45. Daniel P. Logan to J. C. Denis, April 7, 1864, OR, 1st ser., 32, pt. 3:755.

46. Milton Brown Prest to Joseph Johnston, November 4, 1863, Prest to Maury, November 5, 1863, Adjutant General's Correspondence: Letters to Various Commanders, MDAH, RG 9, box 394, vol. 116, folder 4; Dabney H. Maury to T. M. Jack, March 15, 1864, H. Maury to Dabney H. Maury, March 12, 1864, OR, 1st ser., 32, pt. 3:632–33.

47. Thomson to Seddon, March 29, 1864, OR, 1st ser., 32, pt. 3:711–13.

48. W. L. Brandon to D. H. Maury, August 14, 1864, OR, 1st ser., 39, pt. 2:776–77; H. C. Kelley to Col. T. H. Taylor, July 30, 1864, OR, 1st ser., 32, pt. 2:736–37; Petition from Citizens of Jones County to Clarke, September 1, 1864, Hamilton Cooper to Governor Clarke, December 26, 1864, Lt. W. H. Quarrels to Clarke, January 1, 1865, Mississippi Governors' Collection, Ramsdell Collection, CAH, microfilm reel no. 786.254B, series E, vols. 66 and 68; Jas. B. Chalmers to Clarke, September 25, 1864, Charles Clarke, 1861–1865, Telegrams, Letters, Ramsdell Collection, CAH, microfilm reel no. 786.254B, series E, vol. 64.

49. Leonidas Polk, A Proclamation (issued by T. M. Jack), April 16, 1864, L. Polk to Col. Baker, April 26, 1864, OR, 1st ser., 32, pt. 3:785–86, 824.

50. Polk to Major-General French, April 26, 1864, Polk to Major-General Lee, April 26, 1864, Polk to Col. J. S. Scott, April 26, 1864, OR, 1st ser., 32, pt. 3:824–26; Douglas West to Maj. J. D. Bradford, May 2, 1864, OR, 1st ser., 38, pt. 4:657–58.

51. Polk to Hodge, April 28, 1864, OR, 1st ser., 32, pt. 3:836–37.

52. T. H. Baker to J. C. Denis, April 4, 1864, J. C. Denis to Col. T. M. Jack, April 9, with enclosures: D. P. Watson to T. H. Baker, April 2, 1864, A. J. Stewart to Commander Post, March 28, 1864, OR, 1st ser., 32, pt. 3:745–48.

53. S. S. Ives to T. M. Jack, March 23, 1864, S. S. Ives to T. M. Jack, March 28, 1864, OR, 1st ser., 32, pt. 3:668–69.

54. J. J. Perry to T. B. Sykes, April 30, 1864, OR, 1st ser., 32, pt. 3:860.

55. Millon Ashley to Thomas Watts, August 15, 1864, Watts to Capt. James Reull, September 6, 1864, Watts Correspondence, ADAH, SG 22553, microfilm reel 22; Daniel S. Hood to John C. Hood, December 25, 1864, Civil War Soldiers' Letters, ADAH, LPR 78, box 1, container 2, folder 5; D. M. Carrin to Hugh Watson, January 6, 1865, Alabama Adjutant and Inspector General's Records, ADAH, microfilm, SG24872.

56. T. B. Roy to C. L. Stephenson, November 11, 1863, Civil War Papers, ADAH, PB/Range H/Sec 7, shelf C, folder 38 (William Hardee Letterbook). Roy conveyed Hardee's order to Stephenson instructing him to put enough soldiers at Nick-a-jack to hold the area. Weitz, *A Higher Duty*, 65, 116–18.

57. R. S. Davis, "Memoirs of a Partisan War."

58. R. S. Davis, "Memoirs of a Partisan War"; Schroeder-Lien, *Confederate Hospitals on the Move*, 85–86.

59. Carlson, "Wiregrass Runners."

60. Williams, *Rich Man's War*, 141–43.

61. Williams, *Rich Man's War*, 144.

62. Williams, *Rich Man's War*, 145–48.

63. Williams, *Rich Man's War*, 148–50; Carlson, "Wiregrass Runners," 87–93.

64. Carlson, "Wiregrass Runners," 96–102, 120; Williams, *Rich Man's War*, 187.

65. Johns, *Florida during the Civil War*, 124–25, 140–46, 154–56, 159–60; Reiger, "Deprivation, Disaffection, and Desertion," 281–86.

66. Johns, *Florida during the Civil War*, 161–62.

67. Johns, *Florida during the Civil War*, 162–63; Milton to Randolph, August 5, 1862, OR, 1st ser., 52, pt. 2:337, *Tallahassee Florida Sentinel*, December 9, 1862; John C. McGehee to Finegan, October 5, 1863, OR, 1st ser., 48, pt. 2:403; John F. Lay to Jordan, OR, 1st ser., 53:309.

68. Patton Anderson to J. M. Mills, May 15, 1864, OR, 1st ser., 53:337; Patton Anderson to H. W. Feilden, May 14, 1864, OR, 1st ser., 35, pt. 1:368–69; John K. Jackson to Samuel Cooper, August 12, 1864, OR, 1st ser., 35, pt. 2:607; John Shorter to Cobb, August 4, 1863, OR, 1st ser., 28, pt. 2:275; Milton to Seddon, January 11, 1864, OR, 4th ser., 3:16; Reiger, "Deprivation, Disaffection, and Desertion," 294.

69. Reiger, "Deprivation, Disaffection, and Desertion," 294–95; Milton to Beauregard, February 5, 1864, Luke Lott to Milton, February 3, 1864, OR, 1st ser., 35, pt. 1:564, 566.

70. Milton to Seddon, June 30, 1864, Milton to Anderson, June 20, 1864, OR, 1st ser., 53:343, 349–51.

71. Capes to Cross, March 27, 1864, OR, 1st ser., 53:318; Reiger, "Deprivation, Disaffection, and Desertion," 297–98; Johns, *Florida during the Civil War*, 165–67.

72. OR, 4th ser., 3:1109.

73. Lonn, *Desertion during the Civil War*, 71; Reynolds to Johnston, May 26, 1863, Thomas C. Reynolds Letterbook, 1862–1865, Ramsdell Collection, CAH, microfilm reel no. 786.146.

74. Mackey, "Bushwhackers, Provosts, and Tories"; Duggan, *Confederate Arkansas*, 107–8.

75. DeBlack, "1863: We Must Stand or Fall Alone," 68, 87, 103; Report of William F. Cloud, Second Kansas Cavalry, September 20, 1863, Report of Brig. Gen. W. L. Cabell, December 7, 1863, OR, 1st ser., 22, pt. 1:603, 607–8.

76. Frazier, "'Out of Striking Distance.'"

77. Frazier, "'Out of Striking Distance,'" 163–64.

78. Frazier, "'Out of Striking Distance,'" 164–65.

79. Frazier, "'Out of Striking Distance,'" 166.

80. Gov. Henry Allen to Maj. John M. Sandidge, Chief of Ordnance, State of Louisiana, February 15, 1865, Letters Received by the Executive, 1865, LDAH, microfilm reel no. CR.006; for desertion by Louisiana troops in 1865, see introduction herein.

81. A. M. Jackson to Gen. S. A. Hurlbut, April 14, 1865, OR, 1st ser., 48, pt. 2:92–93; S. M. Eaton to Col. C. T. Christensen, January 24, 1865, OR, 1st ser., 48, pt. 1:625; Damico, "Confederate Soldiers Take Matters into Their Own Hands," 194.

82. D. P. Smith, "Limits of Dissent," 134, 136.

83. D. P. Smith, "Limits of Dissent," 137–38.

84. Boatner, *The Civil War Dictionary*, 530; Henry E. McCulloch to J. B. Magruder, January 23, 1864, OR, 1st ser., 34, pt. 2:908–9.

85. Marten, *Texas Divided*, 95; R. Taylor to J. B. Magruder, July 18, 1863, John S. Ford to Edmund P. Turner, July 22, 1863, F. R. Lubbock to E. P. Turner, July 23, 1863, OR, 1st ser., 26, pt. 2:119–21.

86. McCulloch to Magruder, October 21, 1863, OR, 1st ser., 26, pt. 2:344–45.

87. McCulloch to Boren, October 24, 1863, OR, 1st ser., 26, pt. 2:352–53.

88. McCulloch to Edmund P. Turner, November 9, 1863, OR, 1st ser., 26, pt. 2:401; James Bourland to McCulloch, January 21, 1864, McCulloch to Magruder, January 23, 1864, J. W. Hale to James Bourland, January 11, 1864, OR, 1st ser., 34, pt. 2:908–11.

89. McCulloch to Magruder, February 3, 1864, McCulloch to Smith, February 4, 1864, OR, 1st ser., 34, pt. 2:943–45.

90. McCulloch to E. P. Turner, March 15, 1864, E. P. Turner to McCulloch, March 31, 1864, OR, 1st ser., 34, pt. 2:1045, 1107.

91. Marten, *Texas Divided*, 96, 100.

92. Weitz, "Desertion as Mutiny," 15–16.

93. HQ, Hardeman's Brigade to T. C. Edwards, January 10, 1865, William Wimberly to T. C. Edwards, April 25, 1865, T. C. Edwards Papers, Ramsdell Collection, CAH, microfilm reel no. 786.400.

94. Seddon to Davis, November 26, 1863, OR, 4th ser., 2:1000.

95. Martin Halls Burton to Miss Yates, March 20, 1864, C.S.A. Records, 1856–1915, CAH, 2C484, folder 8.

9. The Order of the Day

1. Lincoln, "Proclamation of Amnesty and Reconstruction, December 8, 1863," in *Collected Works of Abraham Lincoln*. 7:53–56.

2. Lee to Cooper, January 4, 1864, OR, 1st ser., 33:1063.

3. Davis, Message of the President to the House of Representatives, January 13, 1864, with enclosures, a communication from the secretary of war, January 11, 1864, with attached letter from the Adj. Gen. Samuel Cooper, January 9, 1864 (with General Orders 15 and 20 attached), and

Report of Quartermaster Gen. A. R. Lawton to Samuel Cooper, January 7, 1864, *Confederate Imprints*, 3517: 20: 1289.

4. Confederate Congress, First Congress, Fourth session, "An Act to Prevent the Procuring, Aiding, and Assisting Persons to Desert from the Army of the Confederate States, and for Other Purposes," *Confederate Imprints*, 3517: 2: 23.

5. T. H. Watts to Joe Brown with Petition from Charles Clarke enclosed, April 27, 1864, Watts Correspondence, ADAH, SG 21977 (SG 24872), microfilm reel 20.

6. Radley, *Rebel Watchdog*, 152, 157–58, 162.

7. Seddon to Bragg, April 11, 1864, OR, 4th ser., 3:284; Watts to Pitman, August 2, 1864, Watts Correspondence, ADAH, SG 21977 (SG 24872), microfilm reel 20.

8. List of Indigents of the Parishes of Claitoose and Concordia who have and are being furnished provisions at the Expense of the State of Louisiana, July 10, 1864, Letters Received by the Executive, 1864, LDAH, microfilm reel no. CR.005; William Allen to Henry Allen, January 9, 1865, Letters Received by the Executive, 1865, LDAH, microfilm reel no. CR.006.

9. Confederate Congress, "An Act to Suspend the Privilege of the Writ of Habeas Corpus in Certain Cases," February 15, 1864, OR, 4th ser., 3:203–4.

10. Confederate Senate, Senate Bill 187, "An Act Declaring Persons Owing Military Service to the Confederate States, and Who Seek to Avoid Such Service by Removing beyond the Control and Jurisdiction of Said States, Alien Enemies, and Subjecting Their Property to Confiscation," January 15, 1864, *Confederate Imprints*, 3517: 5: 136.

11. Francis R. Lubbock, "Address to Members of the State House of Representatives, February 5, 1863," in Executive Record Books, TSA, microfilm reel 6.

12. Reuben Allen Pierson to William H. Pierson, August 22, 1863, in Cutrer and Parrish, *Brothers in Gray*, 209–10. Pierson may have been correct. The Confederate Sequestration Act allowed the property of alien enemies to be seized and sold. An oath-swearing civilian might well fall under the definition of "alien enemy." *Journal of the House of Representatives of the State of Georgia*, March 10, 1864 (Milledgeville: Broughton, Nisbet, Barnes and Moore, 1864), 9.

13. S. S. Anderson, General Order no. 2, January 11, 1864, W. A. Alston, General Order no. 7, January 12, 1864, H. P. Bee to Col. P. C. Woods, February 2, 1864, OR, 1st ser., 34, pt. 2:851, 856, 938–39.

14. Lee to Seddon, February 15, 1864, in Lee, *Wartime Papers*, 671–72.

15. Taylor to Boggs, January 21, 1864, OR, 1st ser., 34, pt. 2:901–2.

16. Taylor to Boggs, January 21, 1864, OR, 1st ser., 34, pt. 2:901; Beauregard, Proclamation, March 4, 1864, OR, 1st ser., 35, pt. 2:331; J. F. Belton, General Order no. 30, May 20, 1864, OR, 1st ser., 34, pt. 3:832; Seddon to Lee, July 30, 1864, OR, 1st ser., 40, pt. 3:817–18; Lee, General Order no. 54, August 10, 1864, OR, 1st ser., 42, pt. 2:1169.

17. *Selma Morning Reporter*, September 14, 1863. The Seventeenth Alabama came from companies formed in Russell, Coosa, Montgomery, Butler, Monroe and Pike counties. See Thompson and Thompson, *The Seventeenth Alabama Infantry*, 13–32; Norton to Friends at Home, September 7, 1863, in Norton, *Army Letters*, 180–81.

18. Humphreys to Gregg, January 29, 1864, OR, 1st ser., 33:441.

19. William Nicholson to Father, May 4, 1864, William Nicholson to Aunt, June 11, 1864, Nicholas-McDowell Family Papers, CAH, 3J306.

20. Enoch Allendale to Watts, March 24, 1864, Sheffield to Watts, April 15, 1864, Watts Correspondence, ADAH, SG 21977 (SG 24872), microfilm reel 20; W. L. Nugent to My Darling Nellie, September 26, 1864, in Cash and Howorth, *My Dear Nellie*, 211; M. I. Cowan to Husband, July 16, 1864, Cowan Family Papers, CAH, 2E555. Floridians are almost completely absent from the

Register, yet correspondence shows that many of the deserters in the state had taken an oath. Soldiers from other states used the region as a sanctuary, which may account for why the issue of oaths comes up so frequently in Florida. Yet Union records do not show men from that state taking advantage of the program in great numbers. Florida's 189 deserters to the Union is the lowest number in the Confederacy.

21. Wm. G. Barth to Brig. Gen. W. M. Gardner, March 30, 1864, OR, 1st ser., 35. pt. 2:390–91.

22. Hawkins, *An Account of the Assassination of Loyal Citizens*, Ramsdell Collection, CAH, microfilm reel no. 786.47.

23. Thomas to Brough, April 7, 1864, James Wilson, Circular no. 3, April 29, 1864, OR, 1st ser., 32, pt. 3:287–88, 537–39.

24. For Georgia numbers see Weitz, *A Higher Duty*, 67.

25. Weitz, *A Higher Duty*, 71.

26. Lee to Cooper, July 19, 1864, OR, 1st ser., 40, pt. 3:781–82.

27. Lee to Seddon, August 14, 1864, Seddon to Lee, August 17, 1864. In September, John Babcock reported to Humphreys that deserters from the Confederate army had come in from the brigades of Wise, Scales, and Thomas. Babcock to Humphreys, September 19, 1864, OR, 1st ser., 42, pt. 2:913, 1175–76, 1182–83.

28. T. A. Henderson, Circular, April 5, 1864, OR, 1st ser., 35, pt. 2:38–39; Grant, General Order no. 82, August 28, 1864, OR, 1st ser., 42, pt. 2:555–56.

29. H. S. Sanford, circular, November 23, 1864, Osman Latrobe to William H. Taylor, November 14, 1864, with Lee's endorsement, November 18, 1864, Davis's endorsement, November 29, 1864, A. A. Humphreys to Brig. Gen. S. William, December 27, 1864 (2 letters), G. W. C. Lee to Maj. T. O. Chestney, October 27, 1864, Winfield S. Hancock to Major General Humphreys, November 15, 1864, Jno C. Babcock to A. A. Humphreys, November 12, 1864, G. K. Warren to General Williams, November 12, 1864, Jno G. Parker to Humphreys, November 12, 1864, Jno W. Turner to A. V. Kratz, December 20, 1864, Jno C. Babcock to G. G. Meade, December 21, 1864, Jno C. Babcock to G. G. Meade, December 28, 1864, A. P. Hill to W. H. Taylor, December 1, 1864, Lee endorsement, December 1, 1864, Seddon endorsement, December 9, 1864, OR, 1st ser., 42, pt. 3:609–11, 623, 692, 1049–51, 1083, 1087–88, 1179, 1213, 1249.

30. Carter to General Webster, July 4, 1864, OR, 1st ser., 39, pt. 2:161.

31. Weitz, *A Higher Duty*, 67, 81–84.

32. Junius Bragg to My Darling Josephine, February 1, 1864, in J. N. Bragg, *Letters of a Confederate Surgeon*, 200–202; Taylor to General Bragg, October 4, 1864, OR, 1st ser., 52, pt. 1:752.

33. Taylor to Clarke, October 8, 1864, OR, 1st ser., 39, pt. 3:806.

34. R. J. Hallett, December 7, 1864, Joseph Brown, Executive Proclamation, December 7, 1864, OR, 1st ser., 44:990–91.

35. Major General Hurlbut, General Order no. 151, October 20, 1864, S. E. Graves to Col. A. H. Ryan, December 7, 1864, OR, 1st ser., 41, pt. 4:127–28, 781.

36. Sutherland, "A Strange, Wild Time," 136–43.

37. J. G. Parkhurst, Report of Rebel Deserters received at Nashville, Tennessee, from September 7, 1864 to January 20, 1865, and Report of Deserters Received outside of Nashville office for same period, February 4, 1865, OR, 1st ser., 45, pt. 1:47–48. Based on the data compilation from the Register, deserters were received and processed at the following cities: Chattanooga, Nashville, Memphis, and Knoxville, Tennessee; Louisville, Kentucky; City Point and Fort Monroe, Virginia; Hilton Head, South Carolina; Little Rock, Arkansas; New Orleans, Louisiana; and Atlanta, Georgia.

38. Watson to Watts, October 31, 1864, Watts Administrative Files, ADAH, SG 24872, microfilm reel 19.

39. "Lorena," in Hill, *Poems and Songs of the Civil War*, 228.

40. Lee to Davis, January 29, 1864, OR, 1st ser., 51, pt. 2:812.

41. Cunningham, *Doctors in Gray*, 90.

42. Register of Confederate Troops, 10 vols., Stout Papers, CAH, 4L248, 4L216, 4L249, 4L250, 4L251, 4L252, 4L253, 4L256, 4L257, 4L258, 4L259.

43. Cunningham, *Doctors in Gray*, 66.

44. Schroeder-Lein, *Confederate Hospitals on the Move*, 141–44.

45. Register of Confederate Soldiers, July 22, 1864–, Stout Papers, CAH, 4L256.

46. Edward L. Wells to Sabina Huger Wells, August 6, 1864, in Smith, Smith, and Childs, *Mason Smith Family Letters*, 125–26.

47. H. C. Lockhart to John C. Burch, November 30, 1864, OR, 4th ser., 3:880–81. In the Third Alabama for example, the company with the fewest men absent counted thirty-seven men missing, and one company counted sixty-nine missing. However, the records do not reflect why these men were missing.

48. Junius Bragg to My Dear Wife, February 14, 1864, in J. N. Bragg, *Letters of a Confederate Surgeon*, 210; *Selma Morning Reporter*, February 5, 1864; Reward Poster 33rd Texas, April 14, 1864, in Irby, *Backdoor at Bagdad*; Watts to Compton, August 17, 1864, Davis to Watts, September 4, 1864, Thomas Watts, To All Soldiers Absent from Their Commands, Watts Correspondence, ADAH, SG 21977 (SG 24872), microfilm reel 20.

49. Petition from Citizens of Jones County, Mississippi to Clarke, September 1, 1864, Lt. Col. John T. Smith to Clarke, September 2, 1864, R. Taylor to Clarke, October 8, 1864, Readmen T. Portwood, Sheriff Sunflower County to Clarke, November 21, 1864, Hamilton Cooper to Clarke, December 26, 1864, Mississippi Governors' Collection, Ramsdell Collection, CAH, microfilm reel no. 786.254B, series E, vol. 66; Jas. B. Chalmers to Clarke, September 25, 1864, Mississippi Governors' Collection, Ramsdell Collection, CAH, microfilm reel no. 786.254B, series E, vol. 63.

50. Alabama Muster Rolls, ADAH, SG 25006 (1st Ala.), SG 25010, 25011 (4th Ala.), SG 25016, 25017 (8th Ala.), SG 25019 (10th Ala.), SG 25048 (38th Ala.). See also Descriptive List of Members Dropped from the Roll of the 28th Alabama, ADAH. This is not all of Fowler's backup, but these are the units where any information was provided on deserters.

51. Alabama Muster Rolls, ADAH, SG 25010, 25011 (4th Ala.).

52. Alabama Muster Rolls, ADAH, SG 25016, 25017 (8th Ala.).

53. List of Confederate Deserters confined in Military Prison in Natchez, Mississippi, United States Military Prison Record, August 17, 1863–September 26, 1864, CAH, 3B59; *Daily Mississippian*, June 14, 1864.

54. Field Returns of Jones M. Withers's and Thomas Hindman's Divisions, April 1862–April 1864, War Department Collection of Confederate Records, NARA, RG 109, microfilm 22,056 reel 6 TXC.

55. J. Little Smith to My Dear Al'd, August 29, 1864, Civil War Soldiers' Letters, ADAH, LPR 78, box 1, container 2, folder 9.

56. B. P. Gandy to Sister, June 4, 1864, Civil War Miscellany, CAH, 2C477, B. P. Gandy file.

57. Lewis E. Parsons to Home, September 11, 1864, Civil War Soldiers' Letters, ADAH, LPR 78, box 1, container 3, folder 4; *Selma Morning Reporter*, September 14, 1864.

58. Watts to Seddon, January 19, 1864, Watts Correspondence, ADAH, SG 21977 (SG24872), microfilm reel 20; Davis to Allen, April 7, 1864, Letters Received by the Executive 1864, LDAH, microfilm reel no. CR.005; Husband to Wife, May 2, October 24, 1864, Civil War Soldiers' Letters, ADAH,

LPR 78, box 1, container 2, folder 9; Sandidge to Allen, December 15, 1864, Letters Received by the Executive, 1864, LDAH, microfilm reel no. CR.005.

59. Morgan to Wife, December 10, 1864, Civil War Soldiers' Letters, ADAH, LPR 78, box 1, container 2, folder 10; R. S. Jones to Aunt Martha, April 13, 1864, David L. Jones to Father, October 9, 1864, D. L. Jones to Father, November 8, 1864, Civil War Soldiers' Letters, ADAH, LPR 78, box 1, container 3, folder 1.

60. Catherine Powell, Greene County, Mississippi, to T. Watts, June 13, 1864, Petition from Citizens of Chambers County to Watts, July 1864, Watts Correspondence, ADAH, SG 21977 (SG 24872), microfilm reel 20.

61. W. Rowe, to Watts, July 22, 1864, C. G. of Tallapoosa County to Watts, August 3, 1864, Watts Correspondence, ADAH, SG 21977 (SG 24872), microfilm reel 20.

62. A. H. James to Father and Mother, May 15, 1864, in Elkins, *Letters from a Civil War Soldier*, 27–28.

63. Watts to Hood, September 19, 1864, Watts to Brown, September 21, 1864, Watts Correspondence, ADAH, SG 21977 (SG 24872), microfilm reel 20.

64. Governor Smith of Virginia to Henry Allen with Enclosed Resolutions of October 17, 1864, of Governor's Conference held at Augusta, Georgia, n.d., Letters Received by the Executive, 1864, LDAH, microfilm reel no. CR.005.

65. T. Watts, September 3, 1864, Request to Convene Extraordinary Session of the Legislature, T. Watts to Alabama Legislature, October 7, 1864, Watts Correspondence, ADAH, SG 21977 (SG 24872), microfilm reel 20; Neely, *Southern Rights*, 5–6.

66. J. J. Cowan to Wife, March 1, 1864, Cowan Family Papers, CAH, 2E555.

67. "A Sermon Preached Before Brigadier-General Hoke's Brigade at Kingston, N.C. on the 28th of February 1864, By Reverend John Paris, Chaplain Fifty-fourth North Carolina Regiment, N.C. Troops, Upon the Execution of Twenty-Two Men, Who Had Been Executed in the Presence of the Brigade for the Crime of Desertion" (Greensborough NC.: A. W. Ingold & Co., 1864), in *Documenting the American South*.

10. "We Conquered Ourselves"

1. Alexander, *Fighting for the Confederacy*, 508–9; David Urquart to Samuel Cooper, December 8, 1864, OR, 1st ser., 53:380–81.

2. S. M. Eaton to Col. C. T. Christensen, January 24, 1865, OR, 1st ser., 48, pt. 1:625.

3. Winik, *April 1865*; W. C. Davis, *An Honorable Defeat*; Calkins, *The Appomattox Campaign*; Lonn, *Desertion during the Civil War*, 124.

4. Jno Withers, General Order no. 18, January 23, 1865, George Thomas to the Adjutant General of the U.S. Army, January 2, 1865, H. W. Halleck to George Thomas, January 4, 1865, A. P. Mason to Lieutenant General Stewart, January 11, 1865, A. P. Mason to N. B. Forrest, OR, 1st ser., 45, pt. 2:482, 504–5, 783, 805.

5. Confederate House of Representatives, Bill no. 319, "A Bill More Effectively to Prevent and Punish Absenteeism and Desertion," January 3, 1865, *Confederate Imprints*, 3517: 8: 501.

6. Confederate House of Representatives, "An Act to Provide for the More Efficient Execution of Conscription and the Arrest of Deserters and Absentees from the Army," January 10, 1865, *Confederate Imprints*, 3517: 8: 509.

7. Confederate Senate, "A Bill to Amend an Act Entitled An Act to Prevent the Procuring, Aiding, and Assisting Persons to Desert from the Army of the Confederate States, and for Other Purposes, approved January 22, 1864," February 2, 1865, *Confederate Imprints*, 3517: 5: 212.

8. Ellis to Davis, January 29, 1865, OR, 4th ser., 3:1041–42.

9. Preston to Lee, February 20, 1865, OR, 4th ser., 3:1122–24.

10. Lee to Davis, February 9, 1865, OR, 1st ser., 51, pt. 2:1082–83; Lee, General Order no. 2, February 11, 1865, *Confederate Imprints*, 3517: 11: 645.

11. Preston to Breckenridge, March 3, 1865, OR, 4th ser., 3:1119–20.

12. Samuel Cooper, General Order no. 18, March 30, 1865, OR, 4th ser., 3:1177–78.

13. G. K. Warren to Major General Webb, March 11, 1865 [received 10:20 a.m.], H. G. Wright to A. S. Webb, February 18, 1865, Henry Wise to Major R. P. Duncan, January 22, 1865, D. Lang to Joseph Finegan, January 21, 1865, Wise to Duncan, January 23, 1865, Lee to Secretary of War, January 27, 1865, B. R. Johnson to R. P. Duncan, February 11, 1865, B. R. Johnson to R. P. Duncan, February 17, 1865, Lee to Breckenridge, February 28, 1865, Lee to Cooper, February 25, 1865, Lee to Secretary of War, February 24, 1865, John Turner to John Rawlins, March 4, 1865, OR, 1st ser., 46, pt. 2:587, 831, 927, 1143, 1146, 1148–49, 1231, 1239, 1254, 1258, 1265.

14. J. Longstreet to W. H. Taylor, March 25, 1865, R. E. Lee, General Order no. 8, March 27, 1865, OR, 1st ser., 46, pt. 3:1354–55; Lee to Vance, February 24, 1865, Breckenridge to Vance, March 1, 1865, Vance to Lee, March 2, 1865, Lee to Vance, March 9, 1865, OR, 1st ser., 47, pt. 2:1270, 1296, 1312, 1353–54.

15. L. S. Ross to Major General Walker, February 20, 1865, W. Stedman, General Order no. 1, January 13, 1865, OR, 1st ser., 48, pt. 1:1323, 1395.

16. Charles Clarke to R. Taylor, April 1, 1865, P. D. Roddey to R. Taylor, March 20, 1865, OR, 1st ser., 49, pt. 2: 1134, 1182–83; G. Thomas to Brig. Gen. R. S. Granger, February 20, 1865, D. S. Stanley to Brigadier General Whipple, February 15, 1865, Reports of Deserters Received at Nashville and Chattanooga for the period January 21 to May 9, 1865, OR, 1st ser., 49, pt. 1:349, 720–21, 750; H. W. Walter to J. W. C. Watson, December 20, 1864, OR, 4th ser., 3:976.

17. Davis, To the Senate and House of Representatives of the Confederate States, February 3, 1864, OR, 4th ser., 3:67–70.

18. Walton, *An Epitome of My Life*, 90–91.

19. Phelan to Davis, October 2, 1864, OR, 4th ser., 3:707–10.

20. The numbers for total desertion cases come from Bunch, *Roster of the Court-Martial*, by manually counting each case. The companion book, Bunch, *Military Justice in the Confederate Army*, 88–132, provides the statistical data on executions, trials of soldiers from specific states, as well as some support for the speculation on the condition of Confederate records. The *Official Records* data are listed in the appendix of Lonn, *Desertion during the Civil War*, 231.

21. General Canby to Edwin Stanton, January 27, 1865, C. A. Dana to William Seward, February 7, 1865, M. Bigelow to Seward, March 15, June 30, 1865, *U.S. Department of State Papers*, 3:371, 386, 398.

22. Lonn, *Desertion during the Civil War*, 232. Lonn's numbers are taken directly from OR, 4th ser., 3:1103.

23. Davis, Address to Congress, February 3, 1864, OR, 4th ser., 3:67–70.

24. Herrington, *The Deserter's Daughter*.

25. Yale to Daughter, May 17, 1865, Civil War Miscellany, CAH, 2C447, J. W. Fale file.

26. Evangeline Crutcher to Father, February 4, 1864, Crutcher-Shannon Family Papers, CAH, 2E511; C.S.A. Records, 1856–1915, CAH, 2C484, folder 8: Jerome Yates.

27. Lizzie to Will, May 27, 1863, Lizzie to Will, May 3, 1864, Maria Neblett to Will, May 13, 1864, Women's Writings, Neblett Papers, CAH, 2F81, folder 3; Nicholson-McDowell Family Papers, CAH, 3J306.

Archives

Alabama Department of Archives and History, Montgomery

Alabama Adjutant and Inspector General's Records
    Alabama Muster Rolls
        Civil War Papers
        Civil War Soldiers' Letters
            William Hardee Letterbook
Hardman Family Correspondence
Military Volunteer Family Assistance Records, 1861–66
    Prisoner of War Records
United States Manuscript Census, Mobile County 1860
Governor Thomas H. Watts Administrative Files, 1863–1865
    Governor Thomas H. Watts Correspondence, 1863–1865

Center for American History, University of Texas–Austin

    Charles Clarke, 1861–1865, Telegrams, Letters
    C.S.A. Records, 1856–1915
C.S.A. Records, 1861–1865
Civil War Miscellany
    James J. Cowan Family Papers
    Crutcher-Shannon Family Papers, 1822–1905
        Henrietta Embree Papers
    Diary of George L. Griscom
    Diary of James Kirkpatrick, 1861–1864
    William E. Moore Papers, 1807–1944
    William M. Moxley Papers, 1854–1901
    Neblett (Lizzie Scott) Papers
    Nicholas-McDowell Family Papers
    Cornelia M. Noble Diary
    Ramsdell Collection
    T. C. Edwards Papers
    Hugh A. McLaurin Papers, 1862–1864
    Mississippi Governors' Collection
        Mississippi Governors' Papers, Military Telegrams for 1861–63
            Thomas C. Reynolds Letterbook, 1862–1865
        Edmund Kirby Smith Papers
    William Adolphus Smith Papers, 1862–1877
    Samuel H. Stout Papers

United States Military Prison Record
J. W. Ward Family Correspondence, 1861–1864

Louisiana Department of Archives and History, Baton Rouge

Letters Received by the Executive, 1860–65

Mississippi Department of Archives and History, Jackson

Adjutant General's Correspondence: Letters to Various Commanders
Rev. B. M. Palmer, *The Oath of Allegiance to the United States Discussed in Its Moral and Political Implications*
Receipts for Deserters of the Army

National Archives and Record Administration, Washington DC

Register of Confederate Soldiers Deserting to the Union Army 1863–65. Record Group 598. War Department Collection of Confederate Records. Record Group 109.

South Carolina Department of Archives and History, Columbia

Adjutant General: Abstracts of Letters Received, 1864–1865
Adjutant General, Scrapbook of Published Orders, 1862–1865
Adjutant General's Order Books, 1861–1865
Governor Magrath, Letters Received and Sent, 1864–1865

South Caroliniana Library, Columbia

Records of the Confederate States Army, Fourth Military District

Texas State Archives, Austin

Correspondence Concerning Conscription, 1862–1864
Executive Record Books, Francis R. Lubbock 1/25/63–11/4/63 to A. J. Hamilton 7/25/65–8/13/65

Other Sources

Alexander, Edward Porter. *Fighting for the Confederacy: The Personal Recollections of Edward Porter Alexander.* Ed. Gary W. Gallagher. Chapel Hill: University of North Carolina Press, 1989.
Anderson, Benedict. *Imagined Communities: Reflections on the Origins and Spread of Nationalism.* Rev. ed. London: Verso, 1991.
Anderson, Fred. *Crucible of War: The Seven Years War and the Fate of the Empire in British North America, 1754–1766.* London: Faber & Faber, 2000.
———. *A People's Army: Massachusetts Soldiers and Society in the Seven Years War.* Chapel Hill: University of North Carolina Press, 1984.
Ash, Stephen V. *Middle Tennessee Society Transformed, 1860–1870: War and Peace in the Upper South.* Baton Rouge: Louisiana State University Press, 1988.
Bardolph, Richard. "Confederate Dilemma: North Carolina Troops and the Desertion Problem." *North Carolina Historical Review* 66, no. 1 (1989): 61–86; 66, no. 2 (1989): 178–210.
———. "Inconstant Rebels: Desertion of North Carolina Troops in the Civil War." *North Carolina Historical Review* 41, no. 2 (1964): 163–89.
Bauer, Jack K. *Zachary Taylor: Soldier, Planter, Statesman of the Old Southwest.* Baton Rouge: Louisiana State University Press, 1985.
Beamer, Carl. "The Galvanized Yankees in Kansas." *Kansas Quarterly* 10, no. 3 (1978): 17–27.

Bearman, Peter S. "Desertion as Localism: Army Unit Solidarity and Group Norms in the U.S. Civil War." *Social Forces* 70, no. 2 (1991): 321–42.

Bearss, Edwin C., ed. *The Louisiana Confederate Diary of Felix Pierre Poche*. Trans. Eugenie Watson Somdal. Nachitoches: Louisiana Studies Institute, 1972.

Bennett, Gerald. *Days of Uncertainty and Dread*. Camp Hill PA: Plank's Suburban Press, 1997.

Bergerion, Arthur W., Jr., ed. *Reminiscences of Uncle Silas: The History of the 18th La. Inf. Regiment*. Baton Rouge: Louisiana State University Press, 1981.

Beringer, Richard. "Confederate Identity and the Will to Fight." In *On the Road to Total War: The American Civil War and the German Wars of Unification, 1861–1871*, ed. Stig Forster and Jorg Naglers. Cambridge: Cambridge University Press, 1997.

Beringer, Richard, Herman Hattaway, Archer Jones, and William Still Jr. *Why the South Lost the War*. Athens: University of Georgia Press, 1986.

Bettersworth, John K. *Confederate Mississippi: The People and Politics of a Cotton State in Wartime*. Baton Rouge: Louisiana State University Press, 1943.

Blair, William. *Virginia's Private War*. New York: Oxford University Press, 1998.

Boatner, Mark. *The Civil War Dictionary*. New York: David McKay, 1987.

Bodnar, John. *Worker's World: Kinship, Community, and Protest in an Industrial Society, 1900–1940*. Baltimore: John Hopkins University Press, 1982.

Bohannan, Keith S. Review of *A Higher Duty: Desertion among Georgia Troops during the Civil War*, by Mark A. Weitz. *Civil War History* 47, no. 3 (2001): 270–71.

Bonaparte, Napoleon. "Military Maxims of Napoleon." In *Roots of War*, ed. T. R. Phillips and J. D. Hittle, 1:401–42. Harrisburg PA: Stackpole, 1992.

Bonner, Robert E. *Colors and Blood: Flag Passions of the Confederate South*. Princeton: Princeton University Press, 2002.

Booth, Andrew B., comp. *Records of Louisiana Confederate Soldiers and Louisiana Commands*. 3 vols. New Orleans: n.p., 1920.

Borgwald, Lucille. "Desertions from the Confederate Army." *Davis and Elkins History Magazine*, March 1950, 15–17.

Bragg, Junius Newport. *Letters of a Confederate Surgeon, 1861–1865*. Ed. T. J. Gaughan. Camden AR: Hurley, 1960.

Bragg, William Harris. *Joe Brown's Army: The Georgia State Line, 1862–1865*. Macon: Mercer University Press, 1987.

Brown, Dee. *Galvanized Yankees*. Lincoln: University of Nebraska Press, 1986.

Bunch, Jack A. *Military Justice in the Confederate Army*. Shippensburg PA White Mane, 2000.

———. *Roster of the Court-Martial in the Confederate States Armies*. Shippensburg PA: White Mane, 2001.

Bynum, Victoria. *The Free State of Jones: Mississippi's Longest Civil War*. Chapel Hill: University of North Carolina Press, 2001.

Calkins, Chris M. *The Appomattox Campaign, March 29 to April 9, 1865*. New York: Da Capo Press, 1997.

Carlson, Robert David. "Wiregrass Runners: Conscription, Desertion and the Origins of Discontent in Civil War Georgia." Master's thesis, Valdosta State University, May 1999.

Carp, Benjamin L. "Nations of American Rebels: Understanding Nationalism in Revolutionary North America and the Civil War South." *Civil War History* 48, no. 1 (2002): 5–33.

Cash, William M., and Lucy Somerville Howorth, eds. *My Dear Nellie: The Civil War Letters of Walter Nugent to Eleanor Smith Nugent*. Jackson: University of Mississippi Press, 1977.

Catton, Bruce. *The Coming Fury: The Centennial History of the Civil War*. Garden City NY: Doubleday, 1961.

Chadwick, Bruce. *George Washington's War*. Naperville IL: Sourcebooks, 2004.

Confederate Imprints, 1861–1865. Microfilm. 144 reels. New Haven: Research Publications, 1974.

Connelly, Thomas. *Civil War Tennessee: Battles and Leaders*. Knoxville: University of Tennessee Press, 1979.

Cooling, B. Franklin. "A People's War: Partisan Conflict in Tennessee and Kentucky." In *Guerrillas, Unionists and Violence on the Confederate Home Front*, ed. Donald E. Sutherland. Fayetteville: University of Arkansas Press, 1999.

Cunningham, H. H. *Doctors in Gray: The Confederate Medical Service*. Baton Rouge: Louisiana State University Press, 1958.

Current, Richard N. *Lincoln's Loyalists: Union Soldiers from the Confederacy*. Boston: Northeastern University Press, 1992.

Cutrer, Thomas W., and T. Michael Parrish, eds. *Brothers in Gray: The Civil War Letters of the Pierson Family*. Baton Rouge: Louisiana State University Press, 1997.

Damico, John Kelly. "Confederate Soldiers Take Matters into Their Own Hands: The End of the Civil War in North Louisiana." *Louisiana History* 39, no. 2 (1998): 189–205.

Davis, Granville D. "An Uncertain Confederate Trumpet: A Study of Erosion of Morale." *West Tennessee Historical Papers* 38 (1984): 19–50.

Davis, Robert S., Jr. "Memoirs of a Partisan War: Sion Darnell Remembers North Georgia, 1861–1865." *Georgia Historical Quarterly* 80, no. 2 (1996): 93–116.

Davis, William C. *"A Government of Our Own": The Making of the Confederacy*. New York: The Free Press, 1994.

———. *An Honorable Defeat: The Last Days of the Confederacy*. New York: Harvest Books, 2002.

———. *Look Away, Look Away: A History of the Confederate States of America*. New York: The Free Press, 2002.

———. *The Orphan Brigade: The Kentucky Confederates Who Couldn't Go Home*. New York: Doubleday, 1980.

DeBlack, Thomas. "1863: We Must Stand or Fall Alone." In *The Rugged and the Sublime: The Civil War in Arkansas*, ed. Mark Christ. Fayetteville: University of Arkansas Press, 1994.

Documenting the American South. Chapel Hill: University of North Carolina Press, electronic ed., 1999.

Dotson, Paul Randolph, Jr. "'Sisson's Kingdom': Loyalty Divisions in Floyd County, Virginia, 1861–1865." Master's thesis, Virginia Polytechnic Institute, May 1997.

Dougan, Michael B. *Confederate Arkansas: The People and Policies of a Frontier State in Wartime*. Tuscaloosa: University of Alabama Press, 1976.

Drum, Brigadier-General Richard, comp. *Laws, Rules and Decisions Governing the Military Crime of Desertion to Which is Added a Compendium of the Disabilities Attaching to Desertion as Regards Claims Against the United States, Citizenship, Etc. Etc.* Ed. Fred T. Wilson. Washington DC: Government Printing Office, 1882.

Durrill, Wayne K. *War of Another Kind: A Southern Community in the Great Rebellion*. New York: Oxford University Press, 1990.

Elkins, Vera Dockery, ed. *Letters from a Civil War Soldier*. New York: Vintage Press, 1969.

Ellsworth, Lois Council. "San Antonio during the Civil War." Master's thesis, University of Texas, August 1938.

Emerson, William E. "Leadership and Civil War Desertion in the Twenty-fourth and Twenty-fifth Regiments North Carolina Troops." *Southern History* 17 (1996): 17–33.

Evans, Clement A. *Confederate Military History*. 19 vols. Wilmington NC: Broadfoot, 1988.

Faust, Drew Gilpin. *The Creation of Confederate Nationalism: Ideology and Identity in the Civil War South*. Baton Rouge: Louisiana State University Press, 1998.

———. *Southern Stories: Slaveholders in Peace and War*. Columbia: University of Missouri Press, 1992.

Fellman, Michael. "At the Nihilist Edge: Reflections on Guerrilla Warfare during the American Civil War." In *On the Road to Total War: The American Civil War and the German Wars of Unification, 1861–1871*, ed. Stig Forster and Jorg Naglers. Cambridge: Cambridge University Press, 1997.

Fisher, Noel. *War at Every Door: Partisan Politics and Guerrilla Violence in East Tennessee.* Chapel Hill: University of North Carolina Press, 1997.

Fleming, James R., ed. *Band of Brothers: Company C, 9th Tennessee Infantry.* Shippensburg PA: White Mane, 1996.

Ford, Lacy K. *The Origins of Southern Radicalism: The South Carolina Upcountry, 1800–1860.* New York: Oxford University Press, 1991.

Franklin, John Hope. *The Militant South, 1800–1861.* Cambridge: Harvard University Press, 1970.

Frazier, Donald S. "'Out of Striking Distance': The Guerrilla War in Louisiana." In *Guerrillas, Unionists, and Violence on the Confederate Home Front,* ed. Donald E. Sutherland. Fayetteville: University of Arkansas Press, 1999.

Frederick the Great. "The Instructions of Frederick the Great to His Generals." In *Roots of War,* ed. T. R. Phillips and J. D. Hittle, 2:301–400. Harrisburg PA: Stackpole, 1992.

Fredrickson, George M. *The Black Image in the White Mind: The Debate on Afro-American Character and Destiny, 1817–1914.* New York: Harper & Row, 1971.

———. "White Supremacy and the American Sectional Conflict." In *The Coming of the American Civil War,* ed. Michael Perman. 3d ed. Lexington MA: D. C. Heath, 1993.

Freehling, William. "The Divided South." In *Why the War Came,* ed. Gabor S. Boritt. New York: Oxford University Press, 1996.

Gallagher, Gary W. *A Confederate War.* Cambridge: Harvard University Press, 1999.

Giuffre, Katherine A. "First in Flight: Desertion as Politics in the North Carolina Confederate Army." *Social Science History* 21, no. 2 (1997): 245–63.

Greene, General Nathanael. *The Papers of General Nathanael Greene.* Ed. Richard K. Showman et al. 12 vols. Chapel Hill: University of North Carolina Press, 1976–.

Griffith, Lucille, ed. *Alabama: A Documentary History to 1900.* Tuscaloosa: University of Alabama Press, 1972.

Grimsley, Mark. *Hard Hand of War: Union Military Policy toward Southern Civilians, 1861–1865.* Cambridge: Cambridge University Press, 1995.

Hallock, Judith Lee. "The Role of Community in the Civil War." *Civil War History* 29, no. 2 (1983): 123–34.

Hanson, Victor Davis. *The Soul of Battle.* New York: The Free Press, 1999.

Harris, Joel Chandler. *On the Plantation: A Story of a Georgia Boy's Adventures during the War.* 1892. Reprint, Athens: University of Georgia Press, 1980.

Harris, J. William. *Plain Folk and Gentry in a Slave Society: White Liberty and Black Slavery in the Augusta Hinterlands.* Middletown CT: Wesleyan University Press, 1987.

Harrison, Jon, ed. "The Confederate Letters of John Simmons." *Chronicles of Smith County, Texas* 14 (summer 1975): 25–57.

Hattaway, Herman, and Richard E. Beringer. *Jefferson Davis, Confederate President.* Lawrence: University Press of Kansas, 2002.

Hawkins, Rush C. *An Account of the Assassination of Loyal Citizens of North Carolina for Having Served in the Union Army Which Took Place at Kingston in the Months of February and March 1864.* New York: n.p., 1897.

Heitman, Francis B. *Historical Register and Dictionary of the United States Army, from Its Organization, September 29, 1789 to March 2, 1903.* 2 vols. Washington DC: Government Printing Office, 1903.

Heller, J. Roderick, III, and Carolyn Ayres Heller, eds. *The Confederacy Is on Her Way up the Spout: Letters to South Carolina, 1861–1864.* Athens: University of Georgia Press, 1992.

Herrington, W. D. *The Deserter's Daughter: Southern Field and Fireside Novelette No. 3.* Raleigh: Wm B. Smith, 1865.

Higginbothom, Donald. *War and Society in Revolutionary America: The Wider Dimensions of Conflict.* Columbia: University of South Carolina Press, 1988.

Hill, Lois, ed. *Poems and Songs of the Civil War.* New York: Gramercy Books, 1990.

Howell, H. Grady. *Going to Meet the Yankees: A History of the "Bloody" Sixth Mississippi Infantry, C.S.A.* Jackson: Chickasaw Bayou Press, 1981.

Inscoe, John, and Gordon McKinney. *The Heart of Confederate Appalachia: Western North Carolina in the Civil War.* Chapel Hill: University of North Carolina Press, 2000.

Irby, James Arthur. *Backdoor at Bagdad: The Civil War on the Rio Grande.* El Paso: Texas Western Press, University of Texas El Paso, 1977.

———. "Line of the Rio Grande: War and Trade on the Confederate Rio Grande." Ph.D. diss., University of Georgia, 1969.

Johns, John E. *Florida during the Civil War.* Gainesville: University of Florida Press, 1963.

Johnson, Andrew. *The Papers of Andrew Johnson.* Ed. Leroy P. Graf and Ralph W. Haskins. 16 vols. Knoxville: University of Tennessee Press, 1967–2000.

Jomini, Henri. "Jomini and His Summary of the Art of War." In *Roots of War*, ed. T. R. Phillips and J. D. Hittle, 2:389–557. Harrisburg PA: Stackpole, 1992.

Jones, J. B. *Rebel War Clerk's Diary at the Confederate Capital.* 2 vols. Philadelphia: Lippincott, 1866.

Kean, Robert Garrick Hill. *Inside the Confederate Government: The Diary of Robert Garrick Hill Kean.* Ed. Edward Younger. Baton Rouge: Louisiana State University Press, 1993.

Lancaster, Bruce. *The American Revolution.* Boston: Houghton Mifflin, 2001.

Leckie, Robert. *George Washington's War: The Saga of the American Revolution.* New York: Harper-Perennial, 1993.

Leckie, William. *Buffalo Soldiers.* Norman: University of Oklahoma Press, 1975.

Lee, Robert E. *The Wartime Papers of Robert E. Lee.* Ed. Clifford Dowdey. Boston: Little, Brown, 1961.

Lincoln, Abraham. *The Collected Works of Abraham Lincoln.* Ed. Roy Basler. 9 vols. New Brunswick: Rutgers University Press, 1953.

Lindermann, Gerald. *Embattled Courage: The Experience of Combat in the American Civil War.* New York: The Free Press, 1987.

Lonn, Ella. *Desertion during the Civil War.* Lincoln: University of Nebraska Press, 1997.

———. *Salt as a Factor in the Confederacy.* Tuscaloosa: University of Alabama Press, 2003.

Maars, Aaron. "Dissatisfaction and Desertion in Greenville District, South Carolina, 1860–1865." Ph.D. diss., University of South Carolina, May 2002.

———. "Dissatisfaction and Desertion in Greenville District, South Carolina: 1860–1865." *Proceedings of the South Carolina Historical Association* (2001): 39–51.

Mackey, Robert. "Bushwhackers, Provosts, and Tories: The Guerilla War in Arkansas." In *Guerrillas, Unionists, and Violence on the Confederate Home Front*, ed. Donald E. Sutherland. Fayetteville: University of Arkansas Press, 1999.

Manarin, Louis H., comp. *North Carolina Troops, 1861–1865: A Roster.* 7 vols. Raleigh: State Division of Archives and History, 1966–77; second printing with addenda, 1988–91.

Mann, Ralph. "Ezekiel Count's Salt Lick Company: Civil War and Localism in the Mountain South." In *The Civil War in Appalachia Collected Essays*, ed. Kenneth Noe and Shannon H. Wilson. Knoxville: University of Tennessee Press, 1997.

Marten, James. *Texas Divided: Loyalty and Dissent in the Lone Star State, 1856–1874.* Lexington: University of Kentucky Press, 1990.

Martin, Bessie. *Desertion of Alabama Troops from the Confederate Army: A Study in Sectionalism.* New York: AMI, 1966.

———. *A Rich Man's War, a Poor Man's Fight: Desertion of Alabama Troops from the Confederate Army.* Reprint, Tuscaloosa: University of Alabama Press, 2003.

Massey, Mary Elizabeth. *Ersatz in the Confederacy.* Columbia: University of South Carolina Press, 1952.

McAnaney, Lt. William D. "Desertion in the United States Army." *Journal of Military Service Institute* 10 (1889): 150–65.

McCarthy, Carlton. *Detailed Minutiae of Soldier Life in the Army of Northern Virginia, 1861–1865.* Richmond: Carlton McCarthy, 1882.

McDermott, John D. "Were They Really Rogues? Desertion in the Nineteenth-Century U.S. Army." *Nebraska History* 78, no. 4 (1997): 165–73.

McKiven, Hugh. Review of *A Higher Duty: Desertion among Georgia Troops during the Civil War,* by Mark A. Weitz. *Journal of Southern History* 17 (2001): 874.

McMillan, Malcomb C. *The Disintegration of a Confederate State: Three Governors and Alabama's Home Front, 1861–1865.* Macon: Mercer University Press, 1986.

McMorris, Edward Young. *History of the First Alabama Regiment.* Montgomery: Brown Printing Co., 1902.

McPherson, James. *Antietam: Crossroads of Freedom.* New York: Oxford University Press, 2002.

———. *Battle Cry of Freedom: The Civil War Era.* New York: Oxford University Press, 1988.

———. "The Distinctiveness of the Old South." In *The Coming of the American Civil War,* ed. Michael Perman. 3d ed. Lexington MA: D. C. Heath, 1993.

———. *For Cause and Comrades: Why Men Fought in the Civil War.* New York: Oxford University Press, 1997.

Middlekauf, Robert. *The Glorious Cause: The American Revolution, 1776–1789.* New York: Oxford University Press, 1982.

Militia Laws of Tennessee Containing the Permanent Constitution and Articles of War of the Confederate States. Memphis: Hetton and Feeligs, 1861.

Miller, Robert Ryal. *Shamrock and Sword: The St. Patrick's Battalion in the U.S. Mexican War.* Norman: University of Oklahoma Press, 1989.

Mitchell, James. "The Civil War Letters of James Mitchell to His wife Sarah Elizabeth Latta Mitchell." *Arkansas Historical Quarterly* 37 (winter 1978): 306–17.

Moneyhon, Carl. "The Die Is Cast." In *The Rugged and the Sublime: The Civil War in Arkansas,* ed. Mark Christ. Fayetteville: University of Arkansas Press, 1994.

Moore, A. B. *Conscription and Conflict in the Confederacy.* 1924. Reprint, New York: Hillary House, 1963.

Morris, James. *America's Armed Forces: A History.* Upper Saddle River NJ: Prentice Hall, 1996.

Murphy, D. F. *Full Report of the Trial of William Smith for Piracy as One of the Crew of the Confederate Privateer Jeff Davis.* Philadelphia: King and Baird, 1861.

Neely, Mark E., Jr. *Retaliation: The Problem of Atrocity in the American Civil War.* Forty-first Annual Fortenbaugh Memorial Lecture. Gettysburg: Gettysburg College, 2002.

———. *Southern Rights: Political Prisoners and the Myth of Confederate Constitutionalism.* Charlottesville: University Press of Virginia, 1999.

Nolan, Alan T. *Lee Considered: General Robert E. Lee and Civil War History.* Chapel Hill: University of North Carolina Press, 1991.

Norton, Oliver Wilcox. *Army Letters, 1861–1865.* Dayton: Morningside, 1990.

Otten, James T. "Disloyalty in the Upper Districts of South Carolina during the Civil War." *South Carolina Historical Magazine* 75, no. 2 (1974): 95–110.

Owen, Thomas McAdory. *History of Alabama Dictionary of Alabama Biography.* 4 vols. Spartanburg: The Reprint Company, 1978.

———. "The Work of William Henry Fowler as Superintendent of Army Records, 1863–65." *Alabama Historical Commission* 3 (1900): 178–91.

Potter, David M. *The South and the Sectional Conflict.* Baton Rouge: Louisiana State University Press, 1968.

Powers, Tracy. *Lee's Miserables: Life in the Army of Northern Virginia from the Wilderness to Appomattox.* Chapel Hill: University of North Carolina Press, 1998.

Radley, Keith. *Rebel Watchdog: The Confederate States Army Provost Guard.* Baton Rouge: Louisiana State University Press, 1989.

Raphael, Ray. *A People's History of the American Revolution.* New York: HarperPerennial, 2001.

Reid, Brian H., and John White. "A Mob of Stragglers and Cowards: Desertion from the Union and Confederate Armies, 1861–1865." *Journal of Strategic Studies* 8 (1985): 64–77.

Reid, Richard. "A Test Case for 'Crying Evil': Desertion among North Carolina Troops during the Civil War." *North Carolina Historical Review* 58, no. 3 (1981): 234–62.

Reiger, John F. "Deprivation, Disaffection, and Desertion in Confederate Florida." *Florida Historical Quarterly* 48 (1970): 279–98.

Rhett, Robert Barnwell. *A Fire Eater Remembers: The Confederate Memoir of Robert Barnwell Rhett.* Ed. William C. Davis. Columbia: University of South Carolina Press, 2000.

Robertson, James I. *Civil War Virginia: Battleground for a Nation.* Charlottesville: University Press of Virginia, 1990.

Rogers, Wayne Warren, Robert David Ward, Leah Rawls Atkins, and Wayne Flint. *Alabama: The History of a Deep South State.* Tuscaloosa: University of Alabama Press, 1994.

Salley, A. S., Jr., comp. *South Carolina Troops in Confederate Service.* 3 vols. Columbia: R. L. Bryan, 1913.

Schroeder-Lein, Glenna R. *Confederate Hospitals on the Move: Samuel H. Stout and the Army of Tennessee.* Columbia: University of South Carolina Press, 1994.

Seymour, Digby Gordon. *Divided Loyalties: Fort Saunders and the Civil War in East Tennessee.* Knoxville: University of Tennessee Press, 1963.

Simpson, Harold B., ed. *The Bugle Softly Blows: The Confederate Diary of Benjamin M. Seaton.* Waco: The Texian Press, 1965.

Smith, Daniel E. Huger, Alice R. Huger Smith, and Arney R. Childs, eds. *Mason Smith Family Letters, 1860–1868.* Columbia: University of South Carolina Press, 1950.

Smith, David Paul. "The Limits of Dissent and Loyalty in Texas." In *Guerrillas, Unionists, and Violence on the Confederate Home Front,* ed. Donald E. Sutherland. Fayetteville: University of Arkansas Press, 1999.

Southern Historical Society Papers. 52 vols. Millswood NY: Krause Reprint, 1977.

Sterling, Bob. "Discouragement, Weariness, and War Politics: Desertion from Illinois Regiments during the Civil War." *Illinois Historical Journal* 82, no. 4 (1989): 239–62.

Sutherland, Daniel E. *Seasons of War: The Ordeal of a Confederate Community, 1861–1865.* Baton Rouge: Louisiana State University Press, 1995.

———. "A Strange, Wild Time." In *The Rugged and the Sublime: The Civil War in Arkansas,* ed. Mark Christ. Fayetteville: University of Arkansas Press, 1994.

Tanner, Adelph. *Encouragement of Food Crops in the Confederacy.* N.p.: n.p., 1928.

Taylor, Ethel. "Discontent in Confederate Louisiana." *Louisiana History* 4, no. 2 (1961): 410–28.

Taylor, Michael W., ed. *The Cry Is War, War, War: The Civil War Correspondence of Lts. Burwell Thomas Cotton and Job Huntley.* Dayton: Morningside, 1994.

Thomas, Emory. *The Confederate Nation.* New York: Harper & Row, 1979.

Thompson, Illene D., and Wilbur E. Thompson, eds. and comps. *The Seventeenth Alabama Infantry: A Regimental History and Roster.* Bowie MD: Heritage, 2001.

Thorpe, Francis Newton. *The Federal and State Constitutions, Colonial Charters, and Other Organic Laws of the United States.* 7 vols. Washington DC: Government Printing Office, 1909.

Trotter, William R. *Bushwackers! The Civil War in North Carolina: The Mountains.* Winston-Salem: John F. Blair, 1988.

U.S. Department of State Papers Relating to the Foreign Relations of the U.S.. 3 vols. Washington DC: Government Printing Office, 1862.

Vandiver, Frank E. *Their Tattered Flags: The Epic of the Confederacy.* New York: Harpers Magazine Press, 1970.

Vargas, Mark A. "The Military Justice System and the Use of Illegal Punishments as the Causes of Desertion in the U.S. Army." *Journal of Military History* 55 (January 1991): 1–19.

Vegitius, Flavius Renatus. "In Re Militari." In *Roots of War,* ed. T. R. Phillips and J. D. Hittle, 1:65–176. Harrisburg PA: Stackpole, 1992.

Walton, Major Buck. *An Epitome of My Life: Civil War Reminiscences*. Austin: Waterloo Press, 1965.

Warburton, A. F., steno. *Trial of the Officers and Crew of the Privateer* Savannah. New York: Baker and Godwin, 1861.

The War of the Rebellion: The Official Records of the Union and Confederate Armies. 128 vols. Washington DC: Government Printing Office, 1880–1900.

Washington, George. *The Papers of George Washington: Colonial Series*. Ed. W. W. Abbot et al. 10 vols. Charlottesville: University Press of Virginia, 1983–95.

———. *The Papers of George Washington: Revolutionary War Series*. Ed. Philander D. Chase et al. 13 vols. Charlottesville: University Press of Virginia, 1985–.

Weigley, Russell F. *A Great Civil War: A Military and Political History, 1861–1865*. Bloomington: Indiana University Press, 2000.

Weitz, Mark A. *Defining a Confederate Nation: The Piracy and Sequestration Cases*. Lawrence: University Press of Kansas, forthcoming.

———. "Desertion as Mutiny: Upcountry Georgians in the Army of Tennessee." In *Rebellion, Repression, and Reinvention: Mutiny in a Comparative Perspective*, ed. Jane Hathaway. Westport CN: Praeger, 2001.

———. "Drill, Training, and the Combat Performance of the Civil War Soldier: Dispelling the Myth of Poor Soldier, Great Fighter." *Journal of Military History* 62, no. 2 (1998): 99–124.

———. *A Higher Duty: Desertion among Georgia Troops during the Civil War*. Lincoln: University of Nebraska Press, 2000.

———. "'I Will Never Forget the Name of You': The Home Front, Desertion and Oath Taking in Civil War Tennessee." *Tennessee Historical Quarterly* 59 (spring 2000): 48–77.

———. "Preparing for the Prodigal Sons: The Development of the Union Desertion Policy during the Civil War." *Civil War History* 45, no. 2 (1999): 99–125.

———. "'Shoot Them All': Chivalry, Honour, and the Confederate Officer Corps." In *The Chivalric Ethos and the Development of Military Professionalism*, ed. D. J. B. Trim. Leiden: Brill, 2002.

Welch, Spencer Glasgow. *A Confederate Surgeon's Letters*. Marietta GA: Continental Book Company, 1954.

Wiley, Bell Irvin. *The Life of Johnny Reb*. Baton Rouge: Louisiana State University Press, 1970.

Williams, David. *The Georgia Gold Rush: Twenty-Niners, Cherokees, and Gold Fever*. Columbia: University of South Carolina Press, 1993.

———. *Rich Man's War: Class, Caste, and Confederate Defeat in the Lower Chattahoochee Valley*. Athens: University of Georgia Press, 1999.

Williams, David, Theresa Crisp Williams, and David Carlson. *Plain Folk in a Rich Man's War: Class and Dissent in Confederate Georgia*. Gainesville: University of Florida, 2002.

Winik, Jay. *April 1865: The Month That Saved America*. New York: Harper Collins, 2001.

Wood, Gordon. *The Creation of the American Republic, 1776–1787*. Chapel Hill: University of North Carolina Press, 1969.

Wood, William. *Reminiscences of Big I*. Ed. Bell Irvin Wiley. Jackson TN: McCowat-Mercer Press, 1956.

Woodbury, E. N. *A Study of Desertion*. Washington DC: U.S. War Department, Morale Division, 1920.

Woodruff, J., comp. *The Sequestration Cases before the Honorable Judge A. G. Magrath*. Charleston SC: n.p., 1861.

Woods, James. *Rebellion and Realignment: Arkansas's Road to Secession*. Fayetteville: University of Arkansas Press, 1987.

Woodworth, Steven E. *No Band of Brothers: Problems of the Rebel High Command*. Columbia: University of Missouri Press, 1999.

affecting (Fabian policy), 54–55, 64–85, 91, 117, 123, 128, 133, 154–55, 171–74, 213–14, 222, 235, 255–56, 258, 275; role of antebellum development in, 11–12; and slavery, 138–40, 165, 280, 287; statistics on, ix, xii–xiii, xvi, 95, 110, 131–35, 221, 245–55, 261–65, 268–70, 288; Union policy regarding, xii–xiii, 53, 56–60, 79, 89, 104, 108, 124, 127, 130–36, 155, 165, 218, 224, 234, 247, 249, 253, 257, 282–83, 291

Dinwiddie, Gov. John, 6

draft. *See* conscription, acts and laws

Early, Gen. Jubal, 199–200, 202, 282
Echols, John, 200–202
Edwards, E. N., 16, 20
Edwards, T. C., 231
Ellis, J. W., 280, 284
Embree, Henrietta, 16
Evans, Gen. Nathan, 174, 197
Ewell, Gen. Richard, 28, 242, 250
Ex Parte Merryman, 144

Farragut, Adm. David, 52, 69
Ferguson, Samuel, 210
Flanagin, Gov. Harris, 28
Flewellen Hospital, 168, 262, 264
Florida: civilian plight in, 218–21; desertion in, 163, 218–21; geography, 22, 217; guerilla activity in, 218–21; troops, 131, 245; Unionism in, 218
Florida Royals (Independent Union Rangers), 221
Ford, J. L., 137
Ford, John S., 228, 231
Forrest, Nathan Bedford, 210
Fort Donelson (TN), 52, 54–55, 68, 292
Fort Henry (TN), 52, 54, 68, 292
Fort Jackson (LA), 163
Fort Sumter (SC), 33, 34
Fowler, William H., x, xv, 267–68
Frayser, James M., 268
Fredericksburg (VA), 117

"Galvanized Yankees," xii
Gammage, Pvt. William, 117, 171
Gardner, W. M., 164
Gates, Gen. Horatio, 7
Georgia: civilian plight in, 41, 213–17; desertion in, 131, 170, 213, 254; geography, 20–22, 212, 214; guerilla activity in, 213–17; troops,

xvi, xviii, 77, 131–33, 135, 170, 172, 180, 245–46, 250–51, 254–55, 261–62; Unionism in, 213–14

Gettysburg (PA), 21
Gettysburg, battle of, 89, 129, 153, 156–57, 236
Graham, William, 105–6, 112, 143, 237
Grant, Gen. Ulysses S., 52–53, 117, 171, 173, 225, 234, 236, 253–54, 279
Greene, Gen. Nathanael, 9–11, 63, 83, 90
Gregg, Gen. David, 245
Grierson, Benjamin, 217

habeus corpus, 144, 239, 284, 289
Hall, Jason, 60, 170
Halleck, Gen. Henry, 134, 188, 244
Halsey, E. W., 69–70, 73
Hamilton, Andrew Jackson, 123–24
Hamilton, James, 206
Hardee, Gen. William, 40, 160, 164–65, 172
Hardeman, R. B., 38, 56
Hardy, P. D., 73
Harris, Isham, 53–54, 133, 179
Harris, Joel Chandler, 31–32
Hawkins, Epheraim, 268
Heigler, Joseph, 164
Heroes of America, 202, 210
Herrenvolk Democracy, 18, 22, 140
Herrington, W. D., 289–90
Heth, Gen. Harry, 95–96
Hill, Alexander Campbell, 175
Hill, Gen. Ambrose Powell, 108, 254, 282
Hill, Gen. Daniel Harvey, 96, 143
Hindman, Gen. Thomas, 60–64, 72, 186, 202, 221, 269–70
Hodge, Gen. George, 210
Hoffman, Col. William, 53
Hoke, Gen. Robert, 190–91, 193, 195, 197, 235, 292
Holder, W. R., 265
Holmes, T. C., 160
Hood, Daniel S., 212
Hood, Gen. John Bell, 206, 255, 258, 271, 274, 279
Houston, Sam, 226
Humphreys, Gen. A. A., 245
Hundervant, Mrs. Alliou, 135
Hurlbut, Gen. Stephen, 257

Imboden, John, 149, 151, 155, 161, 170, 199
Independent Union Rangers (Florida Rangers), 221

Ives, S. S., 211

Jack, T. M., 206
Jackson, Gen. Thomas J. (Stonewall), xvii, 34, 90, 95, 108, 142
Johnson, Andrew, 53, 56–60, 68, 79, 119, 130–31, 186, 259
Johnson, Gen. Bushrod, 242, 282
Johnson's Island (OH), 58, 82, 136
Johnston, Gen. Albert Sydney, 55
Johnston, Gen. Joseph, viii, 172, 174, 178–79, 212, 250, 258, 261, 275, 283
Johnston, W. P., 221
Jones, John B., 29, 37
Jones, Pvt. R. S., 272
Joyner, J. E., 157–59, 170–71, 198–200

Kean, Robert Garlick Hill, xi, xiv, 110, 152, 180, 236, 269
Kelley, H. C., 209
King, H. W., 168
"Kirby Smithdom," vii
Kirk, John, 109
Kirkpatrick, James, 18
Knoxville Daily Register, 173

Lauderdale, Sallie, 76–77
Lay, Col. George W., 155, 192, 194–96, 203, 205, 232
Lee, George Washington, 216–17
Lee, Gen. Robert E., 26, 34, 36, 87–92, 142, 152, 181, 199–200, 202, 204, 238, 279; and desertion in 1862, 87–88, 93–94; and desertion in 1863, 130, 149–51, 155–61, 169–70, 177, 188, 197; and desertion in 1864, 235, 242–44, 250–51, 260–61, 270; and desertion in 1865, 280–83, 292; surrender of, vii–viii, 198; as symbol of nationalism, ix, 86
Lee, Gen. Stephen, 210
Lee's Rangers, 217
leniency, 7–8, 63, 83, 87, 94, 96–102, 156, 188, 219, 244, 254, 256, 279, 285–86, 288
Leory, Henry J., 200–201
Letcher, Gov. John, 90–94, 101, 104, 107, 112, 122–23, 130, 291
Lincoln, Abraham, 144, 253, 270–71; and oaths, 120; and Proclamation of Amnesty 1863, 89, 138, 234–235
Lockhart, H. C., 266
Lonn, Ella, 185, 212, 214, 278
Longstreet, Gen. James, 34, 95, 110, 131

Lorena, 260
Louisiana: civilian plight in, 69–73, 118, 127, 223–25; desertion in, 43, 72–74, 163, 223–25; guerilla activity in, 72, 163, 223–25, 257; troops, xiii–xv, 43, 68, 131, 185, 245–46, 251–52, 257–58, 269, 295; Unionism in, 225
Lovell, Mansfield, 72
Lubbock, Gov. Francis, 75, 123–24, 136–38, 141, 228, 240–41, 291

Magrath, Gov. Andrew G., 198
Magruder, Gen. John, 123–24, 137, 227
Manasass: First Battle of, xi, 28, 46; Second Battle of, 92, 110
martial law, 64
Mason, James, 56
Maury, Col. H., 207
Maury, Gen. Dabney, 207–8, 210, 214
Mayfield, James, 211
McAnaney, William D., 3
McCarthy, Carlton, 51
McClellan, Gen. George B., 88–89, 92, 111
McCullough, Col. Henry E., 79, 227–30
McDaniel, Pvt. E. D., 156
McGowin, Alex, 173–74
McLaurin, Pvt. Hugh A., 67–68, 186–87
Melton, C. D., 195, 197
Memphis (TN), 54–55
Mexico, 79, 123, 175, 288
Miles, William, 183
Milton, Gov. John, 163, 220
Mississippi: civilian plight in, 41, 64–69, 128, 203–11, 272; desertion in, 43, 64, 66–69, 140, 203–11, 267; geography, 22; guerilla activity in, 203–11, 233, 267, 272; troops, xiii, 43, 64–69, 131, 133, 162, 172, 174, 180, 185, 245–47, 251–52, 254, 258, 269, 295–96
Mississippi River, 53–54, 60, 69, 161, 256
Missouri: desertion by troops of, 222, 256, 269; invasion of, 222, 258, 270, 275; troops, 221–22
Mitchell, J. B., 160
Mitchell, James, 174
Mitchell, Robert, 128
Moore, Samuel P., x–xi, 82–83
Moore, Gov. Thomas, 38–39, 70–72, 77, 112, 223
Moore, William, 16
Morgan, Gen. Daniel, 9
Morgan, Gen. John, 198, 260–61
Morgan, Timothy, 272

Morris, R. H., 163
Mortimer, Horace, 174
Mosby, Col. John, 199
Moxley, Emily, 41–42
Moxley, Maj. William, 41–42
Murphy, Col. U. S., 124
Myers, Asbury, 113

Nashville (TN), 54–55
Neblett, Lizzie Scott, 74, 86, 194, 294
Neblett, William, 74, 185
New Orleans, 71–72, 118, 127, 223, 257, 287
Newton, Thomas, 160
Nicholson, William, 187, 247, 294
Nick-a-jack (GA), 213
North Carolina: antebellum, 10; civilian
    plight in, 90, 106–7, 109, 158, 189–95; de-
    sertion in, 109, 141–43, 158; geography, 10,
    20–21, 106, 109; guerilla activity in, 106, 141,
    162, 188–95; Supreme Court, 141–48, 239;
    troops, xiv, xviii, 2, 90, 96–100, 102, 109,
    131–32, 142–48, 155, 170–71, 180, 185, 190,
    245, 246, 250–53, 277, 282, 287, 296
Norton, Oliver Wilcox, 245
Nugent, William, 247

oath of allegiance (oath swearing): by civil-
    ians, 56–60, 88–89, 93, 116–22, 128–30, 234–
    35, 292; by deserters, xii, 56, 82, 117–22, 124,
    130–35, 157, 165, 170–71, 223–24, 245–55, 257–
    59, 268–69, 283, 292, 295–97; ideological
    implications of, 104, 116–22; by prisoners
    of war, xii–xiii, 53–55, 82, 104, 121, 136–38,
    165
Ogden, Jesse, 38
Okefenokee Swamp (GA), 216

Palmer, Benjamin Morgan, 118–22, 124, 127,
    138
Palmetto Ranch, vii
Paris, John, 275–76, 284
Parsons, Lewis E., 271
Payne, George W., 175
Pearson, Richmond, 141–48, 159, 239, 275
Peebles, Thomas W., 68–69
Pemberton, Gen. John, 43, 135, 164–65, 203
Pender, Gen. William Dorsey, xvii, 142, 144
Peninsula Campaign, 110
Perkins, John, 119
Pettus, Gov. John, 38, 41, 43, 45, 64–69, 112,
    140, 203, 209

Phelan, James, 286
Pickett, Gen. George, 248, 253, 275, 287
Pillow, Gideon, 68, 150–51, 154, 162, 175–81,
    183, 188, 193–94, 203, 205–6, 210, 213, 232,
    272, 280–81, 293
Pitman, T. S., 238
Polk, Gen. Leonidas, 124, 206–7, 209–10, 212,
    233, 238, 244, 269–70, 272, 275
Pope, Curran, 58, 69, 77
Pope, John, 93
Port Hudson (LA), 71, 119, 127, 164, 173, 175
Potter, Alonzo, 25, 27
Preston, Gen. John, 178–80, 194–95, 197, 232,
    280–81, 288, 293
Price, Gen. Sterling, 172, 174, 221, 244, 256,
    258, 270, 275
provost guard, 36–37, 101, 165, 238, 249

Quantrill, William, 188, 230–31

Randolph, George, 88, 103, 111
Register of Confederate Deserters to the
    Union Army, 1863–1865, xii, 130–35, 169,
    203, 244, 249, 259, 267, 287
Reynolds, Gov. Thomas C., 221
Richardson, Col. Richard V., 160–61, 170
Roddey, Gen. Philip, 162, 210
Rodes, Gen. Robert, 102, 242
Rosecrans, Gen. William, 117, 134, 171, 173, 188,
    244–45
Russell, Mark, 211
Rutherford, E. H., 187

Sanders, John, 215
San Patricos, 2
Savannah (GA), 132
Searcy, Pvt. J., 173–74, 186
secession, 16, 21, 185, 213
Seddon, James, 161, 164, 169, 181, 195, 208, 220,
    232–33, 236, 238, 271; and Gideon Pillow,
    177–79, 188, 204; and Heroes of America,
    200–202; and Robert E. Lee, 157–58, 197,
    242–43, 250–51; and Zebulon Vance, 142,
    146–48, 190–91, 193–94
Sequestration Act, 240
Seven Days Campaign, 88, 110
Seymour, Pvt. L. B., 99–100, 152
Shenandoah Valley, 149, 155, 181–82, 199, 202
Sherman, Gen. William T., 202, 206, 213–14,
    247, 254, 258, 261–62, 279
Shields, J. C., 159